SECOND EDITION

SOCIAL RESEARCH

An Evolving Process

DON G. McTAVISH
University of Minnesota

HERMAN J. LOETHER
California State University Dominguez Hills

ALLYN AND BACON
Boston ▪ London ▪ Toronto ▪ Sydney ▪ Tokyo ▪ Singapore

Series Editor: *Jeff Lasser*
Series Editorial Assistant: *Andrea Christie*
Marketing Manager: *Judeth Hall*
Editorial-Production Service: *Omegatype Typography, Inc.*
Composition and Prepress Buyer: *Linda Cox*
Manufacturing Manager: *Suzanne Lareau*
Cover Administrator: *Kristina Mose-Libon*
Electronic Composition: *Omegatype Typography, Inc.*

A Pearson Education Company
75 Arlington Street
Boston, MA 02116

Internet: www.ablongman.com

Between the time Website information is gathered and then published, it is not unusual for some sites to have closed. Also, the transcription of URLs can result in unintended typographical errors. The publisher would appreciate notification where these occur so that they may be corrected in subsequent editions. Thank you.

Library of Congress Cataloging-in-Publication Data

McTavish, Donald G.
Social research : an evolving process / Don G. McTavish, Herman J. Loether. — 2nd ed.
p. cm.
Includes bibliographical references and index.
ISBN 0-205-33744-9 (alk. paper)
1. Social sciences—Research. 2. Social sciences—Methodology. I. Loether, Herman J. II. Title

H62 .M337 2002
300'.7'2—dc21

2001022603

Printed in the United States of America

10 9 8 7 6 5 4 3 2 1 06 05 04 03 02 01

Dedicated to the memory of
Evelyn M. Loether and
Ruth S. McTavish

CONTENTS

PREFACE

Research method texts often focus on recipes for "correct" research design or descriptions of appropriate research styles. Accordingly, the reader is given the impression that research is a cut-and-dried set of procedures that, if followed religiously, will produce the desired results. However, actual research rarely meets the standards for an ideal design and is more like an *evolving* inquiry process than text discussions often suggest.

Several anthologies have been published (e.g., Hammond, 1964; Riley, 1988) in which prominent researchers describe the backstage scene of their own research and thus give the reader a flavor of this evolving inquiry process. Although these books do give one a sense of the unforeseen opportunities and pitfalls involved in doing research, they usually do not discuss general principles or the range of options of sound social science research.

We decided to take a somewhat different tack than either of these approaches in our book, focusing on research as an evolving social process and on the options that arise in the process of carrying out a project.

Social Research underscores the process of research as a serious attempt to achieve a desired style of research within the confines of a real social setting. It points to the inevitable tradeoffs that confront researchers and their consequences both for the research that is carried out and for the results of that research. It emphasizes the constant impact of social arrangements and understandings on the findings one may draw from research. Because research is what one does when one does not know the answers, the process inherently is a discovery process even when the style of research is well known.

This book also points to families of flaws that seem to crop up in the very social process of inquiry. It discusses ways in which these flaws may be detected and corrected. Furthermore, it considers ways one might guard against these and other threats to sound research.

In recognition of the fact that they are an integral part of the whole process, research ethics are incorporated into the book throughout the various steps of research rather than being confined to a single chapter. When something is unknown, the ethics of the procedures used to find answers are of persistent concern from the inception to the completion of a project.

The text focuses on patterns of research decisions and their consequences for research findings. We attempt to include a broader coverage of topics of research than is usually covered. We have included a discussion of systematic content analysis, measurement, and other topics not always in vogue in contemporary methods texts. We have also suggested strategies for the integration of qualitative and quantitative research. Believing that current courses ought to prepare students for their careers over the next decade or so, we have included some topics we expect to become more central to the social science inquiry process in the future. In short, the text and associated materials attempt to include a broad range of tools for social scientific inquiry, set in the context of general principles of the sociology and philosophy of science.

Most importantly, we take seriously the role of the human researcher and the social context of research and their consequences for findings. Thus, this book might be characterized as using a *sociology of social research* perspective as well.

The text is designed so that chapters can be selected or omitted depending on the length and level of the course. Chapter 1 presents a general introduction to the subject of social research including a discussion of the social settings in which it takes place. Following this, Section I of the book deals with the basic planning that goes on in developing a research project. Chapter 2 deals with conceptualization of the project, Chapter 3 deals with measurement issues, Chapter 4 discusses the process of selecting a study design, and Chapter 5 covers the integral relationship between inference and sampling.

Section II focuses in more detail on the principal types of study designs used by social scientists: experiments (Chapter 6), surveys (Chapter 7), case studies (Chapter 8), and secondary data research (Chapter 9).

Section III deals with the steps undertaken to evaluate the data once they are in hand. Data analysis is covered in Chapter 10 and options for reporting the results of the analysis in Chapter 11.

Chapters 12 ("The Organization of Research") and 13 ("Resource Considerations") cover topics that are not normally covered systematically in general research methods books. They are included here because of our emphasis on social research as a social process and the consequences of that fact for how inquiry proceeds and how findings of the inquiry are affected. Although the materials covered in these two chapters may be of more immediate concern to graduate students who are involved in research projects, they can also be important to undergraduates, giving them an appreciation of the social process theme developed throughout the book.

Chapter 14 ("Developments and Prospects") attempts to tie the whole book together, focusing on the major themes of the book and on the most likely directions we see social research taking in the future.

Students without a statistical background can readily use this text, although we generally assume that they have had a beginning statistics course. Many college curricula have a prior statistics requirement that helps some with the language of concepts and variables, relationships and inference, and insights into the needs for data that statistical procedures imply. The chapter on data analysis (Chapter 10) includes a discussion of statistical analysis, but it is presented in very general terms, designed merely to provide the reader with an overview of the statistical approach and some of its options. No single chapter in a research methods book can prepare a student to undertake the task of statistical analysis. In fact, a whole course in statistics is often not adequate to provide the student with the statistical sophistication necessary to plan and carry out data analysis independently.

In our experience, a first research methods course may permit and encourage an active researching role for students in teams. This provides insights into the reason for some of the desired research design features and the consequences of the social contexts of research. We have found that students bring rich experiences and insights, excitement, and creativity when given an opportunity to do research first-hand. Admittedly, an academic term is short. We often have sacrificed the polished presentation of findings in favor of conceptual work and fieldwork in data gathering because prior statistics courses often provide write-up experiences based on archived data sets. In any case, it is essential to provide ample opportunity for reflection and discussion about the consequences of research practices and design decisions for research conclusions.

We have included several features in the text we hope you will find useful, such as boxed material to summarize the argument or point to places where relevant discussions can be found. Getting the vocabulary of research is often helpful, so lists of key terms appear at the end of each chapter, with exercises and references. A glossary also provides brief definitions of terms.

This book is the outgrowth of our experiences over many years of research and our observation of research both in the classroom and in professional life. We want to acknowledge and thank the many students, teachers, and colleagues who have shared their inquiry processes with us, and the reviewers who have given us many constructive suggestions for improving the text. For reviewing the second edition of *Social Research: An Evolving Process,* we would like to thank Douglas Forbes, Southwest Texas State University; and Larry Lance, University of North Carolina.

REFERENCES

Hammond, Phillip E., ed. *Sociologists at Work: Essays on the Craft of Social Research.* New York: Basic Books, 1964.

Riley, Matilda White, ed. *Sociological Lives.* Newbury Park, CA: Sage, 1988.

CHAPTER ONE

THE SOCIAL SETTINGS OF SOCIAL RESEARCH

From time to time studies of the effects of secondhand smoke are reported in the mass media. In June 1994, for example, 53 news stories said that the latest research reported in the *Journal of the American Medical Association* had found that women who had never smoked but whose spouses were smokers had about a 30% greater chance of getting lung cancer than women married to nonsmokers (Seligman, 1994:177–78).

Spokespersons for the Tobacco Institute disputed this finding and accused the Environmental Protection Agency and the medical community of selectively using research that fit their preconceived biases and ignoring other research that did not. According to the Tobacco Institute, "There is a very, very low level of risk if there is any at all" (Seligman, 1994:177).

What is the average citizen to conclude from these reports and the ongoing controversy surrounding them? Is secondhand smoke dangerous to one's health or not? The proper answer to this question can be important to a person's social behavior and future health.

Similar conflicting reports appear, from time to time, with respect to whether sugar or butter or decaffeinated coffee or some other food or substance is detrimental to one's health. Another area of controversy centers on the question of whether sexually explicit materials contribute to socially disapproved behavior (such as promiscuity or sexual abuse) on the part of those exposed to them.

It is all very confusing to average citizens. Whom are they to believe? Obviously, an evaluation of the soundness of the research conducted on these matters, and others as well, is badly needed. Do some of these studies even deserve to be labeled research? Those who are going to engage in research certainly must have a clear understanding of what research is if they are to do scientifically meaningful studies. Even those who do not intend to engage in research themselves need a clear notion of what research is in order to make intelligent decisions about their own behavior.

This chapter starts with some examples of studies. Then we ask, "Are these studies research?" Four criteria are used to answer this question. Once the question is answered with respect to the studies described, the chapter goes on to discuss who does research, common social contexts of research and some of their consequences, ethical concerns in researching, and an overview of the typical research process.

EXAMPLES OF STUDIES

Framing Discussions of Political Events

Gamson (1992) wanted to know how working people construct and negotiate shared meanings about political events when they talk to friends and acquaintances. He recruited people from 35 Boston neighborhoods, who then recruited approximately four friends for peer conversations in their homes, ending up with 37 small conversation groups. A leader initiated discussions on each of four issues: affirmative action, nuclear power, troubled American industry, and Arab–Israeli conflict. A trained **observer** also attended the discussions to record what was said. In addition, current newspaper and TV reports on these topics were examined.

Analyzing how the discussions were framed and their use of the media, Gamson reported that three distinct resource strategies were used. A cultural strategy used the media and popular wisdom to frame the discussion. A personal strategy drew on personal experience and popular wisdom. Finally, a mixed strategy combined personal experience and the media to frame the discussion. These three strategies were used differently in conversations on different political issues. Results are described in Gamson's research monograph, *Talking Politics* (1992).

What have we learned? Do the conclusions apply broadly to working people? After all, the study was conducted only in 1990 Boston. How strong is the evidence that these three strategies are the ways in which the meaning of political events becomes established?

Older People's Spending Patterns

A study by Cook and Settersten (1995) helped to provide information about spending patterns of older people and how they differ by income levels. Prior research provided only overall information about older people's spending patterns. The authors noted several myths or images about older people's household expenditures that needed to be examined. One image is that older people formerly had to spend large sums on medical care but now Medicare and Medicaid programs adequately provide for their medical expenses. The authors wanted to see whether such images were accurate. Information was also needed to see whether age or income level had an effect on spending patterns that should be taken into account in making public policy.

Cook and Settersten used already existing data (also called **archival data**) from a survey of consumer expenditures conducted by the U.S. Bureau of Labor Statistics in 1984–1985. The survey was a carefully drawn probability sample designed to represent U.S. households. Cook and Settersten were interested only in older households, so they used data only for households with a head who was age 45 or older. There were 3,933 older households in the Bureau of Labor Statistics survey.

To carry out the study, the authors needed to define carefully the **variables** they were planning to use. For example, they grouped total household expenditures into three categories: essentials (clothing, food, housing, health care, and transportation); giving (to individuals, philanthropic and political contributions); and recreation (entertainment and reading). Expenditure patterns in each area were compared for four age groups (45–54, 55–64, 65–74, and over 75). Households were also categorized into five income groups: those below the poverty line; the near poor, just above the poverty line; middle income; more well-to-do; and the most well-to-do. Comparisons of expenditure patterns were then made for different income groups, different age groups, and both income and age groups combined. (See Box 1.1.)

Cook and Settersten found that income level makes more difference than age in the area of giving, including political contributions. Furthermore, poor older people spend a significantly larger proportion of their income on food and housing. The proportion spent on health care rises by age group, but the proportion spent on transportation and clothing goes down as age increases. The near-poor and middle-income groups spend the highest proportion of their income on health care. Overall, 93% of the income of households under the poverty line and with a

BOX 1.1
ON CONCEPTS AND VARIABLES

Concepts such as "total family income" are ideas an investigator has about important characteristics of some entity such as a family. The concept must be clarified and defined, preferably explicitly, so that researchers can understand and share the phenomenon that is being studied. The concept "total family income" is defined to have a range of possible values. Thus, it is called a **variable** in a given piece of research. To be useful to researchers, however, the abstract definition of a concept is not enough. A set of indicators must be developed in order to actually measure or classify families in terms of their total family incomes. As we shall see in Chapter 3, there are usually many possible indicators of concepts. Some are better than others (reliability and validity are terms that will be defined further in Chapter 3).

A given indicator may be a question in a questionnaire—"What is your total family income from all sources for last year?"—and provide a range of categories such as "below $10,000," "$10,000 to $30,000," and "above $30,000." This is an indicator of the concept "total family income." A measurement procedure is called an operational definition of a concept, and the concept's, formal definition is called a conceptual definition.

In practice, you will find that a shorthand is used. The word variable is sometimes used in a general sense to refer to a concept and any of its potential indicators. A more precise distinction between concept and variable is made when it is needed.

head of household aged 75 or more was spent on essentials, as compared to 78% among the most well-to-do in the 45–54 age group.

This study provides refined descriptions of expenditure patterns among older-aged households. Description is one of the important goals of research. It also provides comparisons (in this case, comparisons across older age groups, across different income levels, and across different types of expenditures). As we shall see, **comparison and contrast** are essential features of good research. How do we know that the results of this study accurately describe older people's expenditures in the United States as a whole? Does anything that the investigators did support such generalizability of their conclusions?

Preparing a Case

The state had instituted a car emission test that was required of all cars each year before they were licensed. Senator Hampton, a state legislator, wanted to convince his colleagues that routine testing should be eliminated or at least curtailed. In his quarterly newsletter to constituents, Senator Hampton indicated his desire to find illustrations of the ineffectiveness and hardship caused by the annual testing. His staff members were instructed to summarize responses and add any other arguments they could find that would help him make the case for elimination of the testing program.

Staff received 230 responses from his constituents. Reasons given by the 20 respondents who argued that the program should not be eliminated were set aside. Among the arguments that were listed for eliminating the program were that it cost too much, only a few cars were rejected, the overall air quality was not very different from before the program started, and it was unnecessary, at least for newer cars that had properly functioning exhaust systems.

Could Senator Hampton's conclusion about the car testing program be seriously challenged by the evidence that was gathered? Is there anything about the way this study was conducted that has an impact on its conclusions?

Studying Gendered Perceptions

One of the consistent findings in the literature on gender differences is the differential evaluation of the two genders in U.S. culture (Golden, 1976). Men and women both tend to value men more highly than women. Golden cites a study by Goldberg documenting this phenomenon among women. The study used a questionnaire that contained six edited articles from professional journals, each followed by nine survey questions asking for the reader's evaluation of how well its author conducted the study and the study's likely impact. Goldberg did an interesting thing. In half of the questionnaires a given article had a male author (e.g., John T. McKay), and in the other half of the booklets the same article had a female author (e.g., Joan T. McKay). The two questionnaires were randomly given to a sample of 40 female undergraduate students at the author's college. Students read each article and answered each evaluation question. Evaluations of male and female authors for the same articles were compared and, as expected, female respondents tended to rate male-authored articles more highly. From the way the study was conducted, it is difficult to think of any other reason except the cultural beliefs female students share about gender that would account for the differences in evaluation that were found. Can you think of any **competing explanations** that might explain the findings?

There are strengths and weaknesses in all research, and the process of deciding what to do often involves tradeoffs. For example, Gamson's study of how political events are framed provided more control over what topics were raised, the size of discussion groups, and the presence of a trained observer to record what was said. On the other hand, the groups were from only one part of the country. Cook and Settersten used a nationally representative, existing data set, but it contained only information that the original investigators decided to include, and those data came from only one society and one particular point in time, 1984–1985. Goldberg's experimental study, as we shall see, permits a rather strong conclusion about the impact of gender on women's evaluation of edited articles, but the findings are limited to a small group of people at one college. Good tradeoffs in research are those that contribute the most to demonstrated knowledge.

Senator Hampton's "study," although parading under the guise of research, was really a selective choice of evidence in support of a preconceived intention to change an existing practice while ignoring any contradictory evidence. This example differs from the other three largely in terms of the lack of motivation on the part of the senator and his staff to collect the facts of the matter objectively and to reach a decision based on those facts.

IS IT RESEARCH?

When is a study to be considered research? To start with, studies focus on some **research topic** of interest: crime, spending patterns, norms and stereotypes, and so on. But this is not enough. Good studies address a specific **research question** that needs an answer. "Why do people commit crimes?" "How do spending patterns differ for older people who have more or less income?" "Do women buy into gender-stereotyped norms and values?" *Without a question, there is no need for research.*

What do you do when you want to find the answer to a question? People develop answers in a number of different ways. Some rely on hunches they have about what is true. Others turn to authoritative sources that they respect. Past experience or wisdom may also be a basis for finding answers to questions.

Scientific research is different from these ways of developing answers to questions, primarily in its concern about how knowledge is gained. It is this focus on *methods* of finding out that is distinctive about a book on scientific research.

If one can show how one came to know something—the methods or procedures used—the resulting knowledge is more likely to be verifiable. Reporting the procedures used permits others to repeat those procedures and demonstrate either that the conclusions are correct or that they need revision. It also permits others to examine the procedures for flaws and errors; things that weren't taken into account that could affect the conclusions reached. It is the methods used to generate the findings that underlie the conclusions reached and establish them as knowledge. Therefore, the care with which the research is carried out and the completeness with which the procedures used in carrying it out are reported underlie the knowledge claims that are made in any scientific field.

This isn't to say that hunches or educated guesses are necessarily wrong. However, how one arrived at those hunches or guesses is not a process that can usually be replicated by someone else in order to verify that the process justifies the conclusions reached. It is the public nature of methods of knowing and the implied encouragement of others to check results that lie at the very foundation of knowledge in scientific fields. Gaining new knowledge is often a difficult process, calling on creativity, a background in theory, a grasp of alternative **research methods,** and skill in carrying out a research plan.

In this book we are interested in conclusions that can be verified, repeated, and examined for flaws. We are interested in the **research process** by which such knowledge is developed and shared. Although these procedures are used widely in many areas of society, our special interest is in how knowledge is developed in the social sciences and in the field of sociology in particular. We will use the word ***research*** to refer to this more systematic inquiry process.

How can we tell which of the four studies described earlier are research in this more systematic sense? Scientific research can be distinguished from other kinds of studies in terms of four general characteristics of the inquiry process.

- **Knowledge-building pursuit.** Scientific research involves some interest on the part of the investigator in developing knowledge beyond what was previously known in some area. This is evident, for example, when studies gather data (new or archived) to use in deriving new knowledge about some stated problem. There are many reasons to seek new knowledge. Research goals include describing some situation; predicting future, past, or otherwise unknown outcomes; controlling some process; or explaining why some phenomenon occurs as it does.
- **Demonstrated knowledge.** Research involves a critical openness about how a study was conducted so that it is available for the independent judgment of others. Other researchers can follow the procedures to check the results.
- **Falsifiability.** Scientific research deals with research questions that can have more than one possible answer. The idea an investigator has about an answer to a question potentially may be true, partly true, or false. There is a careful attempt to make the gathered data fair. Favorable and unfavorable evidence are equally sought out and examined.
- **Generalizability.** The investigator is interested in applying research findings more broadly than to the data that were examined. In principle, the research is intended to apply to other cases at other times and places.

These characteristics lead research findings to be stated in a specific way. There are three kinds of statements that people make. One is a factual statement that something exists, called an *existential* statement. Another type of statement is *evaluative.* It states that something is good or bad according to some criterion. Third, there are *aesthetic* statements that something is pleasing or displeasing, pretty or ugly. Scientific research ends up making existential statements. Something exists, such as the percentage of the population that is below the poverty line or the fact that income levels make a difference in older people's household spending patterns. Outside their research work, scientists make evaluative and aesthetic statements, but the result of research is statements that summarize facts about what exists in the real world.

Thus, the legislator's study is not research because it is not set up to be falsifiable. The desired conclusion was known in advance and the problem was to build a strong case. Negative evidence was not sought and, when it occurred, it was set aside as largely irrelevant and not useful. In all likelihood there was no interest in generalizing beyond the effects of the law in that particular state and time and no interest in building knowledge. How conclusions were developed was not likely to be displayed in the course of the legislative debate.

The other three studies are research in that they all appear to be oriented toward building knowledge, they describe the methods by which results are known, they set up the inquiry process so that evidence on all sides of a problem can be examined, and they are clearly interested in generalizing their knowledge more broadly, beyond the specific instances that are examined. They are driving toward some general principles that are useful beyond the studies themselves. Note that an important part of what makes inquiry *research* is the intent of the investigators to build generalizable knowledge and to do it in a way that can be demonstrated.

Why is this research approach to knowing important? First, it is one possible way in which new knowledge can be generated; it works. It is also a more accurate and fruitful way to build knowledge. This has been shown over the years as scientists have contributed to building scholarly knowledge and solving human problems. Second, it is checkable. Others, following described research procedures, can replicate findings (or show that they are not accurate). This provides an opportunity to correct errors and reinterpret findings. Third, scientific research is driven toward findings that are relevant not just to the instances that are studied but to unknown cases. Thus, the ability to provide descriptions or principles that are valid and useful beyond the study itself is an important advantage of scientific research.

There are logical parts of research, such as developing good ideas, showing how these are related to what is already known, and laying out the steps in reasoning underlying the research. There are creative parts of research that may involve identifying a good research problem or a way to investigate something that has defied investigation. There are planning parts of research that involve laying out the ideas, the reasons for doing research, and ways the research might best be conducted. There are businesslike parts of research that involve the efficient execution of research plans. However, there is a **social context of research** as well. It is this social context of research that this book underscores. After all, the methods that are actually used, not simply the hopes or plans that have been made, underlie the soundness of conclusions that are reported.

WHO DOES SOCIAL RESEARCH AND WHY

Research is a human pursuit, rooted in our curiosity about our universe and ourselves. The topics we find interesting, the skills we have learned, the consequences we anticipate, our biases and foibles, insights and resources all bear on the accomplishment of research. We are allowed to do some things; we have resources that permit some investigations and not others. We have values that guide what we do and how we do it. We also have distractions and preferences. So how is research accomplished? What are its constraints and pitfalls? What conditions promote successful and substantial research?

In contemporary society, research tends to take place in organizational settings and in a very basic sense it is conducted by a **research team.** The ability of an investigator to deal with these facts of social life determines in large part whether knowledge can be produced. Some of the more common social contexts of research are described here.

"Listen to this: 'Extensive research has recently been completed which proves there are other businesses just like show business.' "

Contexts with a Mission to Produce Knowledge

Universities and nonprofit research laboratories are good examples of knowledge-producing contexts. The organization has a mission to produce knowledge that is available to anyone who is interested.

In these contexts, the investigator is often a specialist in some subject who has a position in the host organization. Duties typically involve research plus other responsibilities such as teaching, serving on committees, giving talks, and counseling, but investigators are usually free to choose research topics and design their research. Senior investigators in universities, for example, may have job security that insulates them to some extent from problems that pursuing research on unpopular ideas may inspire.

Grants supporting research are applied for and awarded in a competitive process. The granting agencies (e.g., federal agencies or private foundations) generally are looking for work in a topic area they consider important, but they usually leave the details of the research to the investigator. Results are published and sometimes even the original data are made public. Care is taken to explain research procedures used. Pressures on the grantee are to perform the research well (and within budget), publish the findings in professionally respectable publications, respond to questions about the research, and successfully apply for additional research funding. Indeed, the advancement of researchers in their organization depends on publishing and successful grant getting.

The research team typically involves one or more principal investigators, research supervisors and workers (often students paid as research assistants), and various support staff such as secretaries and accountants. Investigators often find it interesting to devote much more time and effort to their project than is specifically paid for by their grants. In universities there usually is an educational theme as well. For example, research staff gain experience and find part-time support while they pursue a degree. The principal investigators may also be the student workers' academic advisers.

Contexts with a Mission to Solve a Particular Problem

A second major context for research is one in which the purpose is to provide information designed to contribute to the solution of a particular problem or to evaluate the program or activities of some organization. This type of research is generally referred to as applied research. The investigator is engaged to conduct research that will meet the needs of an agency or business. A wide variety of organizations with varying focuses sponsor this type of research. For example, a researcher may be an employee of or may contract with a governmental agency in which the research focuses on establishing rules and regulations, evaluating the consequences of certain practices, developing evidence concerning breaches of the law, or helping with long-range planning. Researchers also may be found in partisan "think tanks." These organizations often have a desired line of conclusions or a set of issues they wish to promote. Researchers for political campaigns or for some value position may work in this type of organizational context.

These contexts have somewhat different pressures. The employee-researcher generally must be oriented toward that which the business or agency finds useful or profitable: new products, new ways of doing business, research supporting the virtues of a product or stand on an issue, and so on. Funding may be largely an internal business investment in research. Other companies do research for paying clients, and the clients' objectives are central to the research endeavor. The researchers are concerned with satisfying their clients, keeping within budget, being on time, maintaining the image of their firm, and retaining and gaining new research contracts.

Here the research team structure may be more explicit, including one or more investigators assigned to a project, assistants, clerical and accounting staff who may be shared with other projects, and the organization's hierarchy of officials and departments. Research staff effort is charged to some project in a more business-oriented accounting system, which may restrict overtime effort. Results of this kind of research tend to be private or in-house working papers and reports (including details of how the study was conducted) that are not readily available to outsiders but are provided to clients.

Student Investigators

One important type of somewhat-independent scholar is students in a college setting who are doing research papers or theses or are participating in a team research effort. In addition to allowing students to practice new research skills, these settings can provide a unique opportunity to create knowledge, in part because of the course and college context.

Consider the (usually) built-in opportunities. The pressures are largely personal but are driven by course or degree requirements. You are generally free to try something new and interesting. You can pick from a wide range of topics that interest you, and you can pursue your topic in the way you think best, taking a few more risks than you could if you were working in some company. Rarely will that happen later in life! At the start, there is an equality among student team members, who have different (and largely unknown) insights and skills. Motivations differ and grades may be more important to some students than others. There is some pressure to excel, driven by grading as well as competition with peers and a chance to show the professor that you have a better idea. The course has a definite ending that must be met. Generally there is little funding, but the college context provides a number of free opportunities. There are many experts around. Most faculty are eager to help someone who has a good idea and is trying to pursue it successfully. Universities are full of people who are usually eager to talk about your ideas. In most other settings such help is limited, either because it is politically risky to have frank discussions or because the chain of command keeps you restricted to those you can "properly" approach. Universities also tend to provide greater access to relevant literature than other settings.

Some students hope to do as little as possible, to seem to gather data but fake it, to overstate what was found, to just get a passing grade in a required course. A missed opportunity! This course is among the few rare opportunities in most students' lives to engage in research they consider important and do it in an idea-sensitive context. Some students have a long-standing line of inquiry they find compelling. Each assigned research paper becomes an opportunity to dig into another aspect of their favorite topic in more detail.

The point is that students are often in a unique position to engage in serious scientific research in a social context that is unique, supportive, and malleable. Sometimes this leads to unusually good research. Almost always it is a good chance to learn valuable inquiry skills. Many scholarly associations take pains to include good student papers in their professional meetings (sometimes with awards attached), and journals publish good papers from students (sometimes coauthored by an adviser). Journals also provide good feedback from their reviewers. Graduate schools and idea-oriented agencies and businesses often take special note of student-initiated research and publications. Careful inquiry is still a rare commodity!

SOCIAL FACTORS IN RESEARCH

Research doesn't just happen. Technical skill and knowledge of the area one is researching are critical. Also critical are social processes such as researchers' and staff members' expectations of each other and their research, research norms, social pressures, and desired outcomes, all of which affect research findings. For example, competition between researchers may lead a researcher to avoid getting useful advice from the other researchers. Students may defer to their mentors, even when they see a better solution or an error. To save face, more problematic aspects of research may be glossed over. Some contexts are exciting and challenging, others spawn low morale and a sense of being ignored and canceled out. There was a report of a research interviewer who didn't like some questions in a questionnaire and quietly omitted asking a whole section of the survey. The point is that social processes lead to strengths and weaknesses in research.

A large, professional research organization had a novel solution to a shortage of time in conducting a piece of contract research. Usually, research involves an extensive literature search as part of initial planning, before gathering data. This helps uncover information that is valuable to the researcher, identifying measures to use, approaches to take, and previous findings. Under a deadline, this research company hired a teacher during the summer to create a bibliography on the topic of their research contract. During this time the research itself was proceeding and it was completed about the time that the bibliography was finished. The final report simply bound the bibliography and the report of the results of the research together. The research could not have been informed by anything found in the bibliographic search! Here, the literature search was only window dressing. A tradeoff had been made between getting the contract finished on time and the potential quality of the research had it been enriched by the literature on prior work in the area.

Each of the organizational contexts listed earlier (and others not mentioned) has a somewhat different combination of social factors that influence research. Researchers have different statuses as employees, consultants, or more independent scholars. Some organizations are flat (everyone can legitimately approach anyone else) and some are hierarchical (with a chain of command that excludes some potentially helpful people from involvement in a study). Some organizations have a mission to make a profit or perpetuate an organization and support a staff. The priority of goals affects decisions about research. For example, sound research is valued differently in different organizational settings, which may lead to time and resource pressures on research. Research output varies. Depending on the social context, the most desired outcome may be a published article or research monograph, a technical report by some deadline, or an answer favorable to the organization's values. Research may be targeted at an immediate application or use (applied research) or it may be a contribution to knowledge in a field with little immediate concern about its use in everyday life (basic research).

Clients also differ. In academic research the audience is the general public or, more specifically, professional peers. Research organizations have government or private clients who contract for research. Some research is for investigators themselves, to satisfy their own curiosity.

The researcher may take an advocacy stance for certain political or social outcomes that may color research decisions. Often funders of research have value positions; the researcher is under pressure to take these values into account in the expression of findings (e.g., drug research funded by drug companies or tobacco research funded by the tobacco industry). In some cases, results are private and not widely available for checking or replication. In other cases data may revert to the public domain after some period of time so that they are constantly available for review.

The social side of research is evident not only in research by inexperienced people but in research by highly trained and able researchers. We will discuss some of the problems that can arise. The antidote is a good research question and research plan, careful reflection about research ideas and consequences of the way in which the research is conducted, knowledge about research options and how they fit together with research problems, bright and insightful researchers, and a social situation that facilitates the human process of inquiry.

In this book we will talk about families of flaws, things that seem to go together not because they must, but because humans are running the process and they make mistakes and work under a variety of pressures. You have undoubtedly seen some of these patterns unfold. Someone wants an answer to a question and is so convinced that he or she has the ultimate answer that the research ends up being a selective process of picking only supportive evidence and ignoring everything else. The "conclusion" was settled upon before any evidence was gathered, and the conclusions often are defended with great passion. You may also have seen people decide to do research without a clear idea of what they are researching. The result is a zigzag process of going from one research problem to another, ending up with data that never quite fit the latest research idea. Conclusions are then vague and confusing at best.

This methods book deals with different ways to set up and conduct research, ways that have proven to be useful in certain situations. It also deals with ways of thinking about research findings and examining them for strengths and flaws. In many ways, research methods help investigators negotiate social contexts in order to accomplish valid and reliable knowledge.

ETHICAL CONCERNS IN SOCIAL SCIENCE RESEARCH

The bottom line for any serious social science research is that the investigator must behave in a respectful and ethical way toward participants. Ethical behavior is determined by two sources: the investigator and the societal context in which the research is being conducted. Most researchers feel two sometimes-contending pressures. One is the desire to do the best possible job of inquiry so that some solid findings are established. The second is a desire to treat those involved in the research in a humane and appropriate way. These are standards that stem from the investigator's own values and background. In some cases these two personal pressures pose a dilemma. For example, an investigator may want to be open about the purpose of a questionnaire or experiment, but being open may bias later responses and work against achieving unbiased research findings. What should an ethical researcher do?

Beyond pressures stemming from the investigator's own ethical standards, the social context in which the research is conducted may have norms and laws governing contractual obligations about how the research is to be conducted (e.g., deadlines, accounting, who is involved, what is to be researched) as well as standards of how research subjects and research staff may be treated. Examples of this latter type of ethical standard are topics judged to be taboo that are not supposed to be researched (and are unfundable), professional society standards guiding ethical behavior of their members, funding agency requirements for the treatment of subjects, legal standards, limitations on the use of subjects imposed by organizations that are concerned about legal sanctions, and other cultural prescriptions and proscriptions. Reynolds (1982) illustrates a number of situations in which ethical issues are raised and suggests how they may be handled.

The ethical behavior of an investigator has consequences not only for the welfare of subjects, staff, and organizations involved in research, but also for the investigator's chances of conducting research again.

The risks of research for participants in social science research are generally not severe. Many research procedures are similar to the everyday experience of people in a society. For example, being sent a questionnaire or receiving repeated follow-up calls from a polling agency, being asked questions about private matters, or being given information that may or may not be true are experiences nearly everyone has had with commercial firms and agencies. Similar behavior by researchers is unlikely to be more upsetting to research subjects. On the other hand, some steps in research may be harmful. Manipulation in experiments, for example, may be experienced as embarrassing or demeaning; disclosure of private information to the wrong party may affect a person's reputation or job prospects. The research process may reveal to an individual certain things that affect his or her self-esteem. Failure to explain one's true intentions adequately may assault the view of proper behavior researchers have for themselves as well as the sensibilities of the subject.

Most investigators want to be known for upholding the highest standards of ethics and scholarly rigor. Being respectful of staff and subjects is likely to be a primary interest. Thus, most researchers try to avoid creating embarrassing situations, avoid demeaning anyone, avoid negative consequences for staff and subjects, respect individual privacy and make good on promises such as confidentiality, and let the subject know the purpose of the study (possibly at the end of data gathering).

Professional societies generally espouse a code of conduct that includes accepted ethical practices in their particular research area. At the end of this chapter, selections from the code of conduct adopted by the American Sociological Association are listed as an illustration.

Finally, the societal context of research often has rules designed to ensure appropriate investigator behavior. In the United States, for example, federal funding agencies require universities to have human subjects review boards that examine research proposals and funded projects for their treatment of humans. Such boards may also act on behalf of the organizations to ensure that the organizations avoid being sued for the behavior of their researchers. Sometimes subjects are asked to sign a statement acknowledging acceptance of any research risk. In the United States, some topics of research are defined as sensitive and intrusive and are subject to greater control. In the United States there is no "client privilege" law for researchers. Thus, promises of confidentiality have no special legal standing, as they do for doctors and lawyers. Researchers need to be aware that their records could be legally confiscated. Ethical issues also arise because of conflicts of interest; for example, a university drug researcher working with funds from a drug company may also own stock in that company. This may exert pressure on the researcher toward successes and away from failures of the drug (Krimsky, 1997).

In the end, certain steps should be taken in investigations to solve most ethical issues.

- When assurances of confidentiality are given, the researcher should plan steps to **maintain confidentiality.** For example, case identification numbers are generally substituted for other personal identification as the data are coded. A matching list of case numbers and personal identifiers is kept in a safe place while data files are being checked for accuracy. Often the original questionnaires, schedules, any matching lists, and recordings that contain personal identifiers are carefully shredded or destroyed once the data file is checked for accuracy. There are steps that can be taken during data gathering that let one know who has responded without identifying a particular response instrument with that person, thus maintaining anonymity when it is crucial.

- Researchers should **disclose** the essential nature of the project in which a subject is being asked to participate. If disclosure would bias the research, then a researcher should disclose essential details early, but perhaps save responses to more detailed questions about the research for later after the subject has had an opportunity to complete a questionnaire or respond to an experiment. Individual subjects need to be informed and consent to their participation in most research.

- Researchers should build in research procedures that help **handle potential negative consequences** of research. One example is planning to debrief (or provide other support) to each person involved in an experiment that may have a confusing or demoralizing effect on a respondent.

- Researchers should **avoid conflicts of interest.** This might take the form of avoiding research in which the researcher has an economic interest (e.g., tobacco research by researchers who are also paid by a tobacco company) and, certainly, informing readers of the sources of funding in any publication of results.

- Finally, researchers should **demonstrate open concern for the ethical problems** of research throughout the research process.

In this text we keep the ethical concerns of researching in the forefront by pointing out potential issues throughout the text, elaborating on ethical concerns as they apply to the various steps in research.

SCHEMATIC OUTLINE OF RESEARCH METHODS

Some have described research as a shuttle between data and thinking, the real world and theory. Riley (1963:4) suggests a four-part model of research (see Figure 1.1). She shows research as a shuttle between a conceptual model and research findings. Research methods guide the empirical phase of gathering data. Methods of interpretation guide the process of reaching conclusions about the implications of research data for a conceptual model.

Guided by one's theoretical ideas and assumptions about the research question, empirical methods are designed to gather empirical data relevant to the research problem. But data do not interpret themselves, so interpretive methods are used to guide the assessment of the data and suggest their impact on one's research question and the conceptual model underlying it. Usually in the process of research there is a continual shuttle between data and ideas, refining the data collection process and elaborating the interpretation of findings.

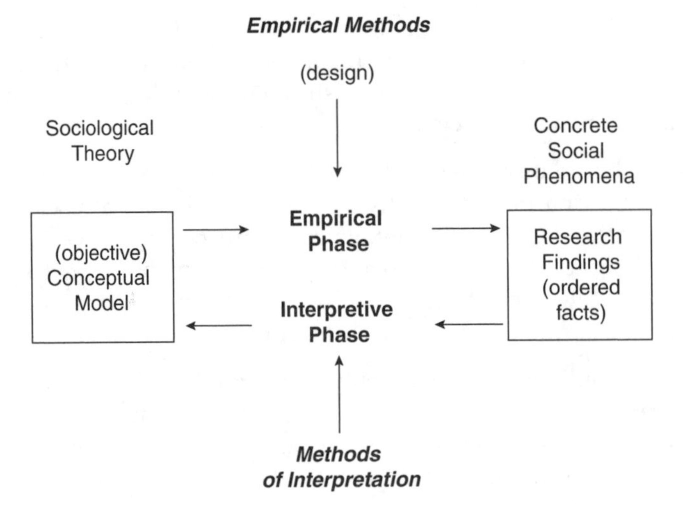

FIGURE 1.1 Riley's Model of Research

Another way to look at research is as a flow of steps that are often taken in the process of doing research. Key parts of research include the following:

1. Settling on a research topic
2. Refining a specific research question about that topic
3. Reviewing literature to identify prior thought and theory relevant to the research question
4. Developing a research plan (i.e., research design) and resources in order to gather and analyze appropriate information to answer the research question
5. Data gathering (a field phase of the research)
6. Organizing data, checking data for accuracy, and analyzing data
7. Interpreting and checking the results
8. Writing the research report

For example, a researcher, having identified a topic, needs to refine a research question that can be answered by research. As we shall see, some potential questions can't be answered. Others are biased toward one outcome. A good research question takes work to refine adequately.

All research is based on assumptions and theory about the subject matter. It is generally helpful if these are explicit and examined. A review of literature on a topic helps locate relevant theory, methods that have been used in similar studies, and findings from prior research in an area. This guides research planning. Research involves identifying and assembling data relevant to the research question. Sometimes this involves use of existing (archival) data; sometimes it comes from a survey, field observation, or an experiment. We will talk about these alternatives later in this book.

Once the data are gathered and checked for accuracy, the analysis takes place and findings are interpreted so that the research question is answered and appropriately qualified. All of this typically is written up in a final research article, book, or report.

Hopefully, in the process of reading this book, you will gain insight into the flow of research decisions and learn about options and possibilities for conducting social science research, how research plans can be accomplished, and the impact of social contexts on research.

SUMMARY

In this chapter we have introduced some examples of studies and raised the question about how to identify research in the sense used in this book. Scientific research is different from hunches, best guesses, and experience alone as ways of knowing. Differences stem from the investigator's intent and skill in building knowledge that can be demonstrated, is falsifiable, and is potentially generalizable beyond the research itself to useful general principles or a description of broader situations.

Underlying research-based knowledge is its social setting or social context, which affects the way in which research is accomplished. Research takes place in organizational settings and is usually conducted by a team, which can be a strength as well as a problem. Research designs are often tradeoffs, always seeking the soundest research within constraints. Investigators work in a variety of settings with different characteristics that affect research. Students are also in a social context that affects the research they do, but often this can be a very favorable context for learning the ropes of social science research and conducting important research. Ethical considerations include standards stemming from researchers themselves and from outside sources. Informed consent of subjects is one important procedure used in most research. Ethics is a feature of all stages of research, and these issues are continually raised throughout this book. Finally, this chapter introduced two overall ways of thinking about research. Riley points out the shuttle between ideas and data that is characteristic of research. There is also a flow of research that moves from deciding on a topic, through formulating a research question, all the way through the final checking and reporting of findings.

The chapters in this book trace out main options and issues involved in the conduct of social science research. We attempt to place the pursuit of research in a social context to highlight the effect of this context on the quality of research findings.

TERMS TO KNOW

Archival data
Comparison and contrast
Competing explanations
Concepts
Investigator/researcher
Observer
Research
Research methods

Research process
Research question
Research teams
Research topic
Social context of research
Variables

ISSUES AND COMPARISONS

Hunches, authority, and experience
Case-building versus research
Riley's model of research
Kinds of statements
- Existential statements
- Evaluative statements
- Aesthetic statements

Impact of organizational settings
Elements of research
- Falsifiability
- Knowledge-building pursuit
- Demonstrated knowledge
- Generalizability

Goals of research
- Description
- Explanation
- Prediction
- Control

EXERCISES

1. Listed here are some examples of studies people might do. What is the person trying to do? Lay out (in words or arrow diagrams) what you see as the most important elements of each project. Which ones are research and why? Which ones are not research and why? How could those that are not research be changed so they are scientific research in the sense used in this chapter?
   a. J. Ustis is an investigator who helps lawyers prepare their cases for court. Ustis's research on a case involves different research methods such as field observation and using data from various records, personal interviews, and surveys of communities. He then writes a report of these findings.
   b. Is speed a factor in highway auto fatalities in rural areas? A researcher examined records of all highway fatalities in the past 2 years for a random sample of 100 rural counties. For each fatality, the researcher recorded the official estimate of speed at the time of impact. The 100 counties in the sample had an average of 25 auto fatalities per 100,000 population, and the average speed at the time of impact was 10 miles per hour over the posted speed limit. The researcher concluded, "Yes, speed is a factor in auto fatalities in rural areas."
   c. Are states justified in barring children who have AIDS from public schools? A researcher says "yes" because no studies have been conducted that *prove* that one cannot get AIDS from saliva or nasal drainage.
   d. Thomas Wilson (1991:117–23) writes that "previous research has found only modest effects of community size on social psychological characteristics (in this case their 'tolerance') of residents. . . . Tolerance is the willingness to allow the expression of divergent ideas and treat others according to universalistic criteria independent of value differences. Tolerance has generally been operationalized as a willingness to extend civil liberties to persons holding deviant religious or political views." Wilson uses data from the National Opinion Research Center General Social Surveys conducted between 1976 and 1989. Regarding urban experience, he writes, "I find that urbanism's impact on per-

sonality may be stronger than previously thought." For respondents whose urban experience is adequately reflected by available community size measures in the data (i.e., not just current city size but the size of cities the person has lived in or moved to), Wilson finds that community size has strong positive effects on tolerance. He also found that migration promotes tolerance regardless of size of destination community.

2. Find several examples in the media in which findings are being reported (print media are probably better for this purpose). Is there anything about the social context—organization, team, sponsorship, values—that might have a consequence for the knowledge that is being put forth? What factors might support its quality as research that one can trust? What factors might undermine the quality of the research? What could be done to change the impact of the study's social context to strengthen the knowledge it produces?
3. Identify one or more topics for research that interest you. Then find a journal or set of books that present research in that area. For three or four research reports, identify the research question that is the focus of the report.
4. Identify one research topic that interests you. State 8 to 10 research questions that you would find interesting to study on the topic. Each question should have more than one potential answer, and it should be possible to do research to answer each question. Note that each question ends in a question mark!
5. Under what circumstances is it appropriate to conduct research without participants' knowledge? What ethical dilemmas are involved and how might they be handled?

CODE OF ETHICS[1] Selected Sections

Dated: Summer 1997
American Sociological Association, 1722 N Street NW, Washington, DC 20036

Introduction

The American Sociological Association's (ASA's) Code of Ethics sets forth the principles and ethical standards that underlie sociologists' professional responsibilities and conduct. These principles and standards should be used as guidelines when examining everyday professional activities. They constitute normative statements for sociologists and provide guidance on issues that sociologists may encounter in their professional work.

ASA's Code of Ethics consists of an Introduction, a Preamble, five General Principles, and specific Ethical Standards. This Code is also accompanied by the

[1]Selected parts of the extensive code of ethics are presented here. The full code is available on the American Sociological Association's Web site (http://www.asanet.org). Most other professional associations maintain Web sites with similar information.

Rules and Procedures of the ASA Committee on Professional Ethics, which describe the procedures for filing, investigating, and resolving complaints of unethical conduct.

Preamble

This Code of Ethics articulates a common set of values upon which sociologists build their professional and scientific work. The Code is intended to provide both the general principles and the rules to cover professional situations encountered by sociologists. It has as its primary goal the welfare and protection of the individuals and groups with whom sociologists work. It is the individual responsibility of each sociologist to aspire to the highest possible standards of conduct in research, teaching, practice, and service.

General Principles

The following General Principles are aspirational and serve as a guide for sociologists in determining ethical courses of action in various contexts. They exemplify the highest ideals of professional conduct.

Principle A: Professional Competence. Sociologists strive to maintain the highest levels of competence in their work; they recognize the limitations of their expertise; and they undertake only those tasks for which they are qualified by education, training, or experience. . . . They consult with other professionals when necessary for the benefit of their students, research participants, and clients.

Principle B: Integrity. Sociologists are honest, fair, and respectful of others in their professional activities—in research, teaching, practice, and service. . . . Sociologists conduct their affairs in ways that inspire trust and confidence; they do not knowingly make statements that are false, misleading, or deceptive.

Principle C: Professional and Scientific Responsibility. Sociologists adhere to the highest scientific and professional standards and accept responsibility for their work. . . . Sociologists value the public trust in sociology and are concerned about their ethical behavior and that of other sociologists that might compromise that trust. . . . When appropriate, they consult with colleagues in order to prevent or avoid unethical conduct.

Principle D: Respect for People's Rights, Dignity, and Diversity. Sociologists respect the rights, dignity, and worth of all people. They strive to eliminate bias in their professional activities, and they do not tolerate any forms of discrimination based on age; gender; race; ethnicity; national origin; religion; sexual orientation; disability; health conditions; or marital, domestic, or parental status. They are sensitive to cultural, individual, and role differences in serving, teaching, and studying groups of people with distinctive characteristics. In all of their work-related activities, sociologists acknowledge the rights of others to hold values, attitudes, and opinions that differ from their own.

Principle E: Social Responsibility. Sociologists are aware of their professional and scientific responsibility to the communities and societies in which they live and work. They apply and make public their knowledge in order to contribute to the public good. When undertaking research, they strive to advance the science of sociology and to serve the public good.

Ethical Standards

1. Professional and Scientific Standards. Sociologists adhere to the highest possible technical standards that are reasonable and responsible in their research, teaching, practice, and service activities. They rely on scientifically and professionally derived knowledge; act with honesty and integrity; and avoid untrue, deceptive, or undocumented statements in undertaking work-related functions or activities.

9. Conflicts of Interest. Sociologists maintain the highest degree of integrity in their professional work and avoid conflicts of interest and the appearance of conflict. Conflicts of interest arise when sociologists' personal or financial interests prevent them from performing their professional work in an unbiased manner. In research, teaching, practice, and service, sociologists are alert to situations that might cause a conflict of interest and take appropriate action to prevent conflict or disclose it to appropriate parties.

11. Confidentiality. Sociologists have an obligation to ensure that confidential information is protected. They do so to ensure the integrity of research and the open communication with research participants and to protect sensitive information obtained in research, teaching, practice, and service. When gathering confidential information, sociologists should take into account the long-term uses of the information, including its potential placement in public archives or the examination of the information by other researchers or practitioners.

11.01 MAINTAINING CONFIDENTIALITY

(a) Sociologists take reasonable precautions to protect the confidentiality rights of research participants, students, employees, clients, or others.

(c) Information provided under an understanding of confidentiality is treated as such even after the death of those providing that information.

11.06 ANONYMITY OF SOURCES

(b) When confidential information is used in scientific and professional presentations, sociologists disguise the identity of research participants, students, individual or organizational clients, or other recipients of their service.

11.08 PRESERVATION OF CONFIDENTIAL INFORMATION

(b) Sociologists plan so that confidentiality of records, data, or information is protected in the event of the sociologist's death, incapacity, or withdrawal from the position or practice.

12. Informed Consent. Informed consent is a basic ethical tenet of scientific research on human populations. Sociologists do not involve a human being as a subject in research without the informed consent of the subject or the subject's legally authorized representative, except as otherwise specified in this Code. Sociologists recognize the possibility of undue influence or subtle pressures on subjects that may derive from researchers' expertise or authority, and they take this into account in designing informed consent procedures.

12.01 SCOPE OF INFORMED CONSENT

(a) Sociologists conducting research obtain consent from research participants or their legally authorized representatives (1) when data are collected from research participants through any form of communication, interaction, or intervention; or (2) when behavior of research participants occurs in a private context where an individual can reasonably expect that no observation or reporting is taking place.

(b) Despite the paramount importance of consent, sociologists may seek waivers of this standard when (1) the research involves no more than minimal risk for research participants, and (2) the research could not practicably be carried out were informed consent to be required. Sociologists recognize that waivers of consent require approval from institutional review boards or, in the absence of such boards, from another authoritative body with expertise on the ethics of research. Under such circumstances, the confidentiality of any personally identifiable information must be maintained unless otherwise set forth in 11.02(b).

(c) Sociologists may conduct research in public places or use publicly available information about individuals (e.g., naturalistic observations in public places, analysis of public records, or archival research) without obtaining consent. If, under such circumstances, sociologists have any doubt whatsoever about the need for informed consent, they consult with institutional review boards or, in the absence of such boards, with another authoritative body with expertise on the ethics of research before proceeding with such research.

(d) In undertaking research with vulnerable populations (e.g., youth, recent immigrant populations, the mentally ill), sociologists take special care to ensure that the voluntary nature of the research is understood and that consent is not coerced. In all other respects, sociologists adhere to the principles set forth in 12.01(a)–(c).

12.02 INFORMED CONSENT PROCESS

(a) When informed consent is required, sociologists enter into an agreement with research participants or their legal representatives that clarifies the nature of the research and the responsibilities of the investigator prior to conducting the research.

(d) When informed consent is required, sociologists inform research participants or their legal representatives of the nature of the research; they indicate to participants that their participation or continued participation is voluntary; they inform participants of significant factors that may be expected to influence their willingness to participate (e.g., possible risks and benefits of their participation); and they explain other aspects of the research and respond to questions from prospective participants. . . . Sociologists explicitly discuss confidentiality and, if applicable, the extent to which confidentiality may be limited as set forth in 11.02(b).

12.05 USE OF DECEPTION IN RESEARCH

(a) Sociologists do not use deceptive techniques (1) unless they have determined that their use will not be harmful to research participants; is justified by the study's prospective scientific, educational, or applied value; and that equally effective alternative procedures that do not use deception are not feasible, and (2) unless they have obtained the approval of institutional review boards or, in the absence of such boards, with another authoritative body with expertise on the ethics of research.

(b) Sociologists never deceive research participants about significant aspects of the research that would affect their willingness to participate, such as physical risks, discomfort, or unpleasant emotional experiences.

(c) When deception is an integral feature of the design and conduct of research, sociologists attempt to correct any misconception that research participants may have no later than at the conclusion of the research.

(d) On rare occasions, sociologists may need to conceal their identity in order to undertake research that could not practicably be carried out were they to be known as researchers. Under such circumstances, sociologists undertake the research if it involves no more than minimal risk for the research participants and if they have obtained approval to proceed in this manner from an institutional review board or, in the absence of such boards, from another authoritative body with expertise on the ethics of research. Under such circumstances, confidentiality must be maintained unless otherwise set forth in 11.02(b).

12.06 USE OF RECORDING TECHNOLOGY

Sociologists obtain informed consent from research participants, students, employees, clients, or others prior to videotaping, filming, or recording them in any form, unless these activities involve simply naturalistic observations in public places and it is not anticipated that the recording will be used in a manner that could cause personal identification or harm.

13. Research Planning, Implementation, and Dissemination. Sociologists have an obligation to promote the integrity of research and to ensure that they comply with the ethical tenets of science in the planning, implementation, and dissemination of research. They do so in order to advance knowledge, to minimize the possibility that results will be misleading, and to protect the rights of research participants.

14. Plagiarism.

(a) In publications, presentations, teaching, practice, and service, sociologists explicitly identify, credit, and reference the author when they take data or material verbatim from another person's written work, whether it is published, unpublished, or electronically available.

(b) In their publications, presentations, teaching, practice, and service, sociologists provide acknowledgment of and reference to the use of others' work, even if the work is not quoted verbatim or paraphrased, and they do not present others' work as their own whether it is published, unpublished, or electronically available.

REFERENCES

Cook, Fay Lomax, and Richard A. Settersten, Jr., "Expenditure Patterns by Age and Income Among Mature Adults: Does Age Matter?" *The Gerontologist* 1995;35:1.

Gamson, William A., *Talking Politics*, Cambridge University Press, Cambridge, UK, 1992.

Golden, M. Patricia, ed., *The Research Experience*, Peacock, Itasca, IL, 1976.

Krimsky, Sheldon, "Who's Minding the Lab?," *Tufts University Health and Nutrition Letter*, 1997.

Reynolds, Paul D., *Ethics and Social Science Research*, Prentice Hall, Englewood Cliffs, NJ, 1982.

Riley, Matilda White, *Sociological Research: A Case Approach*, Harcourt, Brace, New York, 1963.

Seigman, Daniel, "The 30% Solution," *Fortune*, July 11, 1994, pp. 177–78.

Wilson, Thomas C., "Urbanism, Migration and Tolerance: A Reassessment," *American Sociological Review* February 1991;56:117–23.

CHAPTER TWO

CONCEPTUALIZATION: WHAT TO MEASURE AND WHY

The first key to research is a research question (e.g., "Do self-employed immigrants to the United States get greater economic returns than wage/salaried immigrants?"). It's a simple idea, but absolutely basic to research: What do you want to find out? It's easy because a research question is a statement ending in a question mark! It's hard because asking the right question and forming the question in a way that leads to good research requires some experience. It requires clarity and background knowledge of the topic you want to study. This critical start defines what you are after and helps you identify where to start and when you are finished.

Good research questions often presuppose that you have a good deal of interest in and information about the topic you are studying and what others have already found out about it. Behind a good research question is some idea or hunch, or, ideally, a more carefully researched **theory.** As we shall see, these ideas help put the research question in a context and guide how it is addressed.

Research questions involve special **concepts** such as self-employment and economic returns. These are generally technical terms that point to some phenomenon that is an important aspect of the topic to be researched. Such concepts must be defined carefully so that others understand specifically what they mean. A later step in research is the identification and development of indicators of each concept so that researchers can gather data on whether and to what extent the concepts they are interested in exist in some population.

In this chapter we discuss how to form a research question; then we will deal with the technical terms or concepts involved in the research question. Finally, this chapter describes the framework of ideas, assumptions, and theories that are the context of the research question. Chapter 3 discusses how concepts can be defined, indicators found, and measures developed.

FORMING RESEARCH QUESTIONS

It is helpful to make a distinction between a **research topic** and a research question. An investigator often starts with a research topic or general phenomenon of interest such as domestic violence, recidivism, old age, or occupational similarity between parents and children. Research topics may come from an investigator's personal experience or from the investigator's reading of theory, or they may be ideas that arise from examining others' research. Some research topics are suggested by funding sources or organizations that contract for research. Whatever the source, it is useful to clarify what topic one is really interested in investigating. The **research question** specifies what we want to study specifically about a topic and suggests key concepts we need to take into account. Research questions can be about a wide variety of things that pique the investigator's curiosity. Here we discuss some examples to illustrate this variety.

Many research questions are about some kind of outcome that is interesting to the investigator. For example,

> "Is the self-esteem of high school boys and girls influenced by the kind of school they go to?"

Here, self-esteem is the outcome. It is called a **dependent variable** because it is the outcome of interest in the research question.[1] It is potentially influenced by other variables. The question asks whether the kind of school would have an impact on this outcome. School type is another key concept in this research question. Here school type is thought to influence the dependent variable in some way, perhaps as a potential cause (called an **independent variable** because of its potential impact on the dependent variable). The research question could be restated: "Is school type (independent variable) a variable that influences self-esteem (dependent variable)?"

For clarity, the relationship of concepts indicated by independent and dependent variables can be shown in an **arrow diagram** that graphically lays out the relationship between the concepts with which the research question is concerned. Notice that, by convention, the outcome or dependent variable is at the right and the independent variable is at the left. These are connected by an arrow, with the arrow point indicating the direction of influence.

Another common type of research question compares two or more factors that may influence an outcome. For example,

> "Does the family or do peers have more influence on juvenile delinquency?"

[1]Indicators of concepts are called variables in research. In Chapter 3 we discuss the development of variables that are good indicators of concepts. Here, we use the more common research term *variable* and the conceptual term *concept* interchangeably. In Chapter 3 the distinction will be our focus (defining concepts so that variables can be developed as indicators of those concepts).

In this case, relevant research would seek to compare the impact of family with the impact of peers as they may influence the same outcome: juvenile delinquency. Note that there are three important concepts involved in this question: family factors, peer factors, and juvenile delinquency. All would have to be carefully defined in order to be used successfully in research to answer the research question.

Sometimes investigators are interested in an outcome (dependent variable) but are not aware of what factor or factors might result in the outcome. Accordingly, the purpose of the research may be to identify such factors. This might produce a research question such as the following one:

> "Why do some cities have higher crime rates than other cities?"

This research question calls for **exploratory research** to find potential independent variables.

Finally, a research question might simply call for a description of what the true state of affairs is in some respect. An example would be,

> "What was the percentage of Hispanic-owned businesses in Los Angeles in 1997?"

This question points to a concept, Hispanic-owned business, as its focus. It calls for a factual description of the ethnic ownership of businesses in Los Angeles in 1997 by whether they were Hispanic-owned.

What Makes a Good Research Question?

Good research questions have several characteristics. Specifically, they include the following:

- First, the question must be clearly stated. "Is the self-esteem of high school boys and girls influenced by the kind of school they go to?" is certainly better than "I wonder how schools are different?" The first research question is more specific and less ambiguous in pointing to differences that are of interest between specific kinds of schools. It is also stated more directly. Of course, it will be necessary to define in a systematic fashion what is meant by "kinds of schools" in order to carry out the research.

- Second, a good research question must be researchable. It must be a question that can have an answer that is based on checkable, shared evidence that can be gathered. "Why is the Mona Lisa beautiful?" would be a poorer question than, "Why do art connoisseurs believe that the Mona Lisa is beautiful?" The first is not researchable because, as far as we know, beauty is an individual judgment, unlike the percentage of Hispanic-owned businesses. We need questions that can be answered in a way that permits checking and can serve as a basis for agreement among investigators. Another way to put it is that a research question is researchable to the extent that it calls for finding out what exists. If the research question calls for statements about what the investigator thinks is aesthetically pleasing, or asks about his or her personal evaluative opinions, then the research question is not researchable in the framework we are discussing in this text.

▪ Third, good research questions point to important concepts that can be clearly defined. Thus, self-esteem, a long-standing concept in the social sciences, has had considerable effort devoted to its clear definition. Social scientists use many other concepts, such as recidivism, gender, occupational similarity, juvenile delinquency, school type, and aging of a population. Furthermore, as we shall see in Chapter 3, these concepts must be measurable. That is, they must be defined in a way that directs the researcher in observing or asking questions to determine what category of the variable a unit of analysis (case) falls into. We would need to be able to determine, for example, whether a population were aging or, perhaps, how old the population was.

▪ Fourth, it specifies the units of analysis (called cases) to which it applies. A good research question also indicates the kind of case that is involved. This would be the unit to which the concepts apply. If it's gender, then probably an individual person is the unit. If it is organizational centrality, then the unit is probably an organization. In the social sciences there are so many potentially interesting cases, such as individuals, organizations, friendship pairs, societies, or norms, that great care and clarity are needed.

To what does the research question apply? Three things must be clarified before it is clear what case is being referred to. First, the *kind* of case must be made clear. Is it a research question about teenage mothers, people over age 65, carpenters, those who have lived in rural areas all their lives, societies with a high birth rate, or task-oriented groups? Second, it is important to clarify *where* these cases are located. Are they all in the United States or in northern California? Third, it is important that the research question also indicate, in one way or another, *when* the cases that are of interest exist. Does the research question apply to contemporary society or to cases from 1895? Often research questions imply that they apply without regard to time or place to any organization, individual, or dyad (whatever is the unit). In fact, a goal of scientific research is to broaden theories (and questions that they suggest) so they apply to ever broader classes of cases: not only people in the United States but people anywhere; not only in the past, but now and any time in the future. Of course, that knowledge is hard to come by and hard to test.

▪ Fifth, it specifies the relationships that are expected. Often the expected relationships are such that one thing influences another. For example, how an official handles a domestic violence call has an impact on whether the offender does it again. Sometimes the relationship can be indicated in more detail. One might find that the relationship between concept A and concept B is positive and approximately linear, for example. In fact, the relationship may be stated in precise numeric terms (as in "The correlation between A and B is .56 or .79"). Statistics courses explain the various ways in which a relationship between concepts can be described.

▪ Sixth, a good research question focuses on outcomes (dependent variables) or, as a minimum, clearly indicates what the outcome of interest happens to be. A research question that asks, "What influence does a person's self-concept have?" is a poor one for a very practical reason. There is no limit to the range of potential outcomes and, thus, no real end to the research. The question can't be answered in a lifetime! A potentially fatal flaw in research is asking questions that can't be answered.

- Seventh, it involves contrasts that are made explicit. One of the keys to good research is to have contrasts. Usually research questions specify what the contrasts are to be, such as between parents and children or those who return to crime and those who don't, or older people and middle-aged people, or democratic institutions and those that are more repressive. To the ad that says that a food has less fat, the researcher would immediately ask, "Less than what?" (a comparison).

- Eighth, research questions should specify the conditions under which the relationships are expected (e.g., that it applies only to people who live in cities above a certain size, or that the relationship gets weaker as time passes, or that it is relevant only to women between the ages of 20 and 50). Sometimes a relationship is expected to be quite different under some conditions than others. For example, formal sanctions reduce repeat domestic violence, but only under the condition that some informal sanctions also exist.

- Finally, good research questions are those that stem from some idea or theory you have about important things. Sometimes the theory is implicit, but better research questions generally come from explicitly stated theory. Theory that has been used and tested by other researchers is often most useful as a basis for future research.

Good research questions are clearly stated, researchable questions involving important concepts that are related to theory. The research question applies to some kind of case or unit of analysis, involves comparison and contrasts, focuses on outcomes, and may also specify independent variables and conditions that govern expected relationships between concepts.

Examples of Research Questions

Research questions range in quality from poor to good. It is important that you learn to avoid the poor questions and learn to ask the good ones. The following examples illustrate some of the characteristics of these.

POORER

Old people in nursing homes.

This is a topic, not a question.

I think that people are basically good.

This isn't a question. It is merely an opinion of the investigator.

How do ghosts eat?

This is not a researchable question until one can unambiguously identify ghosts. Research must be about things that can be unambiguously identified in some way, such as by observation or by inference from observations.

What is the impact of city size?

This question can't be answered because it asks only about an independent variable and doesn't limit or specify the outcomes of interest. Although some impacts might be identified, all impacts could not be identified.

Do nuclear families have parents?

This is a **tautology**: It's true by definition. Nuclear families are generally defined as parents and their children.

Was income related to education in the United States in 1995?

This is a good question, but hasn't it been settled already? A researcher may have a new wrinkle on an old question, of course, but there are questions that don't really require much expenditure on further research. Checking prior work on a research question helps determine whether further research is needed.

Why do people commit crimes?

This is probably too broad to be answered in a lifetime. A series of more limited, focused questions would be more likely to be resolved by research. An investigator could start with the most important of the questions and keep going, designing research to answer each question as interest, time, and resources permit.

Why do special education classes have an effect on educational achievement?

This might be a good research question if one could narrow it down further, perhaps by looking in the library for ideas others have had and perhaps developing some hypotheses to test. What types of special education are included and what sorts of educational achievement are of interest, and for whom?

BETTER

Why are people in religious settings in the United States at the beginning of the twenty-first century more likely to think people are basically good and people in law enforcement in the United States at the same time more likely to think of people as basically bad?

This clearly identifies two time- and place-limited groups of cases that are to be compared on a specific attitude. Presumably there is some practical or theoretical reason for being interested in this comparison, but it is potentially researchable.

Does separating a feuding married couple reduce later violence more than lecturing them about the consequences of domestic violence?

Here the investigator is interested in comparing the potential effects of two independent variables on a dependent variable. The case appears to be a married couple (the case must be clearly specified, of course). Because no time or place location is mentioned, the investigator apparently is interested in an infinite conceptual population of married couples. For research, a specific, finite population would be the focus of a specific piece of research.

Why does special education have a greater effect on math learning than on English learning for minority 10th graders in the United States?

The investigator in this instance is interested in explaining the difference in impact that an independent variable has in two different areas. Cases are identified in terms of place but not time. Thus, the infinite conceptual population must be narrowed down in terms of cases at some place and time so that cases could be drawn for analysis. In many of these situations the implication is that the time frame is a contemporary one, a focus that would need justification in a research proposal.

A good way to see whether you have the idea of forming research questions is to pick a research topic you are interested in and then state a number of different, good research questions. Have others go over these questions and make suggestions.

FACTS AND HYPOTHESES

A research question calls for an answer. Two approaches to an answer are used in research and both require an examination of facts. The first approach is to gather appropriate factual data and examine them to see whether an answer to the research question can be formulated. The second approach uses prior research and thinking to come up with one or more hypothesized answers (called **hypotheses;** see Box 2.1 for definitions of this and other terms) to the research question. Then, research is designed to gather factual data aimed at testing whether the hypothesized answers are false. If they are not falsified by the factual data, then the hypothesized answers are presumed to be reasonable answers to the initial research question for the time being. Further research may show that the hypotheses are false in some situations.

Although the second approach, **hypothesis testing,** seems more indirect and cumbersome, it is usually the preferred approach. The first, exploratory approach, is preferred when there is little knowledge about potential answers to the research question or the answers are known to be inadequate.

Hypothesis testing is the preferred approach for several reasons. First, there is usually some prior thinking on a research question that one can build on that helps identify concepts and potential answers that can be tested. For example, prior exploratory research may suggest a hypothesized answer to a research question. In some cases, the hypothesized answer is a strictly logical deduction from well-developed theory. We talk about these sources of ideas later in the chapter. A second reason that hypothesis testing is preferred is that the results of this approach are often logically and empirically clearer. In exploratory research the end product sought is a hypothesis that purports to answer the research question. Because the hypothesis is generated from the data analyzed, those same data cannot be used to test whether it is true or false. A whole new database must be collected to do that. In hypothesis-testing research the investigator gathers a new set of factual data, and these data may show that the hypothesis is false or that the hypothesis is not false. Furthermore, factual data needed to test a hypothesized answer to a research question are usually much easier to define, so research can be

BOX 2.1
TERMINOLOGY

A **concept** is a property or characteristic of some case or unit of analysis in which one might be interested. It is, essentially, an idea about some aspect of some phenomenon (e.g., gender, self-esteem, city size, bureaucracy, social stratification).

A **case** (unit of analysis) is that defined entity that is sampled and scored or measured on variables of interest in a research project. A case is defined in terms of its substantive characteristics and their location in time and place. In sociology a case is often a human individual, a group, an organization, or a society. It can also be social entities such as "the father–child role relationship" or "a dyad." In research, a sample or population of these cases is targeted for examination.

A **variable** is an indicator of some defined concept or characteristic of a case (e.g., a response to the question "What is your age?" is a variable that can be used as an indicator of the concept "Age," or years since birth). Cases can be placed in one of several potential categories (or different values) of a variable.

An **independent variable** is a variable that is thought to influence or affect another variable (e.g., education is thought to have an impact on future income).

A **dependent variable** is the outcome or consequence of some process or the focus of interest in a study (e.g., in the last example, future income is the dependent variable because its value depends on other variables).

A **research question** is a question about the existence of some relationship or situation that can be answered by research that gathers relevant facts (e.g., "Do school experiences have the same effect on the self-esteem of boys and girls?")

A **hypothesis** is a proposed answer to a research question. Hypotheses may be derived from theoretical ideas or they may be suggested by exploratory research (e.g., "Why do children from divorced families have higher delinquency rates?" Hypothesis: "They have fewer available family supports and role models").

Facts are the result of observation or questioning, and they document the existence of something (e.g., the correlation between income and education, which was determined through survey research of some population at some point in time, would be a fact). Facts are used to test hypotheses, and facts may provide a basis for proposing new hypotheses.

Exploratory research is research that seeks hypotheses that will be good answers to research questions. It examines facts to derive potentially testable hypotheses.

Hypothesis-testing research is research that starts with a hypothesis, usually derived from prior theory relevant to a research question, and gathers factual data to test whether the hypothesis is likely or unlikely to be false.

designed in a more focused and efficient way and the results of the research can fill a gap in prior knowledge.

Research is the process of gathering the facts that are necessary to answer a research question. **Facts** are (usually systematically recorded) observations of what exists at some time and in some place. For example, we may observe that at street corner X during time period T, 13 cars passed the stop sign, 10 of them coming to a full stop, or that a certain organization started in 1996, or that a positive correlation exists between income and education among adults in the United States in 1998. This information could be checked by other appropriately trained observers and an **interobserver agreement** could be found. What is deemed to exist at some time and place may be something that can be directly sensed, such as A speaking to B. It may also include things that are unambiguously inferred from direct observations, such as the fact that person S holds two roles in his or her family: spouse and parent. We can infer this from answers that S gives to certain questions the investigator asks or by observing what S does, but we wouldn't "see" a role itself. *Role* is an abstract concept.

To sum up our language of research thus far, we need a research question as the basis for research. We may also have a hypothesized answer to that research question, in which case hypothesis-testing research can be designed. If we don't have a hypothesis, then research is usually designed to explore for an answer to the research question. In either case, an investigator examines factual information that is relevant to the research question and to any hypothesized answers. Research involves gathering the relevant facts to answer a research question.

THEORY AND ITS VALUE FOR RESEARCH

Pate and Hamilton (1992) were interested in the question of what police action best deters repeated domestic violence. For example, should officers arrest the offending spouse, attempt to counsel the family about consequences of abuse, or simply send the offending spouse away for several hours? Pate and Hamilton based their research on deterrence theory, a fancy label for reasoning that had been proposed by earlier researchers (ideas that were stimulated by even earlier research). Deterrence theory is the idea that human behavior can be influenced by incentives such as formal punishments contained in laws and enforced by police. Illegal behavior is discouraged most when penalties are more severe and when penalties are highly likely to be applied. This is because those contemplating illegal behavior perceive the consequences as very likely to be too costly to them.

Later, deterrence theory was broadened by other investigators, who stated a condition under which deterrence theory works best. They found that formal sanctions, such as prison terms or fines, are effective only to the extent that they are accompanied by informal sanctions. Informal sanctions are those that go beyond the penalties imposed by law. These include reactions such as embarrassment (called stigma in the literature), loss of valued relationships with others (called attachment costs), and loss of a job or economic opportunities (called commitment costs). Knowing this theory helped Pate and Hamilton investigate practical ways to reduce domestic violence. The theory suggests that increasing formal *and* informal sanctions would be more effective. Their research is an attempt to find out, by examining facts, whether this reasoning also applies to domestic violence.

Theory is the answer to "why" questions. Why do some people not repeat acts of domestic violence? The answer, according to deterrence theory, is that the threat of formal and informal punishment is perceived as too costly by some people; therefore, they are likely not to engage in domestic violence. Why should perceived cost deter a type of behavior? Perhaps a broader theory about human behavior would provide an answer to that question.

There are four important points to make about theory such as that used by Pate and Hamilton.

First, it is about certain kinds of cases, or units of analysis. For Pate and Hamilton, it appears that the case is an abusing spouse in a married pair.

Second, theories apply to only certain kinds of situations (a feature of theory called its **scope**). For example, deterrence theory applies to humans who are contemplating behavior that is defined as illegal in a society that has laws. Because no other limits are mentioned, one might presume that the investigators see the theory as applicable to any illegal behavior wherever and whenever it may be thought about (e.g., in ancient Rome, undeveloped countries in 1980, or New York City in 2020). Furthermore, it appears to be applicable to domestic violence as well as other illegal behavior. Thus, deterrence theory has a rather broad range of situations to which it is applicable, a broad scope.

Third, theories are about the relationship between concepts, such as the extent of penalties and likelihood of doing something illegal. Concepts such as informal penalties or likelihood of illegal behavior must be defined in order for the researcher to know exactly what is being discussed so that measurement of the concepts is possible. Good research carefully defines these concepts and develops ways to measure them (discussed in Chapter 3).

Fourth, the theory makes statements about concepts, linked by implication; it states what influences what. In this case, deterrence theory states that increasing formal and informal penalties or costs will lower the likelihood that the relevant illegal behavior will be undertaken. Furthermore, it states that the effect of formal sanctions may depend on whether there are also informal sanctions. More specifically, the theory might state that the greater the formal penalty for an illegal behavior, the lower will be the likelihood of that behavior happening, and greater informal penalties will make formal penalties more effective. This statement deals with the relationship between three concepts: formal penalties, informal penalties, and the extent to which illegal behavior will occur. To the extent that these statements are verified by research, they are called statements of **scientific law.** Note that the relationship between the penalties and the likelihood of illegal behavior is negative. In each case, the higher the penalty, the less likely the behavior. Some laws state more exactly how much one variable will affect another, sometimes expressing this relationship quantitatively.

Theories are logically interrelated sets of law-like statements about how concepts are related to each other. As you might suspect, there is a push toward more inclusive theories that interrelate many such statements. Theories range from grand theories to middle-range theories to very minimal theories, depending on their scope and the extent to which many statements of law are interrelated. Most theories used in research today probably are of the small to middle-range variety, like the deterrence theory used by Pate and Hamilton.

Theories can be expressed in words, arrow diagrams, and pictures or models to help demonstrate essential relationships between concepts. Groups of theories that are general, not fully developed, and not subject to much prior research may be called a **theoretical perspective.**

Because finding the answer to questions is generally difficult, most researchers use anything that appears to be useful in their pursuit. Prior theory is often very useful as a guide to research, so researchers generally start their research by doing a **literature search** to find out what has been done and how other researchers theoretically approach their work, what concepts are important to include, how others define and measure these concepts, and what questions remain to be answered.

Researchers use theories, whether formal and explicit or informal and implicit, to guide their research. It is better to have theories explicit and, if possible, stated in a formal way to add clarity to the reasoning about research and its implications. For example, knowing what we now know, it would be incomplete to research the effects of formal penalties on deterring domestic violence without taking account of informal penalties. Another function of theory is to let the investigator know when the research is finished! When the research question is answered as far as the theory is concerned, the research is done. Without theory, an investigator can go on and on, finding little details that may be interesting but do not add up to the resolution of a research question.

Sometimes a distinction is made between starting research with a strong theoretical basis and then conducting the research, or the reverse, starting by examining data and then developing and using theory to interpret findings. The **theory-then-research** approach starts with theory, deduces some implications of the theory for testing, then examines factual data to see whether the deductions are refuted. The outcome has implications for the theory itself. On the other hand, the **research-then-theory** approach examines some data, then develops or looks for a theory that may help explain and organize the findings. The first approach results in research that tests theoretical propositions, whereas the second approach is exploratory research designed primarily to develop ideas for theory. In most research the process can be characterized as a bit of both approaches: Available theory is used to start, relevant data are examined, and further refinements are made in theory. Both descriptive and explanatory research involve the use of theory, implicitly or explicitly.

Is theory always true? No. Theories represent an accumulation of knowledge about how things work. Future findings may be inconsistent with current theory, so current theory would have to be revised or another theory substituted to account for our accumulating factual knowledge. Early statements of deterrence theory were amended with new qualifications involving a new concept: informal sanctions. Thus, theory grows and changes in any field.

Can theories be proved to be true? No. This is because other factors or new knowledge that we do not currently have could greatly modify current theory or even show that what we believed is not true. If our theory is that all dogs are brown, then we can disprove the theory if we find even one dog that is not brown. But, having observed thousands of brown dogs, we still do not know that the theory is true. All we know is that we have thus far not seen a dog that was not brown. Tomorrow's observations may be different! With appropriate data we can show that a theory does not fit and, therefore, that the theory as it stands is false. If data do not refute or revise a theory, then we simply go on treating the theory as if it were still appropriate. Data can show that a theory is false (or false in some respect) or that the theory is not yet shown to be false. With repeated tests of all aspects of a theory, investigators have increasingly greater confidence that the theory accurately summarizes what is known.

Kuhn (1970), in summarizing changes in scientific disciplines, noted that at any point in the history of a field there tends to be a predominant or preferred theoretical perspective and its associated methods of researching, or what Kuhn called a **scientific paradigm.** He called research using these theories and methods normal science. As scientific fields develop, new perspectives may develop and these competitive ideas may challenge the old paradigm, perhaps leading to a revolution in the way an area is approached. New theories become preferred or predominant because they seem to explain or predict better than the old ones.

Selected Theoretical Approaches

There is no single predominant and preferred theory in the social sciences. Instead, there are many theoretical perspectives, many theories with a small scope or range of phenomena they cover, an assortment of theoretical concepts that seem to have some promise sometimes, and a lot of work that tries to identify, develop, and test parts of various theories. What is listed here is a sampling of theoretical approaches that have been used by researchers. Each deals with a research question about some topic. Each uses theory as a basis for hypothesized answers to the research question that are then tested in research.

The first example is about research that uses a **macro-level theory,** that is, a theory about large-scale social structures. The second example is about smaller, individual-level units and it draws on **micro-level theory.** There are many other distinctions between theories, but this will serve our purposes of illustration.

Two Examples

Theory about Societies: Why Does Democracy Develop in Some Societies but Not Others? In an introduction to his own analysis of ways in which economic factors affect the development of democracy in different societies, Muller (1995a, 1995b) describes why economic development of a society might be an explanation for the level of democracy one sees. He goes back to thinking proposed by two former researchers. Lipset (1959) explains that economic development increases the likelihood of a country establishing and maintaining democracy because it increases the emphasis on education, which promotes trust and tolerance, and it changes the stratification system of a society from a pyramid shape (with a large base of poor families and a small number of elite) to a more diamond-shaped pattern of a larger middle class, which would have more moderate and democratic tendencies. The other researchers, Rueschemeyer and colleagues (1992), suggest that the size and organizational power of the working class that come with economic development are more important than the size of the middle class as a force supporting democratic development of a society.

But, as part of his own work, Muller advances the idea that yet another factor is involved: the extent of income inequality in a society. His ideas can be shown in an arrow diagram in which economic development leads to an increase in the size of the middle or working classes and in income inequality and that these increases, in turn, raise the level of democratization in a society (Figure 2.1).

His reasoning appears to be useful. First, it helps him focus on why economic factors affect democracy. Second, it indicates conditions and qualifications about when this might be true. For example, he mentions timing of the development of inequality in a society as a factor. Third, the explanation he is using points out a case or unit of analysis (societies) to which his ideas apply and, very importantly, it indicates the variables he needs to measure. The theory also indicates what kind of relationships he might expect between the variables if the theory is true. Note that Muller goes beyond existing theory to suggest another variable that he thinks is involved and that may explain heretofore-unexplained deviations from the former theory: income inequality.

But the line of reasoning is not simply one that Muller thinks up and asserts based on one study. His challengers have carefully gone over his work (the data Muller used were presented in an article reporting his research, and they are available to others for checking). Bollen and Jackman (1995) suggest that Muller's assertions

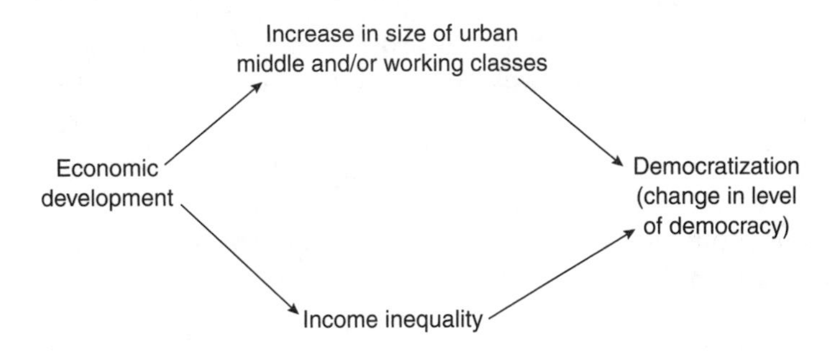

FIGURE 2.1 Arrow Diagram Showing Variables Influencing Democratization

about inequality may be incorrect. They suggest that the data don't adequately support his conclusions and that his ideas must be augmented. As a careful researcher, Muller responds to these comments, reviews the evidence, and comments on their comment. Here we have the process of development of explanations (theory) about why democracy develops more readily in some societies than in others. This is an example of a macro-level theory. The unit of analysis is at the level of whole societies. It also illustrates how prior thinking about "why" questions is very helpful to a researcher and how these ideas can be checked and extended or modified by additional research and thinking. You will find the literature quite useful in your research.

Theory about Individuals: Why Do Working Women Seem to Be Satisfied with Less Than Working Men? Micro-level theories are those that apply to smaller cases (e.g., those that apply to individual people as cases, rather than whole societies). Later we shall see that some analyses involve both micro and macro levels of analysis simultaneously (e.g., individuals within a social context or roles in an organization).

"The Paradox of the Contented Female Worker" (Phelan, 1994) explains research that assesses alternative theoretical explanations of a paradox the author identified. Existing data suggest that although women generally earn less than their male counterparts (about 70% as much), they are equally satisfied with their jobs and their pay and are as strongly committed to their work organizations as men. The finding has been shown in a wide range of prior research, and the paradox is also evident in Phelan's research. Why is this so?

Phelan used the library to examine prior research and reasons given for the paradox, and she found five explanations:

- **Different job inputs.** Women's education, job tenure, effort, and other inputs may be lower, so lower rewards are perceived to be equitable.

- **Own-gender referents.** A woman's reference group to compare job rewards may be other women rather than all who have a similar job. Because other women typically receive lower rewards, the comparison would be seen as satisfactory.

- **Different entitlement standards.** Women may agree that receiving a smaller reward for the same job, as compared with men, is appropriate and fair.

- **Different job values.** Lower rewards do not result in lower satisfaction because women may place a lower value on the income and authority rewards of a job than men.

- **Subjective rewards.** Job satisfaction may not be determined by salary or authority for either men or women. Instead, other intrinsic factors may be more important, and both men and women may share these factors more equally than is the case with income and authority.

Each of these ideas might explain all, part, or none of the paradox, and Phelan's own research was designed to examine the alternative explanations to see which were supported by her data.

THE RELATIONSHIP BETWEEN BASIC AND APPLIED RESEARCH OBJECTIVES

Theory is generally quite practical. It helps answer "why" questions. As in the case of studies of domestic violence, it may have a practical effect on how police handle these cases and on ways to reduce costs by reducing the number of repeat offenders. A good theory has great practical value. It is also scientifically helpful in explaining human social behavior and the relationship between laws and deviance. It summarizes our store of knowledge in this particular area. As in taking a test, it is convenient to have all the needed formulas written down and handy. A good theory is like a shorthand summary of knowledge that is easy to use.

Applied research, as the name implies, is interested in the application of knowledge or, rather, knowledge that has more immediate, practical use. Knowledge about focus groups that can be applied by someone conducting such groups would be useful. Knowing about what causes poor performance in math is useful to educators. Knowledge about what people prefer is useful in business. Knowledge about the attitudes of a group of customers may be vital to the success of a business.

Basic research, on the other hand, is less oriented toward immediate solutions to problems; instead, it tends to deal with ideas of interest to the researcher, theoretical questions that must be answered, or the discovery of knowledge about how something works. Basic research does involve practical outcomes, but these outcomes are generally not seen as immediate reasons for the research. Learning about how norms work may eventually help us to understand teenage violence in urban places.

Conceptualization is necessary, of course, whether research has an immediate, practical or applied focus or is oriented toward basic research on hypotheses that may have no immediate, practical payoff. Theory is helpful and relevant in both situations.

SUMMARY

Research starts with a research question about some topic. A good research question is clearly stated and researchable. It includes concepts that are important for the topic and points to a type of case or unit of analysis to which the concepts apply. It often refers to relationships between concepts such as outcomes and factors that may affect an outcome. A good research question involves comparisons and contrasts as well.

A researcher may also have a hypothesized answer to the research question. Hypotheses come from prior knowledge and experience, especially from a prior body of theory. Facts are gathered to test a hypothesis or to explore for reasonable hypotheses.

Theory is an important part of research; it generally forms a basis for starting out research and also an ending point at which theory is revised or reformulated, serving as a current summary of knowledge on some topic. It is a critical part of research because it helps identify concepts that must be measured, suggests relationships that can be expected between concepts, helps identify conditions under which relationships between concepts are likely to change, helps identify when the research is completed, suggests things to test, and is useful practically and scientifically to explain a relationship or outcome.

In Chapter 3 we deal with concepts and how they can be measured. Clarity about key concepts and how they can be operationalized in the research process is an essential step in conducting research.

TERMS TO KNOW

Applied research
Arrow diagram
Basic research
Case/unit of analysis
Concepts (and measurable variables)
Dependent variable
Exploratory research
Facts
Hypothesis
Hypothesis-testing research
Independent variable
Interobserver agreement
Literature search
Macro-level theory

Micro-level theory
Research question
Research-then-theory
Research topic
Scientific laws
Scientific paradigm
Scope
Tautology
Theoretical perspective
Theory
Theory-then-research

ISSUES AND COMPARISONS

Characteristics of a good research question
Why hypothesis testing is a preferred approach
The value of theory for research
The role of facts in research
Grand versus middle-range versus smaller theories

EXERCISES

1. The abstract of an article is printed here. See whether you can phrase the research question that the investigator seems to be addressing.

   This study explores the role of community characteristics in determining two critical features of adolescent nonmarital sexual activity: the timing of first intercourse and contraceptive use at that event. We specify a conceptual model describing the mechanisms by which the community context affects adolescent behaviors, focusing on the influence of community social and economic characteristics on teenagers' expectations about their adult lives. We test hypotheses derived from this model using a multilevel strategy incorporating both aggregate- and individual-level data for a national sample of white women. The results suggest that the behaviors of adolescents are shaped by the local opportunity structure and normative environment. Social disintegration, socioeconomic status, and the availability of employment opportunities for women emerged as particularly important influences on young women's reproductive choices. (Brewster, Billy, and Grady, 1993)

2. Find a journal article on a topic of interest to you. Then write out the answers to the following questions:
   a. What is the topic?
   b. What is the research question being raised?
   c. According to the criteria listed in this chapter, is the research question a good one?
   d. Are there hypothesized answers to the research question? If so, state them.
   e. What is the case or unit of analysis to which the research question applies?
   f. Is the research case limited in any way (descriptive characteristics, time, place)?
   g. What background in prior research and theory is presented in the article?
   h. Does the research appear to be hypothesis testing or exploratory? Explain.
   i. Can you think of alternative theories that could have been used?

3. Identify a topic in which you have an interest. Then list as many research questions about that topic as you can. Using criteria mentioned in this chapter, evaluate the research questions and indicate which are the best and poorest (and why).

4. Begin to plan your own research project by specifying a research question. Then go to the library and look up three to five pieces of prior research that are relevant to that research question. Describe how the theory and prior work contribute to your thinking about your research question. Revise your research question in light of prior research.

REFERENCES

Bollen, Kenneth A., and Robert W. Jackman, "Income Inequality and Democratization Revisited: Comment on Muller," *American Sociological Review* December 1995;60:983–89.

Brewster, Karin L., John O. G. Billy, and William R. Grady, "Social Context and Adolescent Behavior: The Impact of Community on the Transition to Sexual Activity," *Social Forces* March 1993;71(3):713–40.

Kuhn, Thomas, *The Structure of Scientific Revolutions,* 2nd ed., Chicago, University of Chicago Press, 1970.

Lipset, Seymour Martin, "Some Social Requisites of Democracy: Economic Development and Political Legitimacy," *American Political Science Review* 1959;53:69–105.

Muller, Edward N., "Economic Determinants of Democracy," *American Sociological Review* December 1995a;60:966–82.

Muller, Edward N., "Income Inequality and Democratization: Reply to Bollen and Jackman," *American Sociological Review* December 1995b;60:990–96.

Pate, A. M., and Hamilton, E. E., "Formal and Informal Deterrents to Domestic Violence: The Dade County Spouse Assault Experiment," *American Sociological Review* October 1992;57:691–97.

Phelan, Jo, "The Paradox of the Contented Female Worker: An Assessment of Alternative Explanations," *Social Psychology Quarterly* 1994;57(2):95–107.

Rueschemeyer, Dietrich, Evelyne Huber Stephens, and John D. Stephens, *Capitalist Development and Democracy,* Chicago, University of Chicago Press, 1992.

CHAPTER THREE

FINDING AND DEVELOPING MEASURES

Social distance is an important concept in sociology. It is the degree of social acceptance between given people and some social object such as people of different ethnic backgrounds or people living in different societies (Miller, 1991:329). Social distance studies have been conducted to measure distance from respondents to Blacks, Communists, Russians, older people, and people with other kinds of social labels such as the mentally ill or homosexuals. The concept of social distance is useful to the extent that it can be measured.

PRINCIPLES OF MEASURING

Measurement involves two basic phases. The first phase is deciding what you want to measure—the concept you are interested in and how it varies. For instance, the concept *family income* must be defined, including how it varies (e.g., from low to high income). The second phase involves identifying indicators and procedures that will allow relevant cases to be classified into categories of family income. For example, how might one actually classify families on family income into categories by, say, thousands of dollars of annual family income?

Similarly, in the case of social distance, the concept must be defined in a way that makes it measurable, and the scale used to measure it must be identified. Once this is accomplished, the procedure to be used in assigning cases positions on the measurement scale must be specified. The social distance scale, as developed by Bogardus (1959), ranked people on a 7-point scale measuring their willingness to be associated with people of other social groups. The scale varied from "acceptance to close kinship by marriage" at one end to "would exclude from my country" at the other. In both of these examples, the first step identifies and defines the concept of interest and the second step involves setting up appropriate measurement procedures.

Several important terms are used in talking about measurement. They are defined and illustrated later in this chapter, but the vocabulary is briefly defined in Box 3.1. The most basic term is ***concept,*** which refers to a characteristic or idea about some aspect of a phenomenon a researcher defines, identifies, and (usually) measures. Examples are "social distance," "family income," "gender," "role," "formal

BOX 3.1

FEATURES OF MEASUREMENTS

Concept. A characteristic or idea about some aspect of a phenomenon a researcher defines, identifies, and (usually) measures.

Operational definition. An indicator of a concept that can be used in research to classify cases into categories. Usually there can be many operational definitions of a given concept, some more useful, valid, or reliable than others.

Unit of measurement. The concept or construct of that which is to be subjected individually to the measurement process (e.g., a year or month in measuring age, or a dollar in measuring income). For purposes of calculation, the measurement unit is regarded as single and complete.

Precision. The number of categories that are distinguished in the measurement. A variable that uses only *low, medium,* and *high* would be less precise than one that used 10 categories. Usually, greater precision is sought.

Validity. Whether the formal and operational definitions of a concept correspond to each other. In other words, are you measuring what you intended to measure?

Reliability. The extent to which random errors are involved in the measurement process. The size of the random errors indicates the consistency with which whatever is being measured is measured.

Bias. Systematic error that is involved in measurement due to some known or unknown factor. For example, people may systematically understate their age or overstate their family income.

Random measurement error. Chance errors involved in measurement. These errors average out to zero over a large number of measurements of the same cases because some scores are too high and some are too low.

organization," and "social status." Concepts are known by their names. Although all concepts imply variation, in a given piece of research some concepts are "held constant" (e.g., looking only at high-income families or older people), but most are allowed to vary and are thus called **variables.**

What Concepts?

How do you go about identifying concepts that might be important to measure? There are three basic ways.

- First, you could pick out the key concepts from your research question, perhaps adding other concepts that might be involved. These could then be defined. For example:

  Research question: *"On average, do upper-income families have fewer children than lower-income families?"*

Here, one concept is "family income" and the other is "number of children." With a good research question, the task of identifying concepts is fairly easy because research questions are questions about concepts.

- A second way to identify relevant concepts is to go to the literature on your topic to see what concepts others have found useful. Perhaps their research suggests some concepts that must be included or some that don't make a difference. These sources will probably also identify ways in which these concepts are defined and ways they can be measured.

- Third, if there is little guidance as to the important concepts involved, one may need to engage in exploratory research to identify concepts that can be defined and refined for further use.

Concepts usually are identified by a term or short phrase such as "*self-esteem*" or "*gender.*" Sometimes the same word refers to different concepts, and sometimes different words refer to the same concept. Thus, the precise definition of the concept is needed to clarify what one is looking for.

Conceptual Definitions

Defining a concept is not very different from defining any word. The objective is to make it very clear to some audience what one is dealing with. A good **conceptual definition** is one that clearly distinguishes the properties or characteristics of a concept from those of other concepts. As Cohen and Nagel say,

> Logically, definitions aim to lay bare the principal features or structure of a concept, partly in order to make it definite, to delimit it from other concepts, and partly in order to make possible a systematic exploration of the subject matter with which it deals (1934:231–32).

Definitions often have two segments: how the concept is similar to other concepts and how it differs from them (e.g., "A cat is an animal, but unlike other animals, it meows"). Sometimes concepts are also distinguished from other concepts through the use of examples or analogy.

Although a concept's name, such as "self-esteem," may have wide usage in the media or everyday speech, it is generally a different concept from the one that is carefully defined as a technical term in a scientific field. One reason for using technical jargon in a field is the need to use names that are not in common usage and can be given a single definition. Because multiple terms may be used, a researcher must be especially careful to define the technical concept clearly. Often one will find that important concepts are given a lot of attention in scientific literature. Concepts such as self-esteem, social stratification, and family are the subjects of chapters and books devoted to their definition. Short definitions of many sociological concepts can be found in books such as *The Blackwell Dictionary of Sociology: A User's Guide to Sociological Language* (Johnson, 1995) or *The Intercocta*

Manual: Towards an International Encyclopedia of Social Science Terms (Riggs, 1988). In some cases, there is disagreement within the scientific community as to "the best definition of a concept." Better definitions are those that are more useful and used more often in scientific theories and in research questions. Like most intellectual work, good definitions of key concepts are hard to come by.

A good conceptual definition not only expresses how the phenomenon is similar to and different from other concepts, but it also provides insight into the kind of variability one might expect to find. For example, the definition of *family income* would suggest that income could range from low to high and could, perhaps, be captured in some monetary unit such as the dollar and fractions thereof. It would indicate that the range is continuous. These features of a conceptual definition specify the kind of relationships between categories that are envisioned, which is called the **level of measurement** of the concept.

It is common for researchers to distinguish between four "levels of measurement": nominal, ordinal, interval, or ratio. **Nominal level of measurement** means that the concept being referred to has conceptually defined categories that are distinct, such as "*present*" or "*absent*," or perhaps a larger number of categories that are simply different from each other, such as a list of different occupation titles or different countries of the world. The chief requirement is that the categories be distinct (i.e., mutually exclusive, not overlapping) and that they cover all possibilities for the concept (i.e., the set of categories is exhaustive). An **ordinal level of measurement** includes somewhat more information in that the categories not only are distinct but are also conceptualized to be in some rank order. For example, one's self-esteem may be defined to vary from low to high, or attitudes toward older people may vary from very positive to very negative. An **interval level of measurement** includes an added feature: a conceptually defined unit (e.g., a degree Fahrenheit) that can be distinguished and counted. This means that the categories of the concept are defined so that mathematical concepts such as "the difference between today's temperature and yesterday's temperature" is measured in the same way as "the difference between today's temperature and the temperature a week ago." In other words, intervals between pairs of scores are defined and may legitimately be compared. Although attitudes toward older people may be more or less favorable, there is no conceptually defined unit of such attitudes, as there is for temperature (e.g., degrees Fahrenheit), for example. Finally, a **ratio level of measurement** is one in which (in addition to features of nominal, ordinal, and interval measures) there is a conceptually defined zero point, which means that it is conceptually possible to have none of the property referred to by the concept. Family income would be conceptually defined as a ratio level of measurement because not only are categories of income different, in a ranked order, and identifiable in terms of some defined unit such as dollars or fractions of dollars, but the concept of zero family income is also a part of the conceptual definition of family income. Although the Fahrenheit and Celsius scales to measure temperature are interval-level scales because they do not have an absolute zero point, the concept of an absolute zero point in the Kelvin temperature scale makes it a ratio scale.

Furthermore, a concept's definition usually indicates whether the characteristic in question could vary over an unbroken high to low range of categories such as family income (called **continuous**) or whether the concept has categories that are inherently separated and do not shade off into adjacent categories (called **discrete**). Family size, for example, can be broken down into discrete categories: Families can have 1, 2, 3, or more members, but never 1.5 or 1.73 members (average or mean family size may be fractional because the average describes a group, not an individual score). Level of measurement and continuity are important features of concepts that are examined more closely in texts and courses on data analysis and statistics (see Loether and McTavish, 1993).

In "Changes in Gender Role Attitudes and Perceived Marital Quality," Amato and Booth (1995:58) provide a definition of the concept "gender role attitudes," which is apparently sufficient for their audience of social scientists who read the *American Sociological Review.* They say,

> **Gender role attitudes** of men and women have become less traditional. Traditional attitudes stress the dichotomy between the husband–breadwinner and wife–homemaker–mother, and the differential power relations implied in these specialized roles. Nontraditional attitudes, in contrast, emphasize shared roles and egalitarianism.

In context, one could assume that, like other attitudes, gender role attitudes are beliefs and values that individuals hold but, unlike other attitudes, gender role attitudes refer to beliefs held by individuals about men and women (more specifically, attitudes about traditional or nontraditional roles for men and women). By definition, two extreme categories define the possible range of different gender role attitudes: traditional and nontraditional. Amato and Booth explain, in a brief way, what they mean by *traditional* and *nontraditional.* It appears that the level of measurement involved is ordinal; that is, one could be more or less traditional (there is no defined unit of traditional attitude, but categories are ordered). Possible attitudes range between traditional and nontraditional on an apparently unbroken numeric scale, so the concept they are defining is continuous.

Other examples are given at the end of the chapter.

Operational Definitions

Once a concept has been defined so that it is clearly understandable to some audience, then one needs to devise indicators that can be used to measure that concept. **Operational definitions** are specific ways in which real cases can be classified into the categories of the concept one wants to use in research. There may be several potential indicators for any given concept. Figure 3.1 illustrates the relationship between a conceptual definition of some concept and one of the possible operational definitions of that concept. Age, the lapsed time since birth, might be measured by asking in a phone interview, "How old are you?"

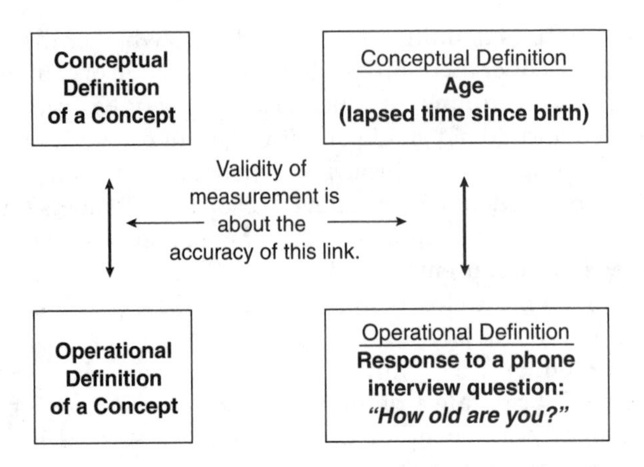

FIGURE 3.1 Validity

Given the usual definition of *gender* as the sex role with which one identifies, man or woman, one could determine a person's gender by asking, "What gender are you?" and writing down the response. Usually there are many potential indicators of the same concept. For example, one could observe a person's dress and grooming, ask the teacher of the person's class, listen to the person's voice (often used in phone interviewing), find out the person's first name, look up birth records, ask the person's parents, or see what form of address the person prefers (Mr., Miss, Mrs., or Ms.). Each of these indicators provides a basis for classifying the person as a man or woman. Not all of these possible indicators of the concept *gender* are likely to be good measures in all situations.

One primary way in which operational definitions vary is in the extent to which they are able to capture the concept the investigator has defined. This correspondence, shown in Figure 3.1, is called the **validity** of the operational definition, or the extent to which it actually measures the concept it is intended to measure. The temperature of a room is not a valid measure of the room's ceiling height. On the other hand, the answer to the question "What is your gender?" is a valid measure of the concept *gender* (assuming that the respondent also understands the question in the way that the investigator expects). Ways to determine whether an indicator is valid are discussed in a later section of this chapter.

The measurement process also generally involves errors. Better measurement processes involve less error. There are two categories of errors in measurement: **systematic bias** and **random measurement error.** Bias is a systematic source of error such that the measurement taken consistently overestimates or underestimates the true value of that which is being measured. For example, there may be a tendency for respondents to give a more socially acceptable answer to a question than they would if they answered objectively or, they may report their ages as younger than they really are. Sometimes an operational definition of a concept may produce a systematic bias because it is measuring something else in addition to the concept that it is intended to measure. For example, if the intent is to measure marital satisfaction and the measurements are taken at a time of widespread unemployment, low satisfaction scores may reflect the strain of unemployment rather than the quality of the marriages themselves.

Random measurement error is the chance of getting an inaccurate reading that does not consistently overestimate or underestimate the true value of that which is being measured. Although each individual measurement may be either an overestimate or an underestimate, these inaccuracies in measurement average out to zero because the probabilities of overestimates and underestimates are equal. The variability of the individual measurements around the true value is an indication of the **reliability** of the measurement instrument. The more these individual measures cluster close to the true value, the more reliable is the measurement instrument.

An analogy is the scatter of holes in a target made by a shooting expert compared with that made by an untrained shooter. In one case, the shots would be grouped more closely around the bull's-eye than in the other. One shooter would be more consistent, or more reliable. Good measures are those that are more reliable; they are more likely to be stable or consistent or very nearly so. Ways to determine whether an operational definition is reliable are also discussed later in this chapter.

Measurement procedures must be both reliable and valid. Accurate measurement of the wrong concept is not helpful, and an unreliable procedure limits the possible validity of measurement.

Another property of measures is involved in decisions about which indicator to use. That is its **precision.** Precision is the number of categories that are distinguished. For example, an indicator of attitudes toward older people might have only two categories: favorable or unfavorable. Another indicator of the same concept might have 10 categories, asking respondents to give a response on a 1–10 scale. The latter would be more precise in this sense. Investigators often prefer measures that are more precise over measures that have fewer categories, although the purposes of research and the cost of greater precision may limit the precision that is ultimately used in gathering data.

An operational definition of a concept includes all of the procedures that are involved in classifying a case into categories of the particular indicator that is being used. For example, age might be measured in a survey by the question, "How old are you?" The operational definition also includes factors potentially involved in the interview process, such as the age and gender of the interviewer, whether the interview is conducted in person or over the phone, how the question is asked and whether it precedes or follows other questions that might affect the response, how the interviewer interprets the answers, and the care with which data are recorded. Because these possible features of classifying the respondent in terms of the concept "age" do not matter (or are handled as part of general good practice in research), they are generally omitted from the way the operational definition is stated. If research shows that some of these factors matter, then the operational definition will probably include some type of specification of the standard conditions that must be observed in making those measurements.

Box 3.1 summarizes some of the terminology involved in measuring. In the rest of this chapter we will describe different ways in which operational definitions of concepts can be developed and ways to examine issues of their validity and reliability. We will also provide some examples of measures that are used in social science research.

MEASUREMENT TECHNIQUES

There are several strategies for developing good measures of concepts. First, there are *single indicators;* a concept is measured by a single variable used as its indicator. However, some concepts are complex enough that two or more variables are needed in combination to capture the concept validly. These measurements use a more complex **property space,** or combination of indicators to correctly classify a case. Finally, some measures use several variables to form a **scale** of items to measure a concept. All measurement involves considerable work to set up the measure and to test it out, to show that it is valid and reliable and worthy of further use. Each kind of measurement typically involves some ways in which it can be checked out.

Single Indicators of Concepts

Usually investigators use a single variable or indicator to measure a concept. This is the simplest and most direct strategy of measurement and generally the least costly. Take the concept of age, for example. Age is usually defined as the lapsed time since a person's birth. It is most often measured in years to the last whole year. So, if you will be 20 next week, today you would probably report your age as 19 years old. As discussed in the last section, many operational definitions of age are available:

- Asking the person's family how old the person is
- Asking the person how old he or she is
- Asking the person for his or her birthdate and doing the subtraction later
- Observing the person's hair color
- Observing the age group in which the person most often mingles
- Examining the person's driver's license
- Using public birth records to see when the person was born

Some of these operational definitions would work better in some situations than in others. For example, if the person were dead, then asking family or using a newspaper account might work best. If the person is shy about revealing his or her age, then one might ask for his or her birthdate instead (actually this is the better approach, at least when asking adults in the United States). Hair color is probably a poorer indicator (less valid and probably less reliable), and using birth records might be too time-consuming if the ages of a large number of people are to be collected.

Each one of these would be considered a single indicator of a person's age. On the face of it, it appears that a single item will probably be valid and reliable, although observing hair color may not be valid in many situations and certainly would be less precise; it would permit classification in only a few, rough categories such as "young" or "old."

Other single indicators that are often used in social science research are as follows:

- What is your marital status?
- What is your gender?
- How many children do you have?
- How many times have you visited a doctor in the past month?
- What is your zip code?

The advantages of using single indicators are that it is usually quite clear what question the respondent is answering and it is easy to record and use the response.

There are two good reasons for combining several indicators into an overall measurement of some concept rather than using a single indicator. First, the concept may be complex and have several facets that must be included in the measure in order to cover the concept adequately. For example, the concept of alienation is usually defined as including the ideas of powerlessness, normlessness, social isolation, and meaninglessness (Neal and Groat, 1974). Many concepts in the social sciences, such as social class, alienation, or self-esteem, are complex and have a number of important facets. Second, a measurement that is made up of several indicators generally has a higher reliability simply because of the number of items. This stems from the multiple measurement of the concept. The result is likely to be more stable than a single indicator of the same concept.

Because researchers strive for more reliable measures to detect smaller differences, you will run across widespread use of multiple-item scales and indices. Here, we look at two ways in which multiple indicators are used: indices and scales.

Indices Made Up of Several Indicators

Indices are usually logical or mathematical combinations of two or more variables designed to accomplish one or both of two objectives. Some indices are designed to include specific facets of a concept and minimize or eliminate the unwanted effect of some other factor or factors. A second objective of an index can be to isolate and identify various combinations of two or more variables because these combinations capture some more-complex concept.

Controlling Unwanted Effects to Make Fair Comparisons. Indices may take out the effect of unwanted factors in a number of ways. For example, the Consumer Price Index is constructed to give the current price of a fixed "basket" of items purchased by families, so a fixed list of products and services is specifically included. By holding constant the "basket" of goods and services, one can examine changing prices and make judgments about the trends in inflation over time. Other indices use the mathematical operation of division to take out the effect of some unwanted factor. An example might be per capita income, in which the total income in a society is divided by the total number of people in that society. One could then compare the income of people in countries of different sizes because size would have been taken into account in the computation of this index. The sex ratio is the number of men in a society divided by the number of women in that society; again, across-society comparisons can be made because the size of the male and female populations is controlled by the way the index is constructed. Sometimes indices called rates take out the effect of age and sex differences between societies; for example, age and sex can be distinguished to form an overall standardized suicide rate. An age- and sex-standardized rate would permit comparison between societies without differences in the number of people in different age and sex categories confounding the comparison. Statistics books often show how rates, ratios, and other indices can be formed (Loether and McTavish, 1993).

Including Facets of a Concept. Indices may also be constructed to capture several important facets that may be a part of the concept that the investigator wants to measure. Some years ago, Hollingshead and Redlick (1958) wanted to measure the concept of an individual's social class position in a community for their classic studies of New Haven, Connecticut. Social class position was defined as an ordinal concept varying from lower class to upper class, and it could be measured if one knew the person's occupation and education level (an alternative index included a third factor: residential area). Hollingshead used an indicator of occupation that distinguished seven levels of occupation from "1. higher executives of large concerns, proprietors, and major professionals" down to "7. unskilled employees." Similarly, education was recorded in seven levels, from "1. Graduate professional training" down to "7. less than seven years of school." Detailed coding instructions were given on the classification of occupation and education. The Index of Social Position, as it was called, was formed by multiplying the occupation score of an individual by a weight of 7 and adding that product to the product of the individual's education score multiplied by a weight of 4. Weights were determined from research involved in constructing the index, giving occupation almost twice the importance in the index as education. Potential scores ranged from 11 to 77, in which 11 $[(1 \times 7) + (1 \times 4)]$ represented the highest social position and 77 $[(7 \times 7)$ plus $(7 \times 4)]$ the lowest. He then divided the 11–77 index score range into five levels or classes, shown in the following table, which he felt represented the structure of that community. The index is described in Miller (1991), in which validity and reliability information for the index are also presented.

CLASS	RANGE OF INDEX SCORES
I (upper)	11–17
II	18–31
III	32–47
IV	48–63
V (lower)	64–77

Forming a Property Space. Other indices (also called **typologies**) may be formed by examining all the logical combinations of categories of two or more variables (sometimes called a Cartesian product), as shown in Figure 3.2. Barton (1964) illustrates this in creating an index for political position from two indicators: usual party affiliation and degree of political interest. The combination of these two variables is called a property space because it shows all the possible combinations of categories of these two variables. Property space is a concept like physical space except that it refers to the "social space" identified by some social concept or the combination of two or more concepts. The phenomena of interest, such as political position, are composed of a combination of other, simpler concepts such as usual party affiliation and degree of political interest.

Barton called people in the two left cells in the top row of this property space Partisans because they were highly involved with one of the traditional parties. People in the upper cell in the right-hand column were labeled Independents because they were highly involved but were not a part of the traditional parties. People in the four cells in the lower left part of the table were called Habituals because of their low to moderate involvement in politics but affiliation with one of the traditional parties. Finally, the two lower cells in the right-hand column were labeled Apathetics because of their low involvement and independent status. Barton now has captured the more-complex concept of political position, which is a logical combination of two other concepts: usual political party affiliation and degree of political interest.

Degree of Political Interest	Usual Party Affiliation: Republican	Democrat	Independent
High			
Medium			
Low			

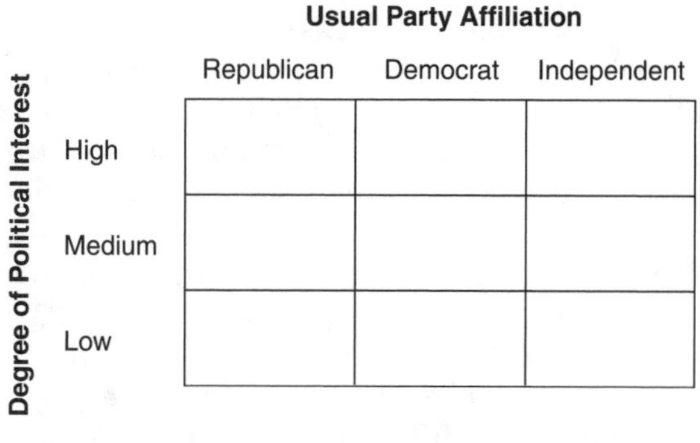

FIGURE 3.2 **Property Space of Political Position**

In Barton's case, the full property space shown in Figure 3.2 has nine cells. However, he decided that some of the cells in the property space could be combined. He chose to partition the property space into four categories that corresponded to his theoretical interests in the more complex concept he called political position. This is called a **reduction** of the property space. Likewise, one could divide up a property space further by adding other crosscutting concepts that would add cells and enlarge the property space. This is called substruction, or further dividing up a property space on the basis of other conceptual distinctions.

Ordered Property Spaces. More-complex property spaces can be created and used in the construction of indices to measure complex concepts. An example is identification of patterns of response to a set of measures on the role involvement of farm women. As shown in Figure 3.3, the concept of role involvement includes three concepts: the extent of involvement in raising children and managing a household, involvement in day-to-day farm operations, and involvement in paid work outside the home and farm context (the original study also added the extent of involvement in community volunteer activities) (Danes and McTavish, 1996). A farm woman could be highly involved, moderately involved, or minimally involved in each of the three areas. Putting these together yields a more-complex property space, but combinations of the three concepts capture the more-complex concept of role involvement.

There are 27 cells implied by the cross-classification of these three 3-level concepts ($3 \times 3 \times 3 = 27$). One could show the property space either by creating a table as shown in Figure 3.3 or by listing the cells shown in the table. For example, the most highly involved farm woman would be one who is highly involved in all three roles:

- Highly involved (3) in homemaking
- Highly involved (3) in farm work
- Highly involved (3) in an outside, paid job

For the sake of simplicity, we could call this a 3 3 3 pattern of involvement.

Other farm women might have other patterns such as 3 3 1 (in which minimal outside work for pay is done), or 2 2 2, down to 1 1 1, in which the farm woman is minimally involved in all three role areas. Notice that in this case the cells in the property space not only are different, but apparently can be ranked from the least involved to the most involved (role involvement is defined as an ordinal concept). All 27 possibilities are listed in Figure 3.4.

In the 27 possible patterns that might characterize a farm woman's role involvement, three are clearly in rank order: the **3 3 3** pattern, the **2 2 2** pattern, and the **1 1 1** pattern of role involvement. The other patterns are mixtures of involvement, and how these patterns are ranked depends on the relative weight we might want to give, conceptually, to the three different kinds of roles. If we treat each of the roles as equal, then some of the patterns of role involvement are essentially

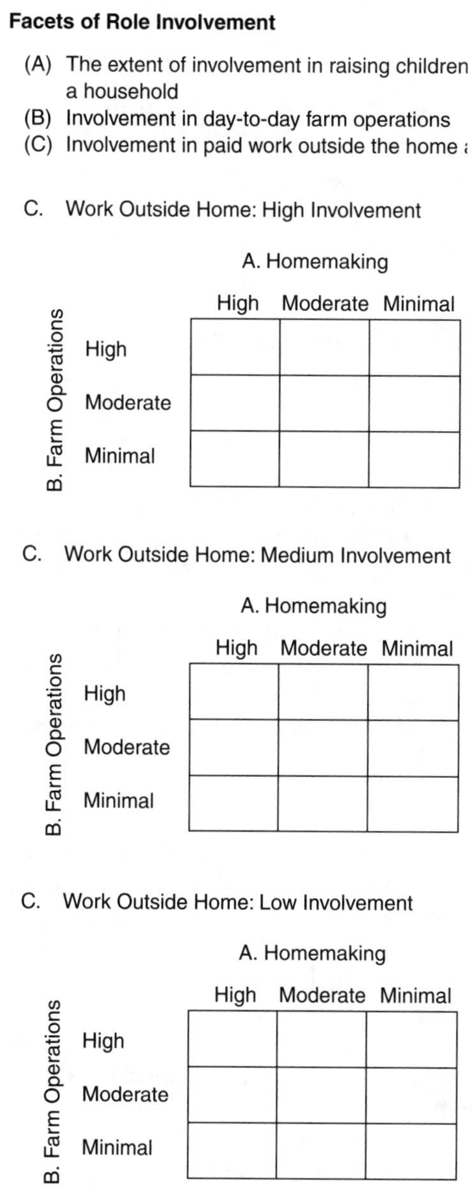

Facets of Role Involvement

(A) The extent of involvement in raising children
a household
(B) Involvement in day-to-day farm operations
(C) Involvement in paid work outside the home

C. Work Outside Home: High Involvement

B. Farm Operations	A. Homemaking: High	Moderate	Minimal
High			
Moderate			
Minimal			

C. Work Outside Home: Medium Involvement

B. Farm Operations	A. Homemaking: High	Moderate	Minimal
High			
Moderate			
Minimal			

C. Work Outside Home: Low Involvement

B. Farm Operations	A. Homemaking: High	Moderate	Minimal
High			
Moderate			
Minimal			

FIGURE 3.3 Property Space Involving Three Concepts, Each with Three Levels

equal. That is, the three ways one could be highly involved in only one role and moderately involved in both other roles. These would be equivalent in role involvement. In fact, we might consider being highly involved in two roles and minimally involved in the third as similar to this involvement pattern.

A	B	C	Sum
3	**3**	**3**	9
3	3	2	8
3	2	3	8
2	3	3	8
3	3	1	7
3	1	3	7
1	3	3	7
3	2	2	7
2	3	2	7

A	B	C	Sum
2	2	3	7
2	**2**	**2**	6
3	2	1	6
3	1	2	6
1	3	2	6
1	2	3	6
2	3	1	6
2	1	3	6
3	1	1	5

A	B	C	Sum
1	3	1	5
1	1	3	5
2	2	1	5
1	2	2	5
2	1	2	5
2	1	1	4
1	2	1	4
1	1	2	4
1	**1**	**1**	3

FIGURE 3.4 List of the 27 Cells in the Property Space Combining Three Concepts, Each with Three Levels

Notice that the scores used to measure degree of role involvement can be summed, and we could use this sum as a way of ranking farm women on role involvement. The higher the sum, the more involved farm women would be in these roles. This would be one way of grouping similar patterns and ranking different patterns on degree of role involvement.

This is an example of creating a more-complex concept out of a combination of simpler concepts by creating a property space, which is then organized along conceptual lines to reflect the more-complex concept. Patterns of response are often useful to examine in order to create indices that capture important concepts.

Scales

When concepts are defined as varying from low to high, multiple indicators may be used, each of which reflects a different level or strength of that concept and, perhaps, different facets of the overall concept. Often a concept is thought of as a single property (variable or dimension) that varies from low to high, such as income, social class, self-esteem, satisfaction with life in general, tolerance, or attitude toward abortion. Measuring such concepts is often done using several indicators, often with several questions about the same concept. These multiple indicators of the same concept refer to somewhat different specific aspects of the concept, and they may tap weaker or more extreme views on the same topic.

An example comes from items used to measure attitudes toward abortion from a survey by the National Opinion Research Center (NORC, 1991). The survey asked a series of questions, including the following:

> Please tell me whether *you* think it should be possible for a pregnant woman to obtain a *legal* abortion . . .
>
> **a.** If the woman's own health is seriously endangered by the pregnancy (88.6% agree)
> **b.** If there is a strong chance of serious defect in the baby (80.0%)
> **c.** If she is married and does not want any more children (43.0%)
> **d.** If the woman wants it for any reason (41.1%)

Notice that the first question listed above is a weak question in that it refers to a less-extreme view about abortion. This can be seen in the fact that (in 1991) about 89% of adult respondents agreed with this question. On the other hand, the last question refers to a more extreme view on the subject as it is discussed in the United States, and only 41% of the respondents in the survey agreed with this question. In measurement language, the first is an **easy scale item** and the last is a **hard scale item.** Including harder and easier items in a scale to measure a concept allows an investigator to identify better what a respondent's views really are. In this case the items also tap different conditions that may be relevant to one's views about abortion.

A distinction is made in measurement theory between the true position of the individual (or other entity) along the scale of some concept and the position of items on the scale of the same concept. Both items and individuals (cases) can be located on the scale. Some individuals are higher or lower on, say, attitudes toward abortion, and some questions one could ask express stronger or weaker attitudes toward abortion. The objective of measurement, then, is to use the pattern of response to indicators (which are located along a scale) to try to recover or identify the place on the scale at which an individual falls. The investigator does not know the true location of the individual on the conceptual scale. All that is typically available is the answers a subject may have given to survey questions (or other indicators). Sometimes the actual responses are called *manifest* data, and the location of the subject on the underlying scale of some concept is its *latent* position on the scale. The job of measurement is to help make inferences from the manifest data to the latent position. Scales help with this task by setting up a manifest scale of questions or other indicators in such a way that a valid and reliable inference can be made about the location of the subject on the underlying scale of the concept being measured.

Several ways of setting up a scale help an investigator gain knowledge about what a pattern of responses may mean for an inference about the location of a subject on some concept of interest. Usually these techniques require the following:

a. A modestly large number of potential questions, all getting at the same concept but perhaps different aspects of it, and questions that are likely to be located at different points on the underlying scale of that concept.
b. A set of data consisting of responses of a sample of individuals to each of the questions. These basic data are then examined statistically for the purpose of weeding out bad items (e.g., they don't seem to behave as if they were measuring the underlying concept).
c. Criteria to identify scale items that discriminate on the concept of interest and are reliable and valid.

Summated Scales. When many items are used to form a scale, respondents might be asked to indicate their opinion to each item along a scale of some type (e.g., from *mild* to *extreme, strongly agree* to *strongly disagree,* or *yes* or *no*). To create a **summated scale,** responses are numbered (with larger numbers representing stronger agreement with the question, for example). Then the numbers for the responses checked by a respondent are summed over all the items in that scale to get a total score for that respondent on that concept. This is similar to counting up the correct responses to a series of (harder and easier) questions on a test that is designed to measure one's knowledge of some course material.

Self-esteem is defined by Rosenberg (1965) as the overall attitude that a person maintains with regard to his or her own worth and importance. It is a **unidimensional** personal predisposition. Ten items were designed to measure this concept. Each item has five response categories referring to how well the statement applies to the respondent: 1, never true; 2, seldom true; 3, sometimes true; 4, often true; 5, almost always true. The items to be rated are as follows:

1. I feel that I have a number of good qualities. (+)
2. I wish I could have more respect for myself. (–)
3. I feel that I'm a person of worth, at least on an equal plane with others. (+)
4. I feel I do not have much to be proud of. (–)
5. I take a positive attitude toward myself. (+)
6. I certainly feel useless at times. (–)
7. All in all, I'm inclined to feel that I am a failure. (–)
8. I am able to do things as well as most other people. (+)
9. At times I think I am no good at all. (–)
10. On the whole, I am satisfied with myself. (+)

The question and response category format used here ("never true" to "almost always true") is sometimes called a Likert item or a **Likert scale.** Other frequently used Likert response formats use three to seven categories of agreement (from "strongly disagree" through "strongly agree"). These and other ways to ask questions are discussed in later chapters.

Notice that items 1, 3, 5, 8, and 10 are stated positively and the other items are stated negatively. We will assign a number to each response category (from 1 to 5); 5 indicates the most positive or highest self-esteem response. Because items 2, 4, 6, 7, and 9 are stated negatively, the "never true" end of the response categories must be changed to number 5 ("never true") down to 1 ("almost always true"). A summated self-esteem scale score could be created by simply adding together the number that a respondent checked for each of the 10 items. Scores could go from 10 (1 for each question) to 50 (5 for each question); the larger the number, the higher the self-esteem (assuming that we have reversed the numbering for the negative items). The logic is that people with highest self-esteem ought to agree with positive items and disagree with negative items. Lower self-esteem would be indicated by a lower total score. Summing the responses is a way to measure the degree of self-esteem.

An advantage of using a scale rather than a single indicator to measure the concept of self-esteem is that the measurement is more stable than a single indicator would be (a feature called reliability, discussed later in this chapter). It also permits an investigator to tap a range of different aspects of self-esteem, which would not be possible unless several questions were asked.

Summated scales can be checked out in several ways. First, the responses that a sample of individuals give to each of the questions could be correlated to see how answers to question 1, for example, correlate with answers to question 2, 3, and so on for all pairs of questions.[1] If each item in the scale is measuring the same thing, then the correlations ought to all be positive and strong. If an item is not correlated with other items, this would be taken as evidence that the item is not measuring the same thing other items are measuring, so it is not a valid item and should be discarded from the scale. Table 3.1 is a matrix of correlations of responses to each pair of self-esteem questions for data presented in Zeller and Carmines's book on social science measurement (1980:92).

The **correlation matrix** in Table 3.1 shows how strongly any given pair of items is correlated in the sample that was used in this study. For example, items 1 and 2 are correlated at .18 (see row 1, column 2), which is low but positive. (Correlation coefficients generally range from –1.0 through 0 for no correlation to +1.0, when +1 or –1 is the strongest possible positive or negative correlation, a perfect match.) Item 2 has a low correlation with items 3 and 8 and a modest correlation with other items. Thus, item 2 ("I wish I could have more respect for myself.") would be a candidate for elimination from the scale, at least on the grounds of its pattern of correlations.

Another way of checking summated scales such as this is **item analysis.** Based on the overall summed scale scores, individuals would be divided into two groups: those with high self-esteem scores (perhaps the top-ranking 25% of respondents) and those with low self-esteem scores (perhaps the lowest 25% of respondents). Then responses to each item would be examined for these two

TABLE 3.1 Correlation Matrix of Self-Esteem Items (N = 340)

ITEMS	1	2	3	4	5	6	7	8	9	10
1	—	.18	.45	.40	.41	.26	.39	.35	.36	.20
2		—	.05	.21	.25	.25	.23	.05	.28	.27
3			—	.35	.40	.31	.38	.43	.28	.33
4				—	.37	.42	.47	.28	.36	.22
5					—	.34	.45	.46	.32	.42
6						—	.47	.21	.50	.19
7							—	.32	.58	.31
8								—	.23	.37
9									—	.23
10										—

(Items are numbered in the order listed above.)

Source: Zeller and Carmines (1980) Table 4.4, page 92.

[1]See Loether and McTavish (1993:230) for an explanation of correlation measures.

groups of respondents. If an item did not show markedly different responses in the low self-esteem group and the highest self-esteem group, one would conclude that the item was unable to discriminate high and low self-esteem and should be thrown out of the scale.

These checks, examining the intercorrelation of items and item analysis, help identify items that should remain a part of the final summated scale used to measure a concept. Other checks can be done to ensure that the items in the scale are unidimensional, that is, that they measure along one dimension rather than haphazardly over many dimensions. Factor analysis is one such scale analysis procedure.

Factor Analysis. The set of responses to items thought to measure a given concept might be analyzed statistically with a procedure called **factor analysis.** This procedure uses a matrix of correlations (such as that shown in Table 3.1) between all pairs of items, using responses to the different questions by a sample of respondents. The factor analysis procedure examines the relationship between responses to the questions and helps determine whether the items can be accounted for by a single, underlying factor or more than one factor. If more than one factor is needed to account for the pattern of item correlations, then the items in the scale and, presumably, the concept they are designed to measure, are not unidimensional, as was supposed. In the example of self-esteem, Zeller and Carmines (1980) conducted a factor analysis of responses to these 10 self-esteem scale items and found two factors. One factor consisted of the positively stated self-esteem items (items 1, 3, 5, 8, 10), and the other consisted of the negatively stated self-esteem items (2, 4, 6, 7, 9). Thus, they suggested that the concept of self-esteem might be considered to be two related concepts: positive self-esteem and negative self-esteem.

With this factor analysis information in hand (especially if other investigators find two factors as well), an investigator could revise the concept of self-esteem to take account of positive and negative self-esteem or throw out items that do not measure self-esteem as one wishes to measure it unidimensionally. Also, when factor analysis showed that some items did not relate very well to a single underlying dimension, an investigator would discard the poor items.

Once the items are revised, the scale is ready for further testing and use. When respondents are asked the scale questions, their scores or locations on the underlying concept are generally some type of sum of the responses to each question (sometimes items are unequally weighted, based on factor analytic results). Good scales are those that have been used and evaluated over and over in different settings and found to behave as they are conceptually expected to behave. Established scales are very helpful to investigators, and finding existing scales is another good reason for a literature search. For example, Bonjean, Hill, and McLemore (1967) provided a collection of scales and other indicators used in the social sciences.

Guttman Scaling. If items designed to measure a concept fall along a scale, then the pattern of responses people give to them ought to help identify the location of individuals on the underlying concept that is being measured. **Guttman scaling**

examines the extent to which responses by individuals show patterns that one would expect if the items themselves were arranged along a single underlying scale. To start with, a higher percentage of respondents ought to agree with easy items and a smaller percentage ought to agree with harder items. Furthermore, the pattern of individual responses ought to reflect the location of the individual and the items on the underlying scale for that concept. Take, for example, a series of three questions about height:

Question 1. *Are you at least 4 feet tall?*	☐ Yes	☐ No
Question 2. *Are you at least 5 feet tall?*	☐ Yes	☐ No
Question 3. *Are you at least 6 feet tall?*	☐ Yes	☐ No

If a person is 5 feet 2 inches tall, the person ought to answer "yes" to the first two questions and "no" to the third. If a person is 6 feet 7 inches tall, he or she should answer "yes" to all three questions. That is, the questions are of different "difficulty." They are also cumulative in the sense that a respondent should check "yes" for all the "easy" questions that refer to heights lower than he or she is but "no" for items that are "harder." If a respondent gives odd answers such as "yes" for question 3 but "no" for questions 1 and 2, one could draw one of two conclusions: the person doesn't understand the questions or instructions or the items are not measuring the concept of height as one had hoped and different indicators should be found. Here, our confidence in the question's clarity would probably lead us to question the respondent's understanding of the questions.

Guttman scaling is a way of examining items in scales that are thought to be cumulative in this sense. The items themselves are thought to be located along the scale at different points, as indicated in Figure 3.5. Individual respondents can also be located on that underlying scale by examining their patterns of response to the items.

To evaluate a Guttman scale, all the possible patterns of response to the items are examined as described here. Notice that there are eight possible patterns

Question Location		Q_1		Q_2		Q_3	
Feet Tall	$3\frac{1}{2}$	4	$4\frac{1}{2}$	5	$5\frac{1}{2}$	6	$6\frac{1}{2}$
Individual's Location				▲ 5′2″			
Expected Responses		**Yes** to Q_1		**Yes** to Q_2		**No** to Q_3	

FIGURE 3.5 Scale Items, as Well as Individuals, Can Be Located on the Underlying Scale of a Concept

because each question is scored as either yes (+) or no (–) and there are three questions ($2 \times 2 \times 2 = 2^3 = 8$).

Pattern 1, in Figure 3.6, is an expected response pattern if the three questions are indeed in the order we expect them to be on the underlying continuum of the concept *height.* The 80 people giving this response are all at least 6 feet in height. Similarly, patterns 4, 7, and 8 are as expected. The 150 in pattern 4 are 5 to 5.9 feet tall, the 86 responding with pattern 7 are between 4 and 4.9 feet, and the 25 with pattern 8 are all shorter than 4 feet tall. Some of the response patterns are not what we would expect if the three questions are located along the height scale as we believe them to be. Pattern 2, for example, shows that 15 people said "no" to question 1 but went on to agree with both questions 2 and 3. Apparently they misunderstood the first question, or the question doesn't measure height adequately. The response for question 1 is an error in the sense that we did not expect such a response given our conceptual notion of height. Similarly, patterns 3, 5, and 6 each show one error. In these three patterns, there is one error each, but it is not clear where the error has been made. Take pattern 3, for example. It could be that question 2 was answered in error and should have been "yes" (+). Alternatively, question 3 might be in error (i.e., the real answer should be "no," or –). For these data we will say it is an error in answering question 3 because there are more + + – responses than there are + + + responses.

Overall, multiplying the number of errors in a given pattern by the number of people making that error, we have a total of 38 errors. The total number of responses is 379 people times 3 questions, or 1,137. The proportion of error responses is 38/1,137 or .033. Alternatively, the proportion of responses that are as expected if the items are cumulative is 1.00 minus the proportion of errors, or .967 (1.00 – .034 = .967). This is called the coefficient of reproducibility, which is one of a number of scores that can be computed to evaluate how well the scale items seem

	Q_1	Q_2	Q_3	Response Errors	Frequency	Total Errors
1.	+	+	+	0	80	0
2.	–	+	+	1	15	15
3.	+	–	+	1	8	8
4.	+	+	–	0	150	0
5.	–	–	+	1	5	5
6.	–	+	–	1	10	10
7.	+	–	–	0	86	0
8.	–	–	–	0	25	0
					379	**38**

FIGURE 3.6 Possible Patterns of Response to Three Dichotomous Items

to fit the cumulative scale idea we had in mind. Here the coefficient of reproducibility is .967, which is very high, sufficient to allow us to conclude that the items do fall along an underlying single dimension, as we had supposed. A coefficient of reproducibility of .80 or higher is desirable. The responses appear to confirm that the scale is measuring the concept of height in the way we expected. Better scales are those that have been evaluated with data from other samples of respondents as well.

Once an adequate scale is developed, responses could generally be scored by simply adding up the number of items to which a respondent agreed. Alternatively, one could evaluate the error patterns and assign individuals making an error pattern to the "correct" (i.e., expected) pattern that comes closest to their responses.

The example of height given here to illustrate the Guttman technique is more clear-cut than most items used to measure social science concepts. The Guttman technique (as well as the others being discussed here) often deals with the measurement of attitudes or other subjective concepts. Consequently, the cumulative character of the items is less apparent and the job of selecting a set of items that will meet the criteria for a scale tends to be much more involved. It sometimes takes a number of attempts to find a set of items that will scale, in the Guttman sense of that term.

The Bogardus Social Distance Scale mentioned at the beginning of the chapter is a good example of a scale containing the kinds of actual items that might be used by social scientists in constructing a Guttman-type scale. Bogardus (1959) used seven items to test respondents' acceptance of different racial, ethnic, or other groups. For example, respondents might be asked to respond with a yes or a no to the following seven items with regard to their feelings about Kurdish people as a class:

I would admit them

1. to close kinship by marriage
2. to my club as personal chums
3. to my street as neighbors
4. to employment in my occupation
5. to citizenship in my country
6. as visitors only to my country
7. I would exclude them from my country

Notice that the order of these items is not as clear-cut as were the three items dealing with height (page 61). Item 1 is assumed to be the most accepting of the seven, and item 7 is assumed to be the least accepting. It is not clear that the items between these two extremes are, in fact, arranged properly so that each succeeding item (from 1 to 7) represents less acceptance than the one immediately preceding and more acceptance than the one immediately following. For example, some respondents might consider item 4 as being more accepting than item 3, whereas others might consider item 3 the more accepting of the two.

It is the purpose of the Guttman coefficient of reproducibility to test whether (1) the seven items can be ordered from most accepting to least accepting, and (2) whether the ordering can be perceived and responded to in a logical and consistent manner by respondents.

Thurstone Method of Equal-Appearing Intervals. Thurstone made extensive contributions to the literature on developing useful scales, and his insights illustrate another approach to developing a scale. Responses to a given item are thought to stem from the location of individuals on an underlying scale of a concept, such that most individuals at a given point on an underlying scale will give a typical response to a given scale item.

Judges are used to construct and test a scale with the Thurstone technique. The investigator also will have at hand a fairly large number of potential items (sometimes up to 100 items selected from the literature or created by the investigator) that could be included in a scale to measure the concept of interest. Judges used in this process are people (usually a small number of people) who are familiar with the phenomenon that is to be measured and who are asked to express their judgment about each proposed scale item. There are at least two ways in which they could be asked to make their judgments. For example, judges could be asked to examine each possible pair of proposed items and judge which item in each pair is higher on the concept of interest (this is called the method of paired comparisons). Because all possible pairings of items are judged, this technique is limited to smaller sets of items. Another approach is to have judges score items (or physically sort items) on a scale of the concept of interest. Often 5 to 11 categories are used. For example, judges could be asked to use scores from 1 (for "highly unfavorable" or low on the concept), through 6 ("neutral"), to 11 (for "highly favorable" or high on that concept).

It is important to note that the judges are not supposed to respond to the items in terms of their own feelings about the concept being measured. Rather, they are supposed to say where they perceive each particular item to fall on a scale from low to high, or highly unfavorable to highly favorable, on the concept. For example, it is assumed that a judge who personally feels very negativly about abortion can, nevertheless, separate his or her personal feelings about the subject from the way he or she ranks a particular statement about abortion on a negative to positive scale. Thus, two judges who have diametrically opposed attitudes toward abortion should be able to agree that a statement such as "Abortion may be a lifesaving procedure for a pregnant woman." is a relatively positive statement about abortion and may rate an 8 on a scale from 1 to 11.

When all judges have completed the task, there will be a distribution of the items along the scale the researcher set up for them to use. As illustrated in Figure 3.7, one judge placed the item in category 4, one in category 5, three in category 6, and so on.

The spread of judgments would be used to eliminate poor items from the final scale on grounds that the stimulus question is too ambiguous if there is too much disagreement about where the item should be placed. Good items are those

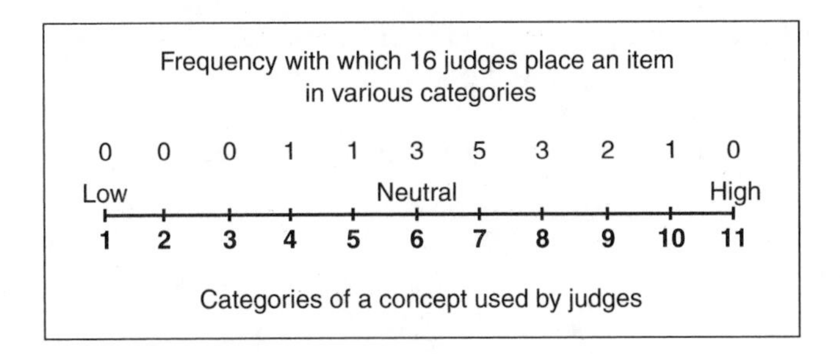

FIGURE 3.7 Illustration of the Distribution of an Item along a Scale of a Concept

with a narrow spread or dispersion. The score of a given item would be the median of judges' responses (i.e., the point on the scale above and below which 50% of the judges placed the statement). Here, more than half of the 16 judges placed the item in category 7 or below, and more than half placed the item in category 7 or above, so the score assigned to this item would be 7 (the median would usually be calculated to a decimal value). According to these judges, the item in question is just above neutral on the scale of the concept we are measuring.

Once items have been thrown out and the best items have been selected, these are used as a scale to give to respondents. The judges have helped select and score items that can then be used in research. One would expect respondents located at, say, point 8 on the underlying scale of the concept illustrated in Figure 3.7 to agree with any item that had a score value of 8 or below (and agree to the item scored at 7, illustrated in Figure 3.7). Looking at a respondent's pattern of response to a set of items created by this Thurstone method, one could assign that respondent the score of the highest-scored item to which the respondent agreed (there are also other ways to use item-score information to assign a value to respondents on the concept measured by this kind of scale). The Thurstone scaling method described here is called the **Thurstone method of equal-appearing intervals.** Notice that this approach assumes that the categories along the scale have equal intervals: 1, 2, 3, on up to 11 (depending on the number of categories used in the sorting scheme). Another method that has some advantages over this method because the spacing of the categories themselves is estimated is called the method of successive intervals (Edwards, 1957).

There are other procedures for creating and evaluating proposed scales to see whether responses are in line with one's expectations for the concept being measured. Often a scale is referred to by the kind of checking it has received or the way in which it was constructed (e.g., Guttman scales, Thurstone scales). Sometimes several of these techniques are used on the same scale. Here, we have illustrated some of the approaches used to create and check operational definitions of simple and complex concepts. The process starts with the creation of many indicators, gathering responses from a number of individuals (sometimes in the role of judges), evaluating the results with the idea of throwing out or revising problematic items, and choosing the best possible set of scale items. The best set of items for one population and era may not be the best in other situations, so the careful investigator constantly evaluates and improves available measures.

MEASUREMENT ISSUES

Beyond the difficult conceptual issues of identifying and defining important concepts that help identify and organize what one ultimately wants to measure, there are key issues to be raised about any proposed measurement. In this section we discuss the issues of validity and reliability.

Validity and Reliability

Any measurement process (classification process) can have two questions raised about it. First, does it make the distinctions that are central to the concept being measured (the phenomenon being classified)? Second, how much random measurement error is involved in the use of the measurement process?

Validity. To measure validity, two things are compared. One is the conceptual definition of the concept to be measured. This calls for a careful and explicit detailing of what is being measured. In the case of social distance as proposed by Bogardus, the description might be "the degree of social acceptance that exists between given persons and certain social groups" (Miller, 1991:378). An early version of Rosenberg's self-esteem measure describes its conceptual intent as "designed to measure attitudes toward the self along a favorable-to-unfavorable dimension" (Robinson and Shaver, 1972:98). Hage and Aiken's concept organizational formalization is described by Miller (1991:407) in a more lengthy way:

> Formalization represents the use of rules in an organization. Some organizations carefully describe the specific authority, responsibilities, duties and procedures to be followed in every job and then supervise job occupants to ensure conformity to the job definitions. A penalty system may be spelled out in writing for impartial monitoring of discipline for infractions. Other organizations have loosely defined jobs and do not carefully control work behavior. The two dimensions of formalization may be specified as *job codification,* or the degree of work standardization, and *rule leniency,* or the measure of the latitude of behavior that is tolerated from standards.

Whatever the concept, some clear conceptual definition is needed. It may take a book or it may be captured in a brief sentence. Whatever it is, the outcome is a communicated understanding of what the concept means. Often these definitions involve explaining how the concept of interest is the same as certain other, known concepts and how it differs from them. Social distance might be likened to physical distance except that it refers to attitudes, opinions, and beliefs about the other individual or group.

The second thing that is needed to examine validity is an actual measurement process. Checking the validity of a measurement process involves comparing the measurement process and the result of using it to the conceptual definition. If one is measuring what one professes to want to measure (e.g., the concept as explained and defined), then the measure is valid. If the measurement process has nothing to do with the intended concept as it has been defined, then the measurement process is not valid. Usually validity is a matter of degree somewhere between these two extremes. For example, the measurement process may measure part of the concept but not all facets of it. Or the measurement process may also include certain systematic biases or errors that would better be avoided.

In his handbook of organizational measurement, Price (1972:90) describes the concept of dispersion in an organization as "the degree to which the membership of a social system is spatially distributed. If all the members of an organization, for example, work at a single location, then spatial distribution is at the minimum; on the other hand, if each member of an organization works at a separate location, then spatial distribution is at the maximum. The dispersion of most organizations, of course, falls somewhere between these two extremes."

In examining the literature for available measures of dispersion in an organization, Price found a potential measure developed by Haas, Hall, and Johnson (researchers generally prefer to use existing measures when possible because some experience in their use is very valuable). This measurement process involved interviewing an executive in an organization, asking for the number of physically different operating sites that organization has (Haas, Hall, and Johnson's measurement procedure involved a careful definition of what an operating site is, which is essential when it comes to counting the number of locations accurately). However, Price (1972) notes that this measurement process has validity problems when it comes to measuring the concept Price calls dispersion in an organization. One of the validity problems is that the definition of dispersion refers to the spread of organization members, not the number of operating sites an organization has. That would not be as much of a problem if organizations tended to create equal-sized operating sites, but organizations often have some huge sites and some small sites. Thus, an organization's membership might be concentrated (low dispersion) even though the organization has many operating sites. The Haas, Hall, and Johnson measurement process, although apparently valid for measuring the number of physically different operating sites, appears to be much less valid as a measurement process for Price's somewhat different concept of dispersion of organization members.

Researchers use a number of approaches to test the validity of measurement processes. The main ones are listed here.

Face Validity. **Face validity** involves professional judgments about the match between conceptual and operational definitions of a concept. Just reading the items in the Rosenberg self-esteem scale and reading his definition of the concept that he intended to measure, one can see a correspondence. It seems, on the face of it, that the scale is measuring the concept. If we read over the items used to measure organizational formalization, we would see that these do not appear to validly measure the self-esteem of individuals in Rosenberg's sense (and should not because self-esteem and formalization are different concepts). Sometimes this judgment is made more systematically by asking two or more judges to look at the operational and conceptual definitions and indicate the extent to which they see an overlap. As a student, you might ask a faculty member who specializes in the phenomenon you want to measure to make a judgment about whether the measurement process you devised is getting at the concept you want to measure. The research literature usually includes many reports of the use of different measures, and this is helpful in picking the measures that are most often used.

Predictive Validity. **Predictive validity** involves using a measurement process in a situation in which it can be compared with the use of some other measurement of the same concept. If there is a previously validated measurement instrument, one could use that and a new one that is being developed to see whether the new measure is as valid. This might happen, for example, when a very long set of items is used to measure some concept such as self-esteem and you need to use a much shorter set of items in your research. You could use both in a preliminary sample and compare results to see whether the short version leads to classifying cases nearly as well as the longer version. If there is a close correspondence, then the new measure is judged to be valid and could be used instead of the longer version in research that could not use the longer version.

Convergent and Discriminant Validity. Sometimes a check on validity can involve comparing the outcomes of the proposed measurement process across groups that are supposed to be similar and also those that are supposed to be different on the concept of interest. There should be greater similarity of outcomes for the similar groups and greater difference of outcomes for the different groups.

Construct Validity. A fourth, important approach to determine the validity of a measurement process is **construct validity,** which involves thinking through the ways in which a concept is theoretically supposed to correlate with different concepts. These expectations can be checked by analyzing the relationship between the concept as measured by the process you are considering and the same cases measured on some other variable. If a new measure of anomie is being checked out, one could go back to the literature to see what it is supposed to be related to. Anomie is related to variables such as social class (the higher the social class, the lower the anomie, theoretically) or suicide (the higher the anomie, the more likely individuals are to contemplate or attempt suicide). Then, if the concept behaves in the way a measure of that concept is supposed to behave, theoretically, the concept is judged to be valid.

All of these approaches to assessing the validity of a measurement process help determine the extent to which a measurement process is valid. The question rarely is answered once and for all, however. Measurements that are good at one point in time may not be good at some other point. An early social class indicator, known as the living room index, asked the researcher to record whether the radio was in the living room. Clearly that is an out-of-date idea in contemporary U.S. society, although it may be useful in some undeveloped countries. Some indicators are great when used by well-trained, experienced interviewers but not very valid if used by someone who doesn't know how to do the measurement; some work with face-to-face interviews but not in a typical self-administered questionnaire. Thus, researchers always carry the validity question around with them as something to be concerned about. One of the real values of looking for prior research that uses a given measure is that one can build on others' experience in using that measurement process. Other researchers may have tested the validity of a measure in situations much like those you will find in the research you plan to do.

Many sources of bias pose threats to the validity of measurement processes. Among systematic biases is **acquiescence bias,** which is a tendency to check the same response category in a series of similar questions. For example, people might generally check the "neutral" category in a series of Likert items (having "strongly agree" to "strongly disagree" response categories). Another source of bias is **social desirability bias,** in which respondents tend to give the response they think is most acceptable or the one they believe the interviewer is looking for. In some cases in which there are a series of questions, the order of the questions may have a systematic effect on the answers to a question. Finally, the situation in which measurements are made may be a sensitive one in which the respondent is unwilling to provide a response that overstates the strength of his or her views. The undercount of crimes in a city, based on crimes known to the police, and inaccurately low counts of suicides when this is thought to be a source of embarrassment are examples of bias in measurement. Bias can also occur during the process of coding, in which a coder might decide, for example, that all "neutral" responses ought to be coded as being in agreement with the question that was asked. One of our favorite examples of systematic bias is an opinionated interviewer who felt that it was inappropriate to ask certain questions in a scale about sexual attitudes; none of the interviews by this interviewer had complete information. In each case, there are research procedures that help minimize these and other sources of invalidity. Validity of measurements is a constant concern for investigators.

Reliability. Reliability of measurement refers to the stability of the measurement process. A reliable measure is one that measures in a consistent manner. Hence, one can expect to get the same value of a concept if the same case is measured again (assuming no real change in the concept being measured). Random error is an indicator of the reliability of the measurement of a concept. The more reliable the measure, the smaller the random error.

It should be noted, however, that a reliable measure is not necessarily a valid measure. Your measurement instrument might be reliable but measuring the wrong concept. Reliability is a necessary but not sufficient condition for validity.

There are a number of ways in which evidence can be gathered to see whether an operational definition is sufficiently reliable.

Test–Retest Reliability. One of the most direct approaches to testing reliability is to use the same measurement procedure on the same cases at two points in time (assuming that there has been no change in the concept of interest). The most reliable measures are those in which the second measurement is very highly correlated with the first measurement, and this correlation would be used as a reliability coefficient.

Unfortunately, the **test–retest** procedure has a number of difficulties associated with it. For example, there may actually be change. Having little time lag between the first and second application of the instrument tends to minimize the amount of change. If the change is uniform for all subjects, then the correlation of time 1 and time 2 would not be affected. There may also be sensitizing effects of being measured with the same instrument at two points in time; this effect may not be uniform for all individuals. Sometimes this effect can be minimized by mixing scale items in with other items so that they may not be recognized at the second use.

Split-Half Reliability. When one has a scale with many scale items, the reliability of the scale can be examined by a technique called the **split-half** technique. Here, the total number of items is divided into two equal groups (randomly or systematically). Responses given by a sample of subjects are scored on each half of the items. If the scale is reliable, a score developed from half of the items should correlate highly with a score developed from the other half. In this case, the correlation coefficient used takes into account the decrease in reliability expected from a score based on only half as many items as the total original scale.

What are sources of random error? This is a difficult question to answer. If one could point to specific factors that produce differences between a true score and the score based on some measurement process, then one would probably have identified a validity problem: a systematic source of error. Reliability problems stem from inherent instability in measurement, which nets out, on average, at the true score. Mistakes and carelessness, miscellaneous effects of poor recall, questions that aren't quite clear or don't quite apply to all subjects are among the likely factors conspiring to make a measurement process less reliable.

Ethical Concerns of Social Science Measurement. Research ethics applies all along the research process, including measurement. Areas of concern include concepts that should or should not be raised with different populations, measurement procedures that pose a threat to individuals, and the scientific quality of proposed measurements. Some question topics are generally avoided with vulnerable populations. For example, questions on sexual activity are often avoided for the very young without special study contexts and prior approval of custodians. Questions on income, ethnic identity or race, and private codes (e.g., social security numbers) are generally considered sensitive subjects even among adults. Although those most sensitive to certain question topics may simply choose not to answer the questions, ethical research generally restricts questions to those that are absolutely needed and clarifies for the respondent how his or her responses will be protected and used. Most measurement procedures used in the social sciences are unlikely to be a threat to most individuals. On the other hand, particularly in laboratory situations in which the effective concept is simulated or created, there could be embarrassment, anxiety, and fear, which would be inappropriate or, if necessary, would necessitate special protective conditions. Finally, there is the ethical concern that sound knowledge be produced. Investigators attempt to measure validly and reliably concepts that they will use in drawing conclusions, an ethical responsibility for good work that underlies a professional approach to a topic.

SUMMARY

In this chapter we have made a distinction between the conceptual definition of a concept, such as income, self-esteem, or social distance, and operational definitions. Conceptual definitions explain the concept one has in mind, including how one expects cases to vary in terms of the concept. For example, a good conceptual definition indicates the range of categories and their relationships to each other (including potential precision, whether they are continuous or discrete, and the level of measurement). It is important to define concepts clearly, often by indicating how a concept is like other concepts and how it differs from them.

Operational definitions, on the other hand, are the specific procedures (indicators) used to classify real cases into categories of the concept. Often this comes down to procedures for assigning a category name or a number to a case, depending on its value on the concept of interest. Any concept will have many potential operational definitions, and these differ in validity (how well they get at the concept that has been defined conceptually) and reliability (the stability of measurement). Thus, there are better and poorer ways to measure family income in different situations. Operational definitions include all of the procedures that result in a case being classified in a certain way in terms of the concept of interest.

There are several approaches to measuring a concept. Some concepts are measured by single indicators, such as single questions in a questionnaire. Others are made up of several indicators in combination, such as indices, typologies, and scales. In this chapter we have explored several ways in which indices, typologies, and scales can be created and assessed, including indices that control some unwanted source of error, indices that combine indicators of different facets of a concept, and property spaces that capture more-complex concepts by identifying patterned logical combinations of categories of indicators (typologies). Summated scales can be examined by procedures such as item analysis and factor analysis. Scaling procedures such as Guttman scaling and Thurstone scaling are other ways in which potential scales can be constructed and evaluated.

Finally, we discussed two basic characteristics of any operational definition: validity and reliability. There are several ways in which evidence can be brought to bear on the assessment of an indicator's validity, such as face validity, construct validity, and predictive validity. There are also several ways to examine reliability, such as test–retest reliability and, when there are scales, split-half reliability. Concern with checking the validity and reliability of indicators occupies a considerable part of an investigator's attention. Good operational definitions are demonstrated to be valid and reliable and are generally more precise.

Because the development of a good indicator of a concept is a substantial intellectual and research task, investigators spend considerable time searching the literature on concepts they want to measure in order to identify clear definitions and the most useful measures they can find. The next section of this chapter provides some illustrations of common concepts and their operational definitions. Foundation issues of study design are addressed in Chapter 4.

EXAMPLES OF CONCEPTS AND THEIR MEASUREMENT

EXAMPLE 1: Powerlessness

Powerlessness is defined as low expectancy for control over events in the political system. It is a continuous, ordinal variable and a property of individuals. Neal and Seeman (1964) have developed a scale to measure this concept. The Neal and Seeman powerlessness scale is described in Miller's handbook, which lists many scales used in sociology (Miller, 1991).

The scale consists of seven pairs of statements; a respondent is asked to check the statement in each pair that most closely approximates his or her own view. The "most powerless" statement in each pair is scored 1 and the "least powerless" is scored 0. A respondent's score is the sum of his or her responses to the seven pairs of statements. The higher the sum, the more powerless the person.

Miller (1991) indicates that research on validity has shown that the pattern of responses to the seven pairs of statements appears to fall along a single dimension, as indicated by a Guttman scale coefficient of reproducibility of .87. A split-half reliability test yielded a coefficient of .70. Both are reasonably high. Validity was assessed by comparing powerlessness scores for organized and unorganized workers and other known groups, and the scores discriminated between these groups. There was also research indicating correlations between powerlessness and other variables that were as one would theoretically expect them to be (construct validity).

Check the statement in each pair that is closest to your own view.

1. ☐ I think we have adequate means for preventing runaway inflation.
   ☐ There's very little we can do to keep prices from going higher.*

2. ☐ People like me have little chance of protecting our personal interests when they conflict with those of strong pressure groups.*
   ☐ I feel that we have adequate ways of coping with pressure groups.

3. ☐ A lasting world peace can be achieved by those of us who work toward it.
   ☐ There's very little we can do to bring about a permanent world peace.*

4. ☐ There's very little people like me can do to improve world opinion of the United States.*
   ☐ I think each of us can do a great deal to improve world opinion of the United States.

5. ☐ This world is run by the few people in power, and there is not much the little guy can do about it.*
   ☐ The average citizen can have an influence on government decisions.

6. ☐ It is only wishful thinking to believe that one can really influence what happens to society at large.*
   ☐ People like me can change the course of world events if we make ourselves heard.

7. ☐ More and more, I feel helpless in the face of what's happening in the world today.*
   ☐ I sometimes feel personally to blame for the sad state of affairs in our government.

*Statements in each pair indicated with an asterisk are coded 1 (the *more* powerless response); the others are coded 0.

EXAMPLE 2: Occupation

The U.S. Census and most social science researchers ask about a person's occupation for several reasons. One reason is that the general type of occupation may help understand the kind of skills and experience the respondent has (farming is different from clerical work). Occupation is also used as an indicator of a person's (or family's) social status in a community (janitors versus Supreme Court justice).

Here we focus on the use of occupation type rather than occupational status or prestige. Occupational prestige measures are described succinctly by Delbert Miller in his *Handbook of Research Design and Social Measurement* (1991:section A).

The 11-category occupation measure used by the U.S. Census and social scientists is listed here, with some illustrations of each category.

Professional, technical, and kindred workers (accountants, scientists, teachers, chemical engineers, pilots, musicians)

Managers and administrators, except farm (bank officers, health administrators, office managers, sales managers)

Sales workers (sales clerks, real estate agents, advertising agents)

Clerical and kindred workers (bookkeepers, file clerks, computer operators, secretaries, clerks)

Craftsmen and kindred workers (carpenters, concrete finishers, dental technicians, plumbers, electricians)

Operatives (furnacemen, drillers, graders and packers, butchers, bus or truck drivers)

Laborers, except farm (carpenter helpers, fishermen, garbage collectors, freight handlers)

Farmers and farm managers (farm owners and tenants, managers)

Farm laborers and farm foremen (including unpaid family farm laborers)

Service workers, except private household (janitors, dishwashers, barbers, firemen, policemen, school monitors)

Private household workers (child care, private household housekeepers, laundrypersons, servants)

Although sometimes the categories are simply listed for respondents to check, the better and more rigorous classification of occupations requires considerable information. The U.S. Census has developed a detailed process that assigns each occupation a six-digit code. Three digits are for the occupation category itself, an elaboration of the preceding categories, and three digits are for the industry in which the occupation is located. The brief classification listed here is a grouped version of this extensive code. The U.S. Census coding manual lists about 23,000 occupational titles and indicates how they should be assigned the occupation codes. In many cases the occupation is difficult to classify and special rules are devised for handling these cases. Books and coding instructions are available from government labor statistics sources (Web site: http://www.fedstats.gov/). The U.S. government has devised a new occupation classification called O*NET, which classifies occupations in terms of general facets of the skills needed to perform a job (see Web site: http://www.doleta.gov/programs/onet/).

In general, it takes several questions to provide sufficient information for classifying occupations in terms of occupation category. One survey organization (NORC, 1991) uses the following questions as a basis for creating the occupation code. Respondents are asked seven questions during a typical interview so that occupation coding can be accurately made:

1. What kind of work do you (did you normally) do? That is, what (is/was) your job called?
2. What (do/did) you actually do in that job? What (are/were) some of your main duties?
3. What kind of place (do/did) you work for?

4. What (do/did) they (make/do)?
5. (Are/Were) you self-employed or (do/did) you work for someone else?
6. (Are/Were) you employed by the federal, state, or local government or by a private employer (including nonprofit organizations)?
7. About how much time (does/did) it usually take you to travel to work—about how many minutes?

From these questions, a detailed occupation code can be established. The occupation can also be used to create a prestige index. The prestige index is based on the education and income levels associated with different occupations. The research on which the prestige code is based involves not only aggregate census data but also research on how people judge the ranking of various subsets of occupations (Ganzeboom and Treiman, 1996; Stevens and Cho, 1985; Reiss, 1961).

EXAMPLE 3: Hollingshead's Two-Factor Index of Social Position (see Miller, 1991:351)

Hollingshead's two-factor index of social position is intended to measure the position individuals occupy in the status structure. The two factors used are occupation and education. Both use a rating from a high score of 1 to a low of 7. Occupation scoring is guided by an extensive list of occupation titles and organizational characteristics. For example, higher executives in larger firms score 1, small business owners and commercial artists score 3, and unskilled employees score 7. Education scoring uses seven categories from "graduate professional training," which is scored 1, down to "less than 7 years of school," which is scored 7.

The index is formed as follows:

Occupation score is multiplied by a weight of 7 (3 × 7 = 21).
Education score is multiplied by a weight of 4 (2 × 4 = 8).

These results are summed to get an individual's index of social position (21 + 8 = 29). It is possible to have scores ranging from 11 [(1 × 7) + (1 × 4)] to 77 [(7 × 7) + (7 × 4)]. Hollingshead then divided scores into five social classes for the purpose of his studies:

Class I: scores of 11–17
Class II: scores of 18–31
Class III: scores of 32–47
Class IV: scores of 48–63
Class V: scores of 64–77

EXAMPLE 4: Illustration of Commonly Used Single Indicators

These operational definitions might be used in a mailed questionnaire.

Size of Household
How many people are living in your household now, including yourself? ____ people

Gender
(Please circle one) Male Female

Age (or birth cohort)
In what year were you born? 19 ______

Education
What is the highest level of school you have completed? (circle one)

- **a.** Less than high school
- **b.** Some high school
- **c.** High school graduate
- **d.** Some technical school
- **e.** Technical school graduate
- **f.** Some college
- **g.** College graduate
- **h.** Postgraduate or professional degree
- **i.** Other (please specify) ______

Family income (an operational definition used for phone interviewing)
Was your total household income in 1995 above or below $35,000?

1. Above (If above, go to question *a*)
2. Below (if below, go to question *b*)
   DK (don't know)
   RA (refused to answer)

a. (If above) I am going to mention a number of income categories. When I come to the category that describes your total household income *before* taxes in 1997, please stop me.

$35,000 to $40,000
$40,000 to $50,000
$50,000 to $60,000
$60,000 to $70,000
$70,000 to $80,000
$80,000 or more
DK, RA

b. (If below) I am going to mention a number of income categories. When I come to the category that describes your total household income *before* taxes in 1997, please stop me.

Under $5,000
$5,000 to $10,000
$10,000 to $15,000
$15,000 to $20,000
$20,000 to $25,000
$25,000 to $30,000
$30,000 to $35,000
DK, RA

TERMS TO KNOW

Acquiescence bias
Bias
Concept
Conceptual definition
Continuous
Correlation matrix
Discrete
Easy/hard scale items
Factor analysis
Guttman scale
Index
Item analysis
Levels of measurement
- Nominal
- Interval
- Ordinal
- Ratio

Likert scale
Operational definition
Precision
Property space
Random measurement error
Reduction
Reliability
- Split-half reliability
- Test–retest reliability

Scale
Social desirability bias
Summated scale
Systematic bias
Thurstone method of equal-appearing intervals
Typology
Unidimensional
Unit of measurement
Validity
- Construct validity
- Face validity
- Predictive validity

Variable

ISSUES AND COMPARISONS

Single indicators versus multiple indicators of a concept
Ethical concerns in measurement of social phenomena

EXERCISES

1. Find a concept that interests you and look up a current conceptual definition of it. Critique the definition and add to it any elements that are implied rather than explicit so that the definition is as complete as possible.

2. Now, list 8 to 12 different potential indicators of the concept. Briefly explain them and rank them in order from most likely to be valid to least likely to be valid.

3. In the literature, find a measure of your concept that corresponds to the most valid measure you have listed. How has it been tested and used?

4. Find a scale that is supposed to measure some concept in which you are interested. Provide the conceptual definition for the concept being measured, show the operational definition, then write an evaluative paragraph summarizing how the scale was constructed, how respondents are scored on the scale, and what your assessment is of the validity and reliability of the scale.

REFERENCES

Amato, Paul R., and Alan Booth, "Changes in Gender Role Attitudes and Perceived Marital Quality," *American Sociological Review* February 1995;60:58–66.

Barton, Allen H., "The Concept of Property Space in Social Research," in Paul F. Lazarsfeld and Morris Rosenberg, eds., *The Language of Social Research,* Free Press, Glencoe, NY, 1964, pp. 40–53.

Bogardus, Emory S., *Social Distance,* Antioch, Yellow Springs, OH, 1959.

Bonjean, Charles M., Richard J. Hill, and S. Dale McLemore, *Sociological Measurement: An Inventory of Scales and Indices,* Chandler, San Francisco, 1967.

Cohen, Morris R., and Ernest Nagel, *An Introduction to Logic and Scientific Method,* Harcourt, Brace, New York, 1934.

Danes, Sharon M., and Donald McTavish, "Role Involvement of Farm Women," *Journal of Family and Economic Issues* 1996;18(1).

Edwards, Allen L., *Techniques of Attitude Scale Construction,* Appleton-Century Crofts, New York, 1957.

Ganzeboom, Harry B. G., and Donald J. Treiman, "Internationally Comparable Measures of Occupational Status for the 1988 International Standard Classification of Occupations," *Social Science Research* September 1996;25(3):201–39.

Hollingshead, August B., and Frederick C. Redlick, *Social Class and Mental Illness,* Wiley, New York, 1958, pp. 387–97.

Johnson, Allan G., *The Blackwell Dictionary of Sociology: A User's Guide to Sociological Language,* Blackwell, Oxford, UK, 1995.

Loether, Herman J., and Donald G. McTavish, *Descriptive and Inferential Statistics: An Introduction,* 4th ed., Allyn & Bacon, Boston, MA, 1993.

Miller, Delbert C., *Handbook of Research Design and Social Measurement,* 5th ed., Longman, New York, 1991.

National Opinion Research Center, *Surveys General Social, 1972–1991: Cumulative Codebook,* University of Chicago, Chicago, 1991.

Neal, A. G., and H. T. Groat, "Social Class Correlates of Stability and Change in Levels of Alienation: A Longitudinal Study," *Sociological Quarterly* 1974;15:548–58.

Neal, Arthur G., and Melvin Seeman, "Organizations and Powerlessness: A Test of the Mediation Hypothesis," *American Sociological Review* December 1964;27:772–82.

Price, James L., *Handbook of Organizational Measurement,* D.C. Heath, Lexington, MA, 1972.

Reiss, Albert J., Jr., *Occupations and Social Status,* Free Press, Glencoe, NY, 1961.

Riggs, Fred Warren, *The Intercocta Manual: Towards an International Encyclopedia of Social Science Terms,* United Nations Educational, Scientific and Cultural Organization, Paris, 1988.

Robinson, John P., and Phillip R. Shaver, *Measures of Social Psychological Attitudes,* Survey Research Center, Institute for Social Research, University of Michigan, Ann Arbor, 1972.

Rosenberg, Morris, *Society and the Adolescent Self Image,* Princeton University Press, Princeton, NJ, 1965.

Stevens, Gillian, and Joo Hyun Cho, "Socioeconomic Indexes and the New 1980 Census Occupational Classification Scheme," *Social Science Research* 1985;1:142–68.

Zeller, Richard A., and Edward G. Carmines, *Measurement in the Social Sciences: The Link Between Theory and Data,* Cambridge University Press, Cambridge, UK, 1980.

CHAPTER FOUR

STUDY DESIGN: BASIC CONTRASTS AND PLANS

Bazargan and Hamm-Baugh (1995) were interested in the relationship between chronic illness and depression among urban, Black older people. They note from prior research that physical health status has been found to predict emotional distress and symptoms of depression. Their study examined the effect of selected chronic diseases on depression beyond the effect of variables that other studies have found to be relevant. To gather data on Blacks with different chronic diseases and symptoms of depression, Bazargan and Hamm-Baugh identified a sample of independently living Black older people (62 years and older) living in New Orleans. The list of households was obtained from various housing and senior citizen centers. After identifying 1,040 Blacks who were willing to participate in the study, these researchers conducted personal interviews to gather information on background characteristics (age, sex, education, etc.) and a checklist of chronic illnesses (e.g., arthritis, kidney disease, lung and heart trouble), and they used an existing scale measuring depression symptoms. In addition, they asked subjects questions about other factors such as social supports, stressful life events, and perceptions of themselves and their abilities. The researchers compared the level of depression for those who did and did not have each chronic illness. Other potential explanations of the impact of various physical illnesses were statistically controlled so that differences in depression for those with various illnesses could be compared correctly.

The **research design** used in this study is a cross-sectional survey. As we shall see, there are characteristic strengths and weaknesses of such a design. For example, because of the way the sample was gathered, it is likely that findings can be generalized to the population from which it was drawn (independently living, older Blacks in New Orleans between 1989 and 1991, the dates of the study). On the other hand, as we shall see, because information was gathered on all variables at the same point in time, it is hard to determine what is the cause and what is the effect. This chapter describes some of the issues and options of research design.

Once a research question is formulated and the conceptualization process has been completed, a plan must be developed to answer the research question as efficiently and thoroughly as possible. The conceptualization of the problem is a crucial prerequisite to the development of the study design or plan because, if it is done properly, it provides a list of the concepts that must be studied and suggests the appropriate population on which to focus the research. Regardless of which study design is developed, an essential ingredient of that design for answering the research question is **comparison.** Without comparison it is not possible to answer the research question satisfactorily.

THE BASIC LOGIC OF VALID COMPARISON

Increasing concern about the state of the health care system in the United States led to a number of proposals to reform the system beginning in the early 1990s. Concerns focused on rapidly accelerating costs and increasing numbers of citizens without access to health care. In partial response to these concerns, a trend toward managed care, particularly in the form of health maintenance organizations (HMOs), developed.

The concept of the HMO was pioneered by Kaiser-Permanente in the 1940s. In the Kaiser-Permanente model, members are given prepaid services by doctors and other health care staff who are employees of the organization at facilities that are owned and operated by the organization. A large number of other HMOs started during the 1990s. Most of these used a model somewhat different from the Kaiser model in that they contracted with a variety of doctors and hospitals that also worked with other insurers. As with Kaiser, however, their members prepaid their medical insurance so that they would have access to care at little or no extra cost when they needed it.

By emphasizing preventive medicine and employing gatekeepers (usually general practitioners) to monitor the care of patients and refer them to specialists when necessary, these HMOs sought to make health care a profitable enterprise. They set up guidelines about the kinds of services they would provide, excluding services that were considered experimental, ineffective, or unnecessary. In addition, they sought to put more and more treatment on an outpatient basis and to limit hospital stays.

Increasingly, the HMOs were attacked by the mass media, politicians, and a range of public organizations on issues of quality of care. The January 1996 issue of *U.S. News and World Report* published an article titled "How Your HMO Could Hurt You." HMOs were also investigated by the *Los Angeles Times* and the TV news program *60 Minutes* (Olmos, 1996). The HMOs responded to these attacks by asserting that the claims of poor quality of care were based on anecdotal evidence.

Although the incidents used in the media to criticize the HMOs were not based on scientific studies of such organizations, a number of studies were conducted earlier to assess members' satisfaction with their HMOs. One such study by Dozier and his colleagues surveyed the experiences of California state employees who participated in the Kaiser-Permanente HMO. When members who had received medical care the previous year were asked whether they were satisfied with the quality of care they received, 87.8% reported that they were (Dozier et al.,

1987:106). Furthermore, 88.7% of the survey respondents said that they were satisfied with the courtesy and consideration shown them by nurses and 87.0% with the courtesy and consideration shown them by doctors (Dozier et al., 1987:109).

At first glance one is left with the impression that members of the Kaiser-Permanente HMO are, in general, well satisfied with their health care plan. After all, percentages in the range of 87% or more are high. However, these findings are incomplete and, in their present form, prevent the reader from determining the quality of the HMO studied.

What is missing is comparison data. One might ask how the Kaiser results with respect to member satisfaction compare with the results for members who were participants in other health care plans. In fact, the Dozier study also surveyed state employees who belonged to other health care plans about their levels of satisfaction.

One of these other plans was BlueCross BlueShield, which was not an HMO. When members of BC/BS were asked about their satisfaction with the quality of medical care they received in the previous year, 88.5% of them reported that they were satisfied. Their level of satisfaction with the courtesy and consideration shown them by nurses was 88.2%, and their satisfaction with level of courtesy and consideration shown them by doctors was 89.4% (Dozier et al., 1987:274, 278). Given these additional figures for comparison, the Kaiser-Permanente findings can now be put in their proper perspective. Although levels of satisfaction with the Kaiser-Permanente HMO were high, they were not unusually high compared to BC/BS[1] and were lower on some items. Comparing the Kaiser-Permanente figures on satisfaction with the figures for other health care plans puts the Kaiser-Permanente responses in a different light. One could conclude from the comparison of plans that satisfaction with health care was generally high; therefore, the reported satisfaction with the Kaiser-Permanente plan did not indicate that that particular HMO was better than the other plans.

To make a definitive comparison of satisfaction with health care plans, it would be desirable to survey people who use a number of different HMOs, a number of preferred provider plans, and a number of fee-for-service plans and then compare the results. Comparison is an essential element of good research.

Types of Comparisons

Many types of comparisons may be made in research. The types of comparisons used by researchers include the following.

Category-to-Category Comparisons. The HMO example is essentially a **category-to-category comparison:** a comparison of categories of people classified according to some characteristic they share. In the case of this example, what they share is membership in the same health plan. In the Bazargan and Hamm-Baugh

[1]The Dozier study did include findings for other plans that were available to state employees. The percentages for these others were comparable to those for Kaiser-Permanente and BC/BS and some were even higher.

(1995) study, comparisons were made between categories of respondents with similar chronic illnesses. This kind of comparison is common in social science research. Whenever ethnic group is used as a basis for comparison, for example, the comparison being made is essentially of categories of people sharing the characteristic: the same ethnic group. Whenever males and females are compared this, too, is a comparison of categories of people with a shared characteristic. The term *category* is used here in preference to the term *group* because *group* implies interaction over time among group members. People who are identified with a particular ethnic status or gender do not necessarily interact with each other over time; most do not interact with each other at all. Therefore, in sociological terms, they do not belong to a common group.

Group-to-Group Comparisons. A second type of comparison is a **group-to-group comparison.** For example, a research project that compares the members of a number of different school clubs (e.g., chess club, computer club, stamp club) would be a group-to-group comparison. The same would be true of a study that used the family as its unit of analysis. If the meaning of *group* is extended to include social organizations or social systems, then the number of possibilities for research is greatly increased. A study that focused on organizations that administer health care plans, for instance, rather than on the satisfaction of members of those plans would involve a group-to-group (social system–to–social system) comparison. The difference between this type of study and the Dozier HMO study is that in the former study, the organizations would be the sources of data needed to answer the research question, whereas in the Dozier study the sources of data were the individual members of the plans.

Individual-to-Group Comparisons. There is a third type of comparison possible in which individuals are compared with groups or organizations. For example, you might want to determine whether groups or individuals are more efficient in solving certain kinds of common problems. In an **individual-to-group comparison,** the problem to be solved might be presented to groups of three people for a collective solution and then to a number of individuals working alone.

Individual- or Group-to-Standard Comparisons. An **individual- or group-to-standard comparison** involves the comparison of individuals or groups against some established standard. For example, consider a study that compares the intelligence quotients (IQs) of a sample of high school students against the average score of 100. Or consider a study in which the annual incomes of a sample of four-person American families are compared to the federally defined poverty level for a family of four.

Comparison of the Same Individual or Group at Different Points in Time. A fifth type of comparison that can be made is a **comparison of the same individual or group at different points in time.** For example, the annual family incomes of a sample of American families might be compared at 10-year intervals over a period of 30 years, starting when the breadwinner of the family is in his or her 20s. This comparison would necessitate keeping track of the individual families in the sample and determining their incomes at each designated point in time.

Cohort Comparisons. Because it is sometimes difficult or impossible to keep track of individuals or family units over time, it might be necessary to substitute a **cohort comparison** for a specific individual or group comparison. In a cohort comparison, rather than collecting the necessary data from the same individuals or the same groups at each point in time, the data are collected from a cohort. A cohort is a number of people or groups who share some characteristic (the same date of birth, for example). When a cohort is studied at different points in time, it will generally contain many, but not necessarily all, of the same members at each point in time. For example, the annual family incomes of families in which the breadwinner is 25 years of age might be compared 10 years later with the annual family incomes of families in which the breadwinner is 35 years of age. The assumption in this kind of comparison is that the cohort at the second measurement includes many of the same people as it did at the first measurement. Of course, there are bound to be differences in the two time periods because some families that were studied initially may no longer be in existence 10 years later and some families that were not in existence initially may be included in the cohort 10 years later.

Mixed Comparisons. Although the six different comparisons just discussed can be made separately, in an actual research project two or more of these types of comparisons may be used. For example, in discussing individual-to-group comparisons, an example was given in which groups of three people were pitted against individual subjects in solving common problems. A reasonable extension of this study might combine such an individual-to-group comparison with a group-to-group comparison. Consequently, the problem-solving ability of individuals might be compared with that of groups of two, three, four, and five people. In addition to comparing the performances of individuals with groups of these different sizes, therefore, the performances of the groups of different sizes could also be compared.

Which type of comparison is appropriate for a study depends on how the study is conceptualized. One of the payoffs of conceptualization, in fact, is that it indicates which comparisons are necessary in order to answer the research question. Research planned without comparisons is fatally flawed from the start, and it usually unfolds as a family of related flaws by the time the research project ends, resulting in a distorted project that may not address any of the initial research questions.

THE ROLE OF TIME IN RESEARCH DESIGN

Two time-based approaches are used in sociology: cross-sectional studies and longitudinal studies. A **cross-sectional study** is one in which the data are collected at one point in time and an answer to the research question applies only to the phenomenon at the particular time it is studied. This type of study might be compared to taking a snapshot of something. The Bazargan and Hamm-Baugh (1995) study was of this type. A **longitudinal study,** on the other hand, involves data collection at different points in time in order to document change in the phenomenon of interest and to answer the research question of how the phenomenon evolves rather than to determine the state of the phenomenon at one point in time. This type of study might be compared to making a video or a movie of something. A crucial question is, "Which of two models—a static one or a dynamic one—is more appropriate for sociology?"

Static versus Dynamic Models for Sociology

When cross-sectional studies are conducted in sociology, it is often implied that social phenomena are best represented by **static models.** For example, if it is found that certain benefits are attached to higher socioeconomic status, such as better health, more education, and higher income, then it is assumed that those findings can be applied not only to the population studied at the time at which the data were collected, but also to that population at other points in time. Hence, it is assumed that the relationship uncovered is a stable one.

Social phenomena are basically dynamic. They are in a constant state of change. Consequently, no two events are exactly alike. What appears as stability is attributable to a steady rate of change that is slow enough to give the perception that no change is taking place. In order to understand social phenomena and predict their future courses, it is necessary to establish the rate at which change takes place as well as the nature of the change taking place, using a **dynamic model** (see Tuma and Hannan, 1984, for discussions of dynamic models).

Dependence on a stable or static paradigm of social behavior is common in sociology, as witnessed by the number of cross-sectional studies that are conducted and appear in the literature. This may be so because sociologists have often adopted an orientation toward social behavior analogous to the orientation geologists use in relating to geological phenomena. Despite the fact that the surface of the earth is in a continuous state of change, geological phenomena usually change at such a slow rate that road builders can assume that any change will be inconsequential, so they build a road with the expectation that the surface will endure. Usually such an expectation is a reasonable and workable one. Occasionally, however, there can be a sudden, unanticipated occurrence such as an earthquake or a landslide that may wipe out the road surface. Such an occurrence is considered an anomaly, and the surface is restored to its previous state in the expectation that it will again endure.

The problem with applying this static model to social phenomena is that they are more dynamic and they generally change at a rate much faster than the surface of the earth. As a consequence, a finding based on a cross-sectional study is unlikely to retain its explanatory and predictive ability for a social phenomenon over time as well as it does for a geological phenomenon. Note that time is a part of the evidence for establishing a causal relationship between variables (see Box 4.1).

BOX 4.1

THE TIME FACTOR IN CAUSAL RELATIONSHIPS

The idea of cause includes the idea of time. There are three elements to the idea of cause:

1. The cause and effect are correlated in some way as one of the following:
   a. A **necessary** condition. If an effect is present then the causal factor must be present.
   b. A **sufficient** condition. If a cause is present, then the effect must be present.
   c. A **necessary and sufficient** condition. If the cause is present, the effect will be present, and the effect will not be present unless the cause is present.
2. The **cause must precede the effect.**
3. **Other factors** antecedent to cause and effect **do not explain away** their relationship.

Although there are instances of longitudinal studies in sociology, they are less common than they should be. One might argue that sociologists should devote less effort to testing theories that describe the states of social phenomena at specific points in time than to those that describe the orderly (or disorderly) changes that take place in social phenomena over time. That is, there should be a shift in focus from static to dynamic models of social systems.

Consider the example of the relationships among socioeconomic status, health, education, and income. It is important to establish that such relationships exist at a certain point in time, but it is equally or more important to determine whether such relationships are getting stronger or weaker as time passes. In the 1990s the data available indicated that the income gap between the wealthy and the poor in the United States widened rather than narrowed, as it had been doing for some time in the past. If the relationship between socioeconomic status, health, and education indicated by cross-sectional studies is examined longitudinally, it might be expected that the increasing income gap will be accompanied by an increasing gap between the wealthy and poor in health and education as well.

Although an isolated cross-sectional study tends to emphasize a static model, cross-sectional studies need not be limited to static models of social phenomena. As a matter of fact, one way of conducting a dynamic, longitudinal study of a social phenomenon is to carry out a series of cross-sectional data-collecting exercises over time (**trend studies**). The General Social Survey is such an effort. Although each annual survey is cross-sectional, once the data are compiled over time (as they have been since 1972) the total database allows for a dynamic, longitudinal analysis of selected aspects of American society. One can determine, for instance, whether citizens' support for capital punishment is waning or increasing by comparing the percentage of those in favor of capital punishment for each of the annual surveys that have been conducted and that have included a question on the subject.

Of course, a longitudinal study of this sort falls into the category of cohort comparison discussed earlier because, although they may be representative of the American people at the time of each survey, the individual respondents within the samples differ from year to year. What this sort of analysis makes possible is such statements as "Over the years studied, American support for capital punishment has increased." The implication of this statement is that a larger percentage of American citizens favored capital punishment as time passed. However, it does not allow the researcher to conclude that individuals who previously did not support capital punishment came to support it as time passed. In order to make this sort of statement it would be necessary to question the same people at different points in time. Or, conversely, cohort analysis could be refined by questioning a cohort of people 1 year older each time a new survey was conducted, with the expectation that those who were 29 years of age last year will be 30 years of age this year (and so on) and will be, for the most part, the same people sampled last year when they were a year younger. This latter type of cohort analysis would reduce the likelihood of change in cohort composition and make it possible to make some statement about whether people have changed their positions with respect to the issues they were questioned about. A better option is a **panel study,** in which the same individuals are reinterviewed through time.

When cross-sectional studies are considered in the larger context of longitudinal research, they may be compared to a single frame of a motion picture or videotape. A motion picture consists of a series of snapshots taken in sequence and then shown quickly, one after the other, to produce the impression of motion.

When put in this context, a cross-sectional study is just one part of a larger study waiting to happen. If research does not move beyond the cross-sectional study, then the research may be considered incomplete. Why, then, should cross-sectional research stop at one point in time? There are a number of reasons why this occurs in sociology. First, the very practical matter of funding a project may limit the collection of data to one point in time. Second, the results of the cross-sectional data analysis may fall short of the researcher's expectations and, thus, discourage the researcher from pursuing the subject further. Third, the primary reason for conducting the study in the first place may have been to generate a publication; once the study results in a publication, the researcher may lose interest in pursuing the subject further. Finally, if the researcher adopts the static model of social phenomena as being the proper model, he or she may not consider the study incomplete.

The whole line of reasoning being advocated here (that is, a dynamic or process approach) suggests that much more emphasis must be put on **replication** of research in sociology than it generally receives. For many researchers, it seems that the goal is to research topics that have not been well researched in the past, rather than replicate existing research. This tendency exacerbates the problem of sociological research being dominated by too many cross-sectional studies and not enough longitudinal ones.

When a cross-sectional study conducted by one researcher is replicated by another, there is the danger of confusing change with a lack of validity or reliability. If a static model is assumed and the second researcher does not get the same results that the first researcher got in the original study, the claim may be made that one of the studies fell short of accepted standards of research. In fact, the differing results between the original study and the replication may just be a reflection of change that has been taking place in the phenomenon under investigation rather than an indication that there were validity or reliability problems with the procedures used in one of the studies. Further replications beyond the first one could actually be useful for sorting out the effects of change in a phenomenon from problems of validity or reliability. Thus, a number of replications over a period of years might allow researchers to detect trends and to distinguish such trends from apparent defects in research procedures.

Time Constraints on Sociological Research

One factor that has had an adverse effect on longitudinal research in sociology has been the short life expectancy of humans, including researchers, compared to the social phenomena being studied. Because social phenomena are generally in the process of changing and the rate of change may be reasonably fast, a fairly large number of **data points** over time may be necessary to establish the nature of trends. A researcher who initiates a longitudinal study of some social phenomenon in hopes of discovering principles with regard to rates and directions of change of the phenomenon may not live long enough to bring the research to fruition. In fact, a trained researcher will not be able to study a normal single human life course during his or her professional lifetime! This fact has the effect of encouraging researchers to undertake studies that give more promise of short-term payoff in results. This may explain, in part, the plethora of cross-sectional studies.

Although long-term studies are difficult to find in the literature, they are not completely absent. Perhaps the best known of these in psychology is Lewis Terman's study of gifted children. In 1921, when he was in his forties, Terman began a longitudinal study of 1,521 children who scored 135 or higher on an intelligence test (Hothersall, 1984:318–321). He and his coworkers focused on the physical, mental, and personality traits of these children as they matured. Teachers were asked to nominate the three brightest and the youngest student in their third- through eighth-grade classes in California. From these the subjects were selected. A total of 850 boys and 671 girls were chosen for the study, with a mean IQ of 151 and a mean age of 11. Their IQ scores ranged from 135 to 200, with 77 of them scoring over 170. "Detailed information about their family backgrounds, educational history, physique, health, interests, preoccupation, character, and personality was collected, thus allowing the first comprehensive portrait of the gifted child" (Hothersall, 1984:319).

The first volume of a series documenting the development of these children was published in 1926 and was followed over the years by a number of other volumes reporting follow-up studies of their progress (Terman, 1926, 1959; Burks, Jensen, and Terman, 1930; Terman and Oden, 1947; Oden, 1968; Sears and Barbee, 1977; Sears, 1977).[2] Although Terman died in 1956, the studies continued for more than 50 years. In general, it was found that the gifted children became healthy, educated, successful, and well-adjusted adults. Furthermore, most of them seemed to age gracefully.

Terman knew when he started the study that he would not be able to follow his subjects throughout their lives, but he could reasonably expect to be involved in the research long enough to see them in their adult years. If he had been in his 70s in 1921, when the study started, he might never have started it in the first place.

Sources of Longitudinal Data Points

Because of the need for numerous data points over time to establish trends in social phenomena, sociologists have increasingly turned to available historical records. For example, census records in the United States go back to 1790. A federal census has been conducted from that date to the present at 10-year intervals. Furthermore, census records over 75 years old are now in the public domain in their original form. Unfortunately, the earlier censuses did not collect very detailed data about people, their families, or their households. This greatly limits the kinds of research that can make good use of these data. There are other historical records that go back many years (such as birth, death, and marriage records), and these are generally available for researchers' use. The increasing popularity of historical sociology

[2]Volume II of the series was a retrospective study of 301 men and women who lived in earlier times and were judged to have been gifted.

reflects sociologists' recognition of the need for more emphasis on longitudinal analysis.

When we can reach back into the past and find relevant data, it is possible to overcome the problem of career longevity of researchers themselves. However, the sorts of data available are limited in coverage. Few attitudinal data, for example, are available for the distant past. Fortunately, sociologists and other social scientists are increasingly building longitudinal databases that include these variables. These include the General Social Survey mentioned earlier, social indicator databases, polling databases, public health databases, and others that go beyond mere fact-gathering. Many of these databases are being stored as computer files that make them easily accessible to researchers with a need to use them (Box 4.2). As a consequence of the development of these data archives, in future years it will be much easier to do longitudinal analysis.

DESIGN OPTIONS: DECISION PATTERNS AND TRADE-OFFS

The plan for researching a question, generally known as the research design, involves a series of decisions. Of course the process starts with deciding the research question to be answered. Once the research question has been chosen, conceptualization must proceed, with attention to the concepts to be investigated and consideration of how those concepts are to be measured. Another result of conceptualization is the specification of the kind of research case and the population of such cases to which the research question applies. Once the conceptualization is accomplished and the relevant population has been specified, the

BOX 4.2
SOURCE OF LONGITUDINAL DATA AND DATA FROM REPEATED SURVEYS

Several Web sites provide information about longitudinal and cross-sectional surveys. At the time of this writing, the following sites were operational:

http://www.asanet.org/data.htm is the American Sociological Association Web site, which includes a good list of major studies and the data they provide.

http://www.psc.lsa.umich.edu/SSDAN/ provides access to U.S. Census data.

http://www.icpsr.umich.edu/gss/ contains information on the General Social Surveys; the International Consortium for Political and Social Research (ICPSR) also maintains a large archive of secondary data.

researcher must develop a strategic plan to collect the data necessary to answer the research question. The process of deciding what must be done involves a number of key decisions.

Matilda Riley (1963) characterized research design as a pattern of decisions that are made explicitly or implicitly in the course of designing and conducting a study. These decisions determine what the research design is. In the end, these decisions also determine what can be claimed as the results of the research. Figure 4.1 lists the 12 main research design decisions Riley lists. You will notice that decisions about the role of time in research are included in the fifth decision in her list. Here we will summarize the design decisions she identifies. These are described in greater detail in other chapters.

FIGURE 4.1 Main Research Design Decisions (From Matilda Riley, 1963)

- **Nature of the Research Case**
  Alternatives include: an individual in a role in some collectivity, a dyad or pair of interrelated group members, subgroup, group, society, or combinations of these.
- **Number of Cases**
  Alternatives include a single case, a few selected cases, or many selected cases.
- **Sociotemporal Context**
  Alternatives include cases from a single society at a single period or cases from many societies or many periods.
- **Primary Basis for Selecting Cases (sampling)**
  Alternatives include cases selected to represent some population, cases selected for some analytical purpose, or both.
- **Time Factor**
  Static studies (covering a single point in time) or dynamic studies (covering a process or change over time).
- **Extent of Researcher's Control over the System under Study**
  Alternatives include no control, unsystematic control, or systematic control.
- **Basic Sources of Data**
  Alternatives include new data collected by the researcher to answer the research question or available data that are relevant to the research question.
- **Method of Gathering Data**
  Alternatives include observation, questioning, or combinations of these.
- **Number of Properties Used in Research**
  Alternatives include one, a few, or many properties.
- **Method of Handling Single Properties**
  Alternatives include unsystematic description or measurement of variables.
- **Method of Handling Relationships among Properties**
  Alternatives include unsystematic description or systematic analysis.
- **Treatment of System Properties**
  Alternatives include unitary (properties such as "type of government," which cannot be broken down into some sum of individual properties) or collective (properties such as "crime rates," which are aggregated from properties of individuals within the system).

■ **Research case** (see Chapter 2). Clarity on the exact **research case** or unit of analysis is especially important in the social sciences because of the variety of units that can be used. For example, one could study individual social actors, dyads, interacting group members, and various levels of groups including a whole society as the case. Sometimes there is interest in occupations or roles or a type of relationship (dating) as a case. These are sometimes combined in levels, such as individuals within groups within communities. Clarity and consistency in defining the case are essential. Confusion sometimes arises because in most studies individuals provide the data on whatever unit the investigator has chosen: respondents themselves, their groups or families, their society, or the occupation they have. In some instances, respondents are *informants* about a case, and in other studies they are *subjects* reporting on their own attitudes and behavior.

■ **Number of cases** (see Chapters 5 and 8). Studies call for different skills and permit different procedures depending on the number of cases selected. A single case may be selected for analytic reasons and studied over time in detail. Alternatively, there may be a small number of cases or a large number. Certain statistical procedures help with handling a large number of cases, and this permits a range of detailed, quantitative analyses, for example. Quite different analysis strategies are implied for case studies.

■ **Sociotemporal context.** Often studies deal with a contemporary era and with the researcher's society simply because of convenience of access. Research that uses historical records and secondary data may extend the context to a number of eras of historic time. Depending on funding or opportunities for developing networks of collaboration among scholars, cross-societal research may be possible. One weakness of current theoretical knowledge is that its tests have tended to be from one era and one society or subpart of society.

■ **Selection of cases** (see Chapter 5). Although some studies select cases for their analytic value alone, many studies have an interest in generalizing sample findings to a broader population. In the latter case, researchers need to use methods that will allow them to get a representative sample and will support their logic of making an inferential leap from a description of a sample to a description of a population.

■ **Time** (see earlier sections of this chapter). This refers to the extension of time in any given study. Some studies, as you have seen, are cross-sectional, dealing with data from one point in time. Longitudinal studies seek data from cases through time (panel studies) or from a series of cases from the same population at a series of different points in time (trend studies).

■ **Researcher's control** (see Chapter 6). By choice but mostly because of possibilities, researchers may have little control over the subjects and phenomenon being studied. A researcher's control extends mostly to the choice of research topic or question and control over the investigator's behavior in observing, questioning, and reflecting on the data. However, some topics and situations permit a researcher to exercise considerable control over a study, especially over who does and doesn't experience some condition or treatment. Ethical considerations limit control in some instances. In others, the nature of the phenomenon being studied is simply not amenable to researcher control. For example, it would be impossible to assign people to different types of families or to different ages or genders or to create different societal contexts. Many of the research methods discussed in this book address the possibilities and consequences of researcher control.

- **Data sources.** New data can be tailored to the investigator's needs, but archived data or historical records may not include exactly what an investigator needs to answer a research question. Today archived data sets are more available, and costs of gathering extensive new data may be too high for a researcher who needs to write a paper in a quarter or publish a paper before salary review time each year. This has consequences for the state of knowledge in a field.

- **Method of gathering data** (see Chapters 6 and 7). Data come from questioning or observation, either done by the investigator or left as a record by someone else. Questions can be efficiently asked of respondents who are anywhere in the world: questionnaires in class, mailed questionnaires to a national sample, or phone interviews across the world. Observation, on the other hand, requires that the researcher be positioned to perform systematic observation (or perhaps view video records made by others).

- **Number of variables (properties) used** (see Chapters 6, 7, and 8). Some research designs permit an investigator to introduce and measure very few variables, simplifying the analysis considerably. Other types of research demand that an investigator include many variables so that those that might make a difference in interpreting results can be taken into account. The number of variables, depending on what they are, can lead to methods for combining and summarizing the data in an efficient way to facilitate further analysis.

- **Method of handling variables (properties).** Studies of few cases, particularly if the cases are more complicated (e.g., a whole social situation, historic periods in a society, or in-depth analysis of an individual's perspectives), often involve a careful summary description of observations or textual data. In other instances an investigator may develop systematic measurement tools to use in classifying a case in terms of some variable. How variables are handled (or how they can be handled) affects how the results are described and the possibility of replication of findings.

- **Method of handling relationships between variables (properties).** When systematic measurement tools are used, often resulting in large amounts of quantitative data, the complexities of relationships between variables can be examined statistically. When variables are handled in a more unsystematic, summary, or descriptive way, the relationship between properties is often handled in a similar summary way, depending on the insights and judgment of the investigator.

- **Treatment of system properties.** When an investigator deals with some social system or larger aggregate, characterizing that system can be approached in a number of different ways. One way is to make an overall observation or measurement of the whole system or aggregate. The other way is to record data on subcomponents of the system and then aggregate these measurements to reach a characterization of the aggregate itself. For example, one might measure how friendly an organization is by asking the leader for a judgment (or by having the investigator make an overall observation). On the other hand, one could ask individual members of the organization for their rating of how friendly the organization is and then aggregate their responses (perhaps by computing the percentage who say it is friendly) and use that as the characterization of the system itself.

Research designs can be characterized by a pattern of choices across these basic alternatives. Thus, different designs stem from different patterns of choice, and these patterns determine what needs to be done in a study and what can be concluded from the data that are analyzed.

Two points should be made about design decisions. One is that the alternatives chosen for these dozen key decisions in a research project must work together as a pattern. The problem of research design is selecting the alternatives that contribute to an answer to a research question. In a way they are like the instruments in a symphony: They must fit together into the desired, overall plan. Second, it is usually the case that resource limits (e.g., time, money, skill, access), as well as ethical considerations, mean that an investigator must make some tough decisions about trade-offs. For example, would research objectives be better served by measuring many variables on many cases that represent a population or measuring fewer variables and dealing with fewer cases at more than one point in time. Or would more be learned if a highly controlled laboratory experiment were used in which cases must be gathered locally (to avoid transportation costs to the laboratory) rather than a research design that drew more cases in a way that represented a broader population but required a much less controlled data-gathering process? Not everything can be done in one research project.

These trade-offs have consequences for what is known from a research project. Thus, few research projects are ideal, and most can be criticized for shortcomings from the ideal. Good research makes trade-offs to advance knowledge at a given point in a field of study. Again, theory and past research are important because they help identify gaps in what is known and guide researchers in making the best trade-off decisions.

As Riley's 12 key research design decisions suggest, there are many potential patterns of decision, so there are many possible forms of social science research. However, four general patterns have dominated most contemporary research: experimental research, survey research, case study research, and secondary data research. Section II of the book covers these four approaches in more detail. Which of these is most suitable for answering a research question is still another decision that has to be made. The decision, in this instance, is based on the particular characteristics of the data needed to answer the research question and the fit of those data to each of the design possibilities.

The decision to use experimental design depends, to a large extent, on the ability of the researcher to exert enough control over the situation to be able to manipulate experimental stimuli. This constraint greatly limits the number of experimental studies found in sociology because of the kinds of phenomena sociologists study. **Laboratory experiments** in sociology are generally limited to small group phenomena. However, **field experiments** on larger social units are possible occasionally. For example, in the American soldier studies carried out in World War II, platoons of Black soldiers were introduced into White infantry companies to see whether the attitudes of White soldiers toward Black soldiers would be affected (Stouffer et al., 1949:586–95). It was found that White soldiers from the companies that included Black soldiers generally had more favorable attitudes toward them than those whose companies did not include Black soldiers.

Survey research, the second typical pattern of decisions for research design, is much more common than experimental research in sociology because of the frequent focus on large populations and because of measurement considerations. The concepts of interest to sociologists often lend themselves most easily to data collection by means of interviews or questionnaires. A typical example of survey research is the General Social Survey mentioned earlier.

Case study research (often **field observation**) is by its very nature longitudinal. It lends itself to research situations in which it is of interest to describe the operation of a social system over time. A classic example of case study research in sociology is William Foote Whyte's field observation study of a street-corner gang in a slum area of Boston (Whyte, 1943). For 2 years he studied the activities of a group of men he characterized as "corner boys." For comparison, he also collected data on a group of "college boys" in the same neighborhood.

Secondary data research is a likely design choice when appropriate, high-quality data are already available. Some data archives such as the U.S. Census have been available for many years, but the number and variety of other archives has rapidly increased as computer technology has advanced. Longitudinal data are available both from a series of cross-sectional studies and from panel studies that repeatedly interview the same individuals over time. Increasingly, secondary data research is reported in the professional journals, particularly when the focus of the research includes international or national comparisons of large social systems.

ISSUES IN THE CHOICE OF RESEARCH DESIGN

Whichever research design is chosen, questions of comparisons to be made and time periods to be considered are fundamental and must be addressed before the actual research can go forward. Although comparison and process analysis are not necessarily built into each of the four design types, they can be provided for in the final study design adopted for use. How are comparison and process analysis handled by each of the four types?

Experimental research satisfies the need to make comparisons by the use of **experimental and control groups.** The process or time question is handled, in part, by before-and-after measurements, although the time periods used between the before-and-after measurements are often not long enough to establish trends in relationships. This shortcoming of experimental studies must be handled through the use of further replication of the experiments.

In the case of survey research, relevant comparisons are generally carried out through questionnaire items designed to assign respondents to different categories or groups (e.g., gender categories) that can then be compared with respect to the independent and dependent variables of the study. As was mentioned previously, surveys often take the form of cross-sectional studies, but by repetition of the surveys over time, changes and trends may be investigated. Increasingly, survey research is carried out in many societies at similar points in time.

Case study research often has the virtue of taking place over extended periods of time, with the potential for documenting changes in process in the social systems being studied. However, such studies often are found wanting when the question of comparisons comes up, in part because of a decision to focus on a single social system. Whyte made a gesture toward comparison in his study of the corner boys by also collecting data on college boys. Nonetheless, that particular comparison is subject to criticism by modern standards because it still leaves unanswered the question of how typical (i.e., representative) Whyte's corner boys are of street-corner gangs in general (or, for that matter, how representative his college boys were of college boys in general). Ideally, a case study includes a representative sample of the social units being studied over time. Thus, Whyte's study of the Norton Street gang is only one of many such studies of a representative sample of such gangs. Given this sort of sample of gangs, they could be legitimately compared and the characteristics that are particularly relevant to the research question being posed could be identified.

In a way, the problem of case studies is the reverse of the problem of the survey. In the case of the survey, the data are collected from a representative sample of the relevant population making comparison possible, but at only one point in time, thus neglecting the requirement that processes be accounted for. Often in case studies, processes are handled by collecting data over time, but representativeness is often lacking, undermining the possibility of broader generalization.

In the case of secondary data, the possibilities for comparison and process analysis depend on the nature of the data that are available for use. If archival data have been collected over a long period of time from a representative sample of the relevant population, then secondary data may meet the study requirements most efficiently of any of the design alternatives. Unfortunately, however, secondary data are often lacking in either sufficient data points over time, in representativeness, or in having detailed records about how the data were gathered. To complicate matters even further, secondary data archives may not include data on the exact variables called for by the study being undertaken. That issue is addressed in Chapter 9.

To study change in societies over extended periods of time, however, social scientists have turned to an analysis of historical records, a special kind of secondary data that is often the only source of long-term longitudinal data. These research designs face problems of access, bias, and incompleteness as well as representativeness. Surprising records are available, however, and are increasingly used in social science research.

Further Consideration of Replication

Earlier in this chapter, replication was discussed as a way to handle the analysis of change, and numerous replications were suggested as remedies for the shortcomings of experiments in establishing trends. This particular use of replication has a different slant than it is usually given in the research literature.

The most common meaning of the concept of replication is the repetition of a study to confirm that the findings of the original study are further supported by additional research. Although this is an important use of replication, it risks perpetuating a static model of social phenomena and undermining the dynamic model.

It is proposed here that more attention be given to replication as a means of carrying out process analysis in sociology. Given this perspective, a replication that does not arrive at the same results as an earlier study does not necessarily invalidate the earlier study. If there is a change in the results, it may reflect a change in the phenomenon under investigation. Consequently, this possibility argues for a careful interpretation of the results of replication to sort out shortcomings of the research and distinguish such shortcomings from changes in the phenomenon studied. The virtue of numerous replications over time is that the numerous resulting data points may allow the researcher to discern trends, thus making it easier to distinguish between research shortcomings and actual changes.

The alternative to a series of replications in which the results change over time is a series in which very little change is apparent. This is also important because it can indicate that the phenomenon under study is stable and resists change or that any change that does occur occurs at a barely perceptible rate.

Although replication was discussed earlier with particular reference to its use in experimental research, the same principle applies equally well to the other design alternatives. It is often used in survey research, particularly in public opinion surveys. It is also used in secondary data research when such archives as census data or vital statistics are the data sources. It is used less often in field-observation case study research, probably because such research is perceived to be longitudinal anyway. However, one might ask whether a study that extends over 2 years at a particular point in history provides enough data points to establish trends over the long run. Would William Foote Whyte's corner boys behave today as they did in the 1930s, for example? This question must be pondered and studied by replicating such research at various points in time.

SUMMARY

This chapter has addressed the selection of a research design that most effectively provides the information needed to answer a particular research question. Attention was drawn to the importance of building comparisons into the research design, whatever form that design takes. It was pointed out that no research question can be answered definitively without making comparisons of some kind.

The point was also made that social phenomena, by their very nature, are dynamic. This fact makes it particularly important to approach the study of social phenomena from a longitudinal perspective that will focus on the change that takes place and uncover patterns of change that will serve as a basis for the explanation and the prediction of the future courses of those phenomena.

Riley's list of main decisions that are always involved, explicitly or implicitly, in any research design illustrates the potential variety of research designs. Like a symphony, however, the selection has to be coordinated and focused on what is needed to answer a research question. There are four typical patterns of decisions about cases, properties, time, control, sources of data, and approach to analysis that characterize most social science research. In this text, these typical patterns of choice are examined.

Four basic research designs—experiments, surveys, case studies, and secondary data studies—were discussed in general terms as alternatives for answering research questions. How comparison and process analysis relate to each of these alternatives was considered.

In Section II, each of these four design alternatives is discussed in more detail, focusing on important issues involved in their use. These discussions should give the reader sufficient information to make an informed decision about which design is most appropriate to answer a particular research question and what flexibility is available.

TERMS TO KNOW

- Comparisons
  - Category-to-category comparisons
  - Cohort comparisons
  - Comparison of the same individual or group at different points in time
  - Group-to-group comparisons
  - Individual- or group-to-standard comparisons
  - Individual-to-group comparisons
  - Mixed comparisons
- Cross-sectional study
  - Static models
- Data points
- Design options
- Experimental and control groups
- Longitudinal study
  - Dynamic models
  - Panel studies
  - Trend studies
- Replication
- Research case
- Research designs
  - Case study
    - *Field observation*
  - Experiments
    - *Field experiment*
    - *Laboratory*
  - Secondary data research
  - Surveys

ISSUES AND COMPARISONS

Other potential patterns of Riley's 12 key research decisions
Trade-offs and issues in selecting research designs
Consequences of time constraints on research

EXERCISES

1. Select a social science research report from one of the leading journals. Examine the report (especially the methodology section) and list the research design decision made for each of Riley's 12 key research design decisions. Critique the decisions in terms of their impact on the conclusions the study is able to draw. Do you have suggestions for better decisions? How do you think the researcher's various limitations and preferences affected the research design?

2. Select a research article from one of the leading journals. Analyze the research that was done and explain how comparison was used in the study. Try to fit the comparisons used into one or more of the six types discussed in this chapter. Would you characterize the study as cross-sectional or longitudinal? Why?

3. If you are to do a research design or project in this class, sketch out two or more research designs, using Riley's paradigm, that would address your research question (survey, case study, experiment). Which design is best/worst for your research? Why?

REFERENCES

Bazargan, Mohsen, and Vereda P. Hamm-Baugh, "The Relationship Between Chronic Illness and Depression in a Community of Urban Black Elderly Persons," *Journal of Gerontology: Social Sciences* 1995;50B(2):S119–27.

Burks, B. S., D. W. Jensen, and L. M. Terman, *Genetic Studies of Genius: The Promise of Youth: Follow Up Studies of a Thousand Gifted Children*, Vol. III, Stanford University Press, Stanford, CA, 1930.

Dozier, Dave, et al., *1970–71 Survey of Consumer Experience Report of the State of California Employees' Medical Care and Hospital Program Prepared Under the Policy Direction of the Medical Advisory Council to the Board of Administration of the Public Employees' Retirement System.* State of California, Sacramento. Cited in Harold S. Luft, *Health Maintenance Organizations: Dimensions of Performance,* Transaction Books, New Brunswick, NJ, 1987:274–78.

Hothersall, David, *History of Psychology,* Temple University Press, Philadelphia, 1984.

Oden, M. H. "The Fulfillment of Promise: 40-Year Follow-Up of the Terman Gifted Group," *Genetic Psychology Monographs* 1968;77:3–93.

Olmos, David R., "Image Therapy," *Los Angeles Times,* March 16, 1996, Section D, p. 3.

Riley, Matilda White, *Sociological Research: A Case Approach,* Harcourt Brace, New York, 1963.

Sears, P. S., and A. H. Barbee, "Career and Life Satisfaction Among Terman's Gifted Women," in J. Stanley, W. George, and C. Solano, eds., *The Gifted and the Creative: Fifty-Year Perspective,* Johns Hopkins University Press, Baltimore, 1977.

Sears, R. M., "Sources of Life Satisfactions of the Terman Gifted Men," *American Psychologist* 1977;32:119–28.

Stouffer, Samuel A., Edward A. Suchman, Leland C. DeVinney, Shirley A. Star, and Robin Williams, Jr., *The American Soldier: Adjustment During Army Life,* Princeton University Press, Princeton, NJ, 1949.

Terman, L. M., *Genetic Studies of Genius: Mental and Physical Traits of a Thousand Gifted Children,* Vol. I, Stanford University Press, Stanford, CA, 1926.

Terman, L. M., *Genetic Studies of Genius: The Gifted Group at Mid-Life,* Vol. V, Stanford University Press, Stanford, CA, 1959.

Terman, L. M., and M. H. Oden, *Genetic Studies of Genius: The Gifted Child Grows Up,* Vol. IV, Stanford University Press, Stanford, CA, 1947.
Tuma, Nancy B., and Michael T. Hannan, *Social Dynamics: Models and Methods,* Academic Press, Orlando, FL, 1984.
Whyte, William Foote, *Street Corner Society,* University of Chicago Press, Chicago, 1943.

CHAPTER FIVE

SAMPLING AND INFERENCE

One of the characteristics of a profession is autonomy. It is usually defined as "the ability to initiate and conclude action, to control the content, manner and speed with which a task is done" (Spenner, 1983). Meiksins and Watson (1989) wanted to study the consequences for professional engineers who worked in organizational settings in which autonomy was restricted. They decided to draw a sample of 800 engineers from the Rochester, New York, area (near their New York University), and they wanted the sample to be representative of all engineers in the area who worked for commercial firms.

Many cities have a city directory that lists workers and their family members, with occupation and place of employment, among other items. They used the 1986 city directory for the Rochester area to identify all engineers in Rochester who worked in for-profit, commercial organizations. Because they were worried that engineers outside the two very large firms in the area might not be adequately represented in their study, they decided to divide the list of engineers into three separate lists: two lists of engineers in each of the two large firms and a third list of all other engineers. Then they numbered each engineer on each list and randomly selected 800, making sure that the number drawn from each of the three lists was in proportion to the number of engineers on each list. Questionnaires were then mailed to the home address of each of the 800 engineers in the sample. Responses indicated that a number of engineers had retired, moved, or died (and thus were not part of the defined population), so they randomly selected replacement engineers from their lists. Overall, 585 of the 800 engineers responded, making a response rate of 73.1%. Meiksins and Watson discussed their findings as representative of engineers (in for-profit organizations in 1986) in the Rochester area, not just descriptive of the 585 engineers who responded. How can it be legitimate to make statements about all Rochester engineers from the responses of only 585 of them? The reasons for sampling and the answer to this question are the subjects of this chapter.

TERMINOLOGY

Sampling is one of the areas in which topics from a statistics course become most relevant to research methods. In this chapter we do not pursue the details of statistical inference but instead provide an overview of the reasons for sampling and its logic. Before we start, some terms must be defined.

Meiksins and Watson were interested in the responses of individual engineers. Thus, an engineer is the case or unit of analysis for their study. Information on each engineer was gathered. The set of cases (e.g., engineers) they wanted to study was all engineers in for-profit organizations in the Rochester, New York, area at the time of their study in 1986. This is their definition of the **population** they wanted to study. In this case their population was finite (bounded in time and place), not infinite, as it is for some studies. A study's population is all relevant cases, and the investigator has to define what is relevant. Each case in a population (or sample) is called an element of the population (or sample). The list of engineers found in the Rochester city directory is called a **sampling frame.** It is simply an available list of all cases in the population that can be used to draw a sample. Ideally, an available sampling frame lists all cases in the defined target population (and only these cases). In this example, they divided engineers in their sampling frame into three groups depending on where they worked, groups that are called **strata.** The 800 engineers selected from the sampling frame (by a special technique called random sampling) constitute the desired **sample** for their study. However, the **achieved sample** included responses of 585, or 73.1% of the 800 to whom questionnaires were sent. The most desired situation, of course, is one in which the sampling frame exactly matches the defined population and data are available from all elements of the desired sample.

Researchers often use various *statistical descriptions of data from a sample* (called **statistics**) to make estimates of what the values of the same *descriptions would be for the population from which the sample was drawn* (called **parameters**). A statistic may, for example, be a percentage or an average computed from sample data that is used to estimate a corresponding percentage or average for the population. Using sample statistics to make estimates of unknown population parameters involves some expected sampling error. **Sampling error** is the amount of variation in sample statistics that is expected if, instead of only one sample, many samples of the same type and size are drawn from the same population (or sampling frame) and compared. In general, the larger the random sample, the smaller the sampling error. As we shall see, it is important to be able to compute the size of sampling error. Here, we do not present formulas for doing so. There are different formulas for different descriptive statistics and different kinds of samples. You can look up the appropriate formulas in a standard statistics text (e.g., Loether and McTavish, 1993), and most computer statistical programs provide the necessary computations. Here we describe the logic of sampling and sampling error.

WHY SAMPLE?

An ultimate goal of research is to arrive at findings that have general applicability. The more general the applicability of the findings, the more impact they are likely to have on sociological knowledge. When research involves testing hypotheses (as is the case with theory-testing research), those hypotheses are meant to apply to some significant population. In the ideal case, the hypotheses apply to an **infinite**

population (i.e., to a population such as all human groups or human beings who existed in the past, are in existence now, or will exist in the future). However, when sociologists find evidence bearing on their hypotheses, that evidence typically applies to some **finite (limited) population,** such as the current population of the United States.

If the data used to test hypotheses come from a complete **enumeration** of the cases in a population, then analysis of those data provides parameters that are descriptive of the population and presumably are accurate. In brief, a parameter is a number that describes some characteristic of a population (e.g., the average age of the people in the population). When parameters are examined, the hypotheses can be verified or rejected directly. No inference is necessary. Obviously, then, whenever it is possible and practical to do a complete enumeration of a population, that is the course that should be taken. However, it is not always possible and practical to do so. This may be because the population is too large or too complex, an accurate list of all of the elements in the population is unattainable (as in the case of an infinite population), or the cost of carefully collecting data from all of the elements in the population (either in time or in money) is prohibitive. When cases are contaminated or destroyed in the process of testing (e.g., in a time-one test that may oversensitize subjects to later testing, or when testing lightbulbs on a production line in which tested bulbs are destroyed in the process), sampling is obviously required.

The next best thing to a total enumeration of a (small) population is the selection of a representative portion or **sample** of it. If selected properly, the data from a sample may be analyzed and the results of that analysis may be used to make generalizations about the population. In fact, to ensure the quality of data, a carefully drawn sample may be far superior to enumeration as a basis for estimating population parameters.

THE LOGIC OF INFERENCE

Sampling from a population, analyzing sample data, and generalizing the results of that analysis to the population sampled make up the process of **inference.** The third step, generalizing the results, is the one in which the inferences are actually made. **Sampling theory** provides the rationale for optimizing the representativeness of a sample, and **probability theory** provides the rationale for generalizing the results of the data analysis to the population sampled.

A sample is a partial enumeration of the elements constituting a population. For example, all the registered voters in a state would represent a population of registered voters, so one might select a sample of 100 of those voters. As you will find later, the 100-voter sample is not constituted of simply any 100 voters. Rather, the 100 voters must be selected to maximize the chance that they represent the total population.

Analysis of sample data results in the computation of statistics. A statistic is generally a number that describes some characteristic of the elements in the sample.

For example, in the case of a sample of a state's registered voters, one statistic of interest would be the percentage in the sample who said they were going to vote for candidate A. This statistic would be descriptive of the voting intentions of the people (elements) who constituted the sample. Note that the resulting statistic is, in itself, not of interest. Interest in the statistic depends on whether it is possible to generalize from it to a corresponding parameter of the population the sample is meant to represent. The corresponding parameter for this example would be the percentage of *all* of the registered voters in the state who said that they were going to vote for candidate A.

Sampling theory deals with strategies for selecting a sample of the elements (cases) in a population to instill confidence that those elements are representative of the population and that any statistics computed from the sample data are optimal estimates of the corresponding population parameters. This sampling theory is based on probability theory. A **representative sample** of a population that justifies generalization to the population is a **probability sample.** Such a probability sample is called a **random sample.**

In probability terms, *random* means that every element in the population sampled has a known probability of being included in the sample (thus, haphazard selection is not random). In the simplest case, every element in the population would have an equal probability of being included in the sample drawn. Furthermore, every possible sample of a given size would have an equal probability of being the sample drawn. A sample meeting these two criteria is known as a **simple random sample (SRS).** Of course, in addition to the SRS there are other types of random samples. Some of these are described and discussed later in this chapter.

Although a properly drawn random sample can be assumed to be a representative sample of the population, that does not mean that statistics computed from such a sample will have exactly the same values as the (usually unknown) population parameters they are used to estimate. However, statistics based on a random sample are likely to be close to population parameters, so they are very good estimates of a population parameter. Furthermore, it is possible to calculate how much those parameter estimates are likely to be in error. In other words, because random sampling is based on probability theory, the random sampling process allows one to compute estimates of sampling error. This is important because it supports the logic of making inferences from sample statistics to population parameters. When a sample is not drawn randomly, we cannot legitimately argue that estimates based on the sample are most likely to be close to the population values, nor is it legitimately possible to compute sampling error. Thus, it is not possible logically and legitimately to support one's inference about a population parameter from nonrandom sample data. Recall that a key feature of scientific research is that one is able to show, by the methods one uses, how one logically draws conclusions based on data.

It is possible in a given instance that an estimate from a **nonrandom sample** may be more accurate than from a random sample. Strengths of the random sampling technique are that estimates are most likely to be accurate or close to the true population parameter, and that it is possible to calculate how much the estimate is likely to be in error. Larger random samples generally have less sampling error. Of course, if the kind of feedback is available that allows one to eventually determine the actual population parameter, then the accuracy of the estimate from even nonrandom samples can be gauged. For example, if a quota sample (a type of nonrandom sample in which quotas are filled by any means available) is used to sample registered voters and the percentage of those voters saying that they would vote for candidate A is computed, then that percentage can be compared with the actual percentage vote when the election takes place.

The problem with most research is that there is no definitive feedback such as a final election tally with which to compare a sample estimate. In fact, if the actual population parameter being estimated through the sample data were accessible to the researcher, then there would be no point in doing a sample estimate in the first place.[1]

RANDOM SELECTION

As mentioned earlier, a random sample is one in which every element in the population has a known probability of being included. In the case of an SRS, every element in the population has an equal probability of being included, and each possible sample of a given size has an equal chance of being the sample chosen.

The SRS is the basic sampling technique in statistics and is the model assumed when most statistical formulas were derived. The procedures used to draw an SRS are described first. Later on, variations on the SRS are discussed.

Because every element of a population is supposed to have an equal probability of being included in an SRS, it is necessary to have a list of all of the elements in the population and to assign a number to every element on that list. This is generally done by assigning the number 1 to the first element on the list and continuing, assigning numbers consecutively, until all elements have unique case numbers. Once the list has been obtained and the elements have been numbered, the next step is to select a given number of those elements through some **random selection** procedure. **Sample size** is often abbreviated as *N*, the number of cases.

In earlier days a printed table of **random numbers** was created and used as a basis for random selection. Perhaps the earliest of these tables was constructed by L. H. C. Tippett, an English statistician who collected about 40,000 four-digit numbers from British census reports and shuffled them thoroughly so that the order in which they appeared would approximate random order (Hagood and Price, 1952:274). Since computers have come on the scene, they have been programmed to generate pseudorandom numbers on command. Truly random numbers are

[1]Election polls are a special case in that the intent of the poll is to estimate a final vote tally that will become known in the future. In other words, an election poll is a device for predicting a parameter that will be known in the future but is not known when the poll is conducted.

those in which each of the single digits from 0 through 9 has a 10% probability of occurring but whose sequence of occurrence is unpredictable. The pseudorandom numbers produced by computers meet the first criterion, and the sequence of digits behaves much as if the second criterion were true as well. The appendix provides a table of random numbers and shows how one might create random digits using a spreadsheet program such as Excel.

To have a computer select a random sample, a program called a random number generator is used. The computer is commanded to select a given number of cases (or percentage of cases) from a range of numbers representing the numbers assigned to the cases in the population list. The computer program randomly generates the requested number (or percentage) of case numbers from the population and prints those case numbers. Cases bearing those numbers are then included in the random sample. For example, if there were 10,000 cases in a population and you wanted to draw a sample of 500 ($N = 500$), you could assign the cases numbers in the range from 00001 to 10000 then have the random number generator select 500 numbers in that range.

Recall that an SRS is one that meets two criteria: Every case in the population has an equal probability of being included in the sample selected and every sample of a given size has an equal probability of constituting the sample drawn. Use of a random number generator fulfills the first criterion for an SRS, but the fulfillment of the second criterion depends on whether restrictions are placed on the case numbers that are drawn. If the 500 case numbers drawn by the computer must be 500 unique numbers (that is, no case number appears more than once), then the sample is said to be drawn **without replacement.** On the other hand, if there is no requirement that the 500 case numbers all be different, then the sample is said to be drawn **with replacement.**[2] If a sample is drawn without replacement, the number of possible samples of a given size (500, for example) is much smaller than the number possible with replacement because replacement allows for all of the samples in which individual cases are included in the resulting sample more than once.[3]

Some random number generators draw only samples without replacement. Others allow you to decide whether to sample with or without replacement. Strictly speaking, sampling theory calls for sampling *with* replacement; however, in sociology both types of random samples are drawn. Later in this chapter we discuss the ramifications of sampling without and with replacement.

[2]The term *replacement* refers to the time, before computers, when pseudorandom samples were drawn by putting all of the case numbers in a container, thoroughly mixing them in the container, and drawing case numbers from the container by hand. If a case number drawn was not put back in the container after it was selected, it was selected without replacement. If the case number was returned to the container after being drawn, it was selected with replacement. For an explanation of the probability principles involved in sampling with and without replacement, see Loether and McTavish (1993:382).

[3]In the extreme case of sampling with replacement, it would (and should) be possible to draw a sample of size 500 in which a single case occurred 500 times. Of course, the probability of occurrence of such a sample is extremely small.

OTHER SAMPLING CONSIDERATIONS

The SRS is the base model used for the process of inference. Presumably, whenever population parameter estimates are needed, the simple random sampling technique would be the one used. As described earlier, it is necessary to obtain a list of all **population elements.** Even before obtaining the list of population elements, however, it is necessary to specify which population is the appropriate one to sample.

Specifying the Population

If the research is theory testing, then the theory being tested should include a scope statement pointing to the population or populations to which the hypotheses of the theory apply. That population, or at least one of the populations specified by the theory, is the one that must be described.

As an example of how specification of an appropriate population might work, consider the theory of homogamy (Burgess and Wallin, 1943) as it is applied to mate selection. Basically, this theory states that when people select mates, selection of those whose backgrounds, interests, attitudes, and values are similar to their own will result in lasting relationships. Furthermore, the more similar the mates are in these characteristics, the more stable and lasting their relationships will be. To what population or populations should this theory apply? Implied in this particular theory is the assumption that the duration of a relationship is problematic. Therefore, the theory would be expected to apply only to a society in which there is provision (such as divorce) for terminating a relationship. If all relationships established in a given society were permanent (at least until death), then the theory would not apply to that society.

Even in cases in which the research is not theory testing, it is important to identify the population to which the findings are meant to apply and use that population as the sampling base. The population so identified should be an important population in terms of what is being researched rather than just a population that happens to be available. Unfortunately, some research is conducted using samples of populations that are selected not because they are the most relevant ones for the research being conducted, but primarily because they are conveniently available. For example, researchers studied the seeming contradiction between poll reports of regular church attendance (in the 40% range) and other indications that regular church attendance is actually lower. As one of their data sources, the authors conducted a random telephone survey of 602 residents of Ashtabula County, Ohio. With respect to their data collection strategy as it applied to the analysis of Protestant church attendance, the authors say,

> The first step in our research strategy was to compare actual counts of church attendance to self-reported church attendance. We collected three types of data in a circumscribed area: (1) poll-based estimates of religious preferences for residents

> of the area; (2) poll-based estimates of church attendance for Protestants; and (3) actual counts of church attendance for all Protestant churches in the area.
>
> We selected Ashtabula County, located in extreme northeastern Ohio, because of its manageable-sized population (100,000 persons) and the location of its population centers. The two largest towns in the county are situated near its center, and there are no large towns near the county line. Thus, the number of persons from Ashtabula County who attend church in other counties should be offset by persons from other counties attending church in Ashtabula. (Hadaway, Marler, and Chaves, 1993:743)

In addition to the telephone survey, the researchers obtained estimates of actual church attendance from the Protestant churches in the area. Because they were not able to get comparable data from Catholic churches, the authors turned to data collected from 18 dioceses scattered throughout the United States to compare with the 53% attendance figure reported by the Catholic respondents to their telephone survey.

The telephone survey of the Protestant churches produced a reported attendance figure of 35.8%, compared with their estimate that the actual attendance was closer to 19.6%.

Their study led the authors to conclude,

> We have shown that the church attendance rate is probably one-half what everyone thinks it is. But the practical difficulties involved with this research limited our data collection efforts. Although the evidence is compelling because it is so uniform, the fact remains that our data pertain to fewer than 20 Catholic dioceses and to Protestants in only one Ohio county. To confirm the existence of this "gap" and to determine if it has widened in recent decades, researchers should examine existing time-series data from local churches, denominations, regional polls, and religious censuses—any data that permit a comparison of poll-based and count-based measures of religious activity. (Hadaway et al., 1993:750)

Why did Hadaway et al. choose Ashtabula County, Ohio, as the population for their study? It appears that a major consideration for the choice was that the senior author of the article was based in Cleveland, which is situated very near Ashtabula County. In their conclusions the authors recognize their choice of population to be sampled as a weakness of their study. Nevertheless, they state, "We have shown that the church attendance rate is probably one-half what everyone thinks it is" (1993:750).

The abstract to this article also suggests an interest in generalizing findings to the whole population of the United States, based on a sample of residents of Ashtabula County, Ohio. The abstract to the article says,

> Characterizations of religious life in the United States typically reference poll data on church attendance. Consistently high levels of participation reported in these data suggest an exceptionally religious population, little affected by secularizing trends. This picture of vitality, however, contradicts other empirical evidence indicating declining strength among many religious institutions. Using a variety of data

> sources and data collection procedures, we estimate that church attendance rates for Protestants and Catholics are, in fact, approximately one-half the generally accepted levels. (1993:741)

Such a broad generalization is certainly not warranted. If the authors wanted to study church attendance of the U.S. population, they should have sampled that population.

The article cited here is an example of the common practice of researchers setting out to study and to reach conclusions about one population, then collecting data from another population because the second population is easier to sample. The authors would have been on sounder ground if they had stated, up front, that the population they were studying was the population of Ashtabula County and that any resulting findings could be applied only to that particular population.

Identifying a Sampling Frame

Once the appropriate population to be sampled is specified, it is necessary to obtain a list of the elements of that population. Such a list is known as a sampling frame. A sampling frame is distinguished from the population it is meant to represent because the elements listed in the sampling frame are probably not an exact duplication of a list of the elements in the actual population to be sampled. This is generally the case because the elements in some populations are in an almost constant state of change. New elements are continually being added, and existing population elements are continually being lost. For example, the population of Chicago changes constantly. At any time of the day or night babies are being born, people are dying, and others are moving into or out of the city. Any sampling frame that could be assembled for the city would necessarily include elements that are no longer in the population and exclude elements that were added to the population while the sampling frame was being compiled.

Of course, some populations are more stable than others. The population of a prison, for example, changes at a slower rate than the population of a city. Furthermore, because of the nature of a prison, the authorities have more complete information about who is in the prison than would be the case for an organization in which people are free to come and go. In addition, compared to the population of a city, the population of a prison is small, and it is easier to compile a reasonably accurate list of a small population than of a large one. In the case of the prison, then, one could compile a sampling frame that should vary little from a list of the actual elements of the population.

Another factor that affects the accuracy of sampling frames is the level of the unit of analysis represented by the population elements. When the elements are individual people, the rate of change in the population is greater than when the elements are collectivities. For example, if one were interested in studying 4-year colleges and universities in the United States, it would be possible to compile a fairly accurate sampling frame of that population because collectivities such as colleges and universities do not appear and disappear as often or as quickly as individual people.

Sampling frames may be different from the intended population in many ways. First, the sampling frame may include elements that are not in the targeted population and must be screened out. For example, if a study called for a sample of people aged 65 and older but sampled households, some screening procedure would have to be used to rule out those under age 65 who live in the same household. Second, the sampling frame may not include all of the desired cases (e.g., those with unlisted phone numbers). Available lists tend to better represent nonmovers than movers, or fully processed cases rather than cases in process, or populations of some public policy interest rather than populations that are not. Finally, if one is interested in an infinite population, a population limited in time and place would have to be specified so that a sampling frame could be identified. Repeated sampling (in time and place) and development of tested theory help to establish propositions that apply to the infinite population in which the investigator was initially interested.

At any rate, the researcher must endeavor to compile or gain access to the most accurate sampling frame available because it forms the base from which the random sample is selected. Once an acceptable sampling frame has been obtained, the researcher may proceed with the selection of a random sample. However, the researcher must never lose sight of the fact that a sampling frame is not a population; when the results of the study are evaluated, possible flaws in the frame should be taken into consideration.

The Sampling Procedure

The sampling frame from which the actual sample is selected is essentially an approximate list of the elements in the population. The elements or cases listed are numbered consecutively, then a previously determined number of those cases is selected randomly by number for inclusion in the sample. The numbers randomly selected are drawn from a range of eligible numbers between 1 and ***N***, where ***N*** is the total number of cases listed in the sampling frame. (Here we use a boldface capital ***N*** to symbolize the population or sampling frame size and a lightface capital *N* for the sample size.) A computer program that generates random numbers or a carefully prepared table of random numbers is used to select the case numbers to be included in the sample; consequently, each case in the sampling frame has an equal chance of being included in the final sample.

Assume that the predetermined sample size will be 500 cases. Then 500 random numbers between 1 and ***N*** are selected for inclusion in the sample. Because the SRS is drawn with replacement, the first 500 random numbers selected would constitute the sample. Should one or more of those numbers be selected more than one time within the 500 cases drawn, that case or those cases would be counted more than once in the sample. In an interview study, for example, if a case appeared in the sample twice, then the responses to the interview for that case would be treated as two separate cases in the final analysis of the data. Typically, the interview results would be entered in the database twice and assigned two separate case numbers.

Because random numbers were used to select the sample cases, each case in the sampling frame would have an equal probability of being included in the sample. Furthermore, because the sampling of cases was carried out with replacement, each possible sample of N cases (in this example, $N = 500$) would have an equal probability of constituting the final random sample to be used for the research. Meeting these two criteria of an SRS justifies the estimation of sampling error and allows the researcher to generalize the results of the study from the sample to the population (or sampling frame) within the sampling error computed.

Sampling Without Replacement

Strictly speaking, the usual formulas used to measure sampling error are based on the premise that the random selection of sample cases is carried out with replacement. However, social scientists often select random samples without replacement. That is, they select cases in such a way as to eliminate the possibility that any single case from the sampling frame will occur more than once in the sample. Although the first criterion of the SRS, that every case in the sampling frame has an equal chance of appearing in the sample, is still satisfied when sampling is done without replacement,[4] the second criterion, that every possible sample of a given size has an equal chance of constituting the final sample, is no longer met. Sampling without replacement restricts the possible samples that may constitute the final sample to those in which no single case appears more than once. If the population represented by the sampling frame is small, then sampling without replacement can significantly influence the makeup of the final sample.

For example, assume that a sampling frame consists of 1,000 cases. If a sample of 200 cases is selected from that frame without replacement, the number of different samples of 200 cases will be much smaller than the potential number of different samples that could be selected if sampling is carried out with replacement. Furthermore, because the pool of cases from which the sampling is carried out (the sampling frame list) is smaller, it is more probable that one of the samples with duplicated cases will appear if sampling is done with replacement.

On the other hand, if the sampling frame is very large in proportion to the number of cases to be selected for inclusion in the sample, then the probability that any one case in the frame will be selected more than once in the sample is low. Assume, for example, that a sample of 500 cases is selected from a sampling frame consisting of 50 million cases. Whether sampling is carried out with or without replacement, it is unlikely that any single case will be repeated in the sample drawn. In such cases, therefore, the decision whether to sample with or without replacement is of little consequence.

Sometimes the decision to sample without replacement is made in order to ensure an adequate spread of the cases. For example, if a sample of 20 states is drawn from the 50 U.S. states and the sampling is done with replacement, it is highly likely that one or more states will be drawn at least twice in the sample. For

[4]See Loether and McTavish (1993:382) for an explanation of why this is so.

the purposes of the study, it might be considered undesirable to count data from a state more than once in analyzing the database. For instance, California's population constitutes more than 10% of the total population of the United States. If California were drawn twice in the sample, data from California would constitute more than 20% of all of the data in the study. For this reason a researcher might decide that sampling without replacement is warranted. In cases such as this, a correction factor can be applied in computing sampling error (see Loether and McTavish, 1993:445).

Although sampling without replacement may be justified in specific research situations and it may be a moot consideration when drawing small samples from large populations, the practice should not be followed merely because the researcher feels uncomfortable about counting a case twice in the analysis of data. This is so because it is not the *case* that is significant in the analysis of data. Rather, it is the *distribution* on variables of interest for the study that is significant.

Perhaps the easiest way to explain this statement is through an example. A traditional illustration used to explain the sampling procedure deals with red balls and black balls in a container. Assume that there are 100 balls in the container and that 60 of the 100 are red and the others are black. To sample with replacement from the container, one would reach in and draw out a ball. There would be a 60% chance of drawing a red ball and a 40% chance of drawing a black ball. Once the color of the ball drawn from the container was recorded, the ball would be returned to the container and a second ball would be drawn.

Note that the important fact is the color of the ball. When the second ball is drawn, its color is recorded and it is returned to the container. The same procedure is repeated until the desired sample size is obtained (say, 20 balls). Each time a ball is drawn from the container, the only bit of information that is gleaned is the color of the ball. No consideration is given to the fact that it is possible to draw the same ball from the container more than once. Thus, what the sampler is paying attention to is the distribution of red and black balls in the container, not which particular ball is red or black.

This same reasoning applies to random sampling with replacement when the elements being drawn are people or collectivities rather than balls. In the case of people, for example, the researcher might be interested in the distribution of a characteristic of the people in the population such as gender. If 60% of the people in the population are female and 40% male, random sampling with replacement from that population should result in a sample that is representative of the population with respect to gender (within sampling error). Furthermore, the example can be extended to the case in which the researcher is interested in the joint distribution of two or more variables in a population. If gender and level of education are related, for example, the relationship would be reflected in the joint distribution of those two variables, regardless of the specific cases included in the sample. When one looks at the situation from this point of view, it is not really essential that the cases in a sample all be unique. Consequently, random sampling should be executed with replacement unless there are good reasons to do otherwise.

OTHER TYPES OF RANDOM SAMPLES

Because the SRS is the basic sampling procedure underlying statistical inference, it should be the sampling procedure of first choice in doing research involving generalization from a sample to a population. In order to draw an SRS, it is essential that a single accurate sampling frame be available. Unfortunately, it is often not possible to acquire such a sampling frame. This is particularly true when the population that the sampling frame is meant to represent is a large population. The population of the United States is over 280 million. Obviously, no accurate sampling frame available lists all those cases, nor is it possible to compile such a sampling frame. Because the composition of the population is constantly changing, any attempt to gather an accurate sampling frame would be futile. The composition of the population would change faster than the identity of the cases for the sampling frame could be ascertained. Various probability sampling strategies provide alternative ways to achieve a representative sample when there are problems obtaining an overall sampling frame list.

The Random Cluster Sample

Fortunately, it is not necessary to abandon the notion of random sampling in drawing a sample for a large, volatile population. An alternative random sampling strategy is available in place of the SRS. That strategy, called the **random cluster sample,** involves obtaining a series of sampling frames (nested from broader to narrower) from which random samples may be obtained. The random cluster sample is essentially a **multistage random sample,** with each stage corresponding to its own sampling frame or frames.

The procedure involves starting with a first-stage sampling frame that is accessible, sampling elements (**primary sampling units**) from that frame, and then compiling additional stages of sampling frames within the selected broader frames (at levels less general than the original one) and sampling from them until the random sampling procedure culminates in a sample or samples of cases (**ultimate sampling units**) at the level at which the data are to be collected.

Perhaps an example of such a random cluster sample will make it easier to understand the sampling process. Assume that we want to draw a random cluster sample of all the high school seniors in the United States as of May 1 of this year. It would not be practical and probably not possible to compile a single sampling frame that suitably identified all high school seniors in the United States as of the designated date.

However, it would be possible to compile a list of all of the states plus the District of Columbia (DC). This list would constitute the primary sampling frame and would accurately replicate a list of the population of states and DC. The states and DC could be listed, numbered from 1 to 51, then randomly sampled. States and DC would be the primary sampling units. Perhaps 20 of the 51 would be selected through the use of random numbers (see Appendix 1).

Once the 20 states (or states and DC) were selected from the original sampling frame, each of these 20 units could be used to generate a sampling frame consisting of a list of the counties in each. California is divided into 58 counties; therefore, if California were one of the 20 states selected, these 58 counties could be listed in a second-stage sampling frame and these could be sampled randomly. The other 19 units selected in the first stage of sampling would be treated similarly. For each, the counties would be listed and then a random sample of those units would be drawn. When the counties sampled from the 20 states had been determined, they would constitute the sampling units for the second round of random cluster sampling (i.e., secondary sampling units).

The third stage of sampling frames would consist of lists of all of the high schools in each of the counties that had survived the second round of sampling (third-stage sampling units). For each of these lists (third-stage sampling frames), a certain number of high schools could be randomly sampled.

For each high school selected at this third level of random sampling, we might sample high school seniors (the ultimate sampling unit), or we might decide to collect data from all seniors in each of those schools. The high school seniors from whom data were ultimately collected could be considered a random sample of all seniors in the United States because they were selected randomly for inclusion in the study.

In an actual cluster sampling procedure, the number of units sampled at each stage would be carefully worked out to fit the needs of the study and to arrive at a final sample of the appropriate size. In the preceding example it was suggested that 20 states (or 19 states and DC) might be sampled from the first sampling frame. This number was selected arbitrarily in order to describe a possible cluster sampling technique. The number of units drawn from the primary sampling frame for an actual study would be considered carefully and would be decided upon in terms of such factors as the desired spread of states, the cost of collecting data from different states, and the heterogeneity of the cases in the different states. Often at this stage of a complex sampling project, a specialist in sampling statistics would be consulted.

It should be noted that the heterogeneity of the cases in a sampling frame is often an important consideration in deciding how many of those cases to sample because the more heterogeneous the sampling frame is, the larger the number of cases from that frame must be drawn to ensure a given level of sampling error. In order to increase the homogeneity of cases to be sampled, some primary sampling frames are divided into a number of separate frames and samples are selected from each of those. For example, the states in the United States might be arranged into nine regions (the South, New England, the Midwest, etc.), then random samples of states would be selected from each of those regions. This strategy is based on the notion that states within a given region are more homogeneous than states from different regions.

This and some of the other considerations (e.g., geographic spread) mentioned earlier would enter into the determination of how many counties would be sampled as secondary sampling units from each of the 20 states sampled as the primary sampling units. As a matter of fact, sampling proportions would be very carefully determined at each sampling level so that the final sample arrived at would be optimally representative of the population to which we wanted to generalize our findings.

The random cluster sample derives its name from the fact that the cases from which the data are finally collected are (usually geographically) clustered. For example, in the case of the cluster sample of high school seniors, the seniors from whom the data would be collected would be clustered in a given number of high schools. Numerous cases would be located at each high school that ended up in the cluster sample, thus making it less expensive to collect data than if cases were spread all over the United States. In this sense the random cluster sample is more economical than an SRS for collecting data.

As a matter of fact, the cluster sample enjoys at least two advantages over the SRS: It is feasible to do when the SRS may not be, and the cases from which data are to be collected are conveniently geographically clustered (if clusters are geographic units), often saving travel costs.

On the other hand, the SRS enjoys the advantage of having a smaller sampling error for a given sample size. Because the cluster sample involves the selection of a series of random samples from the various sampling frames, sampling error is risked each time another random sample of units is selected. Thus, the sampling error is generally compounded.

The consolation to be gained from the random cluster sample despite its generally larger sampling error is that it is feasible when an SRS may not be. Consequently, random samples of large populations are usually cluster samples or some variation thereof. Furthermore, although the formula used to estimate sampling error for an SRS does not apply to a random cluster sample, the procedure for determining the proper formula for estimating sampling error has been worked out (Kish, 1965).

The Stratified Random Sample

Another variation on the SRS is the **stratified random sample.** This type of sample was used in the study described at the beginning of the chapter. The motivation for using a stratified random sample rather than an SRS is quite different from that for the random cluster sample. Furthermore, whereas the random cluster sample requires less detailed information about the population to be sampled than the SRS, the stratified random sample requires more.

In order to use a stratified random sample, it is not only necessary to have a single primary sampling frame, but it must also be possible to divide that sampling frame accurately into separate strata based on some characteristic or characteristics of the cases in the population. For example, suppose we wished to draw a random sample of all institutions of higher education in the United States. There are approximately 3,000 of these. Because it would be possible to get a fairly accurate primary sampling frame of all of these, it would be possible to draw an SRS. However, institutions of higher education fall into a number of different categories. There are 2-year community colleges, 4-year colleges limited to undergraduate education, colleges and universities that offer graduate degrees but not doctorates, and universities that offer a full range of degrees from the baccalaureate to the doctoral degree. If an SRS of all institutions of higher education were drawn from a single sampling frame, some of the possible SRS sample outcomes might include only a few or none of the less common types of institutions. Although this is less likely than getting a proper proportion of each type of institution, a researcher may not want to risk drawing a sample with too few of the more uncommon types of institutions because comparisons may need to be made between types of institutions.

Because of the nature of the study being conducted, it might be very important not only that the full range of institutions be included, but that they be included in the sample *in the same proportions* as they are represented in the population. In order to ensure that the resulting random sample meets these criteria, a stratified random sample could be drawn instead of an SRS. To draw such a sample, the primary sampling frame would be divided into a number of subframes (called strata), each of which would consist only of institutions falling into a single category. Thus, one stratum could consist of all of the 2-year community colleges in the country, another of all of the 4-year undergraduate institutions, a third of all of the colleges and universities offering graduate degrees but not the doctorate, and a final stratum of all of the universities offering the doctorate.

If the study being planned required a sample of 300 institutions of higher education in the United States (approximately 10% in this instance, called the sampling fraction), once the separate strata were compiled the same proportion of cases (here about 10%) from each stratum would be randomly drawn. Because the numbers of institutions falling into each stratum would differ, using the same sampling fraction (here 10%) in drawing a random sample from each stratum would result in an overall random sample that would match the population in terms of proportions of institutions of higher education of each type.

Suppose that it was desirable to divide the institutions not only into the four types mentioned earlier but also in terms of whether they were public or private. The primary sampling frame would be divided into eight strata representing the four types of institutions, public and private. Again, a random sample of the same proportion of the cases (here, 10%) would be drawn from each of the strata; however, in this case there would be eight strata rather than four.

The stratified random samples described thus far are called **proportionate stratified random samples** because the sample strata use the same sampling fraction (have the same proportions of cases) as the population strata from which the cases are sampled. This proportionate sampling is important in generalizing sample results back to the population sampled because it ensures that no stratum in the combined sample has undue influence on the overall results of the study.

Disproportionate Sampling. If one purpose of a study is to make comparisons between strata on a variable such as religious affiliation, in which strata sizes vary greatly in the population, the small strata may deliberately be oversampled so that the sizes of the sample strata being compared are equal. When this is done the resulting sample is called a **disproportionate stratified random sample.** This type of sample is drawn in order to ensure that there will be enough cases in the smaller sample strata that the comparisons of interest can be performed.

The minimum number of cases needed in any stratum in a sample, of course, depends on the nature of the analysis. Suppose that the study being conducted dealt with attitudes toward capital punishment. If the effect of religious affiliation on attitudes toward capital punishment were of interest, in order to compare Protestants, Catholics, and Jews (a breakdown of religion used in the U.S. Census), a sufficient number of Jewish respondents would need to be sampled. Because most people in the United States identify themselves as either Protestant or Catholic, a proportionate stratified sample drawn from a population of Americans would be most heavily weighted with cases from these two categories. Because Jews constitute the smallest population for these three particular religious denominations, the needed size of the sample for Jews could be the determinant of how many cases were needed for the overall sample. For example, if the Jews constituted 10% of the religious population and 500 cases were needed for the analysis of their attitudes toward capital punishment (a need determined by such things as distinguishing gender or income in the analysis of each religious group), an overall sample of 5,000 would have to be drawn by proportionate random sampling. The analysis may not need such a high number of Protestants and Catholics (i.e., 4,500), and funding may not permit such a large overall sample. In this instance a disproportionate stratified random sample could be used to provide for analysis needs and still minimize the overall sample size. For example, a sample of 500 could be drawn from each stratum for an overall sample size of 1,500 rather than 5,000 cases (500 each from Jews, Catholics, and Protestants).

Weighting Responses. An important caution is necessary with regard to generalizing results from a disproportionate stratified random sample. Because disproportionate sampling leads to overrepresentation of some strata, in generalizing results from the overall sample to the population sampled it is necessary to **weight** the responses of subjects from the various strata. Thus, greater weight should be given to the responses of the respondents in the larger population strata and less weight to those of respondents from smaller population strata. If such an adjustment is not made, generalizations will be misleading. For example, assume that an overwhelming proportion of the Jewish respondents are not in favor of capital punishment. Because a third of the cases in the overall sample are Jews, the impression might be given that a third or more of all those in the population, regardless of religious affiliation, are not in favor of capital punishment. Reweighting responses as shown in Box 5.1 accurately represents the overall percentage opposed to capital punishment by properly balancing the views of all strata.

Optimum Allocation Sampling. A third type of stratified random sample technique, called **optimum allocation sampling,** combines features of both the proportionate and disproportionate techniques. This technique takes into account

BOX 5.1

REWEIGHTING DATA FROM A DISPROPORTIONATE STRATIFIED RANDOM SAMPLE

If a sample has used disproportionate stratified random sampling and the results from all strata are to be combined for an overall description of results, then the cases in each stratum must be reweighted so that the overall results accurately represent the population. If each stratum is analyzed separately and an overall description of the total sample is not needed, then reweighting is not needed.

To reweight a sample, the following procedure is used:

1. *Determine the sampling fraction used in each stratum.* That is, the proportion of available cases in the sampling frame for that stratum that were drawn into the sample for that stratum. For example,

	Number of cases in the		
Stratum	*Sampling Frame*	*Final Sample*	*Sampling Fraction*
Protestants	100,000	500	.00500
Catholics	50,000	500	.01000
Jews	15,000	500	.03333
	165,000	1,500	**.00909**

If 15,000 Jewish people were in the sampling frame for that stratum and 500 were drawn in the sample, then the sampling fraction would be 500/15,000 = .033. Notice that the sampling fractions differ by stratum with disproportionate stratified random sampling. Overall, Jews are overrepresented in the $N = 1{,}500$ sample. Catholics are overrepresented as well.

2. *Reweight each case in each stratum by the reciprocal of its sampling fraction times the overall sampling fraction.* For Protestants, the reciprocal of the sampling fraction is 1/.005 = 200. This is multiplied by the overall sampling fraction, which is 1,500/165,000 = .00909: 200 × .00909 = 1.818. Each Protestant case would be multiplied by 1.818, so 500 cases would be reweighted to 909 (1.818 × 500 = 909). As shown in the following table, the weighting factor for each other group is computed in a similar way:

Weight for Protestants = (1/.005) × .00909 = 1.818
Weight for Catholics = (1/.01) × .00909 = .909
Weight for Jews = (1/.03333) × .00909 = .2727

In doing statistical summaries of the overall sample, data for any variable would be weighted for each case, using the weight for the appropriate group. This would preserve the overall sample size [(1.818 × 500 = 909) + (.909 × 500 = 455) + (.2727 × 500 = 136) = 1,500].

both the sizes of the strata being sampled and the homogeneity of the cases in the strata on one or more important variables. Consequently, a larger stratum that is homogeneous in the characteristics of the elements in that stratum would result in the selection of fewer cases than a smaller stratum or a stratum that is more heterogeneous. For example, assume that a study of attitudes toward abortion is being conducted in which a comparison is being made between Protestants and Catholics. It is decided that the desired sample size would be achieved with a sampling fraction of 5% of the population of interest. Assume further that the stratum of Protestants is one-third larger than the stratum of Catholics, but the stratum of Catholics is more homogeneous on attitudes toward abortion than the stratum of Protestants. Given these conditions, it would not be necessary to sample the same proportion of Catholics (5%) as of Protestants. Because Catholic attitudes are more homogeneous, the proportion of cases sampled from the Catholic stratum might be smaller than 5%, and the proportion sampled from the Protestant stratum might be somewhat larger than 5% despite the fact that the stratum of Protestants is larger.[5]

Advantages and Disadvantages of Stratified Random Samples. Under certain conditions stratified random samples may be preferable to SRSs because smaller sampling error may be achieved. The conditions that would make stratified random sampling preferable include the following:

- **Enough accurate information about the population of interest is available to divide the sampling frame into strata based on variables that are relevant to the study being conducted.** That is, it must be possible to identify variables that are relevant to the study, and the representation of those variables in the population must be known so that appropriate sampling frames may be constructed. For example, if religious affiliation is a relevant variable for studying attitudes toward abortion, then the religious affiliation of cases in the population must be known so that the overall sampling frame can be divided into subframes based on religious affiliation. If gender is a second variable relevant to the study, then the distribution of cases in the population by gender must also be known so that the subframes on religious affiliation can be divided further into subframes for males and females. If religious affiliation is divided into Protestant, Catholic, and Jews, and males and females are distinguished, six subframes must be identified.

- **The resulting subframes from which to select the sample will be more homogeneous on variables relevant to the study than is the overall population sampling frame.** If the resulting subframes are not more homogeneous, then the sampling error of the stratified random sample will not be any smaller than the sampling error would be for an SRS and all the effort put into stratification would be futile.

[5]See Kish (1965) for a comprehensive discussion of optimum allocation sampling.

▪ **No variables relevant to the study being conducted would be overlooked in the stratification process.** If the researcher is unaware of some variables that are relevant to the study being conducted and, for that reason, fails to take them into consideration in the stratification process, a stratified random sample might be inferior to an SRS. An important virtue of an SRS is that it generally accounts for relevant variables of a study, whether they are anticipated or not, and results in a sample in which those variables are represented proportionately.

If these conditions are met, a stratified random sample has an advantage. A stratified random sample equal in size to an SRS will have smaller sampling error than the SRS because of the greater homogeneity of the sampling frames of the strata constructed for the sample as compared to the sampling frame of the SRS. This fact makes it possible for the researcher to choose between drawing a stratified random sample equal in size to an SRS, but with a smaller sampling error, or a stratified random sample smaller than an SRS, but with a sampling error equal to that of the larger SRS.

A major disadvantage of the stratified random sample is that it requires more information about the elements of a population being sampled than an SRS. It is necessary not only to be able to access an overall sampling frame, but also to have enough accurate information available to divide that sampling frame into subframes based on information on relevant variables in the population. Furthermore, it is necessary to have enough information about the variables involved in the study being undertaken to be able to identify all that are relevant to the study so that they can be used as a basis for stratification. If the wrong variables are selected as a basis for stratification or a stratifying variable is inaccurate, then the process of stratifying can be a waste of time and money. Furthermore, if variables that are relevant to the study are overlooked in the stratification process, then the process of stratification can likewise be futile.

Although the optimum allocation stratified random sample is the most efficient stratification design (resulting in the smallest sampling error), it is even more difficult to accomplish than the stratified random sample because, in addition to having all the information necessary for the stratified random sample, one must also be able to estimate the degree of homogeneity present in each of the population strata to be sampled.

NONRANDOM SAMPLES

Given a choice, the random sample is always to be preferred over a nonrandom sample. For various reasons, however, nonrandom sampling techniques are used. Sometimes researchers resort to nonrandom samples because they cannot draw random samples. In other cases nonrandom samples are used because they are cheaper or more convenient, or because of ignorance of sampling principles. In any case, several nonrandom sampling designs appear in the literature. Some of these nonrandom designs are described here, and problems of using them are discussed.

Systematic Samples

A sampling frame usually takes the form of an organized list of cases alphabetized by name, arranged chronologically, or arranged by some other characteristic (such as age). If for some reason the list cannot be sampled randomly, a **systematic sample** may be drawn by selecting some interval (such as every twentieth case) from which to draw sample cases. The interval selected determines what proportion of the cases in the population will appear in the sample. Thus, every twentieth case will provide a sample of 5% of the cases in the population.

For the sake of illustration, assume that the file folders of all 2,000 clients of a social service agency are arranged alphabetically in a set of file cabinets. If it were decided that a sample of size 100 of the 2,000 clients was to be drawn in order to provide interviewees for a study, then the **sampling interval** would be computed as 2,000/100 = 20. Thus, every 20th file folder in the drawers would be selected (the 20th, 40th, 60th, etc.). Note that the resulting sample would *not* be a random sample because the particular cases drawn for the sample would depend on the system used to arrange the file folders in the drawers, the interval used to sample them, and the starting point used for determining which file folders were in the proper interval. File folders that did not happen to fall on the interval selected would have *no chance whatsoever* of being included in the sample, and those on the interval would be *certain* to be included. Therefore, there would be no legitimate basis for estimating sampling error.

A variation of the systematic sampling technique introduces an element of probability into the selection of cases for the sample. This variation is called a **systematic sample with a random start.** For example, if the decision is made to select every twentieth file in the list, the starting point for the interval might be determined randomly. Thus, a number between 1 and 20 might be selected randomly as a starting point for drawing sample cases, and the remaining cases might be set at the interval of 20 following the location of the first case. If the random number drawn happened to be 13, for example, then that would be the first case in the sample and the other cases would be arrived at by adding 20 each time to the number of the last case. The second case, therefore, would be the thirty-third, the next would be the fifty-third, and so on.

This random start procedure has the effect of dividing the cases in the population into a number of sets, each with an equal probability of constituting the sample. If the interval being used is 20, then there are 20 sets of cases or 20 different samples that might be drawn. Which set is drawn for the sample depends on the first number drawn randomly and the size of the interval to be sampled. In this example, the set consists of case 13 and every case in the population separated by an interval of 20, starting with that thirteenth case. The 20 sets (or potential samples) would be those beginning with the first case, the second case, and so on through the set beginning with the twentieth case. Each of these 20 sets of cases would have 1 chance out of 20 of being the sample set; therefore, each individual case in the population would have 1 chance out of 20 of being included in the sample drawn.

Although the random start provides a basis for assigning a probability of selection to the cases in the sampling frame, it does not solve some of the basic problems involved in systematic sampling. For example, the arrangement of the cases in the list might be a biasing factor that would produce a sample that was unrepresentative of the population. If the list was arranged alphabetically by name, there could be a bias in the nationalities of the subjects because the first letters of the surnames of some nationalities tend to be concentrated in just a few letters of the alphabet, whereas those of other nationalities are widely spread across the alphabet. If both spouses in a couple should have a chance of being drawn in the sample, an alphabetical list might present problems because spouses tend to share the same surname, so their names would be likely to be near each other or even adjacent to each other in the list. A list arranged chronologically might also present problems of bias. Depending on how the cases in the list were spread across time, cases falling on the sampling interval might overrepresent certain times of the month or the year and underrepresent others. For example, this would happen in sampling a chronological list of elections in which all presidential elections could be included or omitted, depending on the starting date and the sampling interval (4 years).

Obviously a researcher must look critically at a list to be used for a systematic sample to try to determine whether the arrangement of the cases in the list presents problems. If the cases in the list are randomly arranged, then a systematic sample of that list is the equivalent of a random sample. Unfortunately, it is seldom the case that the list to be sampled is randomly arranged.

Quota Samples

A second type of nonrandom sample is the **quota sample.** To execute a quota sample it is necessary to determine how variables relevant to the study being conducted are distributed in the population. This can often be determined by consulting census data or other research conducted earlier on the same population. Once the distributions of relevant variables are determined and the sample size is decided upon, specifications for sampling are prepared and distributed to interviewers. Thus, a given interviewer might be told to find 10 married women between the ages of 40 and 45 to interview. Finding respondents who fit these criteria is left to the initiative or convenience of the interviewer.

Perhaps an example of a quota sample design will clarify what is involved in the technique. Assume that a researcher is to conduct a study of the inhabitants of a city to determine their attitudes toward the police force. It is decided that the respondents of the survey should match the population with respect to gender, ethnic group, and age distributions. By consulting the latest census data, the researcher might find that 53% of the inhabitants are female; 15% are Black, 20% are Hispanic, and 65% are White; 30% are young, 50% are middle-aged, and 20%

are old. Given this information and having decided that the sample should include 500 respondents, the researcher could draw up a list of specifications for interviewers that would guide them in finding respondents. Thus, an interviewer who is to interview 25 respondents might be directed to find 25 who are middle-aged White women. These specifications would be assigned to the interviewers so that when all of the interviews are completed the sample will match the population proportions on age, ethnic group, and gender.

A properly drawn quota sample may give accurate estimates of the parameters of interest in the population sampled. The problem is that because the technique is nonrandom, it is not possible to estimate sampling error legitimately. Unless there is final feedback, as in an election poll, it is not possible to judge the accuracy of estimates the sample statistics provide.

Furthermore, the efficiency of the quota sample depends on astute selection of the variables used to provide specification criteria for the interviewers. If the variables used are not relevant to the study or if equally or more important variables are overlooked, the sample may turn out to be a distorted representation of the population sampled.

A particularly risky aspect of the quota sample design is allowing interviewers to find the subjects of the study on their own. There is no assurance that the interviewers will make any attempt to find respondents who are representative of the population. Rather, they may seek out those who are most accessible, those who are concentrated in a small geographical area (e.g., a mall or section of a city), or those who are most willing to cooperate in answering questions.

Snowball Sampling

In some situations it is not possible to acquire a sampling frame to represent a population. This is often the case when the population of interest engages in some sort of deviant behavior. For example, if one were interested in studying swingers (couples who exchange sex partners with other couples), it would be difficult to find an extensive sampling frame. One might be able to contact a swingers' club and seek to collect data from the club's members, but the club might have a very small membership and there might be a suspicion that the members of that particular club are not very representative of the larger population of swingers.

An alternative would be to execute a **snowball sample** of swingers. A snowball sample is accomplished by finding one case from the population of interest, collecting data from that case, and then having the respondent (or respondents) from that case refer the researcher to one or more other cases. Once the second case is contacted and interviewed, the respondent from that case is asked to refer the researcher to additional cases. Thus, the researcher goes from one case to another, being referred each time to additional cases that belong to the population of interest. Once the researcher exhausts the cases available or decides that he or she has enough interviews to proceed with the data analysis, the sampling is discontinued. This technique makes it possible to obtain data from subjects who would otherwise not be accessible to the researcher. However, it should be remembered that a snowball sample is not equivalent to a random sample. Hence, there is no assurance that the subjects from whom the data are collected are representative of the population of interest. Consequently, a snowball sample should not be used if it is possible to obtain a random sample.

Other Nonrandom Sampling Techniques

In addition to the three nonrandom sampling techniques just mentioned, other types are found in the literature. One type of nonrandom sample is an **analytic sample,** which may be a case or a small set of cases that are selected because they fit some analytic specifications. They may be a classic example of some phenomenon or a current instance of a rare phenomenon (e.g., a prototypical small town or a tornado disaster). Case studies often select a case or a few contrasting cases because of their theoretical relevance. An in-depth analysis of the cases may provide useful description, an example of the operation of some principle, or a basis for elaborating hypotheses for future testing.

Another type of nonrandom sample is what might be called the **convenience sample.** This technique uses cases that are available without regard to the question of their representativeness. When interviewers in a shopping mall stop passersby and ask them to participate in a survey (perhaps of their breakfast cereal preferences), chances are that the agency sponsoring the interviews is a market research company compiling a convenience sample. This type of research is aimed at collecting data that can be used to satisfy the terms of a contract with some company and provide the company with information about the popularity of its product. Often there is little concern about whether the data are representative of the population of current or potential purchasers of the company's product.

In fairness it should be noted that companies that put interviewers in shopping malls sometimes give them guidelines as to whom they are supposed to interview. Thus, interviewers may be given specifications with respect to the personal characteristics of the people they are supposed to interview. This results in a sample that has many of the characteristics of a quota sample, with the difference that the interviewers are assigned to specific locations from which they must find their subjects.

Shere Hite used another version of the nonrandom sample to collect data on the sexual behavior of American women (Hite, 1976). She describes the distribution of her questionnaire as follows:

> Great effort was put into mailing and distribution of the questionnaires in an attempt to reach as many different kinds of women, with as many different points of view, as possible. Early distribution was done through national mailings to women's groups, including chapters of the National Organization for Women, abortion rights groups, university women's centers, and women's newsletters. Soon after, notices in *The Village Voice, Mademoiselle, Brides,* and *Ms.* magazines informed readers that they could write in for the questionnaires, and later there were also notices placed in dozens of church newsletters. In addition, *Oui* magazine

> ran the questionnaire in its entirety, and 253 replies were received from its women readers. Finally, the paperback *Sexual Honesty by Women for Women,* which contains forty-five complete early replies, has asked readers to send in their own replies since its publication in 1974. All in all, one hundred thousand questionnaires were distributed, and slightly over three thousand returned (more or less the standard rate of return for this kind of questionnaire distribution). (1976:xxi)

Even though Hite received completed questionnaires from 3,019 women (a sizable sample), one might legitimately ask whether women who belong to the organizations to which she sent questionnaires or who read the magazines, newsletters, and the book from which she solicited respondents are representative of American women and whether the 3,019 women who filled out the questionnaires are even representative of those to whom the questionnaires were distributed. In a follow-up of the original study, Hite also distributed questionnaires to organizations (Hite, 1987). As she explains,

> Clubs and organizations through which questionnaires were distributed included church groups in thirty-four states, women's voting and political groups in nine states, women's rights organizations in thirty-nine states, professional women's groups in twenty-two states, counseling and walk-in centers for women or families in forty-three states, and a wide range of other organizations, such as senior citizens' homes and disabled people's organizations, in various states.
>
> In addition, individual women did write for copies of the questionnaire using both the address given in my previous works and an address given by interview programs on television and in the press. . . . All in all, one hundred thousand questionnaires were distributed, and four thousand five hundred were returned. (1987:777)

She touted her 4.5% rate of return as "almost twice as high as the standard rate of return for this kind of questionnaire distribution" (1987:777). She states, "A probability method of sampling might have yielded a higher rate of return, but then an essay questionnaire would not have been possible" (1987:777). This statement is followed shortly by another curious statement: "But an even more important reason for not using random sampling methods for this study is that a random sample cannot be anonymous; the individuals chosen clearly understand that their names and addresses are on file" (1987:778).

It appears that Hite goes to great trouble to justify a nonrandom sampling technique so that the reader will be left with the impression that her findings have much wider generality than they deserve.

Evaluation of Nonrandom Samples

Nonrandom samples such as the ones just described are common. There are times when it is not possible to draw a random sample; in such cases a nonrandom sample might be preferred to no sample (and no data) at all.

Because there are no legitimate techniques for estimating sampling error from nonrandom samples, there is no basis for inference to larger populations. Generalizability is sacrificed as a trade-off. It should be kept in mind that the principal reason for sampling is to use the sample data to make inferences about a population. Therefore, whenever feasible, random samples should be drawn. Unfortunately, however, nonrandom samples are often used in lieu of random samples because they are cheaper or easier to execute. These are not valid reasons for using nonrandom sampling techniques.

When random sampling is not feasible, if the study is still pursued using nonrandom sampling, the results of data analysis are limited in application to the subjects who contributed the data. Of course, it is legitimate to describe the subjects of the study in terms of personal characteristics, but this does not ensure that they are even representative of other people who share those same characteristics.

SAMPLE SIZE

A question often asked is, "How large does a sample need to be in order to be representative of the population?" The obvious answer seems to be "The bigger, the better." However, it must be remembered that one purpose of sampling is to get representative data at a reasonable cost. Each additional case sampled adds to the cost of the overall sample. In fact, there is a point of diminishing returns in sampling whereby each additional case beyond a certain point adds smaller and smaller increments to the accuracy with which the sample data estimate the population data. Consequently, it does not pay to increase sample size indiscriminately.

Typical national opinion polls are based on approximately 1,500 cases. When such polls are used to predict national election results, for example, the sample size used can be seen to be a very small segment of the total electorate. Nevertheless, sampling error for such polls is often as small as plus or minus 3 percentage points. This is so because the size of the sampling error does not depend on the proportion of the total population included in the sample.[6] Rather, the sheer number of cases in the sample affects the size of the sampling error (Loether and McTavish, 1993:388, 416–17). Therefore, it is generally the case that the larger the sample is, the smaller the sampling error will be. Because the efficiency in sampling and inference comes from making satisfactory estimates from samples that are small segments of the populations sampled, it is in the interest of the researcher to draw a sample large enough to suit the purposes of the study, but not any larger than needed.

Three important considerations in determining needed sample size are the degree of sampling error tolerable in making inferences from the sample to the population, the number of cases needed in order to carry out the data analysis nec-

[6]An exception to this rule occurs when the sample is nearly an enumeration of the whole finite population, in which case sampling error becomes less. This can be taken into account by a finite population correction factor described in many statistics books.

essary to test the hypotheses of the study, and the response rate or percentage of those sampled who end up providing data.

The tolerance level in sampling error depends on what is being studied. For example, if the purpose of the research is to predict an election result, a 3% sampling error is tolerable in a campaign in which the two candidates are widely separated in popularity, but it might be considered too large in a closely contested campaign. If one candidate were leading the other in a poll by 10%, even with a 3% error it would be fairly clear that the leading candidate had a comfortable margin. On the other hand, if the poll results gave 51% of the vote to one candidate and 49% to the other, a 3% error would be too large to enable the pollster to predict who really had more support.

Thus, the researcher must decide what a tolerable level of sampling error is for the particular study being undertaken. Once a decision is made on how much sampling error can be tolerated it may be possible to compute the necessary sample size. In order to do this, it is necessary to be able to gauge the degree of homogeneity of the population being sampled. If it is possible to estimate how homogeneous the cases in the population are, then this information can be entered into an estimation formula, along with the maximum tolerable sampling error, to solve for sample size (Loether and McTavish, 1993:496–99).

Table 5.1 shows the effect of sample size on sampling error for percentages, assuming that an SRS has been used. Notice that the sampling error gets smaller when the population percentage in question is further from a 50%–50% split. Sampling error is also larger for smaller samples. If we expected a 51% to 49% split in voting for two candidates, for example, we would need a sample of size 10,000 to reduce the sampling error down to .5%, which might be needed to predict a very close election outcome.

With respect to the second consideration mentioned—the planned analysis of data—the more elaborate the data analysis, the more sample cases are required to do the analysis. If a simple univariate or bivariate level of analysis is planned, then a small sample may be adequate. However, if the researcher intends to do a multivariate analysis, then more cases will be required because the data must be spread

TABLE 5.1 Random Sampling Error as a Function of Selected Population Percentages and Sample Sizes

	ANTICIPATED POPULATION PERCENTAGE				
SAMPLE SIZE	90%	70%	50%	30%	10%
10	9.5%	14.5%	15.8%	14.5%	9.5%
50	4.2	6.5	7.1	6.5	4.2
100	3.0	4.6	5.0	4.6	3.0
1000	0.9	1.4	1.6	1.4	0.9
10000	0.3	0.46	0.5	0.46	0.3

over more score categories of the variables being analyzed. As mentioned earlier in this chapter, a study of attitudes toward capital punishment that compared the responses of subjects classified by their religion, gender, and age would require a sample large enough to distribute the cases over all of the cells in the tables used for the analysis. Given two response categories on capital punishment, two for gender, three religious categories (Protestants, Catholics, and Jews), and three age categories (young, middle-aged, and old), there would need to be enough cases in the sample to distribute over 36 different combinations of scores, or 36 cells in the tables used for analysis of the data (the number of cells is the product of the number of categories of the variables, here, $2 \times 2 \times 3 \times 3 = 36$). If all variables in the study were evenly distributed, it would take a minimum of 720 cases to get 20 cases in each of the 36 cells. Given that variables are not generally evenly distributed, a considerably larger sample size would need to be used.

Response rates from samples vary by the way in which data gathering is approached. In well-done surveys, a response rate of 70% to 80% is achievable, but poorly done studies or studies of difficult topics and populations may result in considerably lower response rates. As we shall see in later chapters, nonresponse is generally not a random behavior on the part of subjects. Thus, samples with high nonresponse are likely to reflect biases in addition to reducing the desired sample size. Researchers take account of expected nonresponse and boost the sample size so that the achieved sample size is sufficient for their analysis.

It should be obvious that the decision about the size of sample needed for a study is not simple. It requires careful consideration and much advanced planning of all stages of the research project, including data analysis, to determine an adequate sample size. Computer programs called expert systems are available to help an investigator think through factors that affect sample size in the process of determining how many cases to draw (Brent, Scott, and Spencer, 1988).

SUMMARY

When population data are available for study, it is possible to reach conclusions about the population directly. The purpose of a sample is to collect data from a representative portion of the population of interest and use those data to make inferences about that population. Random selection of the cases in a sample provides a basis for measuring sampling error and using that information for making inferences about population characteristics that are not directly observable.

The basic random sampling technique is the simple random sample (SRS), in which every case in the population has an equal probability of being sampled and every sample of a given size has an equal probability of being the sample selected for study. SRSs are drawn with replacement. Random samples drawn without replacement are also used and, if the population being sampled is very large in comparison to the size of the sample drawn, then there is little difference between the random sample drawn without replacement and that drawn with. However, random sampling with replacement is generally preferred unless specific reasons necessitate sampling without replacement.

Because an SRS requires a single sampling frame, it is sometimes not possible to draw an SRS. In lieu of an SRS, a random cluster sample may be drawn because it is feasible when the SRS is not. The random cluster sample is essentially a multistage random sample, drawn through a series of accessible sampling frames.

Another alternative is the stratified random sample. Although stratified random samples often have smaller sampling errors than SRSs, they are usually harder to accomplish because the technique requires more information about the population than the SRS. The primary stratified random sampling technique involves sampling proportionate to the presence of sampled characteristics in the population. Variations on this primary technique include the disproportionate stratified random sample and the optimum allocation stratified random sample.

Alternatives to random samples include such nonrandom sampling techniques as systematic samples (with or without a random start), quota samples, snowball samples, and convenience samples. These techniques all share the shortcoming of lacking a basis for estimating sampling error; therefore, they do not support generalization to a population. Nonrandom samples are generally frowned on as sampling techniques except in cases in which random sampling of any kind is not a viable alternative and a more limited description of sample data is acceptable.

Determining the optimum sample size for a study is a somewhat complicated procedure that depends on how large a sampling error can be tolerated and how elaborate the data analysis contemplated will be. The goal is to select a sample large enough to suit the requirements of the study being undertaken but not so large as to waste research resources.

Random sampling and inference are two closely related processes, and one should not be undertaken without the other. Studies in which nonrandom samples are used as a basis for inference should be looked on with suspicion.

Even when a random sample is used as a basis for inference, it is necessary to ask whether the population sampled is the appropriate one for the study being conducted. A crucial consideration in any research is whether the target population studied, either directly or inferentially, is the one to which the researcher wants to apply the findings.

TERMS TO KNOW

Achieved sample
Analytic sample
Convenience sample
Disproportionate stratified random sample
Enumeration
Finite (limited) population
Inference
Infinite population
Multistage random sample
Nonrandom sample
Optimum allocation sampling
Parameter
Population

Population elements
Primary sampling unit
Probability sample
Probability theory
Proportionate stratified random sample
Quota sample
Random cluster sample
Random numbers
Random sample
Random selection
Representative sample
Response rate
Sample
Sample size
Sampling error
Sampling frame
Sampling interval
Sampling theory
Simple random sample (SRS)
Snowball sample
Statistic
Strata
Stratified random sample
Systematic sample
Systematic sample with a random start
Ultimate sampling unit
Weighting
Without replacement
With replacement

ISSUES AND COMPARISONS

Strengths of random sampling
Logic of inference about populations on the basis of samples
How to draw a simple random sample from a finite population
Problems in creating an accurate sampling frame
Advantages and disadvantages of different kinds of samples

EXERCISES

1. Discuss the pros and cons of using a telephone directory as the sampling frame for a study of city residents' attitudes about their community's public services (e.g., fire, police, parks, streets, and other public programs).
2. Design a sampling procedure that would enable one to compare the number of hours worked per week for minority and majority men and women in your college's freshman class. What are its strengths and limitations?

REFERENCES

Brent, Edward E., Jr., James K. Scott, and John C. Spencer, *EX-SAMPLE, An Expert System to Assist in Designing Sampling Plans,* Idea Works, Columbia, MO, 1988.

Burgess, E. W., and P. Wallin, "Homogamy in Social Characteristics," *American Journal of Sociology* 1943;49:109–24.

Hadaway, Kirk, Penny Long Marler, and Mark Chaves, "What the Polls Don't Show: A Closer Look at U.S. Church Attendance," *American Sociological Review* December 1993;58(6):741–52.

Hagood, Margaret Jarman, and Daniel O. Price, *Statistics for Sociologists,* revised ed., Holt, New York, 1952.

Hite, Shere, *The Hite Report,* Macmillan, New York, 1976.

Hite, Shere, *Women and Love: A Cultural Revolution in Progress,* Knopf, New York, 1987.
Kish, Leslie, *Survey Sampling,* Wiley, New York, 1965.
Loether, Herman J., and Donald G. McTavish, *Descriptive and Inferential Statistics: An Introduction,* 4th ed., Allyn & Bacon, Boston, 1993.
Meiksins, Peter F., and James M. Watson, "Professional Autonomy and Organizational Constraint: The Case of Engineers," *Sociological Quarterly* 1989;30(4):561–85.
Spenner, Kenneth, "Deciphering Prometheus: Temporal Change in the Skill Level of Work," *American Sociological Review* December 1983;48:824–37.

CHAPTER SIX

EXPERIMENTAL RESEARCH

Investigators are often interested in establishing whether some specific factor (independent variable or stimulus condition) had an influence on specific outcomes. Experimental research designs often serve as a model to answer this kind of question.

You will recall that the idea of a **causal relationship** between two variables requires three kinds of data:

- Evidence that the variables are related (correlated) to each other
- Evidence that the presumed causal variable preceded the outcome
- Evidence that no other variable explains or accounts for the observed relationship

Experimental designs are especially valuable in handling the problem of time-order of variables and the problem of eliminating other variables as potential competing explanations of observed outcomes. These designs permit one to focus on whether a stimulus is related to a specific outcome.

Experimental research designs involve the investigator's control, especially control over who is and who is not exposed to the effects of some level of an independent variable or stimulus. At a minimum, this involves two groups: one that gets the stimulus (called the **experimental group**), and the other that does not (called the **control group**). If there are different levels of the experimental stimulus, then there may be several experimental groups to compare with one or more control groups.

Suppose you wanted to study the effect of reading a computer manual (independent variable or stimulus) on the ability to operate a computer (the outcome or dependent variable). You might create an experimental group who would get the manual (and time to read it), and a control group who wouldn't get the manual. The outcome or dependent variable would be some test of subsequent ability to operate a computer. If those who got the manual did better on the computer operation test, one might conclude that reading the manual improved performance.

But could the two groups in this example have been different to start with in ways that produced the effects, rather than reading the manual? For example, could many in the experimental group (but few in the control group) already have known how to operate a computer? Perhaps more of those in the experimental group than the control group were interested in learning about computers. The problem is that the two groups may have been different to start with, so it is unclear whether reading the manual or some other factor (e.g., interest or prior experience) actually created a difference in the computer operation test.

The solution is to try to make the experimental and control groups as identical as possible on all other potential causes of difference in computer skill. As discussed in this chapter, there are several ways to make experimental and control groups equivalent. If we exercise this control, then the comparison of experimental and control groups constitutes the minimum basis for an experiment.

PRINCIPLES

Internal validity of a study refers to whether conclusions for a study are supported by data and procedures that were used. Can the claim that the independent variable influences the dependent variable be supported for data included in the study? **External validity,** on the other hand, refers to whether the results of a study can be legitimately generalized to some specified broader population. Internal validity is primary. Several experimental designs help ensure the internal validity of a study.

A Model

The **after-only control group design** is the primary model for experiments because it helps attain internally valid studies. It can be symbolized as follows:

(Experimental group)	R	x	O_1
(Control group)	R		O_2

Here, the *x* symbolizes the experimental stimulus that only cases in the experimental group receive. The *O*s are observations or measurement of the dependent

variables. In this experimental design, the main comparison is between O_1 and O_2, and differences, if any, are attributed to the experimental stimulus, *x*. The *R* symbolizes the fact that the pool of available cases is randomly assigned to the experimental and control groups (usually so that groups are of equal size). Why might random assignment to groups be helpful?

Random Assignment

Random assignment accomplishes the objective of eliminating any preexisting condition such as a systematic difference between groups involved in the experiment. This is because random assignment ensures that the chance of any particular kind of case getting into one group is exactly equal to the chance of its getting into the other group. Thus, the difference between experimental and control groups could not be systematically caused by any other preexisting factor. To start with, any difference between groups would result only from chance. The advantage of this is that there are **statistical tests** that help one examine **chance differences** in outcome to see whether observed differences in outcome between experimental and control groups are more than one would expect by chance. These are called significance of difference tests. If there is a statistically significant difference in outcome between experimental and control groups, then the differences that are observed between experimental and control groups are judged to be large enough to be caused by factors other than chance, and the stimulus or independent variable is the main contender.

It is important to note that statistical tests such as these may only be legitimately used if the subjects of the experiment constitute a random sample of some population. This is so because tests of significance refer to differences in the population rather than differences between specific experimental and control groups. If the subjects do not constitute a random sample, then the differences observed between experimental and control groups may still be evaluated but tests of statistical significance cannot be used as criteria for reaching conclusions about hypotheses posed.[1]

Matching

Matching is another way to make experimental and control groups similar by ensuring that there are similar subjects in each group. This can be done on an individual **case-by-case** basis. For example, if one group has a 20-year-old male, a 20-year-old male is sought for each other group. Making groups equivalent can also be done by matching the **overall group distribution** of cases on various variables so that the groups have, say, equal proportions of men and women or are equal on average age. Variables chosen for matching include all those that are thought to be important **alternative explanations** of differences in outcome.

[1]For a discussion of statistical tests and an explanation of the concept of statistical significance, see a statistics book such as Loether and McTavish, (1993).

Randomization is generally preferable to matching because with random assignment one does not have to know which other variables should be controlled. In matching, one must not only know which variables are crucial to ensure relevant similarity of groups but also must have information from subjects on each variable used in matching.

However, making groups similar at the start does not completely solve the problem of internal validity. There may be differences between experimental and control groups that arise *after* cases have been assigned to groups. To minimize or eliminate this possibility, the investigator typically controls the way in which the experiment proceeds to avoid extraneous differences between the experimental and control groups. This is one reason why experiments tend to use controlled laboratory situations in which influences can be standardized.

Differences between the groups may arise during the process of giving an experimental **treatment (stimulus).** Researchers attempt to make the groups identical in everything except the critical features of the experimental stimulus. For example, if the experimental stimulus involves giving computer information to the experimental group, an investigator could give the control group a manual on something else to read so that both groups are similar on having something to read and it is only the critical *content* about computers that is the difference in treatment. Giving the control group a treatment that is like the experimental stimulus in everything except the critical stimulus factor is called a **placebo.** In experiments with new drug treatments, for example, the control group would get a pill that does not have the active ingredient being tested. Experimental research design involves careful examination of ways in which differences between groups might be compromised, making conclusions ambiguous.

A classic example of an internal validity problem occurred in a study of the effects of changes in lighting in a telephone equipment assembly plant in Hawthorne, Illinois (Roethlisberger and Dickson, 1939). Experimental groups of workers were placed in a room in which lighting could be controlled and work productivity measured. As lighting intensity was raised, production went up. But when lighting was lowered again, production went still higher. Experimental subjects felt that they were receiving special treatment; because of this attention, apparently, their performance continued to increase. Called the **Hawthorne effect,** it is a further argument for standardizing the experience of participants in different groups for all factors except the critical independent variables.

The setting for an experiment is usually a controlled setting or laboratory where the investigator can systematically introduce the stimulus, systematically record the outcomes, and monitor the ongoing process. This helps eliminate extraneous disruptions and maintains the independence of the various experimental and control groups. Laboratory settings are also helpful in nonexperimental social science research because they help minimize disruptive outside events and keep a focus on the substantive problem (Couch, 1987). Experiments can also be conducted in larger social settings. For example, a researcher studying the impact of a school funding program might be able randomly to assign school districts selected from across the United States to an experimental group that is provided funding and a control group that does not receive this funding. Outside the laboratory, it is harder to control possible sources of contamination, such as talk among school administrators that might lead a school that didn't get this outside funding to take funds from elsewhere to do what the program would have done. The investigator would probably never know that this happened.

Other Experimental Designs

A wide variety of experimental designs address specific design problems facing an investigator. Each has strengths and weaknesses.

Some experimental research involves several treatment conditions and control groups because there are several different levels of treatment. For example, one group might receive information in written form, one in verbal form, and a third in a video form, all compared with a control group that is not given the critical information. This would involve four groups: three experimental and one control.

There are two other research designs that we briefly describe here for comparison with the after-only design. One is an experimental design and the other is a **one-group, pre–post design** that, by contrast, illustrates some of the strengths of experimental designs. In later chapters we illustrate other research designs that include some but not all of the strengths of an experimental design (these are sometimes called **quasi-experimental designs**).

If an investigator wanted to ensure that experimental and control groups started out similarly on the dependent variable, an early measure of the outcome variable could be made. A design in which a premeasurement of both the experimental and control groups is used is called the **classic experimental design.** It involves adding a premeasurement for both the experimental and control groups, as shown here:

$$\begin{array}{llll} R & O_1 & x & O_3 \\ R & O_2 & & O_4 \end{array}$$

Again, the *R*s indicate random assignment to groups from the pool of participants. *O*s are measurements of the dependent variable. In this design a number of comparisons can be made. For example, O_1 and O_2 can be compared to see whether there are differences in the randomly assigned groups. O_3 and O_4 can be compared to see whether there are differences attributable to the treatment. Also, the difference between O_1 and O_3 can be compared to the difference between O_2 and O_4. Presumably, the difference between the pretest and posttest in the treatment group would differ from that in the control group, implying the impact of *x* on the outcome *O*.

Although the classic experimental design takes account of differences of the outcome variable that were present before the treatment, it also can **sensitize** participants to the focus of the study and may interact with the stimulus to produce effects that would not be found among non-pretested subjects. This limits a second kind of validity, external validity, which concerns the generalizability of findings to broader populations of subjects. In this case, findings may apply primarily to pretested or sensitized subjects. Pretesting may increase the Hawthorne effect.

In a very useful treatment, Campbell and Stanley (1963) listed a number of factors that may diminish the internal validity of a research design. These can be illustrated by contrasting the classic and after-only experimental designs with a one-group, pre–post design (a quasi-experimental design), shown here:

$O_1 \quad x \quad O_2$

An example of this research might be a study of the effect of taking a class. The instructor might hand out a test at the beginning of the school term to measure knowledge in the subject area that students have before taking the class. At the end of the class, the same or a comparable test on the same knowledge would be given. Differences between O_1 and O_2 might be said to result from the class. Are there any alternative explanations of the difference? Yes!

First, there are many other things happening over the course of the study between the time the two measurements are taken. History continues in terms of political and personal events, news reports, other classes, and special events. These could produce the observed effect, rather than the class itself, especially over the time of a school term (historic events could also counteract any effect of the class, perhaps by distracting students from their studies). In addition, the participants are maturing and gaining perspective and experience. Concern for effects of maturing and history may lead investigators to minimize the time over which an experiment occurs. The control group in the classic or after-only experimental designs discussed earlier allows one to sort these effects out by comparing outcomes with those in a control group who have matured and experienced history in the same way, except for the treatment itself.

There are other potential problems with this one-group design. Some students might drop out, creating a problem called experimental mortality. Usually those who drop out are a special subgroup in some respect, so they leave an experimental or control group that is biased, which distorts comparisons later on. Although this could be a problem with any study over time, with a one-group study it is difficult to take this factor into account. Even in studies with a control group, there may be differences in the dropout rate for one group compared with others, confounding conclusions about differences between experimental and control groups on the outcome variables.

Another potential problem for the internal validity of the pre–post one-group design that Campbell and Stanley point out is an instrumentation problem. This happens when the measuring instrument used in the pretest is different in some way from the one used in the posttest. If human observers or interviewers are involved in the testing, they could become sloppy or change questions over time. The tests themselves might not be exactly equivalent or they might be unreliable. The way a standardized test is given at two points in time may also differ. All of these differences in instrumentation would be reflected in differences between the pretest and posttest and impossible to disentangle from the effects of the experimental stimulus. The investigators may also be a source of instrument error stemming from their knowledge of who has received the treatment. An investigator could selectively pay attention to effects of a treatment and neglect examining the presumably uneventful control group as carefully. **Experimenter bias** can sometimes be handled by using a **double-blind experiment** in which neither the subjects nor the experimenter know ahead of time which groups received the treatment.

Finally, Campbell and Stanley call special attention to a common research design fallacy that involves selecting a group for study specifically because it is extreme on the outcome variable. If some of the reason the subjects were extreme to start with was random measurement error, then one would expect a second measurement to have different measurement error that would probably be less extreme than that which led to the case's selection as an extreme case. This apparent change from extreme scores to somewhat less extreme scores over time is called regression toward the mean, or statistical regression. Scores tend to regress to the true mean of their distribution. Statistical regression can also be a competing reason for differences in scores over time. It is expected when groups are selected because they are extreme on a premeasure of the outcome variable.

Statistical regression problems are not uncommon. For example, assume you were interested in treatments that might improve the performance of students who are poor in mathematics. You might give a math pretest, select students who performed poorly on that test, then give them some "treatment" such as a special makeup class. Students would again take a math exam after the treatment. In this case, statistical regression is likely to be a problem. One reason is that the extremely low scores on the pretest might result partly from random measurement error. In general, one would expect a second measurement to "balance out" the measurement error, but there is only one way to go, namely toward higher scores (or toward the mean of the distribution of outcome scores). This appears to be an improvement over time, resulting from the treatment, when it is actually an expected regression toward the mean resulting from picking an extreme group to study. In general, it is a poor practice to select extreme groups for study based on scores of a dependent variable.

Experimental designs such as the after-only control group design or the pretest–posttest control group design are logically better because they control for many of the possible alternative explanations of causes of difference in an outcome variable. Threats to internal validity include selection of cases into experimental and control groups, history, maturation, reactivity of pretesting, instrument change or decay, experimental mortality or dropouts, and statistical regression effects. Sometimes combinations of these internal validity problems also produce further problems for the investigator. A careful analysis of a study design is needed to identify and minimize the possibility of contaminating alternative explanations of results.

Ross and Smith (1965) have pointed out that interaction effects may present interpretation problems even with the most sophisticated experimental designs. For example, when the pretest–posttest control group design is used, observed differences between control group and experimental group results may not be attributable strictly to exposure to the experimental stimulus. There is also the possibility of (1) interaction between the pretest and the experimental stimulus, (2) interaction between the pretest and uncontrolled events, (3) interaction between the pretest, the experimental stimulus, and uncontrolled events, or (4) some combination of these.

A hypothetical example of the simultaneous interaction of pretest, experimental stimulus, and uncontrolled events might be the following: You set up an experiment to determine whether an educational program dealing with the danger of infestation of fruit flies to cherry crops can be beneficial to cherry farmers. You select a group of cherry farmers to serve as subjects for the experiment. All of the farmers are administered a pretest to assess their knowledge about fruit flies and steps they can take to control them. You divide the farmers into experimental and control groups and subject those farmers in the experimental group to an educational program dealing with fruit flies. The control group is not exposed to the educational program. After the educational program has been completed, both the farmers in the experimental group and those in the control group are given a posttest to assess their knowledge about fruit flies and to determine whether they have taken any steps to control fruit flies.

While the educational program is being administered to the experimental group, an infestation of fruit flies occurs in the area where all of the cherry farmers have their farms. The infestation is reported in the local newspapers and on the local TV stations. These news reports not only detail the infestation but offer advice about how the fruit flies may be controlled.

When the study is completed and the results are in, you find that knowledge about fruit flies has increased in both the experimental and control groups and both groups have taken steps to control fruit flies. However, the change in the experimental group exceeds the change in the control group on both counts. The question is how much of the change can be attributed strictly to the experimental stimulus (the educational program) and how much to interaction effects? It is possible that the pretest sensitized both groups to the question of danger to crops from fruit flies, the uncontrolled infestation of fruit flies to their crops further sensitized both groups, and the educational program administered to the experimental group had an additional effect on the experimental group.

In this particular example it would not be possible to attribute observed differences between the experimental and control groups strictly to the effects of the experimental stimulus. Even if the after-only control group design had been used for the experiment, there would still have been the possibility of interaction between the experimental stimulus and the uncontrolled events.

What this example points out (thanks to Ross and Smith) is that experimental research does not ensure that an experimental stimulus can be credited with being the sole cause of an experimental effect.

External validity is also a concern for investigators. This is the extent to which findings from an experiment (or other type of study, for that matter) can be generalized more broadly to some target population. Experimental designs encounter two general problems in generalizability.

One generalizability problem stems from the way the pool of subjects is selected. To generalize to a larger population, one would like a sample to be selected in such a way that all members of the population have a known, nonzero chance of being drawn into the sample. Because of the need for control over the application of the experimental stimulus in experimental research designs, investigators typically conduct experiments in the controlled conditions of their laboratories. It would be prohibitive to have a representative sample of people (or dyads, families, groups, or other units of analysis that are relevant to the study) from throughout the United States or the world travel to the researcher's laboratory. Thus, investigators often advertise for local volunteers who are willing to participate, sometimes with pay. Available subjects in academic research are often undergraduate students. In the end, the experimental results may apply only to local cases, and then only to those who volunteered for whatever reason.

A second type of generalizability problem stems from experimental procedures themselves. For example, if both experimental and control groups are pretested, then findings may apply only to pretested subjects. Or the effect of a stimulus may result from special attention that is drawn to the phenomenon by a pretest or preliminary disclosure of the nature of the experiment during subject recruitment. The laboratory is also a special social setting, which may mean that findings from such studies may not apply to subjects in other types of social settings. In many cases the "reality" of the laboratory setting is not a primary problem because the social phenomenon of interest may not be adversely affected by laboratory conditions. For example, small groups making decisions quickly come to ignore the setting and focus on their discussion.

Replication

Replication of research using other subjects, techniques, and settings, plus continued testing of relevant theoretical principles, ultimately contributes to generalizability and the scientific status of knowledge gained from experiments. One advantage of an experimental design is that it is often of a scope that permits replication to be done easily by the original investigator or others.

Ethics of Experimental Research

Largely because of the more controlled setting of an experiment and the possibilities for greater manipulation of subjects during an experimental treatment, a number of ethical issues arise. For example, an investigator may be torn between fully informing the subject of what the experiment will involve (which may bias findings) and disguising the nature of the experiment. Good practice adequately informs subjects ahead of time so they can make reasoned judgments about whether they want to participate. Researchers often present the essentials of an experiment and seek written acceptance and willingness on the part of the subjects to participate. If students were the subjects and grades were related to their participation, for example, they would probably not feel free to avoid participation in the experiment. When full prior explanation of the essentials of a treatment seems methodologically problematic, other careful monitoring and full disclosure after the experiment are used. Subjects are usually informed that they may withdraw without consequences at any time during an experiment.

Social behavior in small groups does have consequences, and these may be minor or major and positive or negative. For example, an experimenter might want to study prison guard behavior by setting up a simulated prison, using students as prisoners and as guards. The social process could unfold in a way that encouraged harsh guard behavior, which could have harmful consequences. The task of the experiment might also introduce embarrassment or cause subjects to become alarmed by the insights they gained into behavior they might not have thought they would do. Ethical research requires that subjects have a realistic basis for being informed about an experiment and have full freedom to participate or withdraw. In addition, the careful researcher is alert to unwanted consequences the subject might not even recognize at the time and takes steps to avoid any negative consequences. Most social science experiments are not greatly different in their consequences from an interesting and harmless game or usual behavior in a social group.

TECHNIQUES AND EXAMPLES

Doing Experiments

Experiments involve considerable setup work. Once it is designed, the problem of experimental research is to make it work. A researcher must be very clear about the **unit of analysis** that is of interest. Is it a study of the social behavior of individuals, the interaction of a dyad, social activity of a larger group, or group reaction to events? In social science research a dyad or larger group is often the important unit to study, although the social behavior of an individual in a social context may also be of interest.

With clarity about the unit of analysis, the stimulus or independent variable must be operationalized. That is, some means by which the independent variable can be clearly produced under the investigator's control is needed. For example, a study may create a choice situation in which the subjects are asked to discuss applications or case files and make a decision according to some criterion. Sometimes a social setting is simulated in which individuals have to perform some task that incorporates the independent variable. Many approaches have been used and a good deal of scientific ingenuity is usually evident, as you can see in the following examples.

A further, essential step is to find subjects who are willing to participate in the experiment. Because an experiment is usually conducted in a special setting or laboratory, investigators often decide to use available volunteers who are nearby. For academic researchers this is often undergraduate students, but it may be volunteers from the larger community. Only rarely is a study funded well enough that a broader sample of cases can be identified and brought to the study site. As we have seen, this poses problems for external validity but it is often a necessary trade-off. Ads may be placed in a local newspaper, or announcements through various groups may be effective in getting volunteers. Often volunteers are offered a small token payment or reward for participation. Once a sufficient pool of volunteers is available, the investigator can assign them to experimental and control groups, schedule their participation, and conduct the experiment.

The experiment, like other study designs, is a social encounter that results in data. The overall setting of the experiment usually receives a lot of attention to make the experiment flow smoothly, allow accurate data collection, provide explanations of the process before and debriefing after for all participants, and ensure that the desired treatment effects actually happen as planned. Experiments usually take two or more staff to run, so pretesting of the whole process is critical, before the final experiment is conducted. Data checking and analysis follow the series of experiments.

A laboratory setting often provides a range of possibilities for careful control and standardization of procedures. For example, typical small-group experimental laboratories may have one-way mirrors or video cameras to minimize the effect of assistants who are observing and coding relevant behaviors. There may be multiple observers so that **intercoder reliability** can be assessed. Measurement of outcome variables may make use of standardized instruments such as questionnaires or special observational coding forms. In fact, a special observational language may be developed to help capture the theoretically relevant behaviors in a comprehensive fashion.

The following examples of experiments illustrate some of the problems for which experimental designs have been used. They also illustrate the usefulness of a laboratory setting as a place for social research that seeks to create social contexts and samples of various kinds of social phenomena in which much of the "clutter" of the real world is reduced or controlled.

STUDY 1: Gender and Double Standards: An After-Only Experimental Design

Three Canadian investigators were interested in the operation of social norms and stereotypes in the workplace (Foschi, Lai, and Sigerson, 1994). In particular, they were interested in gender and double standards in the assessment of job applicants. They hypothesized that the gender of a job applicant communicates different ideas of competence to men and women who review the applicants. They expected men rather than women to exhibit a greater difference in gender-based judgments. After a discussion of the relevant theories about expectation states, they described their experimental design.

The outcome variable was a choice between two applicants made by a subject. Each subject was given three choices to make. The first was between two men applying for an electrical engineering job. One of the two applicants was substantially superior. The second choice was between a same-gender pair of applicants who were applying for a mechanical engineering job. In this case, although the applications were slightly different in many respects, they were identical in grade point average (GPA). A subject would be given either a male–male or a female–female pair of applicants to judge. This was used as a control condition in later comparisons. Finally, the critical third decision was about a male–female pair of applicants for a nuclear engineering/physics job. For some pairs, the male was slightly higher in GPA, and for some pairs the female was slightly higher. A subject would be given only one of these two pairs to judge. For each folder, a person would be asked to select one applicant or the other or neither person.

Each judgment was represented in a folder that had the two applications and the description of the job for which they were applying, plus a form on which to record the decision. All applications were fictitious, but great care was taken to make them look realistic, including having slightly higher past income for men, which was felt to add realism to the applications. All subjects received the judgment folder for the first choice (two unequal male applicants). The study then called for randomly assigning male and female subjects to receive the male–male or female–female applicants folder. Subjects were also assigned randomly to receive the male-higher or female-higher folder. Thus, the experiment is called a "2 × 2 × 2 design: 2 subject genders, 2 same-gender alternatives (male–male or female–female), and 2 unequal applicant (male-higher or female-higher) alternatives. Because it involves all combinations of the three variables, it is also called a **factorial design.**

The subjects were first- and second-year undergraduates in arts and sciences from the authors' Canadian university in about 1990. They were offered a chance at one of three "lottery" prizes worth about $30–$40. Volunteers who had been involved in a social psychology experiment or had taken more than introductory psychology were eliminated from the pool. There were 43 men and 42 women available for the experimental groups.

Foschi and her colleagues portrayed the study as the final stages of a joint effort by industry and the university to provide professional internships (the cover story). Two women helped administer the experiment by handing out folders and managing the administration. The experiment was "double blind" because neither the researchers nor the subjects knew who was in which experimental group until after the experiment was over. After participants finished the three decision tasks, they were given a detailed questionnaire (adapted from a reliable instrument used before) to check on remembered aspects of the experiment, the subject's background characteristics, and whether the experiment was understood and realistic. Then each person was given a written statement explaining the study and the need for the cover story. There was also a group discussion, and subjects were offered the opportunity for individual private consultations in case they wanted to pursue issues raised by the experiment. They were then thanked and informed about the lottery draw outcome for the incentive prizes.

Analysis of their data included extensive checks on the experiment itself. For example, the postquestionnaire data and the data from the first folder that everyone received suggest that participants understood instructions, felt the task was important, and took it seriously. Data from the second folder (with similar same-gender pairs) showed no differences for either men or women making the judgments. The third folder, with mixed-gender applicants, revealed the effects of a gender double standard in judgments. For women, the better performer, whether male or female, was more likely to be chosen. For men, if the male applicant was superior in a male–female pair, he was likely to be chosen 80% of the time, but if the female in a mixed-gender pair had the better record, she was chosen only 45% of the time. That is, they concluded, men used gender of the applicant as an indicator of competence in selecting job applicants.

Do the findings support the conclusions? Yes: For participants involved in this experiment, the gendered judgment difference is evident. The authors reviewed various possible explanations, but the experimental design they used helps rule out these alternatives. However, the findings may not apply more broadly to subjects who are different from those used here, to different eras than the early 1990s in Canada, or to judgment processes that are different from those used in this study.

STUDY 2: Prison Treatment and Parole Completion: A Field Experiment

Kassenbaum, Ward, and Wilner (1971) were interested in the potential effects of different kinds of group treatment programs for prisoners, a topic that had been debated and around which there were strong claims but little data. Evidence was needed on whether these programs made a difference in the likelihood of completing parole without a repeat offense (i.e., recidivism). Group counseling involved inmates having periodic meetings to talk over matters of concern, often with professional guidance but in a group setting. A number of claims about the effectiveness of these programs led Kassenbaum and colleagues to identify three outcome types they would study. In addition to recidivism, they were interested in whether group treatment programs lessened endorsement of the inmate code and reduced the number of disciplinary problem reports an inmate would receive.

An unusual opportunity arose to examine these hypotheses. At the time in California, where the investigators were located, new prison construction was under way. They were able to convince the Department of Corrections to use the opportunity to conduct an unusual study of group counseling programs, using an experimental design.

One of the new facilities, a medium-security prison, was just being built, and design was capitalized on in the study design. The building was divided into four largely autonomous quads, each housing 600 men with state-of-the-art facilities. Each quad had two buildings, and each building had three floors of 100 men, separated into two groups of 50 by the central control area (Kassenbaum et al., 1971:77). This permitted the use of a number of separate treatment situations within the facility.

The study began before any inmates had been assigned to the new facility. One quad (quad D) was reserved for special inmate cases who had to be transferred or processed through the prison in some special way; this quad was not a part of the study. The other three quads were used in the experimental design, and those in charge of inmate assignments permitted the researchers to create an unbiased, largely random assignment process for those who were a part of the study. Each of the three quads received a different type of treatment program. Quad A was largely voluntary small-group counseling (voluntary participation and those who did not participate—a voluntary "control"). Quad A also had 150 men assigned to a mandatory large-group counseling program that used the dayroom in their 50-man wing for four mandatory 1-hour meetings per week. In Quad B, 300 of the 600 men were assigned to mandatory small-group counseling, and the other 300 men were given a voluntary small-group counseling program (again, divided among those who participated and those who didn't—the voluntary controls). Finally, Quad C housed the mandatory controls, receiving all the usual prison treatment but no organized group counseling program.

The researchers' description of the implementation of the study is very interesting reading and a good example of the issues researchers must address in carrying out a study (see Kassenbaum et al., 1971:74–75). One key to their success is the way they planned the study in conjunction with the corrections system staff. This led to the implementation of the assignment procedure even though funding for the research grant had not been received by the time the new prison opened. Data were gathered from a number of sources: a summary of prison records for those released to parole, questionnaires dealing with inmate values (first given to a 50% random sample and given 6 months later to the same men), a questionnaire about group counseling, a psychological inventory for those about to be paroled, and interviews conducted with 75 randomly chosen inmates. Finally, there was a 3-year follow-up of those who were paroled. The study started in June 1962, data collection ended in June 1967, and the analysis was completed in late summer, 1969. The book describing their landmark study came out in 1971.

The general conclusion from the study was that no significant impact of group counseling could be found. Treatment and control groups did not have significantly different outcomes. These results had substantial implications for prison treatment policy and provided basic information for the study of crime. This study is an example of a longitudinal experimental design conducted in a field (rather than special laboratory) setting.

STUDY 3: Observing Social Processes: The Lab as a Context for Reproducing Social Phenomena

Carl Couch (1987) suggests that the laboratory context is a good one for studying social processes because of the possibilities of creating a social context and making careful records of the processes with minimal distractions or "clutter." He was especially interested in social processes involving at least two people, such as the processes of cooperative activity or coordinated social action.

He suggests using an ordinary room (on campus it would be like a classroom), without two-way mirrors or other features that may raise suspicion and distrust. Couch cautions that one must keep the focus on the social phenomenon being studied and not get distracted by technology. Assistants, whom he calls "positioners," help set up the context and introduce the participants to their tasks. The room, he suggests, ought to be large, well-lighted, and comfortably but minimally furnished in ways that help participants engage in the task at hand, minimizing distractions. He uses a video camera to capture the sociologically interesting processes and cautions that it should be positioned so that dyads or larger groups are viewed (rather than close-ups of individuals). The tapes are transcribed for analysis, and although high quality may not be critical, clear voice and visual images are needed for transcription. In this type of setting, social contexts can be created for eliciting samples of targeted social processes. Contexts are created by various means, such as giving simple instructions or creating a more elaborate setting.

For example, a study of "social openings" was designed that involved two people in the laboratory, initially acting independently. Half of the trials involved stranger dyads and half involved friends. Volunteer subjects were found and provided with some type of reward. In this study the two people in the laboratory room were asked to fill out a questionnaire. As they worked independently to answer the questionnaire, a recording of a staged accident was played in the next room so that they could overhear it. The action of the pair of people in the lab room was recorded on videotape (they were told about the recording as part of their initial introduction to the experiment, and the camera was not disguised but it was unobtrusive). Transcripts of the videotapes were examined for evidence of joint activity and how this arose between the two types of dyads. Recordings enabled the researchers to review the interactions and systematically compare social processes across groups.

A study of authority relationships involved setting up a "factory" in which participants were to produce things from "toy" parts (sticks and knobs with holes) in an assembly-line fashion. A positioner played the part of a "distributor," but participants had roles such as boss and workers. Participants had 30 minutes to make products, and a bonus structure was created so that workers and the boss received a 50-cent bonus for each product that the "distributor" found acceptable. Production and inspection sessions provided information on authority relationships. Another excellent example of the use of an experimental design to study difficult-to-capture social processes can be found in Lauderdale (1976), who studied changes in moral boundaries of small groups.

Although these studies involve elements of experimental design and certainly involve the examination of contrasts, they are an example of using the lab setting because of its possibilities for controlling clutter and efficiently producing clean samples of social processes for analysis.

ISSUES IN EXPERIMENTAL RESEARCH

The chief question about experimental research is whether it can indeed be achieved. A social scientist encounters special limitations on the possibility for control in an experiment. For example, some phenomena simply cannot be manipulated. Randomly assigning birth year, family of origin, age, or race is beyond our control. Some factors conceivably could be controlled (i.e., the investigator could decide who gets the experimental stimulus), but doing so is not ethically possible. For example, randomly assigning married people to those who divorce and those who do not or randomly assigning people to high-paying or poverty-level jobs is not permissible. Finally, there are situations in which random assignment conflicts with other values. For example, randomly assigning convicted criminals to paroled and incarcerated groups or randomly assigning eighth graders to superior and inferior instruction is likely to be limited by a society that wants each child to receive the best possible education or is concerned about equal legal treatment of offenders.

A final category of problems includes those that have consequences for the subjects that are not ethical or acceptable. Some experiments that require subjects to punish "prisoners" severely or that shock and disorient subjects so that they have longer-term problems dealing with what they did in an experiment would be examples. This means that many phenomena of interest to social scientists cannot be controlled in the rigorous way that experimental research demands. Thus, investigators need other ways to research many of the social phenomena in which they are interested. Chapter 7 discusses one such alternative.

Strengths of Experimental Research

Experimental research, when it is possible, has primary strengths in establishing the control needed to achieve internal validity: to be able to say with some certainty that an independent variable had an effect on a specified outcome. The after-only control group design is a model for this kind of control, in large part because of random assignment to experimental and control groups. Experimental designs are usually prospective; that is, from start to finish they are under the investigator's control, giving the investigator more opportunity to maintain a less cluttered and more logical research process. Experiments are usually compact enough in time and resource needs that they can be replicated by others.

Weaknesses of Experimental Research

Weaknesses of experimental design are in the area of external validity (generalizability). It is difficult to assemble a representative pool from which to assign subjects to groups randomly. This illustrates one of the trade-offs in research: seeking internal validity but sacrificing external validity. Experimental designs also tend to focus on independent variables that have few categories so that specific experimental and control groups can be established for study. Independent variables studied are generally those that have an effect within a reasonably short time rather than those that may take years or decades to produce an effect.

SUMMARY

The hallmark of an experimental design is control over who receives some defined stimulus. Ideally, this control is exercised by randomly assigning cases to experimental and control groups, although in some research matching is used.

In Riley's terms (Riley, 1963; Chapter 4 of this book), experimental research involves control by the investigator over the administration of the experimental stimulus and, usually, control of other conditions of the experiment. This design is often called a forward-looking or prospective design (as opposed to a retrospective design) because the investigator needs to set up the experiment and assign the "treatment" (e.g., level of an independent variable) to cases that are later measured on outcomes (e.g., dependent variables). Because of the nature of an experiment, other design choices generally involve selecting a few cases and then choosing those that are analytically interesting rather than attempting to select cases to represent a larger population. Experiments generally take place in a single society and era, which is convenient to the investigator, but they are dynamic studies in that they extend over a (usually brief) time period. Few properties are measured, in part because few need to be measured (because of random assignment to groups) and in part because the outcomes are usually focused and clear. Properties are usually measured systematically in order to detect differences and change, and data are generally new rather than archived (because there must be control of the experiment from the start). Data gathering typically involves both observation and questioning, both done in a systematic, structured way. Later analysis is usually statistical, and the relationship of interest is between the stimulus conditions and the outcome variables. Analysis of variance (ANOVA) and its related statistical procedures is often used in the analysis of experiments. This statistical technique is described in statistics books such as Loether and McTavish (1993). When this level of control is possible, the payoff for the researcher is in the ability to make clear statements about what causes what. This profile of design choices reflects the trade-offs that research often requires.

The internal validity of experimental research designs stems from designs that avoid a number of alternative explanations of study results. Campbell and Stanley (1963) list a number of these threats to internal validity. *Selection* refers to biases resulting from the way cases are selected and assigned to experimental and control groups. *Mortality* is the problem of dropout, which erodes the control that careful selection provides. *History,* or the events that happen in addition to the stimulus, is another threat to internal validity, and the maturation of human subjects is always going on when an experiment extends over time. *Pretesting,* if it is used, may sensitize subjects unduly, as might other reactive aspects of the experimental setup. *Instrumentation* or instrument change may also account for pre–post differences that are erroneously credited to the experimental stimulus. *Statistical regression* may also occur when experimental groups are selected because they are extreme on the dependent variable being studied. Other threats to internal validity stem from certain combinations of these problematic threats. Good research designs identify and take steps to eliminate each threat as a potential alternative explanation of findings.

External validity is often sacrificed in experimental designs simply because it often is prohibitive in cost and internal validity is seen as of more immediate importance. Generalizability of findings is achieved by future replication of experimental research on other cases and in other situations, as well as by the development and testing of theory.

Finally, experimental research is not possible for many topics of interest to social scientists, either because the phenomenon is not subject to researcher control or because exercising necessary control would be unethical or conflict with values of higher priority in a society. Thus, researchers turn to other research designs that involve trade-offs but will build social science knowledge. Two alternative types of design are discussed in Chapters 7 and 8: survey research designs and case study designs.

Overall, experimental research, like other forms of research, represents a social encounter between a research staff, a socially meaningful setting, and subjects. Therefore, its meanings and consequences for high-quality research data are of central concern.

TERMS TO KNOW

- After-only control group design
- Alternative explanations
- Causal relationship
- Chance differences
- Classic experimental design
- Control group
- Double-blind experiment
- Experimental group
- Experimenter bias
- External validity
- Factorial design
- Hawthorne effect
- Intercoder reliability
- Internal validity
- Matching
  - Case-by-case
  - Overall group distributions
  - Statistical tests
- One-group, pre–post design
- Placebo
- Quasi-experimental designs
- Random assignment
- Replication
- Sensitize
- Treatment (stimulus)

ISSUES AND COMPARISONS

- Data needed to support the theoretical idea of cause
- Ethical issues in experimental research
- Prospective versus retrospective research

Experimental design choices characterized in Riley's decision framework
Experiments as data-gathering social encounters
Strengths and weaknesses of experimental research
Factors affecting the internal validity of experiments
Factors affecting the external validity of experiments

EXERCISES

1. Pick an outcome and a potential causal variable. Then design an after-only control group design to study the problem. What are the strengths and weaknesses of the design?
2. Look through a favorite journal that reports on experimental social research. Pick an article of interest to you and describe how the study is designed. What are its strengths and weaknesses?
3. Find an example of a study in which one or more of the threats to internal validity discussed in this chapter is likely to be a problem. Describe how the problem results from the study's design. How could the problem be avoided?

REFERENCES

Campbell, Donald T., and Julian C. Stanley, *Experimental and Quasi-Experimental Designs for Research,* Rand McNally, Chicago, 1963.

Couch, Carl J., *Researching Social Processes in the Laboratory,* JAI Press, Greenwich, CT, 1987.

Foschi, Martha, Larissa Lai, and Kirsten Sigerson, "Gender and Double Standards in the Assessment of Job Applicants," *Social Psychology Quarterly* 1994;57:4, 326–39.

Kassenbaum, Gene, David Ward, and Daniel Wilner, *Prison Treatment and Parole Survival: An Empirical Assessment,* Wiley, New York, 1971.

Lauderdale, Pat, "Deviance and Moral Boundaries," *American Sociological Review* August 1976;41:660–76.

Loether, Herman, and Donald McTavish, *Descriptive and Inferential Statistics,* 4th ed., Allyn & Bacon, Boston, 1993.

Riley, Mathilda White, *Sociological Research: A Case Approach,* Harcourt, Brace, New York, 1963.

Roethlisberger, F. J., and W. J. Dickson, *Management and the Worker,* Harvard University Press, Cambridge, MA, 1939.

Ross, John A., and Perry Smith, "Designs of the Single-Stimulus, All-or-Nothing Type," *American Sociological Review,* February 1965;30:68–80.

CHAPTER SEVEN

SURVEY RESEARCH

Surveys are a common method of data collection in the United States today. There are many polling organizations, which act as independent businesses or as units within newspapers, government agencies, and universities. By now the U.S. public knows what to expect of polls and surveys. For example, one university-based survey organization conducts an annual survey of households in the state in which it is located to find out about a variety of topics of interest to academic researchers and various other agencies that submit questions for the survey. Topics such as gambling, quality of life, public issues, community, the media, and awareness of different organizations are included, in addition to background and demographic questions such as age, marital status, gender, residential area, social class, and work status.

Survey organizations such as this university-based one typically invest considerable effort in creating a schedule of questions to be asked and conduct a number of trial interviews to test the procedure and question wording. Then the survey is started. This particular survey targets a random sample of households throughout the state and conducts telephone interviews using a staff of trained interviewers in a central university location. A sample of phone numbers to call is purchased from a company that specializes in supplying updated lists of this sort. Interviewers call each number, identify a randomly selected member of the household who is 18 years of age or older (those in institutions such as college dorms, nursing homes, or prisons are excluded from this survey), and then complete an interview schedule. There is a routine for calling back (up to six times) those who do not answer the phone the first time. Interviewing takes several weeks.

In a recent Minnesota household survey, about 2,300 phone numbers were called, of which 1,228 were potential or actual interviews (some refused and some numbers were still active on the callback list by the interviewing deadline). Of the original 2,300 phone numbers used, nearly half (40%) were not households, were not working telephone numbers, or were disconnected. A few were omitted because of language problems or because there was no response after six attempted calls. Overall, 65% of the potential interviews were completed (response rates of 70% to 85% or more are desired and generally achievable with careful follow-up).

In this case, each interviewer sat in front of a computer that automatically presented questions in the proper order and allowed the interviewer to enter answers directly into a computer file (the system is called **computer-assisted telephone interviewing,** or **CATI**). This step is done using a printed schedule filled in by hand when a CATI system is not available. Then the actual interview schedules are assigned a case identification number and edited for completeness, and responses are coded, usually numerically; then data are entered into a computer file for statistical analysis.

From an analysis of these data they are able to say, for example, that 39% of the households were two-person households, 62% would like to work at home at least part of the time, and 52% agree that one of their greatest fears is being financially dependent on their family in old age (Armson, 1997). Within margins of sampling error, the results presumably describe views characteristic of Minnesota households at the time the survey was conducted.

This study is illustrative of the kinds of survey research designs, techniques, and issues involved in surveys that are discussed in this chapter. We start with a discussion of four important principles that underlie the choice of survey research designs.

PRINCIPLES

Like other research strategies, surveys have distinctive features that focus much of the investigator's attention and effort. In survey research, four principles tend to be at the center of planning efforts: representativeness, time, competing explanations,

"A recent survey showed that ninety-five per cent of the nation's high-school students had never heard of Costa Rica, but they all knew about yours truly!"

and the distinctive data-gathering social encounters of survey research. These are considered in turn.

Representativeness

Surveys generally strive to represent a defined population, such as all households in Minnesota in 1996 or all adults in the United States in 1990 or all manufacturing firms in New York in 1997. To do this, a sample is drawn from a defined population of cases of interest. The sample is usually a random sample or one that approximates a random sample, giving each unit in the population a known (often equal) chance of being included in the sample. Sample outcomes are usually described statistically, using procedures of inferential statistics, and findings from the sample are generalized to stand as a description of the entire target population. Chapter 5 describes how this is possible, and statistics books also describe the inferential logic behind random sampling. Box 7.1 reviews the argument.

Survey research designs represent a different research trade-off than the experimental research designs discussed in Chapter 6. Surveys are very good at generalizing a description of characteristics that are measured on a carefully drawn sample of cases. Emphasis is placed on attaining results that are representative of a larger, defined population of cases. Recall from Chapter 6 that representativeness (external validity) is one of the weaknesses of typical experimental designs. Thus, survey designs are a welcome addition to the investigator's toolkit. Surveys, like other methods, have their own strengths and weaknesses.

As described in Chapter 5, surveys stress defining the case (i.e., unit of analysis) and the population to which results are to be generalized, identifying a sampling frame that accurately lists members of the population, and then drawing a suitably sized sample by random sampling (or other probability sampling) procedures. Problems in drawing a sample generally revolve around finding an

BOX 7.1
ON THE INFERENTIAL ARGUMENT

An investigator's educated guess from very little data may be correct. Conclusions based on a carefully drawn random sample also may be incorrect. The problem is that an investigator needs to show how the conclusion is reached: *How* does one know what one claims to know? The value of a random sample (or one derived from another probability sampling procedure) from a population is that it provides criteria for making generalizations and helps an investigator assess the risks of making false generalizations. This line of reasoning has proved useful in reaching conclusions that others can replicate. Educated guesses generally do not provide a basis for replication by others and are thus less desirable as a way to support generalizations about a broader population.

accurate and up-to-date **sampling frame** from which to draw a sample and engaging respondents sufficiently so that the **nonresponse rate** is very small in order to minimize the chance of ending up with a biased sample. There are other ways of sampling (e.g., cluster samples, multistage samples, stratified samples) that help implement the process of drawing a representative sample with a sufficiently small sampling error (see Chapter 5). Questionnaire design, interviewer training, and follow-up procedures that we discuss in this chapter help minimize nonresponse.

Time

Survey research generally is conducted at one point in time and thus is called a **cross-sectional design** (surveys may take weeks to complete, but respondents are generally asked questions at only one point in time). In the symbols used in Chapter 6, a survey design would be expressed as

x O

Only one observation or measurement occasion is used. In this case, any *x* (treatment or causes, known or unknown) will have had its impact before the survey is conducted and, in any event, is generally not under the control of the investigator. Surveys thus must ask about the state of independent variables (the *x*) at the same time that the dependent variables are measured because it is generally not known ahead of time what prior experiences or treatments cases have had. Some information that may help establish time order can be gathered by using retrospective questions, asking the respondent about some event in the past (such as "Was your mother working outside the home when you were sixteen?"), although current circumstances may color reporting of past events.

Sometimes the survey design can track changes over time by including repeated surveys of the same respondents; this design is called a **panel study.** Alternatively, a series of samples might be used, sampling different cases that are nevertheless drawn from a similarly defined sampling frame at one or more later points in time (a **trend study**). Thus, in the United States one can identify trends in attitudes toward the police, for example, by examining successive national surveys that measure this variable. Yet each survey is a time-slice, like a frame in a motion picture. Surveys provide a good description of the state of some variable at some point in time but generally give a poorer picture of the details of an ongoing social process. Time order is especially important in studies that attempt to explain outcomes by identifying factors that may influence or produce certain outcomes under certain conditions, or studies of social processes.

Can surveys be experiments? It is sometimes possible to use a true experimental design in survey research. This would happen when the stimulus is given to a random subset of those surveyed. For example, studies of question order or question wording might involve randomly using different forms of a questionnaire. In this case, the researcher has control of the time order (e.g., question ordering, then the subject's response) and over whom is given the experimental stimulus (e.g., respondents getting questions in one order versus another), a central requirement for experimental designs.

Competing Explanations

Although survey designs are excellent for descriptive generalizations at one point in time, they are problematic for explanatory research. If investigators expect that family type (coming from a divorced home rather than an intact family) has some impact on juvenile delinquency, they could ask in a survey what type of home the respondent came from, and they could ask about participation in delinquency. Then the researcher could determine whether the association of home type and delinquency is statistically significant (see Chapter 6 for a definition of this term). Even assuming that these variables are accurately measured, it would be difficult to claim that type of home causes delinquency. Why?

You will recall that a causal claim needs three kinds of evidence. First, there must be a correlation between the cause and its effect (which may be shown in survey research data); second, the cause must occur *before* the effect in that time order; third, there can be no other competing (alternative) explanations that account for the findings. Survey research has problems providing data for the latter two requirements (time order or causal order, and competing explanations).

First, surveys typically measure all variables at the same time. Thus, it is difficult to determine whether the measured cause occurred before its outcome. In some cases this problem can be handled by looking at what is plausible. For example, if one asked whether the subject's parents were divorced when the respondent was 16 (a retrospective question), one might expect these data to represent accurately the true state of affairs at a point in the past. This would be reasonable even though the question was answered at a later time. But memory could be a problem, and there may be other reasons for giving a false answer to the question. Retrospective questioning works well for such things as "How old were you when you graduated from high school?" and less well when you ask "How did you feel about your parents' marriage before you knew they were divorcing?" Therefore, retrospective questioning poses problems that must be considered.

As Davis (1985) points out, there may be other logical bases for establishing a probable time order of variables. For example, graduation from college comes after graduation from high school, a respondent's parents' first jobs probably came before the respondent's first job, gender socialization usually comes before current views on how best to get a job, religious background might come before one's current attitude toward the death penalty, and being married may or may not come before having a child. But what about work status and job skills ("Do you have a journalism job?" and "Are you good at spelling?"). Notice that the time order is sometimes tenuous when it is based only on reasoning rather than direct measurements. Experimental designs that control when a treatment is introduced and then measure the outcome at a later time make the time order of cause and effect much clearer.

The second problem for survey research, handling alternative explanations of findings, is even more serious. Typically, in experiments both the time order and alternative explanations problems are eliminated by the way the research is designed. The investigator controls when the causal variable (treatment) is introduced and when outcomes are measured, and eliminates alternative explanations by random assignment of cases to experimental and control groups (see Chapter 6). In survey research, such controls are typically not possible. Whatever has caused a measured response by a subject has already occurred, along with many other things. The investigator does not know which of these possible events led to the measured outcomes. In order to rule out alternative explanations, the investigator must develop a strategy to control for these other possible effects. In survey research, this is attempted by using **statistical controls.**

For example, if an investigator finds that boys' self-esteem continues to rise throughout high school but girls' self-esteem does not rise as steadily, the investigator would want to control statistically for other things that might have produced different growth rates of self-esteem. Did the girls come from larger families than the boys? To check this, one could divide the sample into those who came from large families and those who came from small families and see whether the difference in self-esteem development between boys and girls is still evident, controlling for family size. Would intact versus broken families account for differences in self-esteem of boys and girls? Maybe the difference can be explained by the different types of school systems through which the boys and girls traveled. The number of alternative explanations of the findings may be quite large. To do this kind of dividing up into subgroups that are similar on some potential causal variable, the survey must ask questions about each of these potential explanatory variables so they can be statistically controlled. Surveys tend to be longer if there is an explanatory interest because the investigator must ask about all possible alternative explanations. This process is limited, of course, to factors that the investigator can think of or are suggested by relevant literature on the topic. In any event, resources and the length of the questionnaire usually limit the number of potential explanatory variables that can be included. This means that surveys can never be definitive about whether a particular "cause" is really the cause of some outcome. By contrast, experimental research, by random assignment of cases to control and experimental groups, provides greater assurance about whether a particular variable is a potential cause of some outcome (at least for the cases in the experiment).

A strength of survey research is that it can begin to address questions for which experimental manipulation of cases is not possible. One could not randomly assign people to different genders, and even if it were possible, one probably would not randomly assign people to different careers. Practical considerations and ethical norms prevent experimental research on many important research problems. The survey research approach, by statistically accounting for at least the potential alternative explanations that theory or creative insight suggest, permits serious explanatory research on many of the important research questions that social scientists investigate.

The Social Context of the Data-Gathering Encounter

Data are always gathered in some type of social encounter. Social encounters generally involve expectations, certain skills, and various social pressures that may affect the data. This is as true of survey research as of every other type of social science research (and probably all research). What type of social encounter is generally involved in survey research, and what are its consequences?

Survey research usually involves asking questions rather than observing as a way of measuring concepts. Questions are formed, ideally in an understandable and standard way, and posed for the respondent. The encounter is generally a one-time, fairly brief affair between strangers. A minimal level of confidence and trust must be established, and the respondent must feel that it is sufficiently worthwhile to participate in the question-and-answer episode and provide accurate information. Three general data-gathering encounters are typical of survey research: personal interviews, phone interviews, and mailed questionnaires (with a range of other variations).

Personal Interviews. The **personal interview** is an encounter in which an interviewer (someone who is acceptable to the respondent, often a middle-aged woman who is similar in background to the respondent) asks questions and records answers. This encounter usually takes place in the respondent's own location (e.g., at home, work, in school, or on the street). Interviewers often try to find situations that are calm, when the respondent is alone and distractions are minimized. The interviewer has been trained in personal interviewing and is experienced in asking questions and recording answers. The list of questions is called an **interview schedule,** and it often contains various notes and reminders to the interviewer that make asking questions and recording responses easy and accurate. An advantage of personal interviews is that the interviewer can clarify questions that the respondent does not readily understand and can observe the respondent during the interview.

Phone Interviews. In the case of the phone interview, the interviewer may be located anywhere as long as a phone connection can be made with the respondent. Respondents are near phones when they are at home or at work, and this affects the time of the call. Getting a desired person on the phone may involve going through some gatekeeper who screens calls. In fact, many phones are unlisted, many people share the same telephone (some have more than one phone), and some people do not have a telephone. These facts are related to possible contaminating factors such as social class and life stage. In a more remote (but less costly) way, the interviewer must establish rapport and complete the interview. Phone etiquette may keep the respondent from abruptly hanging up. Phones also allow the interviewer (with permission) to make a good recording of an open-ended response. Again, the interviewer is equipped with an interview schedule, which often includes aids to the interviewer who makes the call and fills in responses. Phone interviews are more efficient and less expensive than personal interviews.

Mailed Questionnaires. Although questionnaires are used in many different settings, the more common one is the mailed questionnaire, which the respondent receives in the mail, reads and completes, and returns by mail. Here the encounter occurs entirely through what is said in a **cover letter** and in the questionnaire itself, as well as its general appearance. The measuring instrument is called a **questionnaire** (rather than an interview schedule) because the respondents themselves fill in the answers. The questionnaire must be clear and easy to answer. In most industrialized countries the questionnaire has become so familiar that most respondents know what to expect and how it is handled. In some communities, norms and skills for this type of data-gathering encounter have not been developed, which can pose a problem with this type of research.

Other Data-Gathering Social Encounters. A number of other settings involve surveys in one way or another. For example, as part of some other transaction, the subject may be asked questions and is expected to record answers. Other situations might be surveys sent by e-mail or asked as a part of an application form, or made available in a restaurant or business to get customer satisfaction feedback. There are many others, as well as combinations of those mentioned.

In his total design method, Dillman (1978) suggests that it is useful to think of the respondent going through a cost–benefit analysis: What are the costs of becoming involved in the survey, and is there a sufficient perceived benefit that offsets the costs? Furthermore, the respondent must have a sense of trust that the encounter is what it seems to be. Costs can include many things, such as the time it takes to respond to the survey, the inconvenience of answering at the point the respondent happens to be contacted, the survey's interest or importance to the respondent, the ease of providing responses, the extent to which offensive or intrusive questions are raised, and the annoyance of deciding whether it is really a survey or another disguised sales pitch. According to Dillman, reducing costs might involve reducing the effort of the task, eliminating embarrassment or any sense of subordination, and making the task appear brief.

Benefits are equally subtle and varied. A respondent may be particularly interested in the topic and in voicing his or her opinion about that topic. Answering survey questions may be a nice break in whatever the respondent had been doing. The respondent may simply want to help the investigator complete his or her task. It may even appear to be a very important topic to investigate. An investigator can show positive regard for the respondent, use a consulting approach, and make the survey instrument interesting, according to Dillman. Sometimes an investigator attempts to provide low-cost extra benefits such as offering to send a summary report of the results, or giving a coin, pencil, or coupon of some sort in advance for the respondent's cooperation. A professional-looking questionnaire suggests that the investigator is careful and thoughtful and considers the topic important and cares about the respondent's ease in doing the task. Statements about the investigator's intention to treat the data as confidential or anonymous, an easy-to-answer, well-thought-out instrument, friendliness, and a return envelope with postage affixed are among the many items sometimes used to address the cost–benefit equation (Dillman, 1978). Trust is developed through research sponsors who are known and felt to be legitimate and neutral. Thinking back on the questionnaires you have answered, you can probably recall what led you to decide that it was worth responding.

Investigators and their subjects can be thought of in role terms, interacting according to perceptions of the situation and norms they can draw upon. Often the subject's role changes within the same encounter from one of a subject who is providing personal information to one of an expert informant who is providing factual information about someone or something else with which he or she is familiar (e.g., from "What is your gender?" to "What are your parents' occupations?").

The point is that a survey encounter, like other approaches to research, must be carefully examined as a social event and the implications for research taken into account. The type of encounter has a strong impact on how measuring instruments are created, what types of information and research questions can be addressed through surveys, and the kinds of bias and error that are likely to occur.

Ethical Issues in Survey Research

Typical survey research on adults usually raises few ethical issues. It is usually clear that a potential subject may ignore the questionnaire or refuse to be interviewed. Subjects are generally in their own territory and thus may feel a greater sense of control than in an experimental laboratory, for example. Sensitive questions may be skipped.

There are ethical considerations in the use of subject responses, and generally assurances of **anonymity** or at least **confidentiality** are given. With surveys, particularly those by mail, anonymity can be achieved. Often the identities of organizations and individuals are avoided in reporting specific survey findings.

Survey research on minors or vulnerable adults requires greater care. For example, certain sensitive topics are generally avoided unless prior approval is obtained from responsible caretakers. Harassment during survey research is generally avoided.

Finally, the ethical responsibility to those who use study findings demands the highest standards of care and accuracy in conducting the study and fully reporting findings.

TECHNIQUES OF SURVEY RESEARCH

Survey research typically involves four steps. Beyond the usual conceptualization and problem definition and basic design steps, survey research involves

- Finding a sampling frame for the desired population and selecting a sample
- Creating suitable measurement instruments
- Gathering the desired data
- Analyzing the data and writing up the results

In many respects surveys share these steps with other forms of research. Although many types of research involve identifying a sample of cases, the contexts of survey research give rise to special problems and opportunities. Random digit dialing (RDD) and computer-assisted telephone interviewing (CATI) are two examples discussed here.

Measurement also involves many issues and concerns that are common to all research. Survey research differs in the ability to ask questions and expect good answers. For example, considerable time is devoted to planning question order and keeping the subject's task clear and simple, considering how questions are posed, how they engage the respondent, and how easy they are to answer. Special ways of gathering data may or may not be possible in survey research and, because a large number of cases are typically gathered, analyzing survey data often involves statistical analysis. At each of these steps, survey research design influences the options that are available and the typical choices researchers make. We describe each of these steps in turn.

Establishing a Sampling Frame and Selecting a Sample

Conceptualization of a problem that calls for survey research generally implies that a target population has been identified. It is to this population that sample results are intended to be generalized. Some examples of populations that have been used include adults (or households) in various-sized political units such as cities, counties, states, or the coterminous United States (i.e., the lower 48 states, excluding Alaska and Hawaii). Sometimes definitions of a population are more detailed, such as "owners of Utah firms that employed more than 50 full-time employees in 1997," "people over age 65 whose household income is under the defined poverty level," "customers of various types of services from a specific bank," "upper-income baby-boom generation women who have retired from a career," "blocks in an urban area that are ethnically mixed," or "single-parent families with school-aged children." In addition, an explicit or implicit time frame and geographic location usually define the population of interest (e.g., "firms in Utah in 1997"), which makes it a finite population. Whatever the specifics of the definition, the target population must be clearly identified. Chapter 5 deals with these topics in more detail.

Once the population is clearly defined, a sampling frame (a list that comes as close as possible to identifying all cases in the specified population) must be identified. This is where investigators need to be resourceful. There is no current list of large or specialized populations, so some strategy must be developed that will give each member of the population some known chance of being drawn in the sample.

Usually the sampling frame has some inadequacies that must be corrected. For example, one might think that the current phone directory would be an appropriate sampling frame for households in the area. Unfortunately, phone books go out of date at rates as high as a third of the entries each year. Thus, a phone book does not cover families who have recently moved in or out of the area. Furthermore, some phones are intentionally unlisted, some families do not have private phones in their names, and some families have several phone lines. Some have one or more cellular phones and may not have a listed home phone apart from these. Others have special access codes known only to acquaintances. In the United States as a whole, approximately 92% of families have a phone, but this varies by family characteristics. It is also possible for local numbers to be forwarded to nonlocal households. Finally, several special populations are not covered by phone book entries, such as people who live in group quarters or institutions (e.g., nursing homes, college dorms, prisons, shelters). Thus, phone lists are problematic and likely to be biased toward more settled, conventional, economically secure households.

So how do investigators get their sampling frames? One source is commercial organizations that keep more up-to-date lists from censuses and other public records. These organizations have staff who can collate and organize lists and make them available to researchers. Another way is to sample from a more general list but ask **screening questions,** which allow the researcher to discard those not of the type that the conceptual population calls for. Sometimes this is done in studies of older people; the researcher calls homes and asks whether anyone in the household is, say, 65 years old or older and then asks to talk with that person (or randomly samples from two or more older people in the household). Many popular surveys screen to include only adults aged 18 or older. For studies focusing on formal organizations such as the government, a church, or a firm, there are often good lists of members or customers. Some retail firms ask each customer for his or her name and phone number for their computer database. Lacking a customer or membership list, many other innovative techniques provide an approximate sampling frame. For example, a store might survey car licenses in its parking lot over time and use public records to identify car-owner names and addresses in order to contact a sample of customers.

Multistage sampling procedures are often useful in solving sampling frame problems. For example, because there are usually good lists of geographic areas but not of entire populations of individuals or households, a first stage in sampling might be to select a sample of geographic areas randomly (such as cities or counties), followed by a second stage that establishes a sampling frame of desired cases from the selected geographic areas. This makes the creation of a sampling frame more manageable even if one needs to do a field trip to identify households in the selected geographic areas for purposes of drawing a sample. If a list of households is not available in some target community, one might randomly identify city blocks and assign interviewers in the field to start at a specific point (e.g., the house on the northeast corner of a block) and proceed in a defined direction, selecting households for interviews (according to a predetermined sampling plan). This gets around the need to identify households (e.g., where an up-to-date list is not available) until the interviewer is in the field.

Another technique that telephone interviewing permits is called **random digit dialing (RDD).** A computer randomly generates telephone numbers and thus provides a random sample of those with telephones at the time of the survey. Because many numbers are not assigned or are business numbers, researchers can use lists of telephone prefixes (the first three or four digits in a telephone number) where these have been screened by a commercial list provider to eliminate unassigned numbers. The computer then randomly generates the last digits to complete the phone number. Sometimes, if a list of complete telephone numbers is available, the last digit is increased by one for the purpose of potentially including unlisted numbers and to help ensure the subject's anonymity (i.e., the interviewer would not know the identity of the respondent).

The sampling frame must be examined to ensure accuracy and determine any biases that prevent it from adequately covering the intended population. Checks include comparing survey results with preexisting data from a sampling frame list or known characteristics of the target population (e.g., using census records to compare on relevant, available characteristics such as gender, age, work status, and residential area).

Developing a Survey Instrument

As noted in Chapter 3, measurement involves conceptual clarity about the phenomenon one wants to measure and operational definitions that reliably and validly measure that concept. Different research settings dictate a somewhat different selection among possible ways of measuring any given concept.

Unlike experimental research, the typical data-gathering social encounter in survey research (i.e., telephone or face-to-face interview or a mailed survey) generally takes place in the subject's own home or work context and is a brief, one-time encounter. In most survey research situations, the investigator and the subject are strangers so the investigator must gain acceptance from the subject and establish trust sufficient for getting complete, valid, and reliable answers. Thus, the questionnaire or interview schedule must be designed to help the interviewer establish rapport with respondents. Dillman's (1978) advice on reducing perceived costs and increasing perceived benefits is an important guide to creating a survey instrument. The investigator has several tools to accomplish this goal.

Introducing the Study. Often a brief explanatory introduction is given to the subject that explains what the investigator wants (stated briefly and in a way that doesn't bias future responses), why the subject was selected, for what the data will be used, and who is sponsoring the study. A good introduction also provides cues as to how the questioning will proceed. Sometimes an introductory letter is used, sent before the researcher mails the questionnaire, makes the phone call, or arrives for the personal interview. In the case of mailed surveys, a cover letter is generally included with the questionnaire to give needed explanations.

The purpose of an introductory letter is to alert a respondent to future contacts, help establish the legitimacy of the study (e.g., by the letterhead or signature on the letter), explain the importance of the study and its consequences, explain the tasks to be done, and begin to establish rapport. An introductory letter often is a signal of respect and importance, and it often decreases the nonresponse rate.

The survey instrument is usually in the form of a questionnaire or schedule of questions to be asked, with provision for recording answers. It differs in form depending on the method of data collection (a mailed questionnaire, a personal interview schedule, or a phone interview schedule). Whatever the form, the survey instrument includes measures of the study's dependent variables, the independent variables, and any other variables that may be an alternative explanation or may help in controlling or identifying important conditions affecting the relationship of independent and dependent variables. This list of variables is limited only by the purposes of the research, suggestions found in the literature, and the investigator's ideas.

Asking Good Questions. The survey instrument reflects the hypotheses and topics an investigator is pursuing. The temptation is to include things one is curious about even if they don't relate to the key purpose of the study. Good survey instruments are limited to the concepts that must be measured. To accomplish this, Labaw (1980) suggests that the investigator write down the reasoning and use of each potential question (i.e., questions and rationales side by side in two columns on a page) during the instrument development phase. The reasoning column is not included in the questionnaire, of course. If each question has a purpose, the overall questionnaire is likely to be efficient and effective.

Osgood (1957) identifies a number of ways questions can be asked that involve somewhat different tasks for the respondent and provide somewhat different kinds of information. Chapter 3 shows some of the alternatives Osgood identifies. One could ask respondents to

Rank a small set of items in terms of some criterion

Accept or reject (yes or no) an item in terms of his or her own opinions or internal standards

Indicate (on a scale) the degree to which he or she judges an item to approach some standard

Choose one or more items from a list, expressing his or her judgment of appropriateness for some purpose

Provide his or her own characterization of something posed by the researcher, as in writing down a word or paragraph or giving a verbal response in an open-ended way

Match one or more items in terms of some standard

Questions can be asked about attitudes, beliefs, events, behavior, and characteristics, as illustrated here.

ATTITUDES

1. How much of the time do you think you can trust the government in Washington to do what is right: just about always, most of the time, only some of the time, or almost never?
    1. Just about always
    2. Most of the time
    3. Only some of the time
    4. Almost never

2. Please tell me how much you agree or disagree with the following statement: "The success of my organization depends a lot on how well I do my job."
   1. Strongly agree
   2. Agree
   3. Disagree
   4. Strongly disagree

BELIEFS

3. Do you feel that the quality of life is better in America than in most other advanced industrial countries or about the same, or do you feel that people are better off in most other advanced industrial countries than they are in the United States?
   1. Better in America
   2. About the same
   3. Better in other advanced industrial countries
   4. Don't know
   5. No answer
   6. Not applicable
4. Do you believe that there is life elsewhere in the universe beyond the earth?
   1. Yes
   2. No
   3. Don't know
5. In your opinion, who should be most responsible for paying the cost of an aged parent's medical care, including mental health care and treatment?
   1. The person him/herself
   2. His/her family
   3. Government
   4. Insurance
   5. Private charity
   6. Don't know
   7. No answer
   8. Not applicable

EVENTS

6. Did you have a paying job last week?
   1. Yes
   2. No
7. The following questions are about your sister. If you have more than one adult sister, please think about the sister you have most contact with. How often did you see or visit with your sister in the past 12 months?
   ______ number of times in last 12 months
8. Sometimes at work people find themselves the object of sexual advances, propositions, or unwanted sexual discussions from coworkers or supervi-

sors. The advances sometimes involve physical contact and sometimes just involve sexual conversations. Has this ever happened to you?

1. Yes
2. No
3. Never have worked

BEHAVIOR

9. Listed on this card [in the personal interview, a card was shown to the subject] are examples of the many different areas in which people do volunteer activity. By volunteer activity I mean *not* just belonging to a service organization, but actually working in some way to help others for no monetary pay. In which, if any, of the areas listed on this card have you done some volunteer work in the past 12 months?

☐ health
☐ education
☐ religious organizations
☐ human services
☐ environment
☐ public/society benefit
☐ recreation: adults
☐ arts, culture, and humanities
☐ work-related organizations
☐ political organizations or campaigns
☐ youth development
☐ private and community foundations
☐ international/foreign
☐ informal/alone/not-for-pay
☐ other (specify)

CHARACTERISTICS

10. In what year were you born? _______ year (to compute age, subtract from survey year)
11. How many brothers or sisters did you have? Please count those born alive but no longer living as well as those alive now. Also include stepbrothers, stepsisters, and children adopted by your parents.
    __________ number of brothers and sisters
12. Are you currently married, widowed, divorced, or separated, or have you never been married?
    1. Married
    2. Widowed
    3. Divorced
    4. Separated
    5. Never married
13. What is the highest level of school you have completed?
    1. Less than high school
    2. Some high school
    3. High school graduate
    4. Some technical school
    5. Technical school graduate
    6. Some college

7. College graduate
8. Postgraduate or professional degree

14. What kind of work do you (did you normally) do? That is, what (is/was) your job called? ______________________________

Once the list of concepts to be measured has been developed, specific questions must be developed to measure each concept. Measures may be single indicators of a concept or multiple indicators that are combined in some way (see Chapter 3 on scaling) to form a measure of a concept. Notice that response categories for closed-ended or **structured questions** are mutually exclusive (categories don't overlap each other) and exhaustive (categories cover all substantive possibilities). Researchers prefer to use existing measures that have been checked and published and for which there is information about the measure's reliability and validity for the intended population. Lacking these, investigators must develop questions on their own. There are several good guides to developing questions, such as Payne (1951), Labaw (1980), Converse and Presser (1986), Fowler (1995), and Schuman and Presser (1996). We summarize some considerations they discuss at greater length.

Question Wording. A very large proportion of the words people use come from a fairly short list. Ninety percent of what is said or written comes from a vocabulary of about 5,000 words. These are the words that are known and used by most people and are preferred in phrasing questions for the general population. To communicate effectively with the broadest audience, one needs to phrase questions in simple, direct, and unambiguous language. Asking questions in the investigator's technical jargon rarely works well.

Word choice can have a large impact on responses one gets. For example, the words *could, might,* and *should* denote different things. Payne (1951) gives the example, "Do you think anything [might, could, should] be done to make it easier for people to pay doctor or hospital bills?" When the questions were asked in an early poll, 63% said something "might" be done, 77% said something "could" be done, and 82% said something "should" be done. How these words are used is known to make a substantial difference in outcomes!

Questions can be structured in an open-ended or closed-ended fashion. An **open-ended question** is one in which the respondent provides the answer without benefit of listed response categories. Examples such as age or number of sisters ask for a brief response. Other questions might require a word (e.g., occupation title) or a more extensive description (e.g., "What is the most important problem facing our nation today?"). An advantage of open-ended questions is that they do less prompting and thus reduce the potential bias in suggestive response categories. Open-ended questions may also save space when the number of potential response categories is large (e.g., zip codes, state, occupation). It is also a necessary approach when the investigator does not know what the response categories are (e.g., most important problem facing the nation). Disadvantages of open-ended questions are the coding efforts that are required to go through all the responses to develop categories and then apply those categories to the responses. An investigator may want only certain kinds of information, and providing the categories may help clarify precisely what is wanted. Sometimes a question combines both structured and unstructured responses, as in questions that provide a list of most common responses with an "other, please specify" category.

There are many lists of suggestions for making good survey questions, and the reader is urged to consult with some of the references mentioned earlier. Dillman (1978:96), for example, provides a few rules for desirable features of good questions:

Use simple words	Do not talk down to respondents
Do not be vague	Avoid bias
Keep it short	Avoid objectionable questions
Be specific but not too specific	Avoid hypothetical questions

How these work out in any given question is a matter of experience and pretesting. Ideally, a question will mean the same thing to different respondents. Some examples from Dillman (1978), shown in Figure 7.1, will help illustrate some of these points.

Question wording also depends on how questions are going to be presented. Questions presented in a self-administered questionnaire must stand alone without the possibility of explanations by an interviewer. An appropriate question on a

FIGURE 7.1 Illustration of Questions

POOR	BETTER REVISION
What percentage of your monthly income is spent on rent (or house payments)?	How much is your monthly rent (or house payment)? ________ dollars How much is your average monthly income? ________ dollars
Should the city manager not be directly responsible to the mayor? Yes No	To whom should the city manager be directly responsible: the mayor or the city council? 1. mayor 2. city council
When you go out to restaurants, which kind of restaurants do you most often go to? Those that serve foreign-style foods Those that serve American-style foods	If you were planning to eat out in a restaurant soon, do you think you would probably go to a restaurant that serves Foreign-style foods American-style foods

questionnaire may seem too formalistic and elaborate if spoken over the phone or in person. Phone interview questions must include response categories in the phrasing of the question itself because subjects cannot see the potential responses. On the other hand, personal interviews can present somewhat more complicated response tasks, such as sorting a small stack of cards, each having a response alternative, into some specified order or answering a series of questions with response categories that have been printed on a card given to the respondent for reference. Both telephone surveys and in-person interviews can do much more elaborate branching and skipping to follow-up questions that are relevant to an earlier response by the subject. An example of a question tailored to the different data-gathering encounters is as follows:

MAILED QUESTIONNAIRE

What do you think is the single most important problem facing people in Minnesota today?

____

____

TELEPHONE INTERVIEW

The first questions are about quality of life.

What do you think is the single most important problem facing people in Minnesota today?

(IF "TAXES," PROBE: Is that income taxes, property taxes, or sales tax?)

____

____

(PROBE "DON'T KNOW" RESPONSES)

IN-PERSON INTERVIEW

What do you think is the single most important problem facing people in Minnesota today?

(IF "TAXES," PROBE: Is that income taxes, property taxes, or sales tax?)

____

____

(PROBE "DON'T KNOW" RESPONSES)

Translating Questions into Other Languages. When a survey instrument used in one language is to be used with respondents who speak a different language, the investigator must translate the questions. It is often difficult for a literal translation of a question to capture the same meaning in another language. To accomplish the translation of a survey instrument, a process called **back translation** is used (Marsh, 1967: Chapter 8). This typically involves having a bilingual person who is a native in the other culture carefully translate the questions. This translation (not the original language version) is then given to another bilingual person to translate back into the first language. The back-translated version is compared to the original version to see whether the meaning remained the same.

Question Order and Formatting. The order of questions makes a difference in several respects. First, the flow of the entire survey instrument must help establish rapport and trust. Second, answers to preceding questions may affect answers to later questions. Third, grouping questions on similar topics together avoids the appearance of a confusing and chaotic instrument that has not been well thought out. Finally, some questions logically depend on answers to a prior question in a branching fashion.

The order of questions is one of the main ways in which an investigator can contribute to a respondent's developing interest in responding, build rapport, and engender trust. Usually the flow of questions moves from easier (but topically relevant and important) questions, to more difficult or detailed substantive questions, to background or demographic types of questions. For example, a first question might ask for an opinion on the topic at hand in a way that permits an easy entry into the subject of the survey (e.g., "The first questions are about quality of life. What do you think is the single most important problem facing people in the United States today?"). Selection of the first question is of special significance. Background characteristics (questions such as age, gender, marital and work status, education, and income) are best left to the end of the instrument. One reason for this is that the cover letter probably attempts to make the topic of the survey interesting and important, so starting with basic background information breaks the expectation that the researcher is interested in getting the respondent's ideas on the announced topic of the survey. Questions on similar topics should be kept together, and this may necessitate a statement to smooth the transition (e.g., "Now I'd like to ask you some questions about yourself.").

Similar questions are often grouped together for ease of response and efficiency. For example, a series of questions that have the same response categories may be presented in a **matrix format,** with the response categories listed across the top of a matrix-like form and the questions listed down the rows. Response categories for each question could then be lined up in columns under the proper headings, as in the following example.

Should it be possible for a pregnant woman to obtain a legal abortion under each of the following conditions? Please circle a number to indicate the extent to which you agree or disagree.

	STRONGLY DISAGREE	DISAGREE	AGREE	STRONGLY AGREE
a. If there is a strong chance of serious defect in the baby	1	2	3	4
b. If she is married and does not want any more children	1	2	3	4
c. If the woman's health is seriously endangered by the pregnancy	1	2	3	4
d. If the family has a very low income and cannot afford any more children	1	2	3	4
e. If she became pregnant as a result of rape	1	2	3	4

f. If she is not married and does not want to marry the man	1	2	3	4
g. If the woman wants it for any reason	1	2	3	4

A drawback of this type of format is that respondents may circle the same category by way of convenience (a **response set bias**) rather than considering response alternatives carefully after reading each question.

Some questions apply only to certain respondents. For example, questions on hours of work are relevant only for those who work. Some topics require further **probes,** necessitating follow-up questions relevant to certain respondents. The solution to these situations is to have **branching questions,** in which a respondent is directed to go to other questions depending on his or her answers to earlier ones. The branching structure may be quite extensive and, in the case of a questionnaire, a respondent may be directed to questions several pages later if the intervening ones are not relevant. Simple branching can be used in mailed questionnaires; boxes and arrows or special instructions direct the respondent to the question he or she should answer next. The problem is somewhat easier in the case of telephone or personal interviews because the interviewer (perhaps with the aid of a CATI program) is trained to skip over irrelevant questions easily and present only the relevant ones. The respondent is unaware that questions have been skipped. An example of a simple branching question follows.

Was your total household income in 1997 above or below $35,000? (circle the number that applies)

1. Above (if above, go to question **a,** below)
2. Below (if below, go to question **b,** below)

a. (IF ABOVE) I am going to mention a number of income categories. When I come to the category that describes your total household income *before* taxes in 1997, please stop me.
   - ☐ $35,000 to $40,000
   - ☐ $40,000 to $50,000
   - ☐ $50,000 to $60,000
   - ☐ $60,000 to $70,000
   - ☐ $70,000 to $80,000
   - ☐ $80,000 or more

b. (IF BELOW) I am going to mention a number of income categories. When I come to the category that describes your total household income before taxes in 1997, please stop me.
   - ☐ Under $5,000
   - ☐ $5,000 to $10,000
   - ☐ $10,000 to $15,000
   - ☐ $15,000 to $20,000
   - ☐ $20,000 to $25,000
   - ☐ $25,000 to $30,000
   - ☐ $30,000 to $35,000

There are a number of studies of features of questions, including question order and their consequences (Schuman and Presser, 1996; Schwarz et al., 1991). The sequence of questions may have an effect and must be examined carefully—for example, knowledge questions preceded by the information the next question requires or attitude questions preceded by questions that suggest a particular issue or context might alter responses. In phone interviews it is becoming standard practice to order randomly the sequence of questions within a topic area (e.g., a series of Likert scale items on a topic) so that any order effect is balanced out for the sample as a whole. This is possible when CATI programs are used but not practical (except through multiple forms of a questionnaire) for mailed questionnaires.

Length of Questionnaire or Interview. Well-crafted survey instruments may be very brief, such as one or two questions, or very lengthy. There have been successful questionnaires with several hundred questions. The key is the way in which the instrument is put together and how well it engages the interest of targeted respondents. Nevertheless, the general rule is to keep questionnaires as brief as possible and, by the format and number of questions on a page, to help the respondent feel a sense of progress through the questions. However, instrument length is generally not among the main reasons for nonresponse.

Pretesting the Instrument. The most important step in constructing a survey instrument is **pretesting.** The purpose of pretesting is to see whether respondents understand questions and give responses that can be interpreted by the investigator. In the case of interview schedules, a pretest also helps determine whether interviewers can use the instrument effectively. Pretesting involves giving the instrument to a small sample that includes as much of the variety of potential subjects as possible. Often respondents are observed as they answer a questionnaire or are asked afterward about their understanding, confusion, and frustration in answering the instrument. Dillman (1978) recommends that the investigator's professional colleagues and any users of the survey information also be recruited to review the instrument. All of this information leads to a revision of the problematic items and further pretesting until a satisfactory instrument has been developed. This step is perhaps the most important in creating a measurement instrument that works well in the planned data-gathering encounter.

Deciding on the Data-Gathering Approach

We have seen that the type of data-gathering encounter presents opportunities and constraints on the way questions are formed and put together in a measurement instrument. Here we summarize some of the strengths and weaknesses of each of these typical survey research procedures.

Phone Interviews. The telephone interview is a quick and efficient method of data collection. It is useful for rapidly unfolding events such as election campaigns or shifts in public opinion. Having a live interviewer helps in establishing rapport in a diverse sample of respondents and explaining questions as needed. Having an interviewer also aids in screening and in sampling among potential respondents within a family or small group, for example. Most people can be accessed by telephone, at least in more affluent societies. Computer aids to telephone interviewing can help handle problems of the sequence of presentation of items, complex branching, and direct data entry for more rapid analysis. Computer assistance also helps in randomly selecting numbers to call and in managing repeated callbacks at different times. In fact, telephone interviewing is quite helpful in tape recording open-ended responses because the respondent is comfortably close to a microphone (the telephone) and a tape recorder can be connected to the telephone line (with permission) for higher-quality recording that can be transcribed. The telephone interview helps bring reality to promises of anonymity because the interviewer need not know the identity of the respondent. Telephone interviews tend to have higher response rates than mailed questionnaires.

But telephone interviews also have drawbacks. Most phone lists such as the telephone directory are out-of-date and thus lead to underrepresentation of more mobile people. An increasing number of people cannot be accessed by phone, either because they cannot afford the service or they use various blocks to prevent others from knowing their number. Residents in group quarters may not be contacted directly by phone and institutional gatekeepers pose a problem for accessing the desired party. The telephone interview is a somewhat more remote encounter than the personal interview, requiring somewhat different efforts in establishing rapport. Because it is entirely auditory, the interviewer cannot observe body language, which might be useful in detecting problems with questions. In fact, the interviewer has little control over the respondent's social setting during the interview, which may be a problem when the survey is about sensitive issues. Only a low level of complexity can be readily handled in a telephone interview. No visual cues can be used, long response category lists are difficult to convey, and some forms of questions such as ranking or rating on a graphic scale are not readily adapted to this type of encounter. Phone interviews are more costly than questionnaires because they require the time of interviewers to make calls and, potentially, long-distance telephone charges. Finally, the telephone interview requires a coordination of interviewing time between interviewer and subject. Subjects working odd hours may have little chance of being interviewed, and lengthy interruption of respondents busy at other things may lead to more refusals.

Mailed Questionnaires. Mailed questionnaires are very cost-effective in a society with a good public postal service. Because most people are familiar with questionnaires and can read, most questions can be asked effectively. More-elaborate response formats (e.g., matrix-formatted questions, semantic differential scales) can be used when the mode is paper and pencil. A respondent is able to refer back to prior answers and that may help reduce inconsistencies. Mailed questionnaires can also preserve subject anonymity (the investigator generally does not know who is identified with a particular questionnaire) and confidentiality (a detached matching list of identities can be used to mask the identity of questionnaires when respondents are known). Potential interviewer effects are avoided in mailed surveys. A mailed survey, unlike the personal interview, can take a short time to conduct, depending on mail delays.

Mailed questionnaires also have drawbacks. The response rate is generally lower than for telephone or in-person interviews, but follow-up strategies are effective in increasing response rates. Editing and data entry tasks generally increase the time to compile the final data file ready for analysis. More-complex kinds of data, such as life histories or topics that require extensive probing, are less easily handled by mailed survey. Essentially, the questionnaire must be complete and self-contained.

Personal Interviews. Among the advantages of a personal interview is that the interviewer can do some observing as well as listening. Body language, the setting of the data-gathering encounter, and personal attributes of the subject are all within view and can be noted. Interviewers are more in control of the interview setting and can be sure that the subject is alone and not distracted. Establishing rapport and trust may also be more direct and easier. Interviewers are able to introduce and move through complex topics, probe as needed, and introduce more complex tasks such as having the subject sort cards (e.g., Q-sorts), become involved in data-gathering games and simulations, or give responses to pictures. The ability to follow up and probe unclear responses is especially helpful. Field interviewers may also be able to handle difficult sampling problems, such as randomly selecting an adult from a household or determining how to sample a block of houses when data about the block are not otherwise available. Personal interviews receive high marks for accuracy of information, completeness, ability to handle sensitive material, and overall reliability and validity. The response rate for personal interviews is generally highest among the three survey modes discussed here, generally five percentage points higher than phone interviews.

Drawbacks of personal interviews include the high cost of travel and interviewing time. It is a time-consuming activity that requires skilled interviewers. Unlike the CATI possibility for telephone interviews, personal interview schedules must be edited, coded, and entered in a computer file for analysis. It is harder to make good on promises of confidentiality (and impossible to assure anonymity) because the interviewer knows the location of the respondent and could recognize the person in other settings. Like telephone interviews, in-person interviews require coordinating schedules.

Reducing Nonresponse Bias

The greater the nonresponse in surveys, the greater the likelihood that the resulting sample will be biased in some respect. Nonresponse is unlikely to be random. Thus, it is important to reduce nonresponse as much as possible in order to limit the possibility for bias. Many techniques have been proposed for reducing nonresponse, including using hand-affixed rather than metered postage and using personalized cover letters (Parton, 1950; Dillman, 1978). Managing the cost–benefit problem from the respondent's point of view helps reduce nonresponse. Given an otherwise adequate survey instrument, following up on nonrespondents is the most effective strategy. In personal and phone interviews, repeated callbacks would be used. In mailed surveys it is common practice to send reminder postcards a week or so after the initial mailing and send repeated requests, including new questionnaires, to those who have not responded. Finally, phone calls may be used to identify reasons for nonresponse and to seek more responses. In order to preserve anonymity, an investigator may include a separate response postcard for the subject to return, indicating that he or she has completed the questionnaire. The postcard, not the questionnaire, would have the respondent's identity. Then follow-up efforts could be limited to those who had not mailed in the separate response card. Good introductions, affiliation with trustworthy sponsors, assurances of confidentiality or anonymity, and professionally produced survey instruments all contribute to higher response rates.

Finally, as noted earlier, it is helpful to know the nature of any sampling bias so that this can be taken into account in interpreting the findings. Comparison of the achieved sample with other data taken from census records or prior research helps in this task.

Preparation for Statistical Analysis

Once the survey has been completed, several steps are needed before the data are ready for analysis. Typically, questionnaires or interview schedules are scanned and edited to be sure that they are clear for coders. Coding involves establishing variables and categories, usually including nonresponse categories such as don't know (DK), no response (NR), not applicable (NA), and refused. A codebook that lists variables and instructions for coding them is essential. This is used by trained coders to code the data in preparation for data entry into a computer file. Data entry is followed by preliminary computer runs to identify coding and transcription errors (see Chapter 10 on data analysis).

Open-ended responses generally require more-extensive reading and coding and thus take more time. Computer-assisted content analysis may be helpful when verbatim text responses are used. When coding is done by hand, random recoding is useful to detect errors and measure coder reliability.

A hallmark of good research is thorough checking, both minor and major, that occurs before the analysis begins. This step applies to all research, but survey research often involves some special checks. For example, because surveys strive for good representation of a population, checks are usually used to see whether the sample corresponds to the desired population. Sometimes this is not possible because little is known about a population. In other cases some checks can be made. For example, for a sample that is to represent the general adult population, a comparison might be made of the age distribution in the sample with an age distribution from a recent census, making sure to compare only relevant categories meeting the sampling criterion (adult).

Archives of Survey Data

Increasingly, an investigator may be fortunate enough to find that the relevant data have already been gathered by someone else, perhaps the U.S. Census or an academic or commercial polling agency. The General Social Survey is a nearly annual survey of noninstitutionalized adults in the continental United States, using a questionnaire that includes many of the variables important to social scientists. There are also longitudinal data sets on individual development (see Chapter 9 on secondary data). Cases include individuals as well as organizations of various types. Archives of carefully checked, documented, and maintained machine-readable research data are available from a number of sources, including the Inter-University Consortium for Political and Social Research (ICPSR) at the University of Michigan (Web site: http://www.icpsr.umich.edu). Miller (1991:189–213) provides a useful list of some of these archives.

An investigator who uses **archival data** needs complete information about the context in which the data were gathered and the processes of coding and checking that lie behind the data set.

ISSUES IN SURVEY RESEARCH

Problem of Nonexperimental Design and Trade-offs

The survey strategy generally trades off clarity about cause for representation of a larger, defined population. The consequence is that those interested in causal linkages must go beyond showing a relationship between dependent and independent variables and directly address the two other requirements for documenting causal influences. First, survey researchers must deal with the question of time order (did the cause come before the effect?) and then with the question of other potential causes of a relationship between independent and dependent variables. This leads to the need to measure those other factors and the possibility of missing some, plus the general need for larger volumes of data to analyze more-complex relationships adequately. Depending on the stage of progress on a research question, establishing a probable causal relationship may be less critical than establishing that a relationship is probably a characteristic of the larger population. Descriptive research (such as a public opinion poll) is particularly interested in population descriptions, so the survey trade-off strategy is suitable. Finally, the survey strategy may be the only available strategy if the independent variables cannot or should not be manipulated. Randomly assigning marital status, for example, is probably not possible, so an experimental design may not be possible for studies of the effects of marital status.

Problem of Sampling Frame Availability

Another problem for survey research is finding an adequate sampling frame for the population of interest. Most sampling frames (e.g., the phone book) are quickly dated and exclude important segments of the population. Sampling strategies can often help achieve the goals of representative sampling in the absence of some lists (e.g., multistage samples), but the overall problem remains and inspires creativity among survey researchers.

Problem of Data-Gathering Social Encounters and Sources of Bias

Data-gathering encounters always have an impact on the data that are generated. The objective of survey research, as with other forms of research, is to minimize these influences. Thus, in some situations mailed questionnaires are better than telephone or face-to-face interviews. Data-gathering encounters should be designed to reduce subjects' tendencies to give more socially desirable answers, withhold criticism or sensitive information, and exaggerate or conceal private information.

In this regard, in the case of face-to-face interviewing, it is important to give consideration to possible effects of interviewer characteristics. For some studies female interviewers may be more effective than males. For other studies the ways the interviewers are dressed may be more important than their gender. It may even be necessary to do a pilot study involving some preliminary interviewing to determine what interviewer characteristics are relevant for a particular study.

Confidentiality and Anonymity

Anonymity means that it is impossible (or that no attempt will be made) to determine the identity of a case (i.e., a person or organization). *Confidentiality* means that an investigator knows the identity of the case but will not reveal it. There are no laws in the United States that protect research confidentiality or anonymity. Identity lists can be legally obtained by subpoena. Thus, to make an assurance of confidentiality real, an investigator must take steps to make it real. For example, questionnaires or interview schedules generally request that the respondent not provide his or her name or identity, but each instrument is assigned a sequential identification number. This permits researchers to correct errors in a computer data file by referring to the correct survey instrument (with the same ID number) without using personal identifiers such as the respondent's name. When there is a genuine research need to recontact the respondent, a **matching list** that contains the assigned ID number and the respondent's identity is kept in a safe place. This might be necessary for checking on interviewer performance early in a study, filling in missing information during the instrument editing and coding phase, matching the survey data with variables from other sources, or reinterviewing the same respondents in a panel study. Under threat of disclosure, an investigator would have to decide whether to destroy the matching list in order to protect the assurance of confidentiality. The main point here is that ethical investigators must conduct their research in such a way that assurances given to a subject are carried out.

Myths about Survey Research

The following are claims that are heard about survey research.

- "Only short questionnaires will be answered."

According to Dillman (1978:55), questionnaires up to 12 pages or about 125 items appear to pose no response-rate problem. Unless the mail questionnaire is especially well designed, introduced, and followed up, some drop in response rate may occur for longer questionnaires. Face-to-face or personal interviews do not appear to have the same limitations, although a clear focus on the study's intent is always important. Phone interviews can also be long, although the cost of a separate phone interview may not be very different from the cost of adding additional items to a single interview.

- "It's an easy, quick process that anyone can do well enough."

Any inquiry that hopes to generate findings that will stand critical examination requires a great deal of planning, clarity, and skill. For example, insight into the consequences of a particular type of data-generating social encounter is needed. Knowing steps to ensure high response rates and to carry out sampling so that inference can be made to a population is both a technical specialty and an art. Surveys by uninformed people rarely achieve more than a 50% response rate, but the norm for professionally designed and executed surveys is 70% or higher. Knowing how to select needed measures or convert measures so that they work well in different survey contexts also requires considerable skill and pretesting.

- "It's the method of choice in the social sciences."

Although it is true that many research reports in journals are based on surveys, this design is often not the best option. Surveys are strong when the problem is one of generalizability of findings to a defined, larger population. They are weak in eliminating alternative explanations of an outcome and addressing historic or through-time process issues. Reasons for the survey popularity may have more to do with short turnaround times for reporting findings, the socialization of people who are able to answer short, structured questions, and research funding limitations, rather than requirements of a research question. As a method, it is probably more popular than it should be.

- "Results can't be trusted because people lie."

When properly asked, most questions appear to receive honest answers. One problem is phrasing a question that a respondent is in a position to answer and creating a situation of trust that is as neutral as possible. Some survey approaches raise special problems. For example, face-to-face interviews introduce greater opportunities for a respondent to feel under pressure to give a socially desirable answer. This pressure is diminished by the telephone interview and the mailed questionnaire. Voting polls are very accurate if they are well done. Exit polls often predict the outcome of elections within very, very narrow margins, for example.

- "Some data are better than no data."

Confronted with a low response rate, questions that are ambiguous or misunderstood, or a survey that doesn't include critically needed variables, an investigator may nevertheless be tempted to analyze the findings and report them under the assumption that some data are better than none. But poor data lead to poor conclusions. Defective data should be set aside and not used. Sometimes it is possible to compare the sample with expected population characteristics, and sometimes this comparison may suggest that nonresponse bias is low. In such situations, indicators of data quality (such as a low response rate) may turn out not to indicate response bias problems. Defective data are worse than no data at all.

SUMMARY

In this chapter we have presented a variety of ways in which surveys are designed and conducted. One of the main strengths of a survey trade-off is that of external validity: the generalizability of findings from a sample to a population. The cost of this trade-off is in the need to ask about potential explanatory variables so that statistical controls can be used. There are ethical issues in survey research. Although these are generally less problematic than in other forms of research discussed here, they are important.

Three types of data-generating encounters are usually associated with survey research: mailed questionnaires, phone interviews, and personal interviews. The first requires an instrument that the subject can read and understand. Questionnaires may contain precoding of structured questions and may also include unstructured questions. Design of this instrument so that it provides a proxy dialog between the investigator and the subject requires attention to introductions (sponsorship and instructions), question wording, question order, and the overall professional appearance of the instrument.

Phoned and personal interviews permit the interviewer to probe and explain questions further than is possible in mailed questionnaires. The instrument used in phoned or personal interviews is called an interview schedule. It generally contains considerable information of use to the interviewer, such as suggested probes, space to record responses, and items that the interviewer may fill out but not ask directly of the respondent (observations about the setting, notes on how well the interview went, recording obvious things that can be observed, etc.).

TERMS TO KNOW

Alternative (competing) explanations
Anonymity
Archival data
Back translation
Branching questions
Causal order
Computer-assisted telephone interviewing (CATI)
Confidentiality
Cover letter
Cross-sectional design
Interview schedule
Matching list
Matrix format
Nonresponse rate
Open-ended questions
Panel studies
Personal interviews
Pretesting
Probes
Questionnaire
Random digit dialing (RDD)
Response set bias
Sampling frame
Screening questions
Statistical control
Structured questions
Trend studies

ISSUES AND COMPARISONS

Confidentiality versus anonymity
Respondent as subject versus expert informant
Trade-offs of survey versus experimental design
Methods of handling competing explanations of findings in survey research
Source of sampling frames
Types of samples
Data-gathering social encounters in surveys
Ethical concerns in survey research
Dillman's total design method
Myths of survey research
Costs and benefits for respondents in surveys
Different tasks in questions to a respondent
Advantages and disadvantages of structured versus unstructured questions
Qualities of good questions
Issues of question ordering and format

EXERCISES

1. Find two examples of survey instruments. Perhaps one could be a commercial survey and one could be from an academic survey organization. Critique the strengths and weaknesses of these using the criteria in this chapter.

2. Identify a concept you might be interested in measuring (not a standard one such as age, sex, or income). Then develop an item to measure that concept in a questionnaire and then in an interview schedule. What differences are there between these two questioning formats?

3. If you are to do your own research project in this course, draft the instrument in the Labaw format of question (in one column) and corresponding rationale or use (in a parallel column).

4. Use a questionnaire or interview schedule you have developed for your project (or a questionnaire you have available from some other source) to conduct one or two pretests. What have you learned about the questions from using them? What changes would you make and why?

REFERENCES

Armson, Rossana, *The 1996 Minnesota State Survey: Results and Technical Report,* Minnesota Center for Survey Research, University of Minnesota, Minneapolis, 1997.

Converse, Jean M., and Stanley Presser, *Survey Questions: Handcrafting the Standardized Questionnaire,* Sage, Newbury Park, CA, 1986.

Davis, James A., *The Logic of Causal Order* (Sage University Paper 55), Sage, Newbury Park, CA, 1985.

Dillman, Don A., *Mail and Telephone Surveys: The Total Design Method,* New York, Wiley, 1978.

Fowler, Floyd J., Jr., *Improving Survey Questions: Design and Evaluation,* Sage, Newbury Park, CA, 1995.

Labaw, Patricia, *Advanced Questionnaire Design,* Abt Books, Cambridge, MA, 1980.

Marsh, Robert M., *Comparative Sociology: A Codification of Cross-Societal Analysis,* New York, Harcourt, Brace, 1967.

Miller, Delbert C., *Handbook of Research Design and Social Measurement,* 5th ed., Sage, Newbury Park, CA, 1991.

Osgood, Charles E., George J. Suci, and Percy H. Tannenbaum, *The Measurement of Meaning,* Urbana, University of Illinois Press, 1957.

Parton, Mildred, *Surveys, Polls, and Samples: Practical Procedures,* New York, Harper, 1950.

Payne, Stanley L., *The Art of Asking Questions,* Princeton University Press, Princeton, NJ, 1951.

Schuman, Howard, and Stanley Presser, *Questions and Answers in Attitude Surveys: Experiments on Question Form, Wording and Context,* Sage, Newbury Park, CA, 1996.

Schwarz, N., B. Knauper, H. J. Hippler, E. Noelle-Neumann, and L. Clark, "Rating Scales: Numeric Values May Change the Meaning of Scale Labels," *Public Opinion Quarterly* 1991;55:570–82.

CHAPTER EIGHT

CASE STUDY RESEARCH

Experiments and surveys, the research strategies discussed in Chapters 6 and 7, typically involve many cases, and data on the cases are usually pooled or averaged in some way. Social scientists also conduct **systematic research** using only a single case or a few contrasting cases. Social scientists have conducted **case studies** of slum neighborhoods, various immigrant communities, social movements, drug gangs, neighborhood organizations, small rural communities, religious groups, small friendship groups, and large corporations. Whyte and Gans provide examples of field observation case study research.

A classic line of research on urban slum communities was conducted in the north end of Boston by William F. Whyte, Jr., and reported in his book, *Street Corner Society* (1955). Later, Herbert Gans conducted a similar study of second-generation Italians in the adjacent west end of Boston, reporting it in his book *Urban Villagers* (1962). Both researchers spent considerable time living and working in the communities, participating in events, observing everyday life, asking questions, and keeping copious notes. Gans and his wife lived in this "slum" neighborhood as he carried out his research. His observations identified the kinds of social networks in which the west-enders, young and old, were embedded, which he calls the peer group society. His analysis identified a basic paradox. Although the peer group provided people with a setting to express their individuality, these groups rarely worked together on problems and issues, such as an impending urban renewal project slated for their area.

Data for Gans's study came from observations he made while using the stores and facilities in that neighborhood, attending meetings and public gatherings, visiting with neighbors and friends, interviewing community representatives (formally and informally), talking with **informants,** and generally observing what was going on around him. Overall, he estimates that he actually talked with 100 to 150 of the 3,000 west-enders, intensely with 20 who were most involved in the peer group he joined at the invitation of a neighbor. Because peer groups were generally segregated by gender, Gans's wife provided information about women's groups she attended. Gans wrote his observations and reflections about them in a research journal. Later these voluminous notes served as the data to be coded or organized by the themes and topics in which he became interested (Gans, 1962).

The process of doing case study research by field observation techniques raised a number of problems about gaining access, building trust and rapport, finding a comfortable role that permitted asking questions and recording answers, deciding how much of his research objectives to reveal, and determining whether his observations adequately captured what was going on in Boston's west end. These issues and the techniques used in case study research are discussed in this chapter.

Case study research may lead to new perspectives on old theoretical issues, the discovery of new phenomena, and the development of new concepts and theoretical perspectives. Some of this work provides a detailed description of a setting, illustrates important concepts, fills in the dynamic details of how things influence each other, uncovers reasons and meanings behind behaviors or attitudes, and challenges existing theories and stereotypes.

In this chapter we lay out some of the principles and techniques, key issues, strengths, and weaknesses of case study research as a strategy for systematic social science research. Case study research may use many different types of data (e.g., interviews, secondary data, as discussed in Chapter 9, and surveys or historic records), but in this chapter we emphasize field observation, a data-gathering procedure not emphasized in other chapters.

PRINCIPLES

The Rationale for Case Study Research

Case studies are used in social science research for several reasons. For example, a case study is appropriate when there is only one or a very few cases available to study, perhaps because a phenomenon occurs very rarely (e.g., the study of the impact of a particular program, the development of a social movement, the effects of an earthquake, or why a specific riot occurred the way it did). Case study research might be especially desirable as a way to investigate complex social phenomena such as street gang activity or to find out how things are related in some depth, such as how the social dynamics of bar-hopping friendship groups affects how much people drink, or how lifetime conscientious objectors can maintain their beliefs. Case studies help provide insight into meanings people give to the reality around them. It is also common for social scientists embarking on a new line of inquiry to examine a few cases in detail in order to become oriented to the phenomenon and how it can be studied.

Yin (1994) suggests that case study research is most useful when an investigator is interested in how and why events are interconnected, when the phenomenon under consideration is contemporary (not historical), and when an investigator does not have sufficient control to consider, for example, an experimental design. By studying one or a few contrasting cases, the investigator can often describe something in greater depth than would otherwise be possible.

Case study research often involves considerable personal involvement by the investigator in the day-to-day events of some social setting. This kind of study is often described as **field observation** research or **participant observation** research, even though observation is only one of the data-gathering techniques that might be used. Case studies use data from many relevant sources, including various census and other data archives, published records, diaries, personal interviews, and even surveys. In this chapter we highlight the field observation aspect of case study research. In Chapter 9 we discuss the use of archived data in social science research.

Typical Design Choices for Case Study Research

What distinguishes case study research is the overall pattern of choices across Riley's research design decisions (see Figure 4.1). For example, case study research generally involves work in the settings in which social behavior takes place, with implications for loss of control over what happens. This contrasts with experimental research, in which the researcher is typically in control of a special observational setting and phenomena to be observed are induced. In case study research the investigator needs patience and skill to deal with this lack of control in order to take advantage of opportunities and avoid pitfalls in the process of the research.

Cases are often some kind of collectivity or set of role relationships (e.g., a street corner gang or nursing home), and often the boundaries of a case and its context are blurred or the context is especially important to the understanding of the case itself. By choice or because of the required effort and cost of a large-scale case-by-case approach, case study research involves a single case (e.g., a particular immigrant neighborhood or a single firm) or very few cases. Cases are picked for their analytical value rather than in some random sampling fashion to represent accurately the distribution of some phenomenon in a specified population. This focus on a few handpicked critical cases may be helpful in research addressing some theoretical point, or when the researcher needs to know more about the phenomenon before creating more-formal measurement instruments, or because little is known and exploration is the first order of business in a line of research.

Usually a small number of key **organizing concepts** are at the forefront of case study research, but many phenomena are observed in rich detail. Data are usually original observations made by the investigator rather than secondary data from observations made by others, but existing reports and archives may also be used (e.g., newspaper stories, diaries, second-hand accounts of events). Case study research also tends to involve a longer data-gathering period than the typical experiment or survey. An investigator in the field is able to conduct interviews and observe how things are put together and how they change during the course of the observation. Case study research would be considered cross-sectional to the extent that a complex setting is described as it exists at one point in time regardless of the fact that it may take an investigator some time and repeated visits to a field site to complete the observations or other data-gathering work. On the other hand, case studies often involve some attention to changes through time or dynamic social processes. A case study would be considered longitudinal to the extent that repeated visits to the field site result in an analyzed record of changes through time. Still, the sociotemporal context is primarily contemporary: a specific geographic location and time period that are contemporaneous with the investigator's work.

Finally, analysis of the rich, often voluminous observational record (and any other data) is generally handled in a more summative way by the investigator, weighing the evidence and providing a **thick description** of the findings. That is, key aspects of the case are pulled together in an analytic way, with considerable attention to illustrative detail. Although some systematic tallying may occur, the overall conclusions are often more like an in-depth story or conceptual critique rather than a systematic discussion of tabulated data or statistical findings. As in other forms of research, attention is given to ensuring the **validity** and **reliability** of data and reasoning through **alternative explanations** of the phenomenon, mustering evidence for and against them.

The following are illustrative of the wide range of areas in which case study research has been used:

- Jaber Gubrium (1975) spent several months at a nursing home he called Murray Manor (a pseudonym), taking on several roles as participant–observer from work as a staff gerontologist's aide. His purpose was to examine how care in a nursing home is accomplished by the people who participate in its everyday life.

- Lawrence Wieder (1974) studied a halfway house for ex-convicts in East Los Angeles and became interested in the convict code, the subculture language used by ex-convicts. His job was to conduct an exploratory study to see why ex-convicts going through the program did not improve. He had an office in the halfway house, tried to avoid being thought of as a staff member, and used informants and observation in his work.

- Phyllis Baker (1996) used participant observation and interviewing with 16 White women in a shelter for battered women. The experiences of the women with services they received allowed Baker to trace out how they attempted to control their situations in the face of the professional perspectives of the shelter staff.

- Festinger, Riecken, and Schachter (1956) conducted a largely covert study of how a group that predicted the destruction of the world at a specific time prepared for the end and coped with the fact that the world did not end.

- William Thompson and Jackie Harred (1992) studied how topless dancers manage stigma by interviewing dancers and observing their relationships with managers, waiters, and bartenders in seven topless bars in a southwestern city.

- Hans Mauksch (1966) studied nursing practice in the context of a hospital.

- Loree Guthrie (1996), for her PhD dissertation, conducted a case study of teen parents in a school district by intensively studying four teen parents.

- Maxim Kiselev (1996) conducted a case study of children involved in the Chernobyl radiation disaster in Russia.

- Lumane Claude (1996) did a dissertation in which four rural Pennsylvania communities were compared on various aspects of community activity and well-being.

The focus of case studies is quite diverse, including studies of individuals, types of status or role relationship, an historic event, an occupational category, a community or neighborhood, various organizational settings, a certain category of behavior, or a category of norm or belief. Systematic study of cases, particularly field observation of cases, is a widely used approach to many lines of inquiry in the social sciences. As in other forms of inquiry, there are both strengths and characteristic weaknesses that must be considered. (See Box 8.1.)

Humans Observing Humans: Problems of Observation

As Madge (1965) and others point out, special research problems arise with human observation, particularly when humans observe humans. An initial problem is that of longevity. Given a professional researcher's career of, say, 30 years and current average lifetime of around 80 years, a trained human observer can never observe a

BOX 8.1
ETHNOMETHODOLOGY

Inspired by the works of Schutz (1962, 1964, 1966), Harold Garfinkel (1967) developed a phenomenological approach to the study of the social world that he called ethnomethodology. This approach is mentioned here because it lends itself particularly to the case study approach described in this chapter. Garfinkel rejects the notion that a researcher should study a situation armed with preconceived sociological concepts because people, in their everyday lives, construct their social reality as they participate in social situations. As Turner says, "ethnomethodology is concerned with the common methods people employ—whether scientists, homemakers, insurance salespersons, or laborers—to create a sense of order about the situations in which they interact. I think that the best clue to this conceptual emphasis can be found in the word *ethnomethodology* itself—*ology,* 'study of'; *method,* 'the methods [used by]'; and *ethno,* 'folk or people' " (1991:476). Maleness, for example, is not a status that is assigned to a person and once assigned is a known and taken-for-granted characteristic of that person. Rather, the male through his actions in social situations is in a constant process of establishing and validating his maleness. It is the job of the ethnomethodologist, then, to observe the behavior of the "male" in a social situation in order to identify the actions he uses to establish for himself and others that he is, in fact, a male. Furthermore, the ethnomethodologist is not as interested in the substance of the concept of maleness as he or she is in the method the person uses to establish that the concept exists in the social order. As a result of their perspective, ethnomethodologists generally reject the research strategies of conventional sociologists because they consider it counterproductive to impose preconceived notions about the social world on their observations. They approach a case to be studied with a research question in mind, but they allow the data to evolve out of their observations, then try to make sense of what they are observing.

complete, typical human life course. Thus, of necessity, what a person can observe first-hand is time-limited.

The psychological and physiological characteristics of sight also affect observational findings. We sift through things we see, retaining some as important and discarding others as inconsequential or irrelevant. What humans see is conditioned by who they are and what they have learned. Often this is systematically structured by the researcher's position in the social class structure of his or her society (affected by other status characteristics such as age, ethnicity, and gender; see Bailey, 1996, for a discussion of status effects). For example, certain gestures and nods mean something that we have learned ourselves. Experience in a different society quickly underscores the great potential for error in some of these assumptions.

Furthermore, many social concepts are not readily observable. Concepts such as "peer group," "social class," or "leader" are often based on putting together details that are not all in one place at one time. Looking for relevant patterns takes special training and experience. Good observers of social phenomena are rare.

Human researchers cannot be everywhere all the time. They are caught up in some position in the social setting and can only observe some things from that position at a given time and place. There is an inherent need for triangulation, or looking at the same phenomenon repeatedly from different points of view, but humans can't do this instantaneously. Being a student in a class provides insights but also limits what one can observe about how the class is conducted, a problem shared by teachers and principals, who have different opportunities and limitations on what they can observe.

In the end, not all social phenomena are accessible for observation. Researchers may be barred from observing private behaviors, illegal events, or high-security areas. Researchers may not want to be around when some social behaviors happen, regardless of how important the behaviors are (e.g., an observer would not want to witness a murder or burglary because he or she may be considered an accomplice or be put in great danger).

The act of observing humans affects their social behavior to some extent (Sykes, 1978). If an observer joins a family at dinner to observe family dinnertime behavior, the act of joining itself influences what happens (i.e., a guest is at dinner and family members will be on their best behavior).

Although observations may be readily made, remembering what happened until it can be recorded is a problem. Memory functions to highlight certain things and discard others. Some social settings readily permit the researcher to make a systematic, on-the-spot recording of much of what happened (i.e., taking immediate notes or making video or audio recordings). In other settings, techniques must be developed to aid memory until details can be written down.

Finally, there are difficulties when researchers are attached emotionally or in some other way to the people they are observing, and this will affect the observations that are made as well as their interpretation.

The point is that good observation of social phenomena by human observers is a demanding task that requires specialized training, knowledge, experience, careful placement of the observer, good informants, repeated observations, calm reflection on the consequences of one's observational behavior, a healthy skepticism about one's abilities and conclusions, and a good dose of luck. The techniques of field observation research, as of survey and experimental research, are designed to help investigators avoid pitfalls and improve their chances of collecting useful, accurate data. Some of these techniques are briefly introduced here.

TECHNIQUES

Good field observation involves a keen awareness of the social setting and the role of the investigator in it. It involves social skills on the part of the investigator that are not used in the same way in other styles of research. Patience, empathy, and careful listening are key.

There are several books in addition to Yin's (1994) that provide unusually helpful discussions of field observation research. Habenstein (1970) provides a collection of researchers' explanations of their case study research experience, from gaining access to analyzing results. Lofland and Lofland (1984) describe what to look for and how to proceed in analyzing social settings. In this section we summarize the main steps in case study research, which many of these researchers describe in greater detail.

Preparing for the Field

Although case studies often are exploratory, this does not mean that the investigator can start without a research problem in mind and initial ideas about what to examine and what to look for. To study a specific setting, the Loflands (1984) suggested that the investigator needs to use his or her own interests, background, and experiences as a starting point. Then the possible study sites must be evaluated for appropriateness for the research problem and for accessibility. Prior knowledge of a setting is very valuable, so case studies are often focused around places in which investigators are employed or places in which they have been involved that provoke their intellectual curiosity. It is also important that the investigator have the skills needed to operate in the environment. For example, knowing the language or argot of the site and having necessary social skills or the ability to participate may be important. The Loflands (1984) point out that field observation research may put special demands on an investigator to handle feeling lonely or rejected, being marginal in a group, becoming involved in events that are morally repugnant or dangerous, or feeling anxiety about being in a social setting that is uncertain and not under their control. Not all researchers are well suited for field observation work.

Prior research on the topic of interest and any theory that has been proposed in the literature will be helpful in establishing a background for case study research. This background will help determine which research settings are likely to provide relevant information so that one or more cases can be chosen for analytic purposes. Rarely is there sufficient background information for case study research. In fact, one of the strong motivations for case study research is to gain first-hand, in-depth information that can be used as background for further study.

Many case study investigators use some variant of the Glaser and Strauss (1967) grounded theory approach (Strauss and Corbin, 1997). It is an inquiry process that develops inductively from detailed familiarity with first-hand observational data. But case study research may also begin with alternative hypotheses about what is going on, and these hypotheses can be examined with data from a case study.

Case studies may involve selected, contrasting cases that help eliminate alternative explanations of the phenomenon of interest. Contrasts are almost always helpful in interpreting data. Nevertheless, cases are treated individually rather than averaged, as would be appropriate when estimates of characteristics of some defined population are sought, based on a representative sample of cases.

Gaining Access

Once the investigator has clarified the research problem and selected one or more research sites, the next problem is to gain **access.** The researcher may be able to choose whether to gain access without disclosing the fact that he or she is conducting research (e.g., observing people at a ball game or in a bar, getting hired by a firm, or volunteering at a homeless care center) or by disclosing his or her intent and the nature of the research.

Not disclosing the researcher's agenda may pose minimal ethical problems in public settings, but ethical issues are of more concern when access to private settings is gained by misrepresenting one's intent. An example would be research on a closed group such as the one Festinger et al. (1956) describe. Their team became covert members of a group in order to observe the consequences of beliefs that did not come true.

If the choice is to disclose the nature of the research, then the investigator needs a brief and readily understood account or explanation of what he or she is doing. Often this is not detailed, in part because the investigator may feel that full disclosure might affect the quality of data being gathered. More often it is because the details of one's research are not understandable or of interest to gatekeepers or other participants in the research. Although the story remains the same, how it is phrased may vary depending on the audience. Some investigators choose to account for their work simply by saying that they are writing a book about the setting, for example.

How one moves into a research setting has important consequences for what data can be gathered. For example, when there are traditional tensions between employers and employees, coming in under the auspices of management may make it very difficult to get in-depth information from employees (and vice versa). Often the investigator does not have sufficient information ahead of time to understand the tensions in the setting. Prior familiarity with the site pays off, but the investigator needs the social skill to understand potential problems quickly so they can be avoided.

Gatekeepers guard access to most social settings. Nursing home administrators and families may control access to older residents. School staff and parents guard access to research involving school classes. Prison staff quite literally are gatekeepers for research on prisoners. Higher-level organizational staff control research access to most firms. Research on virtually any group must take account of those who have a strong stake in controlling access. Even research in communities may run amok if appropriate stakeholders are not consulted first. Thus, it is not uncommon for researchers doing research in a community to notify city officials, including the police. A concern is whether to enter a setting from the top down or the bottom up or in some other way. Each has potential consequences for the research process.

Gatekeepers (and others in the research setting) will want to assess the trustworthiness of the researcher and the potential threat of the research. The researcher's genuine interest in the setting and professional commitment to inquiry help. Spending time in the setting is important for establishing trust. The researcher's auspices and connections may also help. University research, for example, usually suggests importance, neutrality, objectivity, and skill. William F. Whyte's study of the street-corner gang in Boston illustrates the importance of the gatekeeper to the success of a study (Whyte, 1955). Whyte sought and received the endorsement of Doc, the leader of the gang, before embarking on his study. Furthermore, his behavior in his role as an observer legitimized his presence.

Sometimes preliminary correspondence is written on official letterhead to convey sponsorship and affiliation. Introductions by appropriate people known to those in the setting also help establish the researcher's credibility and trustworthiness. Assurance of confidentiality helps, but the researcher's behavior is paramount. Specific ways to develop a sense of trust and neutrality include not disclosing to others in the setting things informants from different factions have shared in confidence and inventing pseudonyms for the organizations and informants discussed in a research write-up.

Concern for potential sources of harm and ethical considerations are important for case study research, as they are for all research, although the specific issues vary. Courtesy, respect, open-mindedness, and friendliness help in field research, as they do in most social encounters.

Habenstein (1970) notes that a researcher may "get in," but the real question is, "How far in?" Simply gaining physical access is not sufficient for most case study research; one needs cooperation in getting accurate and full information. Again, "how far in" depends a good deal on how trusted the researcher becomes and how important the researcher's interest seems to be.

What Role to Play

Researchers in a field setting will have one or more roles. These provide opportunities to find out about certain things, and they also limit the extent to which some things can be seen or known. The role also affects research data in distinctive ways. Selecting appropriate and useful roles is important for case study research that uses field observation. Whether the researcher is a participant or a nonparticipant in the social activities of the research setting is a common distinction. If one is a participant, that often improves the sense of trust and openness and it may get the researcher into settings that would otherwise be hard to observe. On the other hand, being a participant often limits observation or possibilities for accurately recording data. One could also decide to be known as an observer or researcher. There often is value in being known explicitly as an observer because questions can be asked that would not be possible if one were only a participant. Field study researchers often underscore the desirability of not appearing to know too much (so one can be "educated"), but not knowing too little (being so uninformed as to not understand what is going on and not being credible). Usually field observers choose to be some combination of observer and participant. The student role is often useful because of the balance it provides between interest, knowledge, and willingness to be taught.

The researcher is unlikely to have only a single role in a setting. For example, in parts of the study or with certain groups or events, an investigator may be a participant–observer, participating in a perfunctory way in unfolding events but being known as an observer too. In other situations the researcher may be simply a nonparticipant–observer, sitting back and observing what is happening. One could be a participant in a community but only an observer of a specific event. Needless to say, an investigator needs considerable social skill to recognize what is going on and behave appropriately to accomplish research objectives. Awareness of the consequences of one's behavior and ability to listen with a trained social scientist's understanding makes the field observer's role difficult.

The experienced researcher in a field setting monitors his or her own emotional reactions and involvement in the setting. It is not difficult to become so engrossed in a setting and the people that one loses some perspective and ability to question events. **Going native** means becoming so much a part of a setting that researchers think of themselves as members, uncritically adopt the perspectives and beliefs, and interpret events like other members of the group. Careful preparation for fieldwork may include a colleague or adviser outside the setting who can help a field worker maintain an analytic perspective and monitor his or her own behavior as a researcher.

Gathering and Recording Data

Case study research may involve data from a variety of different sources, gathered in many of the ways discussed in earlier chapters. Field research often involves data from interviews with key participants. A brief interview schedule or list of question topics may be developed so that the investigator covers the needed topics. Interviews might be conducted with people selected because of the role they play in the setting (e.g., mayor, banker, police officer, leader, "typical" participant), asking about their activities, beliefs, norms, and connections as well as their view of the setting and other actors. Case studies may also involve information from **key informants** who are in a position to know some aspects of the case and are willing to share their information. Selection of qualified informants greatly expands the range of information a researcher can obtain. A range of informants in different positions is one triangulation technique used to check the validity of one's observations.

Both words and behavior are usually included as data. Often it is helpful to have a series of questions in mind to guide observation (e.g., what the setting is like, who is there, what their roles are, why they are there, what time of day it is, how long something takes, what actually happened, what meanings it has for participants, and who communicates with whom). Lofland and Lofland (1984) suggest questions such as, "Who is he? What does he do? What do you think she meant by that? What are they supposed to do? Why did she do that? Why is that done? What happens after ___? What would happen if ___? What do you think about ___? Who is responsible if ___?" Becker (1970) suggests asking "how" questions rather than "why" questions to avoid getting only rationalizations of action.

Data from field observations, information from informants, and interviews must be recorded as close to the time of observation as possible to avoid problems with memory and factual distortion. It is said that if it doesn't exist in one's notes, it didn't happen. Full and careful notes are key. Sometimes note keeping can be aided by tape recordings (video or audio), which are later transcribed and reviewed. Although some investigators worry about the distortion recording equipment might cause in the events being recorded, they often find that with explanation and after a short period of time, subjects ignore or forget about the recording device.

Field notes are usually kept as a journal, chronologically, with care in recording what actually happened and, *separately*, what the researcher thinks it means. As in all research, it is important to identify the time and place of observations. A system is needed to identify actors so that observations relating to a given actor can be pulled together later in the analysis. Although detailed notes are recorded as soon as possible, field researchers usually devote considerable time at the end of each day to go over their notes, write out cryptic abbreviations, fill in gaps that are remembered later (with an indication that it is a later addition), add interpretations and reflections (again, with a clear indication that it is an interpretation), and generally put their notes in order for later use (e.g., adding key words, numbering paragraphs).

If an investigator chooses not to disclose the fact that he or she is doing research, then recording data at the time of observation is more difficult. It would be suspicious to have someone in a group making notes when he or she should be participating in what is going on. When the research role is not disclosed, investigators have a number of ways to do the recording, using mnemonic schemes to aid memory and recall of events until they can be recorded or strategies for going to a private place (e.g., a bathroom) to record notes.

Some rather elaborate techniques have been developed to capture what is going on. One example is research by Richard Sykes and Brent (1980), who developed a computer keypad on a clipboard that could be used to enter codes rapidly for unfolding interaction between police and citizens. This provided a time-marked sequence of codes that were used later to examine how sequences of behavior led to certain outcomes (Brent and Sykes, 1979, 1980; Sykes and Brent, 1980). In this case, field observers had to be trained in an **observational language,** which was used in the recording process.

In a study of the effect of drinking-group interaction on amount of drinking, Sykes and his colleagues used a multichannel tape recorder disguised in a gym bag to pick up the conversation of each member of a drinking group (Sykes et al., 1980, 1993). Groups were recruited and members wore small microphones while they were in the bar. The field observer sat at a different table with the gym bag of recording equipment and kept observational notes. One of the skills that observers had to learn in that study was to judge the amount of alcohol consumed. In preparation for this, Sykes conducted a series of studies of local bar glassware (to determine how much different kinds of glasses typically held, allowing for the style of ice cubes used and the kind of drink). In fact, one of the graduate students who was a key part of the research team was sent to bartending school to attain the skill base needed to identify the kind of drink being served.

Field notes and textual data can be kept in a handwritten journal, but increasingly investigators are entering their data and observations directly into computer files. This saves later transcription so that the investigator can enter field notes into one of the computer programs available for organizing, coding, and retrieving segments of field notes for analysis.

Leaving the Field

Getting out of a field setting with feelings of having ended things in an appropriate way is sometimes difficult. Personal friendships have been established and a participating researcher will have built up expectations and obligations. Should one maintain contact with friends? What if they have come to depend on the investigator as a participant in some planned event? How does one bring a role relationship to an end? The case study researcher may want to return to the community to fill in gaps or see how things have changed. Once the research has been written up (in final or draft form), the researcher may want to have selected informants review the conclusions in order to catch obvious misinterpretations or to add their own reflections on the research. The investigator would have to guard assurances of confidentiality and avoid emphasizing a narrower view based on a single perspective.

Analyzing Findings

Case study research, especially if it involves extensive field observations, generally results in a voluminous file of notes and recordings, identified and time-dated, ready for analysis. Usually the researcher continuously analyzes the data as they are collected so that the research journal or other record contains a growing set of reflections on what is going on (kept separate and labeled as such). It is usually suggested that field observation continue until the researcher has a sense that nothing new is being uncovered. To reach that sense, analysis in some form must occur as the field work unfolds. In the end, once the data are available, the researcher reviews all the material, does any comparison that is needed, and verifies that positive and negative evidence for conclusions has been adequately considered. Illustrative incidents and quotes are often identified for use in the final write-up of the research. How do investigators do this?

There are several discussions of the analysis process, often under the label of **qualitative analysis.** Of course, case study research involves both quantitative and qualitative information, but the process of analysis is often more descriptive and interpretive rather than primarily statistical. For example, the analyst goes over all the data, sorting segments into categories by topics, actors, or important concepts that the investigator has identified. Interpretive memos and comments are added, and the process of organizing and interpreting takes many iterations before the evidence, conclusions, and illustrations are all together. Good discussions of qualitative analysis can be found in texts devoted to the purpose, such as Bailey (1996), Lofland and Lofland (1984), Yin (1994), Cresswell (1994), Coffey and Atkinson (1996), Denzin (1994), and Emerson (1983).

Lofland and Lofland (1984) suggest that in analyzing field notes an investigator should consider 11 "thinking units": meanings, practices, episodes, encounters, roles, relationships, groups, organizations, settlements, worlds, and lifestyles. In each case, they suggest raising seven questions: What type is it? What is its structure? How frequent is it? What are its causes? What are its processes? What are its consequences? and What are people's strategies?

Computer aids to the analysis of field notes and other case study data are increasingly available. Weitzman and Miles (1995), Fielding and Lee (1993), and Richards and Richards (1994), for example, describe many of these programs in detail. With the widespread use of computers, many new procedures are being developed. Chapter 9 describes some content analysis procedures that are useful in analyzing and organizing field notes and verbatim transcripts of conversations. Here we mention two programs that have gained some broader usage in the social sciences.

One is called Ethnograph (Seidel et al., 1995). It is a microcomputer-based program that uses a computerized file of field notes and other textual data as its input. The program permits the researcher to mark off segments of text and assign a code. For example, one could mark instances of prisoners talking about guards. Multiple codes can be assigned to the same text segment (e.g., date of observation, characteristics of the person being observed, topical codes for what is being discussed). Text segments can be retrieved and printed so all data relevant to a particular point can be examined and compared. Ethnograph is particularly useful for organizing and analyzing field observation notes.

NUD*IST (Non-numerical, Unstructured Data Indexing, Searching and Theorizing) is another program that is useful in handling voluminous field notes and transcribed text (Weitzman and Miles, 1995). It is similar in many ways to Ethnograph but it permits a different style of analysis. Codes can be organized hierarchically and viewed in useful graphic tree displays. Memos can easily be embedded in the original text, and the memos themselves can be coded and organized.

More-complex logical combinations of codes can be searched and retrieved so that a researcher can go into considerable detail in examining various special conditions within the data.

Once the data are summarized and the report written with illustrations of events and quotations, the write-up is sometimes shown to other colleagues and sometimes to selected key informants who may have been privy to the purposes of the research in the field setting. Reactions and suggestions help improve and correct the interpretation the investigator has reached. Outside perspectives are often helpful when an investigator becomes highly involved in the research and may take many things for granted.

ISSUES IN CASE STUDY RESEARCH

Three main issues are usually raised about case study research. First is the issue of **generalization.** To what extent can findings from a well-conducted case study be generalized to a larger class of cases? One perspective is that a sample of one case is very unreliable and likely to be biased by any number of selection factors. Cases are generally selected for their analytic value, convenience, or availability and thus are not intended to address the issue of representativeness. The extent to which the case is representative of a larger group of cases is unknown. When generalization to a larger, defined population is important, other research strategies such as a survey would be more appropriate if it could be achieved. It should be noted that many theoretical problems do not have an existing population from which a random sample could be drawn, even ignoring the problem of availability of sampling lists. Most theories refer to a broad class of cases that may exist in an infinite number of times and places. A large random sample of contemporary cases in the United States, as well as a single contemporary case, are only time- and place-bounded instances that may be relevant to a theory. What is needed, of course, is a continuing program of replicated studies in different times and places in order to test theories adequately and establish stable theoretical principles. Case studies often reveal and illustrate general principles, although the question of how broadly these principles may apply requires further inquiry.

A second issue concerning case studies has to do with the **level of rigor** with which they are conducted. Examining only evidence that supports preconceived ideas is not rigorous research. Both confirming and disconfirming evidence must be entertained (see Becker, 1958). It is often difficult for another researcher to examine reports and confirm that alternative explanations were considered unless the case study researchers provide **detailed documentation** of their examination of potential alternatives and how they handle potential biases and alternative explanations (see Liebow's description of his field observations in studying low-income males in Washington, DC, 1970). If a field setting permits an investigator to use repeatable and systematic procedures to observe and record data, greater rigor is gained (e.g., using a standardized measurement process to measure some concept). Systematic research procedures are often difficult to implement in field observation studies, and this may raise concerns about rigor. Validity and reliability of observations, in the case of field observation research, come from a researcher's discipline of checking out interpretations or descriptions of what happened by triangulation, always having more than one source of confirmation. This applies as much to reports by informants as to the observations by the investigators themselves. Finally, most research questions, explicitly or implicitly, involve comparison that give meaning to descriptions and explanations (e.g., whether the observed actions are usual for all groups or unusual for the group being observed). Case study research often involves carefully selected contrasting cases or contrasting expectations. Contrasts may be made with prior descriptions or theoretical expectations found in the literature. Greater rigor stems from relevant comparison.

Third is the issue of **how case study research is implemented.** This includes concerns about unbiased availability of information or access to situations that must be understood. There are practical matters such as the time required, especially for field observation case studies, and the skills the investigator needs to operate effectively as a researcher in a field setting. The discipline and ability needed to record germane and useful field notes accurately and to analyze them systematically raise many practical problems. Finally, there are issues of actually implementing solutions to ethical concerns in field observation studies. Most issues relevant to case studies and field observation are also relevant to other research strategies, although the possibilities for handling them differ.

Strengths of Case Studies

Case study research has a number of important advantages for systematic social science research. The payoff of a case study is that it provides greater detail about one or more instances of some social phenomenon. Case studies can lead to a more holistic, contextualized characterization of a case than is often possible with other research strategies. It is a research design that is particularly well suited to studying contemporary phenomena that call for an in-depth examination or detailing some process of change over time. It is one of the few options for studying rare or inaccessible cases. Case study research is helpful when research questions call for in-depth study of why and how something happened. Study of a single case or a few selected contrasting cases may be especially useful when detailed theoretical contrasts are called for. Case studies are also very useful in exploratory stages of research, when the distinction between a case and its context is contingent and not clear-cut, or when large-scale phenomena are being studied, such as a social movement in a community or society. Case study research permits investigators to follow more-dynamic processes and the detailed interplay between a case and its context. Finally, case studies can be less expensive than surveys and experiments.

Case studies use a number of different sources of data, including field observation, detailed interviews, key informants, surveys, and historic records. In this chapter we have focused on field observation as a somewhat distinctive approach to data gathering often used in case study research. Field observation has some distinctive strengths as well.

Field observation is a flexible inquiry procedure that permits the observation of nonverbal behavior, the shuttle of social interaction, and the relationships and activities of individuals or groups. It is useful in situations in which the researcher does not have control over what is happening. Seeing social phenomena in their natural environment leads to better understanding of the conditions and settings under which they occur. Probes and follow-up questions can be easily modified and adapted in new situations to better understand what is going on. When justified, **covert field observation** permits the study of situations that would be distorted or misreported in other modes of data gathering. It is often less reactive than other forms of data gathering. Field observation and interviewing are often better suited to getting at meanings and emotions. Being closer to the things being observed helps researchers avoid being misled about the meaning of events because further observations (triangulation) can help them decide between alternative interpretations. Establishing **rapport** with an informant permits the investigator to use that relationship to gain understanding.

Field observation reports are often used in other studies as a way of illustrating concepts and helping understand some phenomenon. Good field observation in the social sciences is akin to good observational work in astronomy. A data point is well established and can be used by others. Almost all lines of research include field observations somewhere in their development.

Weaknesses of Case Studies

Case study research cannot support generalization of findings to a broader, defined population. It is generally not possible to use statistical tools for descriptive or explanatory analysis in a case study because of the limit on the number of independent observations. However, in some situations, when a case is composed of a number of subunits, these subunits can be statistically examined. For example, in studying a community, distributions of individual characteristics such as age or income may be statistically handled and used to characterize the community as a whole. Nevertheless, case studies can be used to develop and clarify theory, develop useful concepts, and provide a good basis for generating testable hypotheses about broader populations, which can be used in research based on representative samples.

When field observation is the primary mode of data collection, there are a number of other weaknesses to consider. One is the lack of control over what happens in a field setting. This may make it impossible to achieve the observations one wants. It hampers systematic data recording, and it may make it hard to rule out alternative interpretations of what is happening. The sheer effort and skill of doing superior field observations may rule it out as a viable strategy for some problems and researchers. It may be difficult to measure some variables such as alienation, using standard scale instruments that are not available in a version based on observation. This, coupled with less control, may result in measurements that are less standardized than might be desired. Problems of gaining entry may bias what one can and cannot observe, as can the social skills of investigators and their personal relationships with participants. When anonymity is important (e.g., in studies of deviance), field researchers cannot promise confidentiality beyond what the law permits.

As in all research, the investigator must pick the research approach that maximizes strengths and minimizes problems.

SUMMARY

In this chapter we have described research that uses one case or a few contrasting cases. It is best suited to contemporary cases and settings over which an investigator has little control. Although many forms of data gathering may be a part of case study research, field observation was emphasized in this chapter as a distinctive procedure of many case studies in the social sciences. First-hand observation of instances of some phenomenon is basic to scientific inquiry in many fields. Observation presents some distinctive opportunities and advantages as well as distinctive issues for human observers.

Case study research is widely used in the social sciences even though issues of generalizability, rigor, and implementation have been raised. Case studies are used for descriptive as well as explanatory research, especially when an in-depth examination of more-complex social processes occurring in their natural setting is important.

Field observation involves skill in clarifying one's research interests and identifying one's skills and opportunities. The process of gaining access, developing an **account of researcher intent,** and choosing an appropriate role or roles has very important consequences for the quality of observational data. Field researchers need to decide whether to reveal their research role and whether and to what extent to be a participant in the setting. Case study research generally gathers in-depth information on a wide range of topics. What to observe and how to record it in a timely fashion are special concerns of fieldwork. A chronological research journal of field notes and (separately identified) reflections on their meaning is usually a part of the process. Once the researcher leaves the field (and this also calls for planning), the field notes and other data are analyzed. Often this involves tagging, sorting by topics, finding illustrations that illustrate concepts, and writing a thick description of findings. Computer programs are available to help in organizing and analyzing field notes, although most of these also require considerable time in coding and comparing alternative explanations.

Case study strengths include assembling a more holistic and in-depth description of a case, developing new theoretical and conceptual insights, handling more-complex social situations, and following the details of some social process over time. In field settings, case study research may be less reactive and provide greater opportunities for probing meanings and comparing different perspectives on the same event. Weaknesses of case study research in generalizability of findings have been noted. Field observation has its own problems with gaining access to desired information, achieving systematic data, and assessing alternative explanations. Chapter 9 describes the use of archives and secondary data for research.

TERMS TO KNOW

Access
Account of researcher intent
Case study
Covert research
Detailed documentation
Field notes
Field observation
Going native
Informant
Key informants
Observational language
Organizing concepts
Participant observation
Qualitative analysis
Rapport
Reliability
Systematic research
Thick description
Validity

ISSUES AND COMPARISONS

Participant observation or nonparticipation
Disclosure versus covert research
Computer aids to analyzing field notes
Confidentiality versus anonymity
Alternative explanations of case study findings
Ethics of case study research
Reasons for conducting case studies
Strengths and weaknesses of case study research
Cross-sectional versus longitudinal study
Constraints on the observer role
Mnemonic aids
Analyzing field data
When to stop and how to leave a field setting
Level of rigor, generalization, implementation of case study research

EXERCISES

1. Identify some social phenomenon in which you are keenly interested and a site, convenient to you, in which it can be observed for some time. For example, you might be interested in the way aides in a nursing home interact with each other, or etiquette in white-collar and blue-collar restaurants, or child care behaviors in a daycare setting. Be sure to identify clearly the phenomena you are interested in observing and characteristics of the site you have selected. To what extent and in what ways might this starting point lead to better knowledge about the phenomenon, or to biased or misleading findings about the phenomenon you propose to study.

2. Set up a realistic way to gain meaningful access to the site chosen in exercise 1 and set up a way to record observations you plan to make in that setting.

3. Pretest the procedures you developed in exercise 2. Spend several hours in the setting, recording observations you have made. What role did you play in the field setting? What consequences do you see about how your role affected the observations you were able to make? How comfortable was your chosen role? What would you change about your behavior in the field setting? When you are out of the field, discuss how well the procedures worked and the extent to which you may be recording a biased or selective set of materials.

4. After revising your procedures, spend several more hours in the field setting gathering careful data on the phenomenon you are studying. Briefly summarize your findings, identify and define any new insights or concepts you discovered, and reflect back on the methodological adequacy of this mini–research project.

5. Find an interesting research report that uses field observation. Carefully examine it and lay out the research procedure in terms of the ideas and relevant concepts discussed in this chapter. What can be said to be known, based on the research procedures?

REFERENCES

Bailey, Carol A., *A Guide to Field Research,* Pine Forge Press, Thousand Oaks, CA, 1996.

Baker, Phyllis L., "Doin' What It Takes to Survive: Battered Women and the Consequences of Compliance to a Cultural Script," *Studies in Symbolic Interaction* 1996;20:73–90.

Becker, Howard S., "Problems of Inference and Proof in Participant Observation," in George J. McCall and J. L. Simmons, *Issues in Participant Observation,* Addison-Wesley, Reading, MA, 1958.

Becker, Howard S., "Practitioner of Vice and Crime," Chapter 2 in Robert W. Habenstein, ed., *Pathways to Data: Field Methods for Studying Ongoing Social Organizations,* Aldine, Chicago, 1970.

Brent, Edward E., Jr., and Richard E. Sykes, "A Mathematical Model of Symbolic Interaction Between Police and Suspects," *Behavioral Science* November 1979;24(6):388–402.

Brent, Edward E., Jr., and Richard E. Sykes, "The Interactive Bases of Police-Suspect Confrontation: An Empirically Based Simulation of a Markov Process," *Simulation and Games* September 1980;11(3):347–63.

Claude, Lumane Pluviose, *Community Activeness, Success and Well-Being: A Comparative Case Study of Four Pennsylvania Rural Communities,* Ph.D. dissertation, University Park, Pennsylvania State University, 1996.

Coffey, Amanda, and Paul Atkinson, *Making Sense of Qualitative Data,* Sage, Newbury Park, CA, 1996.

Cresswell, John W., *Research Design: Qualitative and Quantitative Approaches,* Sage, Newbury Park, CA, 1994.

Denzin, Norman K., ed., *Handbook of Qualitative Research,* Sage, Newbury Park, CA, 1994.

Emerson, Robert M., *Contemporary Field Research: A Collection of Readings,* Little, Brown, Boston, 1983.

Festinger, Leon, Henry W. Riecken, and Stanley Schachter, *When Prophecy Fails,* Harper & Row, New York, 1956.

Fielding, Nigel G., and Raymond M. Lee, eds., *Using Computers in Qualitative Research,* Sage, Newbury Park, CA, 1993.

Gans, Herbert, *Urban Villagers,* Free Press, New York, 1962.
Garfinkel, Harold, *Studies in Ethnomethodology,* Prentice Hall, Englewood Cliffs, NJ, 1967.
Glaser, B., and A. L. Strauss, *The Discovery of Grounded Theory: Strategies for Qualitative Research,* Aldine, Chicago, 1967.
Gubrium, Jaber F., *Living and Dying at Murray Manor,* St. Martin's Press, New York, 1975.
Guthrie, Loree Price, *Teen Parents of Millcreek School District: A Qualitative Case Study of Four Teen Parents,* Ph.D. dissertation, Temple University, Philadelphia, 1996.
Habenstein, Robert W., ed., *Pathways to Data: Field Methods for Studying Ongoing Social Organizations,* Aldine, Chicago, 1970.
Kiselev, Maxim Y., *Living with Radiation: A Case Study of the Chernobyl Children,* Ph.D. dissertation, Yale University, New Haven, CT, 1996.
Liebow, Elliot, "A Field Experience in Retrospect," Chapter 12 in Glenn Jacobs, ed., *The Participant Observer: Encounters with Social Reality,* George Braziller, New York, 1970.
Lofland, John, and Lyn H. Lofland, *Analyzing Social Settings,* 2nd ed., Wadsworth, Belmont, CA, 1984.
Madge, John, *The Tools of Social Science: An Analytical Description of Social Science Techniques,* Doubleday, Garden City, NY, 1965.
Mauksch, Hans O., "The Organizational Context of Nursing Practice," in Fred Davis, ed., *The Nursing Profession,* Wiley, New York, 1966.
Richards, T., and L. Richards, "Using Computers in Qualitative Analysis," Chapter 28 in N. Denzin and Y. Lincoln, eds., *Handbook of Qualitative Research,* Sage, Newbury Park, CA, 1994.
Schutz, Alfred, *Collected Papers I: The Problem of Social Reality,* Martinus Nijhoff, The Hague, 1962.
Schutz, Alfred, *Collected Papers II: Studies in Social Theory,* Martinus Nijhoff, The Hague, 1964.
Schutz, Alfred, *Collected Papers III: Studies in Phenomenological Philosophy,* Martinus Nijhoff, The Hague, 1966.
Seidel, John, Susanne Friese, and D. Christopher Leonard, *The Ethnograph v4.0: A Users Guide,* Qualis Research Associates, Amherst, MA, 1995.
Strauss, Anselem, and Juliet Corbin, *Grounded Theory in Practice,* Sage, Newbury Park, CA, 1997.
Sykes, Richard E., "Toward a Theory of Observer Effects in Systematic Field Research," *Human Organization* Summer 1978;37(2):148–56.
Sykes, Richard E., and Edward E. Brent, "The Regulation of Interaction by Police: A Systems View of Taking Charge," *Criminology* August 1980;18(2):182–97.
Sykes, Richard E., Richard D. Rowley, and James M. Schaefer, "Effects of Group Participation on Drinking Behaviors in Public Bars: An Observational Survey," *Journal of Social Behavior and Personality* 1980;5(4):385–402.
Sykes, Richard E., Richard D. Rowley, James M. Schaefer, "The Influence of Time, Gender and Group Size on Heavy Drinking in Public Bars," *Journal of Studies on Alcohol* March 1993;54(2):133–38.
Thompson, William E., and Jackie L. Harred, "Topless Dancers: Managing Stigma in a Deviant Occupation," *Deviant Behavior* 1992;13(3):291–311.
Turner, Jonathan, *The Structure of Sociological Theory,* Wadsworth, Belmont, CA, 1991.
Weitzman, Eben A., and Matthew B. Miles, *Computer Programs for Qualitative Data Analysis: A Software Sourcebook,* Sage, Newbury Park, CA, 1995.
Whyte, William F., Jr., *Street Corner Society,* 2nd ed., University of Chicago Press, Chicago, 1955.
Wieder, D. Lawrence, *Language and Social Reality: The Case of Telling the Convict Code,* Mouton & Company, The Hague, 1974.
Yin, Robert K., *Case Study Research: Design and Methods,* 2nd ed., Applied Social Research Methods Series #5, Sage, Newbury Park, CA, 1994.

CHAPTER NINE

SECONDARY DATA RESEARCH

Secondary data are existing data that were generated for reasons other than those the current researcher has in mind. For example, the researcher might do a study of residential migration patterns using existing census data. Or he or she might study the use of certain value-laden phrases (such as *left-wing radicals* or *right-wing reactionaries*) in newspaper articles. In general, what distinguishes secondary data research from other types of research is the source of the data used to answer research questions. Whereas other types of research require the collection of fresh data, this type involves the use of data that are already available.

Research using secondary data is becoming increasingly common in sociology. One reason for this is the availability of more and more computerized databases. Government data and data from a range of research projects are almost routinely being stored (or archived) on computers in a form that makes them accessible to those wishing to use them for new research projects. A second and more important reason is that sociologists, in keeping with the process model of the social world, are increasingly engaging in longitudinal research that depends on **cumulative data.**

Secondary data may be either **quantitative** or **qualitative;** therefore, the research itself may stress either a quantitative or qualitative approach. Two classic pieces of research in sociology illustrate these two approaches. One, Durkheim's study of suicide (1897), made use of quantitative data, and the other, Thomas and Znaniecki's study of Polish peasants (1918–1920), made use of qualitative data.

Durkheim was interested in the effects of social solidarity, or the lack thereof, on suicide rates. He hypothesized that rates would be lower among those who experienced social solidarity than among those lacking it. Social solidarity implies normative controls and ordering of individual lives, connecting each to the broader social setting. He used published suicide statistics to measure suicide rates and variables such as religious affiliation and marital status as indicators of social solidarity. As Madge explains,

> Many European countries (including Austria, Belgium, Italy, France, Bavaria, Prussia, Württemburg, and other German states) and the United States had started keeping regular official publications giving not only the number of

> suicides but also various related statistics that Durkheim could use for his purposes. He did, in fact, base almost all his analysis on material that had already been published. . . . There was only one point at which he found the published material to be insufficient, and in this case he was able to gain the full co-operation of the French Ministry of Justice, which gave him **access** to unpublished raw material. (1962:16–17)

Therefore, Durkheim's study was based totally on the use of secondary data. Given the statistical tools available to him at the end of the nineteenth century, he did a quantitative analysis of the relationships between several indicators of social solidarity and suicide rates for different countries and regions of countries.

Thomas and Znaniecki were interested in emigration from Poland to the United States, the transformation of peasant society, and the social attitudes of the peasants. In contrast to Durkheim, they sought to accumulate as much subjective information as they could. As Madge says, "They were concerned wholly with documents of various kinds, all of which were either contributed directly by people or contributed very directly about people, as with case histories" (1962:53).

Although they tapped a variety of sources, the largest single source of data was a collection of 754 letters representing 50 Polish families, each of which had members who emigrated to the United States. These letters were to and from immigrants. The researchers gained access to them through an advertisement that appeared in an American–Polish journal in 1914 soliciting such letters.

A second set of materials came from the archives of a Polish newspaper. These were brought back to the United States by Thomas after a visit to Poland in 1909. Other materials included copies of newspapers, letters from Polish people who wanted to emigrate from Poland, histories of Polish parishes and societies that had formed in the United States, and life histories of various emigrants (Madge, 1962:55–60).

All of these documents were analyzed qualitatively as a basis for the production of the five-volume study *The Polish Peasant in Europe and America* (Thomas and Znaniecki, 1918–1920).

PRINCIPLES OF SECONDARY DATA RESEARCH

The preliminary steps involved in secondary data research are no different than they are for any other type of research. The research question to be asked must be formulated, and the research must be conceptualized. The departure from other research occurs at the point at which decisions are made about which data are appropriate and necessary for answering the research question.

In any research it is essential that the very best data available to answer the research question be used. In some cases there is no alternative to collecting new data. In other cases, however, there may be useful existing data. The decision might be made to use these data instead of investing time and resources in the collection of new data. Furthermore, the available data may be superior to (or at least just as good as) any data the researcher could collect anew. The collection of data can be time-consuming and expensive, and the resources available to the researcher may sharply limit the quantity and quality of data that can be obtained firsthand.

On the other hand, government agencies such as the Bureau of the Census or the Bureau of Labor Statistics have the resources to collect large quantities of data dealing with various phenomena of interest to social scientists. These data are generally accessible to those who want to do studies beyond those for which the data were originally collected. There are also nongovernment organizations such as the National Opinion Research Center, The *Los Angeles Times* Poll, and the Gallup Poll that regularly gather data from large samples of people from various populations, including the population of the United States. These data are often made available to researchers interested in doing new studies. Box 9.1 provides some useful Web sites for finding archived data.

In addition, there are numerous databases resulting from routine reports of business activities (such as performance reports of companies in various industries), educational activities (reports on school enrollments, expenditures per pupil), government activities (Uniform Crime Reports, data on Social Security recipients, data on marriages and divorces), health sector activities (vital statistics, morbidity and mortality rates), and consumer activities (sales of products, use of credit cards). Although some of these databases are not computerized, they are generally available to researchers in written form.

In addition, numerous international databases are produced by the United Nations and its various agencies. That these have had their impact on sociology can be detected through the increasing appearance in the literature of articles making comparisons between countries throughout the world.

Advances in computer technology have made it possible to store more and more of these databases and make them readily accessible to researchers with a need to use them.[1] These databases, including data from the U.S. Census, can be accessed through computers at universities and colleges throughout the United

BOX 9.1
SOURCES OF ARCHIVED DATA

American Sociological Association: http://www.asanet.org/data.htm

General Social Survey data: http://www.soc.qc.edu

U.S. Census data: http://www.psc.lsa.umich.edu/SSDAN/

Interuniversity Consortium for Political and Social Research:
http://www.icpsr.umich.edu

[1]The Interuniversity Consortium for Political and Social Research at the University of Michigan is an example of a major repository for such databases. Also see Part II of Miller (1991).

States (as well as other countries). Some of these databases include only data collected at one point in time; others, such as the General Social Survey (GSS), conducted by the National Opinion Research Center, are annual surveys that repeat many of the same questions each year. The GSS has been conducted annually since 1972 (except for 1979 and 1981), and all of the past surveys are included in a cumulative database that is accessible by computer.[2]

Qualitative data for studies are available from a number of different sources, depending on the subject being researched. A great deal of secondary data research has used the mass media as a data source.[3] Analyses of newspaper articles, fiction and nonfiction books, magazines, articles in technical and scientific publications, motion pictures, television programs, and radio programs have been used as sources of data for a number of studies (Armstrong, 1993; Berezin, 1994; Binder, 1993; Chafetz et al., 1993; Forrest, 1993; Spencer and Triche, 1994). Other studies, following research strategies similar to those of the Thomas and Znaniecki study, make use of unpublished personal documents such as letters, diaries, scrapbooks, photo albums, and personal property inventories (see Gardner, 1991).

An extremely important and challenging task in doing secondary data research is to locate existing data that are satisfactory indicators of the variables necessary to answer the research question being asked. Centralized services such as the Interuniversity Consortium of Political and Social Research commonly catalog their databases so that users can examine the availability of different subjects and variables to see whether they meet their needs.

USING QUANTITATIVE DATA

The bulk of the databases available via computer are quantitative in nature and are presented in a format that can easily be imported into statistical packages such as the Statistical Package for the Social Sciences or SAS for analysis. If the researcher is able to locate the appropriate data to answer a research question, it is a simple process to access the variables and subject them to the type of analysis necessary.

Representative of research using available quantitative data is a study conducted by De Graaf, Nieuwbeerta, and Heath (1995) of the effects of class mobility on political preferences. The authors sought to determine the effects of intergenerational class mobility on voters' political preferences in four countries: Great Britain, the Netherlands, Germany, and the United States. *Intergenerational class mobility* refers to the social class differences between parents and children. For example, parents who are agricultural laborers might have children who are small

[2]The GSS is available from a number of different sources. It is conducted by the National Opinion Research Center at the University of Chicago, 1155 East 60th Street, Chicago, IL 60637. GSS and other surveys are archived at the Roper Center for Public Opinion Research, P.O. Box 440, Storrs, CT 06268.

[3]Large databases of newspapers from across the United States are available through the Internet. One public library source is http://www.mpls.lib.mn.us/newspape.htm. Here one can search with key words for relevant articles.

business owners. Mobility could be up or down or show no intergenerational change. They tested three "micro-level" hypotheses (numbers 1–3) and three "macro-level" hypotheses (numbers 4–6):

1. *The economic hypothesis:* "The political preferences of the mobile will be closer to the typical political preferences of their class of destination than to that of their class of origin" (1995:1000).
2. *The acculturation hypothesis:* "The older one is the more the impact of the class of origin diminishes relative to that of the class of destination" (1995:1000).
3. *The status maximization hypothesis:* "Downwardly mobile persons orient themselves more to their origin class, while upwardly mobile persons will orient themselves more to their destination class" (1995:1000).
4. *The compositional hypothesis:* "The sociocultural orientations of a class are simply the summation of those of the individuals that make up the class" (1995:1002).
5. *The contextual hypothesis for the mobile:* "A class with a low level of inflow mobility (and therefore a high level of demographic identity) will have a greater impact on newcomers than will a class with a higher rate of inflow mobility" (1995:1002).
6. *The contextual hypothesis for the immobile:* "The more left-wing mobility into a class there is, the more likely are the immobile members of that class to have a left-wing political preference" (1995:1003).

To test these hypotheses, the authors used 56 data sets from the four countries. From the Netherlands they used data from "13 Dutch representative surveys over the period 1970–90" (1995:1003). The U.S. data were from 17 GSSs conducted between 1972 and 1990. The British data came from seven National Election Surveys conducted between 1964 and 1987. The German data were from 19 representative surveys between 1969 and 1990. From these data sets they extracted data on political preferences (parties voted for), social class (as indicated by occupation), age, religion, ethnicity, and year of the interviews.

The results of the analysis showed that on the "micro-level" the acculturation hypothesis fit the data better than the economic or status maximization hypothesis. On the "macro-level," the data did not support either of the two contextual hypotheses but did support the compositional hypothesis. Interestingly, the effects of class mobility on political preferences were similar for all four countries studied.

Databases such as the annual GSS are a rich source of data because the surveys usually include 500 or more variables. For example, the 1990 survey included data on 585 variables collected from 1,372 respondents nationwide. Given the availability of data on such a large number of variables, it is fairly likely that there will be appropriate data for the variables a researcher wants to study if the topic of the research was one that was specifically addressed in one of the annual surveys. For example, the 1990 GSS (among others) asked questions about capital punishment. If the researcher is studying attitudes toward capital punishment, then the GSS results will probably be appropriate. On the other hand, if the topic being researched was not specifically covered by one of the surveys, then the GSS database may not meet the researcher's needs.

There are two temptations a researcher should resist with respect to the use of secondary data:

- *The availability of secondary data should not be the determining factor in the choice of what to study.* That is, one should not decide to study attitudes toward capital punishment simply because the relevant data are available. The problem to be studied should be selected on scientific grounds rather than on the grounds of convenience. Choosing a research topic based on availability of data is letting "the tail wag the dog." The choice should be based on theoretical grounds, or if not on those grounds, at least on the grounds that the topic being researched will provide information of practical importance.

- If available secondary data do not provide information on all relevant variables of a study, *attempts to construe data from available variables as being equivalent to data that are missing on other variables should be firmly resisted.* For example, if the researcher's study calls for data that measure socioeconomic status, but the **data archive** being used does not include a measure of socioeconomic status, then it is not appropriate to take a variable or variables for which data are available and use it in lieu of a legitimate measure of socioeconomic status. For example, the data archive the researcher wants to use might include information on the mean rental values of respondents' places of residence. Using these data in lieu of a more legitimate measure of socioeconomic status would be hard to justify. Although mean rental value may be correlated with socioeconomic status, the relationship is certainly not a one-to-one relationship, and it may not even be particularly strong. For example, it is known that people with low socioeconomic status often pay higher rents for substandard housing than is justified because of the shortage of housing available to them. This could have the effect of distorting the relationship between rental value and socioeconomic status and result in misleading findings.

Another important consideration in the use of secondary data is the size of the sample for which data were collected. As was pointed out earlier (Chapter 5), the number of cases required to carry out a study depends on the type of data analysis that is planned to test the hypotheses of the study. A simple bivariate analysis requires fewer cases than a multivariate analysis. Furthermore, as more variables are included in a multivariate analysis, more cases are required in the sample in order to distinguish the effect of these variables in the population.

Fortunately, many secondary databases have a large number of cases. However, if the study requires the use of only a subset of cases that share certain characteristics (e.g., women aged 65 and over), this may reduce the available data rather drastically. For example, if a study focused on the ages when women first wed, these criteria (gender and age first wed) would reduce the number of cases because all of the male respondents and all female respondents who had never married would not be used in the study. One reason large archived databases are attractive is because they often make available large samples of rare subpopulations.

When a secondary database does fulfill the requirements of the study being conducted, it confronts the researcher with a number of strengths and weaknesses that must be weighed in conducting the study.

Strengths of Quantitative Secondary Data

Secondary quantitative data enjoy the following strengths that may be useful to a researcher:

- *Data collection costs.* The data are already available in a form suitable for analysis, thus cutting the expense, time, and energy normally expended in collecting and processing new data.

- *Number of cases.* There is probably a large number of cases for which data are available. This makes it possible to carry out more complex analysis than would ordinarily be possible.

- *Representativeness.* Much of the secondary data available represent a complete enumeration of the population of interest (such as U.S. Census data) or a random sample of such a population. This **representativeness** makes it possible to reach definitive results (in the case of the complete enumeration) or to make statistical inferences about the population (in the case of random samples).

- *Repeated measures.* Some secondary databases are cumulative. That is, similar data are collected periodically from the same or comparable respondents. This makes it possible to use the databases for longitudinal process and trend analyses.

- *Data use costs.* Much of the secondary data available are in the public domain, which means that they may be used essentially without cost. When costs are involved (as in acquiring data files from agencies such as the U.S. Bureau of the Census), the costs tend to be minimal. In other words, most agencies in control of such databases are not out to make a profit by making the data available to others for use. However, some sources of data such as large, online newspaper files charge each time the database is accessed.

- *Reactivity.* These sources of data are nonreactive. Because they already exist, the researcher does not have to worry about **reactivity,** or the likelihood that he or she will influence responses or actions of subjects by collecting fresh data from them. However, there may be such influences from the original data collection process.

Weaknesses of Quantitative Secondary Data

There are often inherent or imposed weaknesses in secondary databases that the researcher must be willing to confront. These include the following:

- *Coverage.* The population from which the data were collected may not provide appropriate **coverage** for the study being conducted. For example, if the researcher is conducting a study of child abusers, a database that is limited to incarcerated child abusers would not justify generalization of the results to child abusers who were not apprehended and incarcerated.

▪ *Unavailable data.* The database may not include all of the variables called for by the conceptual model developed for the study. If such is the case, the researcher may decide not to use the database in question. In some cases, information may be available to infer what is missing or it may be possible to match records from two or more different databases. A researcher may decide to drop variables for which there are no data from the conceptual model (which usually results in errors of interpretation of findings called **specification errors**). Each of these options generally leaves something to be desired in terms of an optimal test of the conceptual model.

▪ *Categorization.* The necessary variables may be included in the database, but the way the responses are categorized may not be appropriate for the study being conducted. For example, if marital status is an important variable in a study and the intent is to make comparisons between never married, married, widowed, and divorced respondents, a database that classifies respondents as married, never married, or other will frustrate the intent of the researcher.

▪ *Bias.* There may be hidden **bias** in the data of which the researcher using the data secondhand may not be aware. When a researcher collects fresh data for a study, he or she is likely to be aware of nonrandom errors that arose in the process of procuring the data. If the data were collected by someone else, on the other hand, such biases may not be discussed in the available documentation and may go undetected. For example, there may be a very low response rate that is not reported, or biases in sampling or data-gathering procedures. The researcher does not necessarily know the quality of the available data. The findings of a secondary analysis might be seriously jeopardized by low-quality data that, on their face, may look better than they are.

▪ *Data preparation errors.* Recording errors may have occurred when the data were coded and entered into a computerized or printed database. If there are such errors, the researcher using the data secondhand may not be able to eliminate them because the original data collection instruments (e.g., questionnaires) are not available. Even if there is an adequate **codebook,** there may be errors in reporting the sequence or location of data elements in the data file. When one collects fresh data, the integrity of the database may be ensured with careful data input and data cleaning techniques. In the case of the use of secondary data, the researcher must rely on the original researcher to exercise care in handling the data and accurately describing the data set.

▪ *Out-of-date data.* Available data may be stale by the time the researcher gets around to using them. When a researcher collects his or her own data, he or she knows that those data are current. If the researcher uses available data, on the other hand, those data may reflect responses or a social context that is no longer applicable. If data sets are combined but are of different eras, then comparisons are flawed. It is essential to know where and when the data were gathered.

Obviously, in considering the use of available data, a researcher must weigh these potential strengths and weaknesses against the availability, quality, and costs of collecting new data.

Analyzing Quantitative Data

Once appropriate quantitative secondary data have been located, the data must be put into a form for the investigator to use. This involves several steps. A careful investigator needs to find out as much as possible about the conditions under which the data were gathered. What methods were used? How was the training of interviewers conducted and checked? What exactly were the methods used to identify cases? It is most helpful to have copies of all data-gathering instruments to examine.

An important key to the database is a codebook. This is usually a list of the variables that were measured and how they were coded and recorded. Often a data set includes more than just the original responses. For example, identification codes or dates or coder identification may be added as well as various versions of the same question, perhaps with responses grouped in different ways. A good codebook also includes information on any decisions that are made to resolve ambiguous responses and special coding circumstances that have been encountered.

The codebook or other source is needed in order to decipher the format of the data. For example, is there only one record per case or is it a multirecord case file? Often the physical format of the data on the electronic medium in which it is received (disk, CD, tape, electronic message) requires special procedures to convert the data into a useful form for the new analysis. It may not be simple to convert the data into a form you can use, and time and information are needed for this step. In fact, in using quantitative secondary data, the researcher devotes considerable time to finding an appropriate data set and to checking and converting it.

Early analysis of a secondary data set often includes checking analyses similar to the data checking that is conducted before analyzing original quantitative data. For example, one would examine distributions of each variable to check for reasonableness and out-of-range codes, and some comparisons may be made to see that responses are logically consistent. Then the analysis would generally proceed in the same way as similar original data would be examined to answer one's research question.

USING QUALITATIVE DATA

Amy Binder (1993) was interested in how the media depicted the personal and social influences of heavy metal and rap music. Accordingly, she examined 118 opinion articles appearing in five mainstream publications (*The New York Times*, *Time*, *Newsweek*, *U.S. News and World Report*, and *Reader's Digest*) and two Black magazines (*Ebony* and *Jet*) between 1985 and 1990. With regard to these opinion articles, she says,

> Writers make sense of an issue by conjuring up beliefs and values the larger culture takes for granted. They do this by comparing the object to images of past events in the collective memory or to revered cultural icons. Such referent images are used as metaphors to frame the meaning of the event at hand and provide a compelling interpretation of it. (1993:756)

In analyzing the 118 articles, she came up with nine frames used by the authors to give meanings to the lyrics of heavy metal and rap music. Four of these frames construe the lyrics as harmful, and five construe them as not harmful. The harmful frames deal with the corruption of young people, the need to protect young people, the potential danger to society, and the denial that control of exposure to such music is censorship. The nonharmful frames appeal to freedom of speech, deny that the lyrics are harmful to young people, deny that they are a threat to authority, attribute concern over them to a generation gap, and portray them as communicating an important message or as an expression of art.

When she compared the frames used in articles about heavy metal music that was popular in 1985 with those used in articles about rap music in 1990 she found a difference in emphasis. Whereas the emphasis in the heavy metal period was on the effects of the lyrics on the listening audience, the emphasis during the rap period was on the effects on society at large. She attributed this difference in emphasis partly to differences in the themes of the lyrics, but more importantly to the fact that heavy metal music attracted a largely White youth audience whereas rap attracted a Black youth audience. The implication was that the media were more concerned about the welfare of the youthful listeners when they were White, but they were more concerned about potential violent behavior by the youthful listeners when they were Black.

Because of the nature of her research questions, it was necessary for Binder to turn for answers to the print media and opinion pieces that were not intended to be used as social science data. Furthermore, these opinion pieces, when used, provided qualitative data rather than the kinds of quantitative data provided by surveys or censuses. Accordingly, Binder read the articles and extracted from them what she considered themes pertinent to her research topic.

This particular study is an example of research that focuses on media of different types. In each case the researcher is called upon to extract pertinent information from the original source materials. These source materials may take one of several different forms. For example, they may be articles, books, scripts, music lyrics, photographs, paintings, motion pictures, television programs, radio programs, or even types of architecture. Also, the researcher may use one or more of these sources. The Binder study, for example, depended primarily on opinion pieces but also analyzed song lyrics. Which media are appropriate and how many different media should be used depend on the particular research questions being posed.

The sources used by Binder and the other kinds of sources suggested earlier may be characterized as public sources in that they are generally available and are usually produced for public consumption. However, other secondary data sources of a qualitative nature are more personal. Remember that the Thomas and Znaniecki study of Polish peasants used personal letters as primary data sources. Documents such as personal letters, diaries, financial records, "doodles," and children's drawings have been tapped as sources of data. Other possible data sources of this kind include greeting cards, postcards, personal photographs, grocery lists, and appointment books. These kinds of data are not generally produced for public consumption and may not be intended for use by anyone other than the people producing them. Nevertheless, they may be vital resources for answering certain research questions.

Another whole class of available qualitative data may be found in refuse containers. For many years archaeologists have used refuse sites as sources of data about past civilizations. By examining this refuse they have been able to tell what people ate, what tools and weapons they used, what household utensils they had, and so on. In some cases anthropologists and other social scientists have turned to modern refuse as sources of data. For example, it is possible to study patterns of consumption by examining the things that show up in people's trash cans.

Webb et al. (1981) classify refuse among the **accretion measures** (i.e., things that build up over time) they discuss in connection with nonreactive research. In this connection they discuss the research of Rathje (1979), using garbage as an indicator of food waste. He and his team of researchers arranged to have the contents of garbage cans at specified addresses emptied into plastic bags for later retrieval at the dump. Through an examination of this refuse the researchers concluded that poor people wasted less food than their more affluent neighbors, and Mexican Americans wasted less than European Americans.

In an earlier study, Rathje and Hughes (1975) compared interview data about beer consumption with contents of rubbish cans from the same residences. Although the interview data indicated that beer was consumed in only 15% of the residences and eight cans per week was the maximum consumption, examination of the rubbish cans indicated that beer was consumed in 77% of the residences and more than eight cans were discarded per week in 54% of the residences (Webb et al., 1981:17).

In addition to food scraps and empty bottles, refuse may contain such personal documents as letters, bills, old photos, and junk mail, which may be valuable sources of data for the kinds of studies being discussed in this section. Of course, other issues may be raised by their approach, including ethical issues.

As is the case with quantitative archival data, there are a number of strengths and weaknesses inherent in the use of secondary qualitative data sources such as media data and personal documents.

Strengths of Qualitative Secondary Data

Secondary qualitative data offer the following strengths:

- *Data collection costs.* As is the case with the quantitative secondary data, qualitative secondary data, whether they be from the media or from personal sources, are data that already exist. This saves the researcher the money, time, and effort involved in the collection of new data.

- *Access costs.* Some of these data, particularly the media data, are in the public domain and are readily available to researchers, often at little or no cost. Furthermore, text data may already be transcribed and stored on some computer-usable medium.

- *Sample size.* Often these qualitative secondary databases are large (e.g., if newspapers are the source of data, there are over 1,500 daily newspapers in the United States). As was mentioned earlier, large databases make more complex data analysis possible.

- *Over-time data.* Qualitative secondary databases are often cumulative, making longitudinal and trend studies possible. Often written **historical data** are the only available data about some topic in the past. For example, one could study messages children may receive from a study of children's books published over many centuries and available in certain library collections.

- *Investigator bias.* As is the case with quantitative secondary data, these sources of data are nonreactive. That is, because they already exist, the researcher needn't worry that he or she may influence responses or actions of subjects, as is possible when collecting fresh data. As in the case of quantitative archived data, there are still questions to be answered about biases introduced in the way the data were originally collected, but these would not involve bias stemming from the current investigators.

- *Quality of data.* Often textual data (and this may be true of other forms of qualitative data as well) permits an investigator to see the emphasis and emotion placed on a topic by the writer, unlike most quantitative archive data sets. Furthermore, textual data (and some other forms) avoid the pressures that may be involved in translating a complex response into the "language" of a researcher-specified question-and-answer format.

Weaknesses of Qualitative Secondary Data

The shortcomings of qualitative secondary data include the following.

- *Target Population.* The population for which the data are available may not be the appropriate one for the study being conducted. For example, if a researcher is using personal documents such as letters as a source of data, he or she may have to be content with the letters available for perusal, even though they may not come directly from the population that is the subject of the study. Suppose it were possible to peruse letters being sent to and from a prison in order to study the kinds of subject matter communicated back and forth between inmates and their families to see whether there were systematic differences between violent and nonviolent criminals. Although the inmates would be part of the populations of violent and nonviolent criminals, it would be stretching a point to conclude that they were representative of those populations. There is no good reason to conclude that incarcerated criminals are just the same as criminals who are not incarcerated or who have not been apprehended.

In a similar vein, if one were to turn to the media and study letters to the editor in daily newspapers in order to gauge public opinion about some issue, it would certainly be a mistake to assume that those who write letters to editors are representative of the public. Self-selection operates in determining who bothers to write letters to the editor, and there is likely to be a second stage of selection operating when the editor decides which letters are to be published.

■ *Knowledge of Data Creation.* In the case of personal communications such as letters and memos used in evaluating what is said, one must look to both the writer and the recipient. As Ponsonby (1923:2) said, "Letters may be said to have two parents, the writer and the recipient" (quoted in Plummer, 1983:23).

In other words, the message sent by a letter writer is also shaped by who is to receive the letter. Thus, a person would not write the same letter to a personal friend as to his or her mother. As a matter of fact, it is conceivable that there would be little overlap in the contents of two such letters written one after the other. This fact further complicates the use of personal documents as data sources because the researcher has to know who the recipient was, how the recipient was related to the writer, and what the consequences of that relationship were for the message being sent. In general, documents (and other forms of qualitative and quantitative data) are created in a social context that may have both desired and biasing effects on the resulting archived data.

■ *Irrelevant Data.* Both media sources and personal sources contain what Webb et al. (1981:72) call **dross,** that is, the parts of documents that are irrelevant to the research conducted. The dross rate is likely to be much higher for qualitative secondary data than for fresh data or even for quantitative secondary data. As a consequence, the researcher must wade through the dross in order to select the documents or parts of documents that are germane to the study being conducted.

■ *Accuracy.* Though not limited to the use of qualitative secondary data sources, questions of accuracy of the materials appearing in media or personal documents are important. Writers may deliberately seek to deceive their readers, may have trouble separating imagination from fact, or may have faulty memories. Even in the case of daily diaries, it cannot be assumed that the entry was made on the day the diary was dated. Thus, errors might be introduced into accounts of happenings when the diarist enters several entries at one time. Of course, the same problem could be equally serious for letters, memos, and other forms of documents (as well as quantitative secondary data).

■ *Inference and Response.* Because media sources and personal documents were not originally produced for the purposes for which a researcher wants to use them, they may not include direct information on the variables the researcher wants to tap. This may lead the researcher to make inferences about statements made in the document that may not be warranted. This might be called an attempt to read between the lines.

- *Legibility.* Personal documents written in longhand may be difficult to read. The original document may be illegible or, if it is an old document, it may be faded or smudged. Sometimes one indistinguishable word can drastically change the meaning of a sentence. Furthermore, even printed documents may contain typographical errors, which may make them difficult to understand. This is also a potential problem with audio and video recordings.

- *Timeliness.* Available media or personal data may be stale by the time the researcher gets around to using them. When a researcher collects his or her own data, he or she knows that those data are current. In the case of media and personal sources, this may not be the case. To further complicate matters, when the sources are very old the messages being conveyed may be subject to misinterpretation because of changes in language. A related **timeliness** problem that may be particularly characteristic of the mass media (but could also apply to personal documents) is that events or people alluded to may be meaningful only within the context and the time frame in which they originally occurred or existed.

CONTENT ANALYSIS

The technique most commonly used in the analysis of qualitative secondary data is **content analysis.** Bernard Berelson defined content analysis as "a research technique for the objective, systematic and quantitative description of the manifest content of communication" (1952:18). It is a procedure for systematically examining textual or visual materials to extract information bearing on the message or messages they communicate. In order to carry out such systematic examination of materials, it is necessary to distinguish the different levels of units to be studied. Krippendorff (1980) distinguishes between three types of units that are germane to content analysis: sampling units, recording units, and context units. By **sampling units** he means independent, self-contained elements such as articles, books, films, pictures, or speeches that can be selected for study. In combination, the sampling units constitute a population of interest. For example, one might be interested in all books published in the United States in the twentieth century. Because of the sheer volume of books published, it would not be possible to examine all of them, but it would be possible to sample a certain representative proportion of them to analyze with the intent of generalizing the results of that analysis to the whole list.

Recording units are the aspects of the sampling units that become the actual focus of the content analysis. Krippendorff characterizes these as "the separately analyzable parts of a sampling unit. While sampling units tend to have physically identifiable boundaries, the distinctions among recording units are achieved as a result of a descriptive effort" (1980:58).

Krippendorff claims that most content analyses use one or more of five different ways of identifying recording units:

- **Physical units.** These are units that can be physically delineated in space or in time. For example, one might use the pages of a book as recording units or the individual frames of a motion picture film. In terms of time, one might use the times of the day (e.g., mornings, afternoons, and evenings) to study the mix of television programs offered.

- **Syntactical units.** Syntactical units, he says, are natural units that are relative to the grammar of a particular communication medium. Thus, in terms of a written communiqué, the syntactical unit could be a word, a sentence, or a paragraph. In applying the concept of the syntactical unit, the author says, "Syntactical units in the nonverbal media are the television shows (as listed in the *TV Guide*), the acts in theatrical performances, encounters in drama, news items in broadcasts, or editing shots in film" (1980:61).

- **Referential units.** By referential units the author means those that refer to objects, events, particular persons, ideas, or countries. As an example, in analyzing fiction books one might focus on the characters. In analyzing news articles one might focus on which particular countries are mentioned.

- **Propositional units.** Rather than focus on a single referential unit such as a character in a book, a researcher might focus on a specific structure between characters such as a superordinate–subordinate relationship. Or, in the case of syntactical units, one might look at how words are related to each other in sentence structures such as subjects, objects, and modifiers. Consequently, propositional units are a more complex level of analysis than single referential or syntactical units.

- **Thematic units.** When the purpose of the analysis is to extract the subject or subjects of a sampling unit, one is engaged in thematic analysis. When one concentrates on thematic units one is looking for the essential point or points being made by the communication. For example, a study of the stump speeches of politicians might focus on the themes stressed by the respective candidates. Whereas one candidate might focus on the reestablishment of family values, another might focus on downsizing government and a third might focus on crime reduction.

The third category of units of analysis, **context units,** takes into account the environment within which the recording units occur. The meanings attached to recording units are often meaningful only within the context in which they occur. For example, if the recording units are words, it is obvious that the meaning of a particular word can be understood only within the context in which it is found. The meaning of the word *love* has different connotations depending on the context in which it is being used. Love of a husband for a wife does not have the same meaning as love of a mother for a daughter. Nor does love of one's country have the same meaning as love of God. This word takes on four different meanings in these four contexts.

Which sampling units, recording units, and context units are relevant to a particular study depends on the subject of the study and the way that the study is conceptualized. In a study that is intended to test theory, the content analysis units should be suggested by the theory so the researcher should know what units must be sampled and how the analysis of the sampled units should proceed (e.g., what recording units are to be used and what context units are relevant). Furthermore, the theory should offer guidelines for determining which of the five types of recording units mentioned previously must be used.

On the other hand, if the research is not guided by theory, the recording and context units, at least, may have to develop out of a careful examination of the sampling units that have been collected. When the units of analysis are derived from the data in this way, the results of the analysis are not tests of theoretical hypotheses, but rather the generation of theoretical hypotheses that must be tested later with other data.

Computerized Content Analysis

From the social scientist's point of view, text data and other qualitative data pose important practical problems for research. Two key problems are the costs of handling large volumes of these data and **coder reliability.** Computer technology provides partial solutions to these two problems. The hope is for a solution that will tirelessly handle large quantities of data reliably.

Computers have been used since the 1960s to handle textual data. An early interest was in developing **word counts** automatically. Each unique word in a text (called a type) would be listed alphabetically with a tally of the number of times a type appeared in the text (i.e., the number of tokens there were of each unique type). One could then create a ratio of the number of different types that appeared among the tokens that were used (a **type/token ratio**). This ratio is sometimes used as a measure of the complexity of a text; the higher the proportion of different words in a given length text, the more complex the expression of ideas in the text. A number of **readability indices** can also be computed using the proportion of words in a text that are long words.

Most talk involves the use of a rather small vocabulary of different common words. In English, the 100 most frequently used words account for about half of the words used by speakers and writers, and a vocabulary of the most common 5,000 words covers more than 90% of what is said or written. The patterning of the use of these words carries information about social context and about the ideas and emphases that are important. Vocabulary and use patterns (e.g., word characteristics, words used together, word and sentence length) have been used to aid in identifying unknown authors by matching text characteristics in a text of unknown authorship with those of a text of known authorship.

Another early interest in computer text analysis was in the creation of **concordances** that would indicate where a word could be located in the text (usually by line number) and in displaying some of the text immediately around specific words. **Key words in context (KWIC)** programs list each instance of each word in a text alphabetically, down the center of a page, together with words (often 5 to 10) that immediately preceded and immediately followed each word. This provides some idea of how a given word was used in its sentence context.

In addition to ever-more-complex word processors, some programs were created that would analyze text in a more research-oriented way. Stone and colleagues (1966) at Harvard developed a mainframe computer system called the General Inquirer that served as the basis for a number of early computer content analysis studies of text. The system was based on a computerized dictionary in which words that reflect a given idea were grouped together in a specific category. For example, the category *self* might contain the words *I, me, my, mine,* and so on. Text often was tagged, marking various parts of speech in sentences that would be used in the computer program to classify given words more appropriately. The computer could then go through the text and use rules that had been programmed to categorize words appropriately in the text into the preestablished **computerized dictionary categories.** The result would be category counts (or percentages) for each of the categories in the dictionary. Further analysis would use these counts to see which ideas in the text were emphasized, as compared with other texts in the analysis. The researcher proceeds in a quantitative or qualitative way, based on the computer results, to identify meanings, connections, and examples from the text.

With widespread availability of powerful personal computers, the number of computer programs created to help the content analyst has grown rapidly. In general, current content analysis programs fall into three categories.

Aids in Managing Text. Researchers dealing with text need to transcribe it into computer form, make copies, move text around by cutting and pasting relevant sections together, editing and correcting errors, searching for certain types of words, and counting the number of words. Most of these operations are readily handled by word processing programs. Scanners can help read printed text into a computer file, ready for content analysis.

Aids for Coding Text. There are many computer programs that help the researcher code text.[4] For example, Ethnograph is a widely distributed and maintained program that permits the researcher to mark blocks of text in a transcript file and assign it one or more code categories the researcher creates for the study.[5] A passage might represent a negative statement about a character in a book that is available as a computer file. The researcher could mark that passage and then select the "negative" category and maybe the character being discussed from a list of possible codes that the researcher prepared and described in setting up the computer analysis. The program would remember these codes and the text that goes with them so that the researcher could later ask for a list of all passages that were "negative" (or even some combination of codes) for further examination and analysis.

Different programs accommodate different coding schemes (e.g., *who* did *what* to *whom,* or what event *follows* another event in a sequence of events) and provide a variety of tools for graphic and numeric organization and presentation of the coded data. All of this helps the researcher analyze the relevant aspects of a text.

These aids to coding text intimately involve the researcher in all the decisions about what code to assign to a given text passage. This means that the researcher can bring to bear on the coding decision a broader reading of the text, an understanding

[4]Computer programs that aid in the coding of text include INTEXT (available from ProGAMMA, P.O. Box 841, 9700 AV Groningen, The Netherlands), AskSam (AskSam Systems, P.O. Box 1428, Perry, FL 32347), QSR NUD*IST (distributed by Scolari, Sage Publications, 2455 Teller Road, Thousand Oaks, CA 91320), and TextPack described in Weber (1990).

[5]Ethnograph is available from Qualis Research Associates, P.O. Box 2070, Amherst, MA 01004.

of the social situation surrounding production of the text, and an understanding of the intent of the coding scheme. The computer simply smoothes out the process and makes it more efficient and, in some cases, helps avoid simple coding errors. Coder reliability and bias are relevant concerns.

Content Analysis Programs. A small number of programs build in the rules for coding aspects of the meaning found in text. They provide scores that are used in the process of analyzing textual data. The General Inquirer was an early program of this type. Some programs permit the investigator to develop rules for identifying key words or sequences, which then can be used automatically to identify and record instances of those sequences in a large archive of text such as a newspaper archive. Other programs contain procedures to identify patterns of category usage that are compared with previous data on various social settings so that the way topics are framed—the social context of the text—can be identified and compared between texts. Scores that contrast the emphasis on ideas in a given text with the emphasis generally expected in a broad sampling of English can be computed to help identify ideas that are conspicuously absent as well as those that are overrepresented in the text.[6] These programs increase the reliability of coding and enable an investigator to pursue the analysis in greater detail.

Many social and cultural regularities can be found in an examination of textual data. There is no single true meaning of a text. The meaning of the pattern of word-symbols depends on the theoretical ideas a researcher has in approaching the text. A psychoanalyst may have one theory, a political scientist another, and a sociologist or linguist yet another. The researcher generally is interested in factors that lead to certain kinds of meaning being expressed or to the consequences of these patterns for other outcomes.

Issues in the Use of Content Analysis

Although content analysis is an extremely useful technique for the processing of qualitative secondary data, as is the case with any research technique, there are strengths and weaknesses involved in its use.

Strengths of Content Analysis. Content analysis enjoys a number of strengths that qualify it as the premier procedure for use in the processing of qualitative or textual data.

- *Emphasis.* Textual data often provide insight into meanings and the emphasis the writer or speaker puts on a topic. This comes through by the inclusion of things

[6]One of the programs in this category that scores social context and ideas that are emphasized is called the Minnesota Contextual Content Analysis (MCCA) program, described in McTavish and Pirro (1990). It has been incorporated in a dictionary analysis program for the PC by Ken Litkowski, CL Research, 9208 Gue Road, Damascus, MD 20872-1025 (see http://www.clres.com).

that are pertinent, the omission of things that are not as important, and the way ideas are presented. The way in which ideas are framed is also evident in text.

- *Reactivity.* Because the data being analyzed are nonreactive, content analysis is also nonreactive. No matter what type of handling the data are subjected to, including physical alteration (such as cutting and pasting), the essential substantive nature of the data is not altered because they are existing data beyond the influence of their original creators (e.g., authors, artists, performers). Of course, if original data were collected through open-ended interviews, then the impact of the researcher on the data-collection process would be a concern.

- *Response.* Once the sampling units are defined, it is usually possible to obtain the relevant data for 100% of the units sampled. The problem of nonresponse is essentially nonexistent because the data sampled already exist.

- *Sample units.* Sources of the units sampled are generally identifiable and can be documented. For example, a sample of newspaper opinion articles can be identified by dates of publication, places of publication, and, in most cases, identities of their authors. This makes possible some assessment of the quality of the data being subjected to analysis. Furthermore, these kinds of information make it possible to identify the relevant context units that must be taken into consideration in performing data analysis.

- *Time.* Because the units available for sampling often represent materials produced over time, it is possible to subject them to longitudinal analysis, which may delineate trends and reveal significant patterns of change.

- *Reliability.* Once recording units are defined and procedures are developed for analyzing those units, it is possible to conduct reliability checks on the analysis by having a number of researchers analyze the same data independently and by comparing their separate analyses.

- *Multiple units.* Because of the richness of the data being analyzed, it is possible to subject them to analysis using more than one type of recording unit. For example, a study of opinion articles could focus on single words, sentences, and themes all within the same analysis. Furthermore, these recording units could be analyzed in terms of the various contexts within which they occur.

Weaknesses of Content Analysis. The weaknesses of the content analysis technique include the following:

- *Representation.* The sampling units available for study may not be a fair representation of the population that the study ultimately seeks to speak for. For example, if a sample of newspaper articles is selected over time as a representation of public feelings about various current events, there is no assurance that what gets published is really representative and free of biases. This weakness can be just as troublesome in studies of professional journal articles as in studies that rely on the mass media for data. For example, if a researcher wanted to study trends in medical research throughout the twentieth century, he or she would have no assurance that what appeared in the medical journals fairly represented the research that was undertaken. Editors of journals and editorial boards often have biases in favor of or against certain types of research. Consequently, they might ignore a whole line of research because they were not interested in it or did not approve of it. Personal documents such as letters or diaries might not provide representative data for a general population because some segments of the population might be illiterate and others might be more prone to set their thoughts down on paper than citizens in general.

▪ *Preconceived ideas.* In approaching data with a preconceived set of recording units, researchers might completely miss important information imbedded in the database. The concepts used for analysis of qualitative data structure what researchers find in the data. The conceptualization of the research, therefore, becomes a crucial factor in determining how fruitful analysis of the data will be. Similar drawbacks apply to most research, quantitative or qualitative.

▪ *Misinterpretation.* Because content analysis deals with the processing of existing data, the meanings of materials are determined by the researchers without the benefit of clarifying feedback from the creators of the materials. This can be a particular problem when the sampling units represent materials created over a long period of time. If the recording units are words, for example, it is possible that words appearing in earlier materials may not have the same meanings as the same words appearing in more recent materials. A case in point is the word *gay.* Depending on when a written document was produced, a gay man might be (1) dressed in bright or fine clothing, (2) light-hearted and carefree, or (3) homosexual (*Concise Oxford Dictionary,* 1982:409).

The changing meaning of the word *gay* is documented in the dictionary and, if the researcher took the trouble, he or she might be able to connect a particular meaning of the word to a particular period of time. However, it is also likely that other words or phrases would be subject to misinterpretation without the researcher's knowledge that the misinterpretation had occurred.

▪ *Context information.* Because the content of a personal document is determined not only by the creator of the document but also by the intended recipient, it may be difficult to establish the appropriate context within which to analyze the document because the person or people for whom the document was written may not be known. Of course, the same problem could occur in the process of analyzing mass media data. A book written for a professional audience might be very different from a book on the same subject written for a popular audience.

▪ *Legibility.* Personal documents are often written in longhand. Parts of the documents might be illegible, thus making an accurate content analysis difficult, if not impossible. Particular words that are illegible might be key words that, when not taken into consideration, change the meanings of the sentences.

▪ *Identity.* When pictures, such as photographs, are the medium being subjected to content analysis, problems may arise if the photographs are not identified as to time, place, and people portrayed. These features of the photographs might be crucial to the process of accurate content analysis.

SUMMARY

Research based on the use of existing data is increasingly common in sociology because of the availability of computerized data archives, other kinds of data archives, increasing emphasis on longitudinal research, and an increase in research involving international data.

The kinds of data used in this research may be classified as quantitative or qualitative. Quantitative data are exemplified by census data or survey data. Qualitative data include public and personal documents not originally generated as data. Durkheim's study of suicide rates is a classic example of the use of quantitative data, whereas Thomas and Znaniecki's study of Polish peasants is a classic example of the use of qualitative data.

Studies making use of existing data involve the same research stages as any other study, with the exception of the data collection stage. At the data collection stage the task becomes one of locating existing data that are adequate to answer the research questions. Computer technology has accelerated the development of cumulative data archives that are readily available to researchers. Existing quantitative data are particularly attractive to use because they are usually stored in a form ready for statistical analysis. Qualitative data, on the other hand, usually require considerable analysis and coding before they can be subjected to hypothesis testing.

Quantitative secondary data have both strengths and weaknesses. Among their strengths are savings in data collection and processing costs, the large numbers of representative cases available for analysis, the availability of cumulative data, and the lack of reactivity of the data to secondary analysis. Among their weaknesses are gaps in coverage of representative cases, absence of some relevant variables and meaningful response categories, hidden biases and other weaknesses in the existing data, and lack of contemporaneous data.

Qualitative secondary data also have strengths and weaknesses. Among their strengths are savings in data collection costs, savings in access costs, large numbers of cases available, availability of cumulative data, lack of reactivity of data to secondary analysis, and the richness of the data available. Among their weaknesses are lack of representativeness, lack of knowledge of the circumstances under which data were created, the presence of irrelevant data, questionable accuracy, problems of legibility, and lack of timeliness.

A major data analysis technique for qualitative data is content analysis. It involves the systematic assessment of documents, some of which may not have been originally intended for use as data. The types of data extracted from the documents are determined by the research questions and hypotheses posed.

In the past, content analysis was a long, tedious process; however, the development of computer software is showing promise in reducing the costs involved in handling large volumes of text and improving coder reliability. Current software programs for content analysis fall into three categories: aids in managing text, aids for coding text, and programs that perform the content analysis.

Content analysis shares many of the same strengths and weaknesses as qualitative data. Nevertheless, it is a key technique for bridging the qualitative–quantitative gap.

On the whole, secondary data are attractive to researchers because they provide large databases at a reasonable cost and, consequently, open up avenues of research that have not generally been accessible because of limited resources of time and funding.

TERMS TO KNOW

Access
Accretion measures
Bias
Codebook
Coder reliability
Computerized dictionary categories
Concordance
Content analysis
Context units
Coverage
Cumulative data
Data archives
Dross
Historical data
Key words in context (KWIC)
Legibility
Physical units
Propositional units
Reactivity
Readability indices
Recording units
Referential units
Representativeness
Sampling units
Secondary data
  Qualitative
  Quantitative
Specification errors
Syntactical units
Thematic units
Timeliness
Type/token ratio
Word counts

ISSUES AND COMPARISONS

Ethics of secondary data research
Shortcomings of archived data
Strengths and weaknesses of quantitative and qualitative secondary data
Quality of secondary data, documentation adequacy
Data creation context
Inference and response
Data preparation errors

EXERCISES

1. Search the research literature for an article based on the use of secondary quantitative data. Using the lists of strengths and weaknesses of quantitative data in this chapter, evaluate the article.

2. Search the research literature for an article based on the use of secondary qualitative data. Using the lists of strengths and weaknesses of qualitative data in this chapter, evaluate the article.

3. Select an article from a magazine or newspaper and lay out a plan for doing a content analysis of it. Be sure to define the unit of analysis you would use. What problems do you foresee in attempting to analyze the article?

REFERENCES

Armstrong, Edward G., "The Rhetoric of Violence in Rap and Country Music," *Sociological Inquiry* February 1993;63(1):64–83.

Berelson, Bernard, *Content Analysis in Communications Research,* Free Press, New York, 1952.

Berezin, Mabel, "Cultural Form and Political Meaning: State-subsidized Theater, Ideology, and the Language of Style in Fascist Italy," *American Journal of Sociology* March 1994;99(5):1237–86.

Binder, Amy, "Constructing Racial Rhetoric: Media Depictions of Harm in Heavy Metal and Rap Music," *American Sociological Review* December 1993;58(6):753–67.

Chafetz, Janet Saltzman, Jon Lorence, and Christine La Rosa, "Gender Depictions of the Professionally Employed: A Content Analysis of Trade Publications, 1960–1990," *Sociological Perspectives* Spring 1993;36(1):63–82.

Concise Oxford Dictionary of Current English, edited by J. B. Sykes, Clarendon Press, Oxford, UK, 1982.

De Graaf, Nan Dirk, Paul Nieuwbeerta, and Anthony Heath, "Class Mobility and Political Preferences: Individual and Contextual Effects," *American Journal of Sociology* January 1995;100(4):997–1027.

Durkheim, Émile, *Le Suicide: Étude de Sociologie,* Alcan, Paris, 1897; translated by John A. Spaulding and George Simpson, edited by George Simpson, and published as *Suicide,* Free Press, New York, 1951.

Forrest, Thomas R., "Disaster Anniversary: A Social Reconstruction of Time," *Sociological Inquiry* November 1993;63(4):444–56.

Gardner, Saundra, "Exploring the Family Album: Social Class Differences in Images of Family Life," *Sociological Inquiry* Spring 1991;61(2):242–51.

Krippendorff, Klaus, *Content Analysis: An Introduction to Its Methodology,* Sage, Newbury Park, CA, 1980.

Madge, John, *The Origins of Scientific Sociology,* Free Press, Glencoe, NY, 1962.

McTavish, Donald G., and Ellen B. Pirro, "Contextual Content Analysis," *Quality and Quantity* 1990;24:245–65.

Miller, Delbert C. *Handbook of Research Design and Social Measurement,* 5th ed., Sage, Newbury Park, CA, 1991.

Plummer, Ken, *Documents of Life,* George Allen & Unwin, London, 1983.

Ponsonby, A., *English Diaries: A Review of English Diaries from the Sixteenth to the Twentieth Century with an Introduction on Diary Writing,* Methuen, London, 1923.

Rathje, W. L., "Trace Measures," in L. Sechrest, ed., *Unobtrusive Measurement Today,* Jossey-Bass, San Francisco, 1979.

Rathje, W. L., and W. W. Hughes, "The Garbage Project as a Nonreactive Approach: Garbage in . . . Garbage Out?" in H. W. Sinaiko and L. A. Broedling, eds., *Perspectives on Attitude Assessment: Surveys and Their Alternatives,* Smithsonian Institution, Washington, DC, 1975.

Spencer, J. William, and Elizabeth Triche, "Media Constructions of Risk and Safety: Differential Framings of Hazard Events," *Sociological Inquiry* May 1994;64(2):199–213.

Stone, Philip J., Dexter C. Dunphy, Marshall S. Smith, and Daniel M. Ogilvie, *The General Inquirer: A Computer Approach to Content Analysis,* MIT Press, Cambridge, MA, 1966.

Thomas, William I., and Florian Znaniecki, *The Polish Peasant in Europe and America,* Gorham Press, Boston, 1918–1920.

Webb, Eugene T., Donald T. Campbell, Richard D. Schwartz, Lee Sechrest, and Janet Belew Grove, *Nonreactive Measures in the Social Sciences,* 2nd ed., Houghton Mifflin, Boston, 1981.

Weber, Robert Philip, *Basic Content Analysis,* 2nd ed., Sage, Newbury Park, CA, 1990.

CHAPTER TEN

APPROACHES TO DATA ANALYSIS

Once the data for a study are in hand, it is necessary to determine whether they support the hypotheses of the study, refute them, or fail to do either. Assuming that the data collection phase of the study has gone according to plan and the data are those that were called for conceptually, the next step is analysis. If not, as Box 10.1 suggests, the data must be discarded.

Whether data come from questionnaires, interviews, observation, or personal documents, they are initially in raw form and must be processed before they can be subjected to analysis. Computerized databases such as the General Social

BOX 10.1
ARE THE DATA WORTH ANALYZING?

One of the skills of a good researcher is that of deciding whether the data at hand are worth analyzing. If the data are not adequate, they should not be analyzed! As simple as this seems, it is difficult to set aside a data set in which considerable work and resources have been invested. All too often one hears, "Some data are better than none, even if the data are seriously flawed." To analyze bad data is a waste of time and likely to be misleading—garbage in, garbage out! The following circumstances might lead an investigator to discard a data set:

- Key measures are not reliable (e.g., based on unsystematic guesses).
- Response rate is low (say, 50% or less) or the data set is incomplete.
- Major variables relevant to the study are missing or not validly measured.
- The data do not contain needed contrasts.
- The wrong cases were sampled.
- There is strong evidence that the data are biased (as in research sponsored and run by people who have a strong vested interest in the outcome).
- Key variables do not have needed categories distinguished.
- There is no good record of how the data were gathered, checked, and recorded.

Survey or the U.S. Census are an exception. They have already been processed and can be analyzed without much additional handling.

STEPS IN DATA ANALYSIS

Although the details vary from one study to the next according to the kinds of data that have been collected, several steps in the process of data analysis are standard.

Coding

The first step involves reducing raw data to systematic forms through coding and recording.

Case Identification Numbers. Typically, each response form is given a sequential identification number, which is also entered into a database so that errors that are discovered later can be corrected by tracing back to the original response form. If assurances of confidentiality have been given and identities are known, using ID numbers can help mask the respondent's identity. Often an investigator removes identities from the response form and uses only ID numbers for reference, keeping a matching list of identities and ID numbers in a secure place until the data are checked for accuracy before the list is destroyed. This helps to preserve the promised confidentiality.

Coding Variables. In the case of a questionnaire, an interview schedule, or an observation schedule, the responses to questions or the observational units are often precoded (e.g., with preassigned codes printed on the instrument itself) so that the data can be entered directly into a database for analysis. For example, the question "What is your current marital status?" is asked, and the response categories are as follows:

1. Never married
2. Married
3. Divorced
4. Legally separated
5. Widowed
6. Does not apply to this respondent
7. Refused to answer question
8. NR (no response, blank)

The person processing the data can make note of which category is checked on the instrument being scrutinized and enter the code number (1 to 5) of that category into the database. Codes for types of nonresponse (6 to 8) are added as well ("did not know," "refused to answer," "missing data," or "not relevant for this respondent"). Good practice calls for assigning some code to each variable for each case so that it is clear nothing has been skipped inadvertently. The more precoding that can be done at the stage of instrument construction, the easier it is to process the raw data.

Coding Text. If the raw data are in the form of narratives, then it will take more effort to process them for database entry. For example, if the data are personal letters, it will probably be necessary to perform a content analysis (see Chapter 9) before the data are ready to be coded. Often this means creating a verbatim transcription with a word processor and saving it to a computer file for content analysis. Meaningful categories of data must be developed, and the letters (or other coding units) must be searched for occurrences of those categories. Examples of possible categories include occurrence of certain significant words or phrases (e.g., "money problems"), occurrence of certain themes (e.g., "family responsibilities"), or mention of certain people (e.g., "grandmother").

Even in the case of questionnaires, if some questions are open-ended, it is necessary to do content analysis on the responses in order to develop a coding system for data entry.

Coding Observational Data. If the research involves observational records, these are coded in a way that is similar to coding questions (if an observation schedule has been created that has categories for an observer to check), or content analyzed (if, for example, the observer has narrative field notes or the data are recorded on audio- or videotape). Again, an early decision on the unit to be coded is important.

Codebook. A codebook is usually created that lists the variables and codes and describes any rules for deciding how responses should be coded. The codebook is very useful later in the analysis process because it indicates what the various codes mean.

Data Entry

The second step in data analysis involves entering the coded data into a database. The database is generally organized by case, with the data for each case recorded according to the variables defined for the study. Thus, in a questionnaire study each respondent is identified by a case number, and his or her answers to questions are coded and entered into the database, as illustrated in Figure 10.1. In almost all instances, the database is stored as a computer file to be subjected to computerized analysis.

Checking

The third step involved in data analysis is known as cleaning the data. This involves checking the database to make sure that the data codes entered are consistent with the raw data collected for each of the subjects (cases) of the study. Whenever discrepancies are found between the raw data and the coded data, these are resolved and corrected in the database. Preliminary computer runs are

	Variables					
ID#	var1	var2	var3	var4	...	var-*k*
001	1	34	4	7		9
002	3	17	2	9		3
003	3	25	1	3		1
•						
•						
•						
N	2	29	2	2		8

(Cases)

FIGURE 10.1 Case-By-Variable Data Matrix

usually used to check for data entry errors. Using the current marital status question mentioned earlier as an example, there were five response categories represented by the five numbers between 1 and 5. In order to provide for subjects who failed to answer the question, some code such as the number 8 (or several codes if there are different types of nonresponse that are relevant) might have been assigned to the no-response category. Computer software may be used to produce a simple table that tabulates the number of responses to each code number assigned. If such a table is produced and it includes responses coded with the number 10, for example, that indicates that there are some errors in the database that must be identified and corrected because 10 was not among the valid codes assigned.

Analysis

The fourth step involves using statistical techniques to organize and summarize the data in meaningful ways so that they may be assessed for their relevance in answering the research questions posed by the study. This step is discussed later in this chapter.

Interpretation

The final step is to interpret the results of the analysis and determine whether the data support the hypotheses of the study.

The details and cost of these steps must be planned while the research design is being worked out because the design and the data analysis strategies are interdependent. If the details are worked out while the study is being planned, then the researchers have some assurance that they will collect the data necessary to carry out the analysis needed to answer the research questions. Collecting data and then deciding what analysis is necessary can be disastrous. There have been cases in which data analysis was not planned and researchers discovered that the data they had were incomplete or were not in the proper format for the necessary analysis.

QUANTITATIVE AND QUALITATIVE APPROACHES

Research in sociology is commonly split into two supposedly distinct and separate approaches: the quantitative approach and the qualitative approach. Those who identify themselves as qualitative researchers sometimes imply that the quantitative approach deals strictly with data that have been reduced to their bare minimum so that they will lend themselves to statistical manipulation. They argue that such data are stripped of their very essence, thus sacrificing their social significance in the interests of convenience in processing.

In this book we have made a distinction between quantitative and qualitative raw data in terms of how those data are collected and recorded (see Chapter 9). We pointed out, for example, that diaries, personal letters, and other personal documents are usually not intended for use as data and consequently do not appear in a form that readily lends itself to quantitative processing. In contrast, the example of questionnaire responses to a query about current marital status illustrates raw data that lend themselves easily to quantitative analysis, without the need for further processing. Often the volume of data on many cases calls for techniques (usually quantitative) to simplify the process of understanding the data as a whole.

However, there is an important difference between quantitative and qualitative raw data and quantitative and qualitative analysis of those data. Quantitative analysis does not imply that some sophisticated statistical manipulation of the data is necessary. Rather, it implies that generalizing results from one observation of one case is not justified. Consequently, a number of cases judged to be representative of the population being studied must be observed before one can use random sampling logic to make inferences to the broader population from which it was drawn. Alternatively, if only one case is observed (such as a particular organization), then it must be observed over time in order to collect enough observations to be able to discern patterns of behavior characteristic of that case and make needed contrasts for interpretation. In either event, counting is involved, and the analysis uses quantitative tools.

When statistical analysis is used, the researchers are merely using a set of techniques designed to evoke the essential characteristics of data in a more formal and systematic manner than a researcher's observation that the subjects being studied "usually" behave in a particular way.

In other words, the difference between qualitative and quantitative analysis is not a difference in kind, but merely a difference in degree. The argument that quantitative treatment of data robs those data of their essence is erroneous. The mere exercise of looking for recurring patterns of behavior in qualitative data is, in fact, submitting those data to analysis, and it is at that point that they may be robbed of their essence (if such robbery occurs), rather than when the frequencies with which the patterns recur are recorded. Using statistical techniques to analyze data merely simplifies the task of evaluating the degree to which those data support or fail to support the hypotheses being addressed by the research, particularly when many cases are involved.

STATISTICAL ANALYSIS

After data are organized and stored in a database, they are usually submitted to some type of statistical analysis. Statistics is a set of techniques for making sense of and generalizing from data.

The field of statistics is usually divided into two parts: descriptive (or analytical) statistics and inferential statistics. The descriptive part of the field involves the use of one or more statistical techniques to analyze the data in hand and come to some conclusions about what they reveal. Descriptive analysis is limited to making illuminating statements about the data researchers have already collected.

Once the descriptive analysis has been completed, inferential statistics may come into play. If the data analyzed descriptively constitute a probability (random) sample of some larger population and if the results of the analysis warrant it, then inferential techniques may be used to generalize the results of that analysis to the population represented by the sample (see Chapter 5 for a discussion of sampling and inference). On the other hand, if the data analyzed are based on a complete enumeration of the relevant population, then inferential techniques are not needed. In other words, inferential statistics are used to estimate population characteristics from sample data when population characteristics are not readily available. If population data are available, such estimates are neither relevant nor necessary. If the data are neither a population nor a random sample of a population, then the researchers must limit their conclusions to the subjects in the study and, again, statistical inferences to a population are ruled out.

"Meaningless statistics were up one-point-five per cent this month over last month."

LEVELS OF STATISTICAL ANALYSIS

Statistical analysis of data may be performed on several levels. In **univariate analysis,** one variable is analyzed at a time. The purpose of **bivariate analysis** is to determine whether there is some relationship between two variables. When more than two variables are simultaneously involved, **multivariate analysis** is performed.

When data are analyzed, three general approaches can be used: tables, graphs, and statistical measures. In the first approach the data are organized into tables so that their distributions may be examined. This approach works best with variables for which there are few categories of responses. Although tables can be constructed for continuous variables (e.g., age), collapsing the variables into a few response categories is necessary so that the resulting tables are not too unwieldy. For example, an age distribution might be collapsed into a number of age classes in which each class covers an interval of 10 years.

Tables may be constructed for univariate, bivariate, and multivariate analyses. Multivariate tables may be complicated to analyze, however, if too many variables are included.

Graphs are an increasingly popular way to analyze data. This is especially true because computer graphic programs have become more sophisticated. Some graphic techniques are more useful than others because some focus selectively on key features of the data or permit comparisons most relevant for a given problem (see Loether and McTavish, 1993:Chapter 4, for a discussion of graphic techniques). Graphs can be used for analyzing univariate data and bivariate data without too much difficulty. In the case of multivariate data, graphs may be used for three variables, but beyond that their use is limited because of the problem of working visually in more than three dimensions.

The third approach to data analysis involves the use of statistical measures. Statistics are essentially index numbers that summarize characteristics of data. The discussion to follow, dealing with univariate, bivariate, and multivariate analysis, focuses on this third approach.

Univariate Analysis

When statistical analysis focuses on one variable at a time, the emphasis is on examining the distribution of scores on that variable. What makes scores on a variable interesting is the fact that they do vary. As a matter of fact, it is that variation in scores for which hypotheses and research questions attempt to account.

Four characteristics of a univariate distribution may be significant for the research questions being asked: central tendency, variability, skewness, and kurtosis. **Central tendency** is the proclivity of the scores of a variable to cluster around some central value. If such a central value can be identified, it can be used to represent the distribution as a whole. **Variability** is the tendency for scores in a distribution to take different values and to spread themselves around the point of central tendency. **Skewness** is the tendency for scores in a distribution to vary more in one direction from the central tendency (e.g., in a positive direction) than in the other, thus producing an asymmetric distribution. **Kurtosis** is the degree of sharpness in the peak of a distribution.

Central Tendency. One measure of central tendency is the mode, which is merely the score of a variable that occurs with the greatest frequency. If one were to examine the marital status of adults in the United States, for instance, it would be found that there are more people who are currently married than there are in any other specific score category for that variable (e.g., single, divorced, or widowed). Thus, "married" would be judged to be the most representative marital status with which to identify American adults.

The mode is the most commonly reported measure of central tendency in public opinion polls. For example, a preelection poll may report which of the candidates running for public office has the most supporters among those polled. If the percentage supporting the most popular candidate is greater than 50%, then the mode constitutes a majority. If the percentage supporting the most popular candidate is less than 50%, then the candidate is said to have a plurality, which is also the mode. Of course, the higher the percentage of cases at the mode, the stronger the mode is as a measure of central tendency. (See Box 10.2.)

BOX 10.2
LEVELS OF MEASUREMENT

Recall from Chapter 2 that the information referred to by a number must be understood before analysis can proceed. Four levels of measurement are usually distinguished as a way of highlighting significant differences in what numbers may mean:

- *Nominal:* A mutually exclusive and exhaustive set of categories with no order implied.
- *Ordinal:* A mutually exclusive and exhaustive set of categories that are ordered conceptually.
- *Interval:* A mutually exclusive and exhaustive set of categories that are ordered and have known quantitative distances between categories, which may be continuous or discrete.
- *Ratio:* A mutually exclusive and exhaustive set of categories that are ordered and have a known quantitative distance between categories. The scale of measurement has a defined zero point, which means the absence of the quantity being measured; these too may be continuous or discrete.

Examples include marital status (nominal), pro or con attitudes about something (ordinal), Fahrenheit temperature (interval), and number of siblings (most count-type variables are ratio level). Statistical analysis typically treats interval and ratio variables in the same way and interval and ratio level variables are simply called interval variables.

Occasionally the distribution of a variable has two modes rather than one. Such a distribution is known as a bimodal distribution. A bimodal distribution can have interesting implications for some studies. As a case in point, when international data on infant mortality rates during the 1930s are compared with the rates for the 1960s, it is found that the earlier distribution is bimodal and the later one is unimodal. The earlier bimodal distribution distinguishes clearly between the western, industrialized countries and the less developed countries of the world. Two clear modes appear in the data, with high rates of infant mortality in the less developed countries and low rates in the more developed countries.

In contrast, the 1960s distribution is unimodal, indicating that the clear-cut and dramatic difference in infant mortality between less developed and more developed countries had disappeared by that time. Not only did all of the infant mortality rates decline between the two periods, but the striking difference in rates for the two types of countries disappeared. This change is probably attributable to the work of organizations such as the World Health Organization in combating infectious diseases and improving sanitation in less developed countries.

Of course, it is possible for a distribution to have more than two modes. The more modes there are, however, the less useful the mode is as a measure of central tendency. It is most clearly interpreted as a measure of central tendency when there is only one; and, of course, the larger the proportion of the cases in the distribution represented by that mode, the better it is as a descriptive summary of the data.

Although the mode is particularly intended as a measure of central tendency for nominal scale, categorical variables, it can also be used for distributions of ordinal, interval, or ratio measurements. As a matter of fact, the case of international infant mortality rates with a bimodal distribution illustrates the use of the mode for a distribution of ratio scale scores. When the mode is used to represent central tendency for distributions measured at a level above the nominal level, certain characteristics of those more refined levels of measurement (e.g., order and magnitude) are, in effect, being ignored.

When scores are measured on the ordinal level, the median rather than the mode is the preferred measure of central tendency. The median, unlike the mode, relies on the ability to put scores in order. Basically, the median is the middle score in a distribution of ordered scores. Consequently, there are equal numbers of scores above and below the median. The median represents central tendency in a distribution in the sense that it marks the middle of the distribution.

The arithmetic mean is the appropriate measure of central tendency for data measured at the interval or ratio level, given that there is no serious skewness present in the distribution being analyzed. The arithmetic mean is called that to distinguish it from other means that exist, such as the harmonic mean and the geometric mean. These means are used for special purposes that we will not get into in this chapter (see Loether and McTavish, 1993:Chapter 5).

The arithmetic mean is the summary measure commonly called the average. It is computed by adding up all valid scores for a variable and dividing by the number of valid scores. It is sensitive to differences in the magnitudes of scores and is thus the most comprehensive measure of central tendency. Because differences in magnitude are reflected in the arithmetic mean, it is not an appropriate measure of central tendency for nominal scale or ordinal scale variables. Its use is limited to analysis of interval or ratio variables.

Because the arithmetic mean, the measure of central tendency appropriate for more information-packed levels of measurement than the ordinal level, is a poor representation of central tendency when a distribution is seriously skewed, the median is often used in lieu of the mean. Because it is merely the order in which scores appear rather than their actual magnitudes that is important for computing the median, it is not unduly affected by skewness. On the other hand, the mean is. For example, the distribution of family annual income in the United States is badly skewed toward the high side because of a few extremely wealthy families. If the arithmetic mean is used to represent the central tendency of this distribution, it gives a distorted picture of the distribution because it is unduly affected by those few extreme incomes. The median, on the other hand, is the income above and below which 50% of the family incomes in the country lie.

A median cannot be computed for data measured at the nominal level because nominal scale data do not have order to them. However, it does lend itself to computation with interval or ratio scale data. When it is used as a measure of central tendency for such data, those data are, in effect, being reduced to the level of ordinal data because it is merely their order and not differences in their magnitudes that is being represented. The example of annual family income is a case in which the median rather than the mean is used to measure central tendency.

Measures of Variability. Whenever a measure of central tendency is computed for data, it should be accompanied by a measure of variability. Despite having similar scores on a measure of central tendency, two distributions may differ radically in their variability. For example, suppose that the students in two social studies classes are given an IQ test. The students in class A are found to have an average IQ of 110 and the students in class B average 112. Comparing only the arithmetic means of the classes, one would get the impression that the two classes are very similar and that the same approach may be used to teach both. However, if the variability in IQ scores is compared, it might be found that the IQs of those in class B vary from a low of 105 to a high of 122, and those in class A vary between 88 and 151. Obviously, the measures of central tendency do not reflect the relative heterogeneity of the students in the two classes. The teacher who used the same approach on both classes might do well with the students in class B by teaching to their average. However, if the same strategy were used in teaching class A, the brighter students might find the materials boring and unchallenging, and the slower students might be overwhelmed by the materials and not be able to keep up.

Because the subjects of sociological research are often collectivities such as groups or organizations rather than individuals, the significant characteristic of the subjects often is their variability rather than their central tendency. In such instances data analysis may not even include the computation of a measure of central tendency. Table 10.1 deals with a study by Adams (1953:406) that looked at the occupations of the fathers of physicians born in 5-year cohorts between 1875 and

TABLE 10.1 Trend of Respondents' Fathers' Occupational Prestige for Respondents Who Are Physicians, in Four U.S. Cities, by Respondent's Birth Cohort

DATE OF BIRTH (COHORT)	NUMBER	MEAN NORTH–HATT PRESTIGE RATING	STANDARD DEVIATION OF PRESTIGE RATINGS
1875–1879	9	78.7	7.5
1880–1884	9	77.9	6.7
1885–1889	7	81.6	8.8
1890–1894	15	80.9	7.0
1895–1899	19	74.8	10.4
1900–1904	22	74.6	8.7
1905–1909	24	74.2	14.2
1910–1914	23	74.0	10.6
1915–1920	9	76.4	13.6
Totals	137	76.1	10.7

1920. Scores on an occupational prestige scale (the North–Hatt Rating Scale) were assigned to the fathers' occupations for each birth cohort of physicians, then means and standard deviations (a measure of variability to be discussed shortly) were computed to examine the influence of intergenerational occupational inheritance.

Because fathers' occupations often have an influence on the occupations of their sons, Adams sought to determine the extent to which this phenomenon had an impact on the sons' occupations and whether it had changed over the years (Adams, 1953). He computed the mean prestige rating of the fathers' occupations for each age cohort and compared them. As you can see from Table 10.1, the means fluctuated between a high of 81.6 and a low of 74.0, but there was a difference of only 2.3 points between the mean of the first cohort and the mean of the last cohort. There is no clear-cut evidence of a trend toward either increasing or decreasing mean prestige over the period covered.

An examination of the standard deviations presents a different picture. The standard deviation is a measure of the variability of the scores in a distribution. The larger the standard deviation, the more variable the scores. Notice in Table 10.1 that the standard deviations, although they fluctuated in the short run, increased over the years covered in the study. The standard deviation for the last age cohort, born between 1915 and 1920, was almost twice as large as the one for the first age cohort (1875–1879).

What these results indicate is that although the average prestige rating for fathers' occupations did not change over the years, the variability of those ratings increased. Thus, physicians in the later cohorts came from families in which the range of prestige of their fathers' occupations was greater than it was in earlier cohorts. This indicates an opening up of the opportunity structure so that people who aspired to become physicians had a better chance of realizing their ambitions in later than in earlier cohorts, even though their fathers did not have high-prestige occupations.

As is the case with measures of central tendency, there are measures of variability appropriate to each of the scales of measurement: nominal, ordinal, interval, and ratio. At the nominal level of measurement, for which the mode is the appropriate measure of central tendency, the index of dispersion is an appropriate measure of variability. It is a measure of how much the subjects are spread over the different response categories of a nominal variable. For example, as was mentioned earlier in the discussion of the mode, the most common marital status among adults is married. Other possible categories of marital status include never married, divorced, widowed, and legally separated. If all subjects in a study were married, the mode would be married and the index of dispersion would have a value of 0, indicating maximum homogeneity in the responses. On the other hand, if the subjects of the study were evenly spread over the five categories of marital status, the index would be equal to +1, indicating maximum heterogeneity in the responses. In this case, there would be no meaningful mode to which one could point.

Although the index of dispersion is designed to measure variability of a nominal scale variable, it could also be used with ordinal, interval, and ratio scales of measurement. If it were, however, it would be ignoring characteristics of those scales of measurement that the nominal scale does not possess (e.g., order and magnitude).

If the variable being analyzed is ordinal but there are few response categories, then the index of dispersion would still be an appropriate measure of variability. For example, if the variable were social class and the three response categories were upper class, middle class, and lower class, then the index of dispersion could be used to measure variability, and the class including the central case in the distribution would be the median.

If the ordinal variable being analyzed had numerous ranks, then the appropriate measure of variability would be the interquartile range. The range of a distribution is the difference between the lowest score in the distribution and the highest score. The problem with using the range as a measure of variability is that the two extreme scores may not be generally representative of the overall distribution. The extreme scores may be unusual or errors. For example, the North–Hatt Occupational Prestige Scale (A. Reiss et al., 1961) is an ordinal scale that initially ranked the prestige of 100 occupations in the United States. At the high end of the scale was Justice of the U.S. Supreme Court and at the low end was shoe shiner. If this scale were used to measure occupational prestige of a sample of blue-collar workers at a meeting and there happened to be one physician at the meeting (another high-prestige occupation), perhaps as the featured speaker, the range would give an exaggerated impression of variability because of the presence of the physician. If the physician were not present, the range would be much narrower on occupational prestige.

Because of this problem with the overall range, a measure of variability that focuses on a truncated range is generally used for ordinal data. This measure is the interquartile range. It disregards the values in the lowest 25% and the highest 25% of the distribution of ranks and focuses on those that bound the middle 50% of the distribution. The logic behind this measure is that the middle 50% of the ranks is more likely to provide a representative picture of the variability of the distribution because of the tendency for the scores to cluster around the measure of central tendency (in this case, the median).

The interquartile range cannot be computed for a nominal level distribution because it depends on the ability to rank the score points in the distribution. However, it can be computed for interval or ratio level data. When it is used for either of these, in effect, it reduces the measurement level to an ordinal scale and ignores magnitude of difference in score points. Consequently, about the only time that the interquartile range would be used for interval or ratio level data is when the distribution of scores is seriously skewed, necessitating the use of the median instead of the mean as a measure of central tendency. Earlier it was pointed out that annual family income in the United States is badly skewed. Because of this skewness problem, the median is a more representative measure of central tendency than the mean. Accordingly, the median and the interquartile range could be used to measure central tendency and variability.

When the variable being analyzed is interval or ratio level and the arithmetic mean is used to measure central tendency, the appropriate measure of variability is the standard deviation. The standard deviation shares the philosophy used with the interquartile range: The scores in a distribution that cluster about the measure of central tendency are more representative of the distribution than are more remote scores. Accordingly, one standard deviation (above and below the mean of a distribution) measures the variability of the scores representing, roughly, two-thirds of the scores in the middle of the distribution around the point of central tendency.

Because an interval or ratio scale includes magnitude as a characteristic of measurement, the standard deviation focuses on the magnitude of difference between each score in the distribution and the mean. The difference between the mean and a score is called the deviation score. For example, if the average annual income for a sample of families were $35,000 and the Smith family had an annual income of $33,000, then the Smith family's deviation score would be –$2,000. For reasons better left to a statistics book for explanation (see Loether and McTavish, 1993:Chapter 5), the deviation score of each case in a distribution is determined, these deviation scores are squared, and the sum of these squared deviations is averaged. Finally, the standard deviation is arrived at by finding the square root of the average squared deviation.

The standard deviation is standard in the sense that one of its interpretations is in terms of the normal, bell-shaped distribution. When the actual distribution that researchers are analyzing closely fits the model of the bell-shaped curve, the area ranging from one standard deviation below the mean to one standard deviation above the mean includes approximately two-thirds (68.26% of the cases in a normal distribution) of the cases in the distribution. If the distribution being analyzed is seriously skewed, then the two-thirds rule does not apply, and the interpretation of the standard deviation in this sense is problematic.

As a rule, whenever the mean is used to measure central tendency, the standard deviation should be used to represent variability. As was pointed out in the discussion of Adams's study of occupational inheritance, however, there are occasions when the standard deviation is of primary interest and the mean is not computed at all.

Skewness and Kurtosis. Some statistical measures for skewness and kurtosis require a more technical discussion than can be developed here, but they can be found in statistics books (e.g., Loether and McTavish, 1993). More attention is given here to skewness than to kurtosis. However, kurtosis can also be a distorting factor for a distribution and can lead to problems in the interpretation of central tendency and variability in analyzing a set of interval or ratio data. After all, the interpretations of the mean and the standard deviation are based on the assumption of a normal distribution that is both symmetric and mesokurtic (moderately peaked).

In summary, when analysis of data is univariate, the principal characteristics of the data that are focused on are central tendency and variability. The other two characteristics, skewness and kurtosis, are less likely to appear in reports of results, but they are important, in addition to the measurement level of a variable, in selecting which measures of central tendency and variability to use and in interpreting the results of their use.

Bivariate Analysis

When the purpose of data analysis is to determine whether there is a relationship between two variables and to describe that relationship, the analysis is said to be bivariate. Generally, a distinction is made between the two variables in a bivariate analysis by casting each into separate roles: One is identified as an **independent variable** and the other is identified as a **dependent variable.** Recall that the distinction between an independent and a dependent variable was discussed earlier (see Chapter 2). The dependent variable is the one for whose scores the hypothesis attempts to explain the outcome. The independent variable is the one that serves as at least part of that explanation. If one were to think of the relationship between the independent and dependent variables in cause-and-effect terms, the independent variable would be the **cause** and the dependent variable would be the **effect.**

For example, assume that researchers are interested in the relationship between the amount of education people receive and the amount of money they make during their active work lives. The hypothesis might state that the more education a person receives, the more money that person will make during his or her work life. In this study the amount of education would be the independent variable and the amount of money earned would be the dependent variable.

The Meaning of Cause and Effect[1]**.** A cause-and-effect relationship implies a relationship between the independent and dependent variables. It may be that the causal variable is **sufficient** to produce the effect, the causal variable is **necessary** but not sufficient to produce the effect, or the causal variable is both **necessary and sufficient** (a one-to-one relationship between cause and effect). That is, every time

[1]See Box 4.1, p. 86.

the cause is introduced, the effect will follow without exception, and every time the cause is withheld the effect will fail to follow without exception. Often this latter sense of a cause–effect relationship is what investigators seek. But relationships that are found are generally not certain but probabilistic. A probabilistic relationship implies some level of predictability between the independent and the dependent variable, but not perfect predictability. Bivariate statistics help measure the extent to which a relationship exists between a presumed cause and effect.

Cigarette companies have argued repeatedly that scientists have not established a cause-and-effect relationship between cigarette smoking and lung cancer. In the strictest technical sense of the meaning of *cause and effect,* they are correct in their assertion. A cause-and-effect relationship would mean that every person who smoked would contract lung cancer and that nonsmokers would never contract it. Obviously this is not the case. However, scientists have established that there is a relationship between smoking and the occurrence of lung cancer. Heavy smokers have a higher rate of lung cancer than light smokers, and light smokers have a higher rate than nonsmokers. Furthermore, heavy smokers who quit smoking quickly reduce their chances of contracting the disease.

The problem is that the relationship between smoking and lung cancer is not a simple, bivariate, cause-and-effect one. That is, smoking is one of a number of variables that, in various combinations, may result in the contraction of lung cancer.

It is probably safe to say that no phenomenon of interest to scientists is of the simple, bivariate, cause-and-effect type. Consequently, so-called scientific laws are probability statements rather than absolute statements about relationships. Nevertheless, they are useful for both prediction and explanation.

Bivariate Measures of Relationship. There are many statistical techniques for measuring bivariate relationships. As is the case with the univariate measures discussed earlier, each of these techniques is intimately connected to the levels of measurement of the variables to be analyzed. Also, they focus on four characteristics of bivariate relationships. In this case, however, the four characteristics are the following: whether a relationship between the variables *exists*, the *degree* of relationship that exists, the *direction* of the relationship, and the *geometric nature* of the relationship.

If the values of an independent variable do not provide any information that may be used to predict values on the dependent variable, then there is no relationship between the two; they are said to be independent of each other. If a relationship does exist, then it is important to measure the degree or the strength of the relationship. Strength of relationship may vary from no relationship up to some maximum value. *Direction* of the relationship refers to the scales of the two values being analyzed and how they relate to each other. If an increase in the independent variable is accompanied by an increase in the dependent variable, then the direction of the relationship is said to be positive. If the independent variable increases as the dependent variable decreases (or vice versa), then the direction of the relationship is said to be negative or inverse. The fourth characteristic, the *geometric nature* of the relationship, refers to whether the graphic representation of the relationship between the scores on the independent and dependent variables is best described as a straight line, a stair-step function, or some sort of curved line.

Karl Pearson (1896) pioneered the development of a technique to measure the relationship between two continuous (interval or ratio scale) variables. It is called the Pearson Product Moment Coefficient of Correlation and is still the preferred technique for analyzing interval or ratio variables. In the process of developing his technique, Pearson standardized the resulting coefficients so that they could vary from a value of –1.00 at one end of the scale to a value of +1.00 at the other end. In the middle of the range of coefficients is 0, which indicates that the two variables being analyzed are unrelated (or independent) of each other (no linear relationship). A coefficient of +1.00 is known as a perfect positive correlation, indicating that for each value of the independent variable there is only one value of the dependent variable, and that as the value of the independent variable increases, the value of the dependent variable also increases. A coefficient of –1.00 also indicates a perfect correlation, but increasing values of the independent variable are paired with decreasing values of the dependent variable (or vice versa). In this case, a coefficient of –1.00 is known as a perfect negative correlation or a perfect inverse correlation. Pearson's coefficient, in effect, simultaneously provides information about the first three characteristics of a relationship. The fourth characteristic, geometric nature of the relationship, is fixed because Pearson assumed the relationship between the variables to be linear (straight line) in developing his technique.

In general, the many techniques for measuring bivariate relationships that have been developed since Pearson's coefficient have been designed to duplicate the range of possible values of the Pearson technique.[2] Accordingly, the various techniques for measuring relationships between ordinal, interval, or ratio variables usually can take values between –1.00 and +1.00. Because nominal variables lack order, direction of a relationship is not ascertainable; therefore, techniques to measure nominal variable relationships usually can take only values from 0 to +1.00. (See Box 10.3.)

BOX 10.3
A NOTE ON TERMINOLOGY

Techniques for measuring relationships between variables that are measured at the nominal or ordinal levels and are presented in tables are usually called measures of **association,** whereas those that measure relationships between interval or ratio variables or ordinal variables in which a large number of ranks are involved are called measures of **correlation.** Both concepts infer relationships.

[2]Some techniques do not have a maximum coefficient of +1.00 or –1.00. An example of one of these is the Pearson contingency coefficient for categorical, tabled data. The upper limit of the contingency coefficient is a function of the dimensions (rows and columns) of the table in which the data are presented. Lack of a definite maximum value such as 1.00 is generally considered a shortcoming of a technique because it complicates attempts to compare coefficients across data sets.

The techniques for measuring association between nominal or ordinal variables in which the data are in table form fall into two categories according to the philosophy of measurement used.

The first category of techniques is based on the philosophy that the no-association model should be the standard against which to compare actual data. Using the table containing the actual data of a study, expected frequencies are computed for each cell in the table. These expected frequencies are those that would appear in the table if there were no association between the independent and the dependent variables being analyzed (see Loether and McTavish, 1993:178–79, 576–79). These expected frequencies are compared to the actual frequencies for differences. The more the actual frequencies deviate from the expected frequencies, the more evidence there is for an association.

Table 10.2 is a bivariate table using data taken from the General Social Survey of the National Opinion Research Center in 1990. The variables compared in this table are whether the respondent's mother worked after the respondent was born (MAWKBORN, the dependent variable listed down the side of the table) and the race of the respondent (Race, the independent variable listed across the top of the table). Data for these variables were available from 766 interview respondents. The top entry in each cell of the table represents the actual number of cases for the cell. The bottom number in each cell represents the expected frequency for the cell. As you can see, these two entries in each of the cells do not agree. This fact leads to the conclusion that there is an association between race and whether the respondent's mother worked after the respondent was born. Cramer's *V* is a measure of association that could be used to analyze these data. It is an appropriate technique for examining relationships between two nominal level variables. Note that Cramer's *V* is .27, indicating the degree of relationship between the variables. Because the variables being analyzed are nominal, Cramer's *V* can take values only between 0

TABLE 10.2 Observed and Expected Frequency of Respondents Whose Mother Worked After Respondent Was Born, by Race of Respondent, United States, 1990

RESPONSE TO MAWKBORN		RACE			
		WHITE	BLACK	OTHER	ROW TOTAL
Yes	Observed	275	74	21	370
	Expected	311.1	43.0	15.9	
No	Observed	369	15	12	396
	Expected	332.9	46.0	17.1	
Column total		644	89	33	766

Cramer's *V* = .27.

and +1.00. The coefficient .27 is closer to 0 than it is to +1.00; nevertheless, there is some association between the two variables.

The second philosophy of measurement for nominal or ordinal variables in table form deals with what is called proportionate reduction in error. In this case expected and observed frequencies are not compared. Rather, the question posed is whether collecting data on an independent variable is worthwhile for predicting values on a dependent variable. If the number of errors made in predicting subjects' responses on the dependent variable is reduced by measuring an independent variable and using information about the independent variable to predict values of the dependent variable, then there is an association between the two variables. Furthermore, the more those prediction errors are reduced, the stronger the association is.

Table 10.3 presents the same data as Table 10.2; however, in this case expected frequencies are not included in the cells. The second entry in each cell is the column percentage of cases for that cell. For example, the 42.7% means that 42.7% of the White respondents answered "yes" when asked whether their mothers worked after they were born. Below the table a lambda of .18 is reported. Lambda is an appropriate proportionate-reduction-in-error measurement for nominal data such as these. Lambda has limits of 0 and +1.00. Therefore, a lambda of .18 indicates that there is an association between the two variables. The .18 may be interpreted to mean that knowing a respondent's race reduces error in predicting whether the respondent's mother worked after the respondent's birth by 18% over what the prediction error would have been without that information.

The column percentages in the table are not necessary for the computation of lambda. The use of percentages is actually an alternative that may be used to analyze data. Although not as efficient as a measure of association, examination of percentages has been found to be one of the most popular techniques used by

TABLE 10.3 Frequency and Percentage of Respondents Whose Mothers Worked After Respondent Was Born, by Race of Respondent, United States, 1990

		RACE			
RESPONSE TO MAWKBORN		WHITE	BLACK	OTHER	ROW TOTAL
Yes	Count	275	74	21	370
	Column Percentage	42.7%	83.1%	63.6%	48.3%
No	Count	369	15	12	396
	Column Percentage	57.3%	16.9%	36.4%	51.7%
Column total		644	89	33	766
		100.0%	100.0%	100.0%	100.00%

Lambda: with MAWKBORN dependent = .18.

sociologists. Examination of percentages is not efficient as a measure of association because it is a piecemeal technique involving the comparison of two percentages at a time, and percentage differences do not have a well-defined, standardized range of values similar to those found in the measures of association being discussed here. As a matter of fact, their potential range of values depends on the distributions of the empirical data in the table being analyzed.

To illustrate the use of percentages to analyze data, examine the percentages in Table 10.3. The percentages computed for this table were column percentages. These are the relevant percentages to compare because they show how the dependent variable is distributed over the various response categories of the independent variable. Note that there are six cells in the table, so several pairs of percentages may be compared. For example, we may want to compare the labor force participation of the mothers of White and Black respondents. The percentage of White respondents whose mothers worked after their birth was 42.7%, compared with 83.1% of the mothers of Black respondents. The difference between these two percentages is 40.4% This percentage difference is called epsilon. Whenever any of the epsilons in a table deviate from 0, this is an indication of an association between the independent and dependent variables. This particular epsilon indicates that it was much more common for the mothers of Black respondents to work after the birth of their babies than it was for White mothers. Similar comparisons could be made between the mothers of White and Other respondents and between the mothers of Black and Other respondents. In this sense, the analysis is piecemeal. The more cells there are in a table, the more comparisons are possible. Furthermore, it is possible to find tendencies in the epsilons of a large table that show complex and sometimes contradictory differences, thereby complicating the issue of how much association there is overall and what the nature of that association is. For this reason researchers often use a measure of association that is based on simultaneous evaluation of all of the data in a table for an overall summary of the association.

When the table being analyzed contains data from two ordinal level variables, the process of analysis is basically the same as is used for nominal data; however, the particular techniques used for determining association take advantage of the additional information provided by ordinal scales. Table 10.4 includes data for two ordinal variables. These data also come from the 1990 General Social Survey. The independent variable of interest is the self-identified social class of the respondents and the dependent variable is their perceived health status.

The cells in this table include the actual frequency of cases in the top part of the cell and the column percentage in the bottom part. Again, these percentages are not necessary to compute the measure of association. The measure of association used to analyze this table is Somers's *d*. Because it is a measure for ordinal data, the range of its possible coefficients is –1.00 to +1.00. Note that the Somers's *d* for these data is +.10. This indicates that there is a positive association between social class and perceived health, with a greater percentage of respondents in the higher social classes reporting better health than those in the lower classes. Somers's *d* is a proportionate-reduction-of-error measure; therefore, a *d* of .10 indicates that there is some positive association between social class and perceived health, but it is not

TABLE 10.4 Number and Percentage of Respondents Rating the Condition of Their Health, by Subjective Class Identification, United States, 1990

	CLASS				
HEALTH	LOWER CLASS	WORKING CLASS	MIDDLE CLASS	UPPER CLASS	ROW TOTAL
Excellent Count	10	110	152	13	285
Column Percentage	33.3%	27.0%	34.6%	44.8%	31.5%
Good Count	7	197	201	10	415
Column Percentage	23.3%	48.3%	45.8%	34.5%	45.8%
Fair Count	10	77	68	5	160
Column Percentage	33.3%	18.9%	15.5%	17.2%	17.7%
Poor Count	3	24	18	1	46
Column Percentage	10.0%	5.9%	4.1%	3.4%	5.1%
Column total	30	408	439	29	906
	100.0%	100.0%	100.0%	100.0%	100.0%

Somers's *d*: with Health dependent = .10.

very strong. As a matter of fact, the .10 may be interpreted as meaning that knowledge of a respondent's social class reduces error in predicting that respondent's perceived health status by approximately 10%.

In this table, the column percentages and various epsilons could be used to analyze the data in a piecemeal fashion; however, a single measure of association such as Somers's *d* can do the job more efficiently. Percentages are useful in identifying the geometric pattern of association. (See Box 10.4.)

BOX 10.4
SYMMETRIC AND ASYMMETRIC MEASURES

The various techniques available for measuring relationships between variables are divided not only by level of measurement of the variables being analyzed, but also in terms of whether they are symmetric or asymmetric. A symmetric measure is one that results in the same coefficient regardless of which variable is designated the independent and which is designated the dependent variable. An asymmetric technique results in two different coefficients depending on which of the variables is designated as the independent and which is designated as the dependent variable. Pearson's product moment coefficient of correlation is an example of a symmetric measure, whereas lambda and Somers's *d* are asymmetric measures. Therefore, when an asymmetric measure is used to analyze data it is very important to distinguish carefully between the independent and the dependent variables of the study.

Tables 10.2 and 10.3 include data from two nominal scale variables, and Table 10.4 included data from two ordinal scale variables. Accordingly, techniques designed to measure association between nominal scale variables were used for Tables 10.2 and 10.3, and a technique to measure association for ordinal scale variables was used for Table 10.4. Some tables to be analyzed consist of one nominal scale and one ordinal scale variable. What measurements of association are appropriate for analyzing such a table? The rule is that the measure of association should be determined by the variable that is lowest on the measurement scale. Consequently, a measure for nominal scale data would be the technique of choice.

When two variables are measured on the ordinal level but there are too many ranks on each to put the data into tables, a technique such as Spearman's rank order coefficient of correlation (rho) may be used (see Loether and McTavish, 1993:229–30). For example, if occupational prestige rankings on the North–Hatt Scale for the same population at two different points in time were to be compared, Spearman's rho would be an appropriate technique.

When the independent and dependent variables are measured at the interval level, the ratio level, or a combination of these two, and the assumption that the relationship is linear is justified, Pearson's coefficient of correlation r is the technique of choice. If the assumption of linearity of the relationship is not warranted, then a technique appropriate for a curvilinear relationship (such as eta, an asymmetric measure) should be used instead. For interpretation, squaring r or eta results in a measure that can be interpreted as the proportion reduction in error in predicting one variable from knowledge of the other.

The particular techniques for measuring bivariate relationships that have been mentioned here are only a few of the many available. Which is most appropriate for a particular situation depends on the data to be analyzed and the research question to be answered. The leading statistical computer software packages, such as Statistical Package for the Social Sciences (SPSS) and SAS, offer a wide variety of techniques. In order to choose an appropriate technique and to understand the results of the analysis, the researcher must have sound knowledge of the field of statistics. For this reason, at least one comprehensive course in statistics and, preferably, more than one, is an essential prerequisite for this type of analysis.

Multivariate Analysis

Generally, for sociological phenomena bivariate analysis is an oversimplification. The assumption that one independent variable is sufficient to explain the variability of a dependent variable is usually not realistic. It is likely that a system of several variables must be taken into consideration to account for the scores on the dependent variable. Several multivariate techniques have been developed to handle prediction and explanation for such systems. Furthermore, the computer has made it reasonably simple to use these techniques for analyzing data.

As mentioned earlier, multivariate analysis is performed in any situation in which more than two variables are involved. Variables other than the dependent and independent variables of a study are called **control variables** or test variables.[3] *Control* implies that the variable has some sort of impact on the relationship between the independent and the dependent variable and the nature of that impact can be determined by factoring out or controlling the variable.

The Roles of Control Variables. Control variables may play a number of different roles in the theoretical scheme being analyzed, depending on the time order of their effects relative to other variables used in the analysis. For example, a control variable may precede the independent variable of a study, in which case it is called an antecedent variable. In the example given earlier of a study in which the independent variable is number of years of school completed and the dependent variable is total income received over the work life, the education level of the subjects' fathers might be used as an antecedent variable. In such a case, it would be assumed that the subjects' levels of education would be influenced by the educational attainments of their fathers. Therefore, fathers' educational levels would help to account for the variability in subjects' levels of education. Figure 10.2 diagrams the relationship between an antecedent variable (*Z*), an independent variable (*X*), and a dependent variable (*Y*).

If the control variable comes between the independent variable and the dependent variable, then it is called an **intervening variable.** A variable that intervenes between father's level of education and the respondent's total income during work life, for instance, is the respondent's gender. The respondent's gender, in effect, acts as a filter that alters the relationship between father's education and respondent's income. The way it alters the relationship depends on whether a respondent is a male or a female. A female respondent with the same amount of father's education as a male respondent will generally make less money during her work life, in part because she is female. Figure 10.3 diagrams the relationship between an independent variable (*X*), an intervening variable (*Z*), and a dependent variable (*Y*).

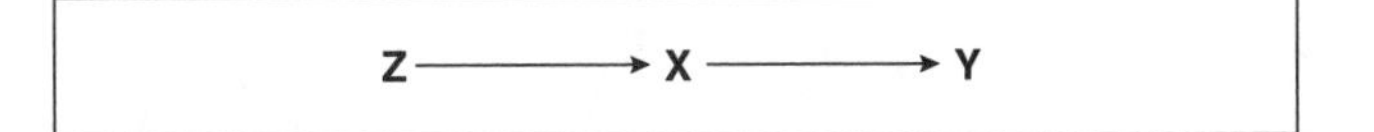

FIGURE 10.2 Role of an Antecedent Variable

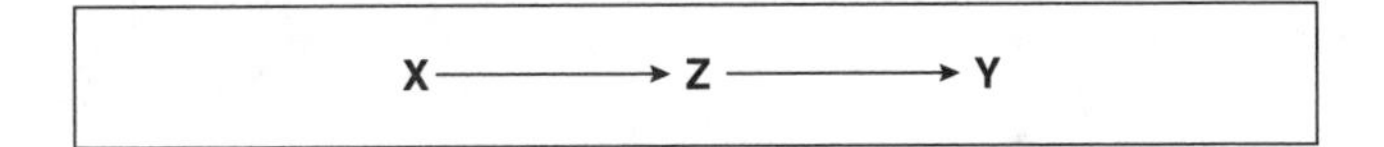

FIGURE 10.3 Role of an Intervening Variable

[3]We call them control variables here. The term *test variable* applies to laboratory experiments in particular. The term *control variable* also applies to nonexperimental situations.

A third possible role for a control variable is one in which it has separate effects on both the independent and dependent variables of the study. This class of control variable is known as an **extraneous** (which may be an **antecedent** or intervening) **variable.** This situation is diagrammed in Figure 10.4.

If the only relationship between the independent variable and the dependent variable is the one diagrammed in Figure 10.4, then there is no direct relationship between the two and the apparent relationship between them is **spurious.** If variable Z were controlled or factored out in this situation, any apparent bivariate relationship between X and Y would turn out to be 0.

Effects of Control Variables. The three kinds of control variables just discussed (antecedent, intervening, and extraneous) may have different consequences for the relationship between the independent and dependent variables, depending on the particular phenomenon under investigation. One type of effect produced by a control variable is known as the **suppressor effect.** The suppressor effect dampens the relationship between the independent and dependent variable so that it seems weaker than it actually is, or even nonexistent.

In a study of sexual permissiveness and social class, Ira Reiss (1967) hypothesized a negative relationship between permissiveness and class. When he analyzed the data on 800 students from five schools in the eastern United States, he got the data shown in Table 10.5.

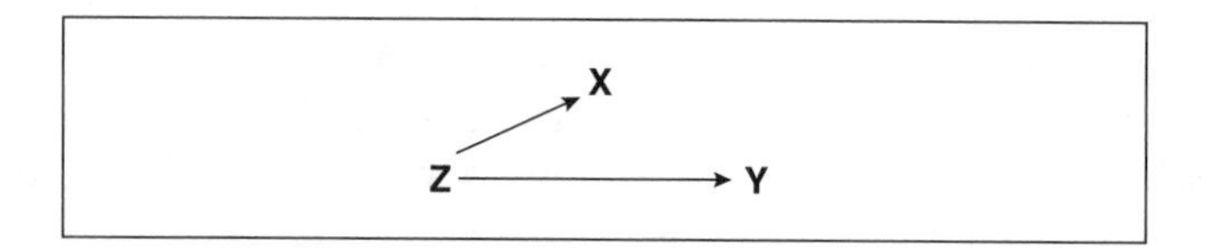

FIGURE 10.4 Effects of Extraneous Variable on Independent and Dependent Variables

TABLE 10.5 Percentage Distribution of Permissiveness Attitudes by Social Class

PERMISSIVENESS ATTITUDE	SOCIAL CLASS: LOWER CLASS	MIDDLE CLASS	UPPER CLASS	TOTAL
High	49%	46%	50%	49%
Low	51	54	50	51
Total percentage	100%	100%	100%	100%
Total *Ns*	383	189	225	797

Somers's $d = -.0001$.

One would conclude from this result that there is no relationship between social class and permissiveness attitudes. However, if church attendance is introduced to this data analysis as a control variable, Tables 10.6 and 10.7 are the result.

As you can see from these tables, high church attendance produces a negative association between social class and permissiveness attitudes, and low church attendance produces a positive association. The negative association is more than twice as strong as the positive association; nevertheless, both associations appear when the control variable is introduced. Tables 10.6 and 10.7 are called conditional tables because the data in each are determined by the value of the control variable.

Note that the role played by the control variable is not clearly delineated by the tables. The control variable could be antecedent, intervening, or extraneous and produce these tables. Which interpretation is assigned to the role of the control variable is determined by the theoretical model being tested.

TABLE 10.6 Percentage Distribution of Permissiveness by Social Class Among Those Who Attend Church Regularly

PERMISSIVENESS ATTITUDE	SOCIAL CLASS			
	LOWER CLASS	MIDDLE CLASS	UPPER CLASS	TOTAL
High	42%	26%	23%	34%
Low	58	74	77	66
Total percentage	100%	100%	100%	100%
Total *N*	262	98	102	462

Somers's $d = -.16$.

TABLE 10.7 Percentage Distribution for Permissiveness by Social Class for Those Who Don't Attend Church Regularly

PERMISSIVENESS ATTITUDE	SOCIAL CLASS			
	LOWER CLASS	MIDDLE CLASS	UPPER CLASS	TOTAL
High	64%	67%	72%	68%
Low	36	33	28	32
Total percentage	100%	100%	100%	100%
Total *N*	113	89	119	321

Somers's $d = +.06$.

A second type of effect produced by a control variable is known as a **distorter effect.** The distorter effect reverses the relationship between independent and dependent variables such that a relationship that is actually positive may appear to be negative, or vice versa.

Suppose that a study were done comparing attitudes toward affirmative action programs with social class. Responses to the item on affirmative action are Favor and Oppose. The class variable is divided into Middle Class and Working Class. Table 10.8 presents the results of the data collected.

Notice that 45% of working-class respondents approve of affirmative action programs, compared to 36% of middle-class respondents. When race is introduced as a control variable, Table 10.9 results. When the control variable, race, is introduced, the relationship between affirmative action attitudes and social class is reversed. In this table it is the middle-class respondents rather than the working-class respondents who are more likely to favor affirmative action. This reversal is due to the fact that Blacks, both middle class and working class, have more favorable attitudes toward affirmative action than Whites. When race is not controlled, as in Table 10.8, the actual relationship between affirmative action attitudes and social class is distorted. Again, as was the case with the suppressor effect, it may result from the influence of an antecedent, intervening, or extraneous variable.

The third type of effect is one in which the apparent relationship between the independent and dependent variables is spurious. That is, there appears to be a relationship when no such relationship exists. When a control variable is an extraneous variable, for example, it may produce a spurious effect. Controlling for the extraneous variable will uncover such an effect.

A hypothetical study of the relationship between the number of firemen at a fire and the dollar loss resulting from the fire provides a good example of a spurious relationship that can be attributed to an extraneous variable. Table 10.10 presents data presumed to have been collected from the sites of 143 fires.

TABLE 10.8 Percentage Distribution of Attitudes Toward Affirmative Action Programs by Social Class

	SOCIAL CLASS		
AFFIRMATIVE ACTION ATTITUDES	MIDDLE CLASS	WORKING CLASS	TOTAL
Percentage who approve	36%	45%	40%
Frequency who approve	86	108	194
Percentage who oppose	64%	55%	60%
Frequency who oppose	154	132	286
Total percentage	100%	100%	100%
Total *N*	240	240	480

Fictitious data.

TABLE 10.9 Percentage Distribution of Attitudes Toward Affirmative Action Programs by Social Class Controlling for Race

	BLACKS		WHITES	
AFFIRMATIVE ACTION ATTITUDES	MIDDLE CLASS	WORKING CLASS	MIDDLE CLASS	WORKING CLASS
Percentage who approve	70%	50%	29%	20%
Frequency who approve	28	100	58	8
Percentage who disapprove	30%	50%	71%	80%
Frequency who disapprove	12	100	142	32
Total percentage	100%	100%	100%	100%
Total *N*	40	200	200	40

Fictitious data.

TABLE 10.10 Frequency Distribution of Dollar Loss from Fires by Number of Firemen Present

	NUMBER OF FIREMEN		
DOLLAR LOSS	NONE	ONE OR MORE	TOTAL
Over $500	24	61	85
$500 or less	42	16	58
Total	66	77	143

Fictitious data. Somers's $d = +.43$.

The Somers's d of +.43 seems to indicate a substantial positive association between the number of firemen present at a fire and the size of the resulting financial loss. In light of this finding, one might pause to think about whether it is wise to report a fire when one occurs. Fortunately, however, the apparent association is spurious. The extraneous variable affecting both size of the financial loss and the number of firemen in attendance is the size of the fire. Tables 10.11 and 10.12 are conditional tables in which the size of the fire has been introduced as a control variable. Taking out the effects of size of the fire reveals that there is no association between resulting financial loss and the number of firemen present. It was the neglected extraneous variable that initially misled us.

Note that an intervening variable could produce the same kind of spurious association if the only relationship between the independent and dependent variables was via the intervening variable. Figure 10.3 is a diagram of such a situation. However, if there is a direct relationship between the independent and dependent variables in addition to the relationship through the intervening variable, the effect produced could either be suppression or distortion.

TABLE 10.11 Frequency Distribution of Dollar Loss from Fires by Number of Firemen Present When Fire Is Small

	NUMBER OF FIREMEN		
DOLLAR LOSS	NONE	ONE OR MORE	TOTAL
Over $500	4	1	5
$500 or less	40	10	50
Total	44	11	55

Fictitious data. Somers's *d* = .00.

TABLE 10.12 Frequency Distribution of Dollar Loss from Fires by Number of Firemen Present When Fire Is Large

	NUMBER OF FIREMEN		
DOLLAR LOSS	NONE	ONE OR MORE	TOTAL
Over $500	20	60	80
$500 or less	2	6	8
Total	22	66	88

Fictitious data. Somers's *d* = .00.

In some instances a control variable may have a combination of effects on the relationship between the independent and dependent variables. Thus, it may distort the relationship at one level and suppress it at another level. Or it may distort the relationship in one direction at one level and distort it in the opposite direction at another level. Appropriate analysis depends on the investigator's conceptual clarity about the research problem and research design.

Multivariate Models. The statistical models that have been developed to analyze multivariate data vary according to both the measurement levels of the variables involved and how the roles of those variables are defined. No attempt is made here to explain these techniques in detail; we describe some of the many models available through SPSS, SAS, BioMed, and a number of other statistical software packages.

- Partial correlation is a technique for analyzing continuous variables measured at the interval or ratio level when there is one dependent variable, one independent variable, and one or more control variables.

- Multiple regression (and multiple correlation) is a technique for analyzing multivariate continuous data measured at the interval or ratio level. The model includes one dependent variable and two or more independent variables. In the optimum situation, the independent variables are uncorrelated with each other and correlated with the dependent variable. The technique is essentially an extension of simple regression techniques and Pearson's product moment coefficient of correlation to the case in which more than one predictor (independent) variable is used.

- Path analysis is a technique for analyzing a theoretical explanatory model consisting of a system of continuous interval or ratio variables hypothesized to be playing independent, dependent, and extraneous roles. Models that extend the ideas of path analysis to a more sophisticated level are called Lisrel models.

- Log-linear analysis is a technique using categorical (nominal or ordinal level) variables to explain the frequencies in a table of empirical data. No distinction is made between independent and dependent variables, but a hierarchy of effects may be tested from a high level of simultaneous influence by all the variables in the model down to a level at which none of the variables has any influence on the table cell frequencies.

- Logit analysis is a technique for testing the effects of a number of categorical (nominal or ordinal) independent variables on a single categorical dependent variable. The dependent variable may be dichotomous (two categories) or polytomous (three or more categories) and may be nominal or ordinal level.

- Logistic regression is a technique for testing the effects of a number of continuous (interval or ratio) variables on a categorical dependent variable. The dependent variable may be dichotomous or polytomous and may be nominal or ordinal.

- Event history analysis is a set of techniques for the analysis of the pattern of occurrence of events (e.g., marriages, deaths) over time. It seeks to identify explanatory variables that determine when events of interest occur. (See Allison, 1984, and Yamaguchi, 1991, for further discussion of event history analysis.)

These are just a few examples of the kinds of statistical techniques that have developed to handle multivariate data analysis. It is largely because of the dramatic advances in computer technology that these techniques have become feasible for testing rather sophisticated and sometimes complicated theoretical explanations of sociological phenomena. It should be noted that, although event history analysis is the only one of these techniques that is specifically geared to the analysis of longitudinal data, all of them may be used in the analysis of such data. (See Tuma and Hannan, 1984, for further discussion of dynamic models.)

A cautionary note is in order here. The availability of these and other statistical models on computers should not be construed as license to use them whimsically. The type of analysis appropriate in a given instance should be dictated by the theoretical model being tested rather than by the availability of statistical techniques and computer software to apply those techniques. Applying inappropriate techniques is likely to lead to misleading or spurious results. If inappropriate techniques are used in an attempt to deceive others about the importance of the findings, then clear ethical problems arise.

SUMMARY

The answers to research questions require a systematic analysis of the data collected. In a well-executed study, the data analysis is planned in the preliminary stages of a project so that, once the data are collected, the steps in processing them will already be determined. Whether the raw data are quantitative or qualitative, they must be processed so that their impacts on the questions being researched can be assessed. When analysis is focused on one variable at a time, the analysis is characterized as univariate. When relationships between pairs of variables are of central concern, the analysis is characterized as bivariate. Analyses dealing with three or more variables are characterized as multivariate. Three different kinds of techniques are used in data analysis: tables, graphs, and statistics. These are often used in combination; in many cases all three are used. In general, statistics provide more detailed information than graphs and more comprehensive analysis than tables.

When statistical analysis is used, the level of analysis that is appropriate and the particular techniques that apply depend on the theoretical model being tested and the level of measurement of the variables being studied. Univariate analysis focuses largely on the characteristics of central tendency and variability. Bivariate and multivariate analysis focuses primarily on relationships between variables. A number of techniques for univariate, bivariate, and multivariate analyses have been developed to handle data measured at the different levels: nominal, ordinal, interval, and ratio. Also, the models addressed by these techniques vary in how their variables are divided into independent, dependent, and control categories. Some techniques handle simple theoretical models, but others are capable of handling sophisticated and complicated ones. Fortunately, the labor involved in using these techniques has been delegated to computers with statistical software. However, selecting and using these techniques requires a rather comprehensive understanding of when they apply and what the resulting analysis means.

TERMS TO KNOW

Association
Bivariate analysis
Cause
Central tendency
Control variable
Correlation
Dependent variable
Distorter effect
Effect
Extraneous (antecedent) variable
Independent variable
Intervening variable
Kurtosis
Multivariate analysis
Necessary
Necessary and sufficient

Skewness
Spurious
Sufficient
Suppressor effect
Univariate analysis
Variability

ISSUES AND COMPARISONS

Ethical concerns in data analysis
Selecting appropriate statistical techniques
Case-by-variable data matrix
Quantitative versus qualitative approaches

EXERCISES

1. Find three different tables from different publications. Describe what each table shows and critique its use of statistical description.
2. Using archival data, create a univariate description of a nominal, ordinal, and interval-level variable. (Optional: Select an appropriate measure of central tendency and dispersion for each variable and interpret what they tell you about the distributions.) Then find two variables to create a bivariate table. Percentage the table and describe what it shows. (Optional: Select and interpret an appropriate measure of association.)
3. Set up a dummy table with columns and rows labeled for two variables in which you are interested, one an independent variable (across the top) and the other a dependent variable (down the side). Put in fictitious cell percentages (percentaging down, in the direction of the independent variable, so each column adds up to 100%) showing that the relationship of the two variables is as you suspect it is. What measure of association would be most appropriate?

REFERENCES

Adams, Stuart, "Trends in Occupational Origins of Physicians," *American Sociological Review* 1953;18:404–409.

Allison, Paul D., *Event History Analysis: Regression for Longitudinal Event Data,* Sage, Newbury Park, CA, 1984.

Loether, Herman J., and Donald G. McTavish, *Descriptive and Inferential Statistics: An Introduction,* 4th ed., Allyn & Bacon, Boston, 1993.

Pearson, Karl, "Mathematical Contributions to the Theory of Evolution, III: Regression, Heredity and Panmixia," *Philosophical Transactions of the Royal Society of London* (A) 1896;187:253–318.

Reiss, Albert J., et al., *Occupations and Social Status,* Free Press, New York, 1961.

Reiss, Ira L., *The Social Context of Premarital Sexual Permissiveness,* Holt, Rinehart, & Winston, New York, 1967.

Tuma, Nancy B., and Michael T. Hannan, *Social Dynamics: Models and Methods,* Academic Press, Orlando, FL, 1984.

Yamaguchi, Kazuo, *Event History Analysis,* Sage, Newbury Park, CA, 1991.

CHAPTER ELEVEN

REPORTING THE RESULTS

Shortly after Julius Roth finished his PhD, he was hospitalized for tuberculosis. But the extended time he spent in hospitals was also an opportunity to pursue his research interests into occupations and organizations. His months of observation in five hospitals resulted in a book that pulls together his research on the way time is dealt with in the thinking of clients and staff in hospitals. He wrote a research monograph called *Timetables: Structuring the Passage of Time in Hospital Treatment and Other Careers* (1963). The book makes available his insights and data not only to other researchers interested in this phenomenon, but also to a much broader audience.

In order to advance knowledge in a scientific field, it is necessary to communicate information about completed research as well as research in progress. In that sense, scientific knowledge is a public commodity. There is an obligation to make results of research available to the scientific community so that other scientists can evaluate those results, incorporate them into their own work, or perhaps seek to validate them through further research.

Researchers who report their results also benefit from making them public. They often get feedback that helps them take stock of where they are and where they need to go next to extend their research. In addition, they get recognition that may advance their careers.

Research grant recipients have a special obligation to make the results of their research public. In the case of a research contract, the funding agency may require a final report whose use it wants to control. In either case, however, a proposal for funding usually requires the authors to state how they intend to make the results available to others.

REPORTING OPTIONS

There are several different options available for reporting research results. Which of these is selected depends on a number of factors. First of all, the guidelines of the funding agency may specify which avenues of **publication** to use. If the funding agency has a publication of its own, for example, it may require that a report of the study results be prepared for publication there. If the funding is through a research contract, the agency may require a report for its own in-house use. Then again, an agency may simply offer general guidelines requiring widespread circulation of the results within the relevant scientific community. Even in this latter case the funding agency may require researchers to obtain its approval of the text and the publication medium before publishing.

Second, the options selected for circulating results often depend on the needs of the researchers who carried out the study. For example, if any of the researchers are academics seeking tenure or promotion, the findings may be submitted in article form to a refereed journal in accordance with university requirements. If there are graduate students on the research team, it is likely that some parts of the results will be reported in master's theses or doctoral dissertations. Presentation of early research findings at professional conferences is also common, and it may also serve as a vehicle for generating financial support to allow researchers to attend professional conventions or other meetings.

A third factor that may help to determine which options for circulating findings to select is the subject matter of the research. For example, a research topic deemed to be of general interest may result in the publication of a trade book (a book written on a popular level and destined for the shelves of a general-circulation bookstore). Thus, a study of prostitutes and pimps might be of enough general interest to warrant its publication in a popular form. On the other hand, a study of professionalization trends among nurses may be limited to publication in a professional journal.

"Tonight, we're going to let the statistics speak for themselves."

Occasionally the selection of a circulation medium might be a matter of chance. A colleague who edits a journal may be seeking materials for a future issue and may invite the researchers to prepare an article for consideration. Alternatively, the topic researched might be of heightened interest to the public because of some current event, leading media representatives to seek findings for publication in the popular media.

Recognizing the importance of making scientists aware of what research is going on in their fields, some disciplines try to report, however briefly, all of the research completed or in progress. Consequently, some studies appear as full-blown articles and others as research notes.

Reports of scientific studies may circulate in one or more of the following forms:

- A **technical report** is a formal account of the research commissioned by the funding agency and designed for its use. Researchers write these with the specific needs of the sponsoring agency in mind. Circulation of the report may be limited to the funding agency, or the agency may make it more widely available.

- A paper for **oral presentation** at a convention or other professional meeting is usually allotted so little time that the presentation can do little more than give a sketchy account of the research. Exposure to such a paper is limited to the audience attending the session at which it is presented, although a written version may also be available to other interested parties. In sociology, the publication *Sociological Abstracts* regularly publishes abstracts of papers presented at large conventions.

- A **research article** in a professional journal offers more opportunity to report a research project in detail, but the text published is still constrained in length and content by the judgment of the editor or editorial board. Circulation of the article is limited to those who have access to the journal in which it appears, by membership in a society that sponsors the journal or through university library collections.

- A **monograph** is a book-length manuscript that reports in some detail the theory behind the study, how the study was conducted, and what the results were. Monographs are made available to professional audiences through publication by university presses or specialty publishers, and circulation is usually limited.

- An **edited collection** is a series of articles published in book form. The articles may be originals solicited from authors who are writing and doing research in the field to which the book is devoted (e.g., gerontological research), or the collection may include both original and reprinted articles.

- **Doctoral dissertations** and **master's theses** are research monographs produced to fulfill partial requirements for graduate degrees. Generally, dissertations and theses are not published. Copies may be available through the library of the university that awarded the degree. Another important source of dissertations and theses is the dissertation and thesis microfilming service at the University of Michigan. The annual publication *Dissertation Abstracts* provides short abstracts of the works produced at universities throughout the United States. Microfilm copies of the complete works are usually available for purchase from the University of Michigan. Occasionally, dissertations or theses are published by university presses or other specialty publishers if the subject matter is considered to be of sufficient general interest to warrant it. Of course, such publication moves them into the monograph category mentioned earlier.

■ Occasionally **textbooks** are used as vehicles for reporting the results of research conducted by the authors. The problem with this medium is that the research is included in a book dealing with a wide range of subject matter related to the course (or courses) for which the book was written. Consequently, the research is not as likely to come to the attention of interested professionals as it would if it appeared separately in a professional journal. Furthermore, because of space limitations, the study and its results probably will be reported in a brief form, leaving out technical details of interest to professionals.

■ **Periodicals** aimed at a broader audience than the professionals in the field are another possible publication medium. This category includes periodicals such as *Scientific American, Science, Civilization, Discover,* and *Society.* This type of periodical has the advantage of reaching a wide mixed audience consisting both of professionals and lay readers.

■ Unpublished materials are circulated among interested professionals in some disciplines or subfields of some disciplines. These materials are sometimes known as working papers and are usually considered to be preliminary versions of reports that will later be published in some form for wider circulation. They are a good vehicle for letting others in the field know what research you are engaged in and for soliciting ideas, suggestions, and critical comments that will be helpful in refining the research or the report. Unfortunately, the limited circulation of these materials prevents interested professionals who are not on the mailing list from being aware of what others are doing.

■ **Trade books** produced for general public consumption and marketed through general interest bookstores are another source of possible publication. However, few research studies have the potential breadth of interest to qualify them for publication as trade books. As mentioned earlier, a study of prostitutes and pimps might qualify for trade publication. However, the final product may be slanted more to the prurient or sensational than to the scholarly aspects of the research in order to increase sales.

■ The **mass media,** such as newspapers and news magazines, may serve as vehicles for communicating research results if the subject of the research is deemed to be of sufficient general interest to warrant a story. However, reports of research in the mass media are seldom covered in enough detail to do the research justice. Such reports tend to dwell on the parts of the research that are considered to be surprising or sensational. Details of research design and data analysis are not likely to be included.

- **Audiovisual media** such as audiocassettes, videocassettes, motion pictures, and slides may serve as vehicles to report research results. However, their use is generally limited to the few studies that lend themselves to such presentations. A study of the interpersonal dynamics of a young children's play group, for example, might lend itself to videotaping as a vehicle for communicating the interpersonal relationships that develop in the course of organized or unorganized play. Of course, such a video must be accompanied by a narrative that interprets what is going on from a sociological perspective. From time to time a master's thesis may be accepted in videotape form. Generally, however, the videotape must be accompanied by a written narrative to meet the requirements for completion of a degree.

- The **Internet** provides researchers an opportunity to circulate news about their research activities to both professional and general audiences. An advantage of publishing on the Internet is that it is possible to reach a large, far-flung audience quickly and inexpensively. Furthermore, readers of the **research report** may easily communicate comments, suggestions, questions, or even critiques to the researchers via e-mail.

As mentioned earlier, reports of research need not be limited to one of these options for communication. Several of them might be used to ensure widespread circulation of pertinent information about a study.

WRITING THE RESEARCH REPORT

The option chosen for reporting research determines the form that the research report will take. An oral presentation must be brief because of time limitations, whereas a report of research that appears in mass media generally will not include technical information about how the study was conducted.

The ideal vehicle for reporting is the monograph or the article appearing in a professional journal because these forms allow for the communication of the technical aspects of the research process as well as the findings. In general, to fulfill its functions a research report should include the following:

1. An **introduction** that clearly states the **problem researched.** This should be accompanied by an account of how and why the problem was selected for study. In addition, the problem should be put in a theoretical context, relevant concepts should be discussed and defined, any assumptions made should be stated, and any hypotheses posed should be listed. Finally, the theoretical and practical importance of the problem should be explained.

2. A **literature review** should be included as the next section of the report. In this section any literature that is relevant to the problem researched, the theory used as a conceptual base for the research, or the methods used to carry out the research should be reviewed and its relationship to the study being reported

should be made clear. The literature review is usually an analytic critique, not just a list of studies, organized around the variables or conceptual needs of the research report. It may be a creative scholarly contribution in its own right, and it often serves as a starting point for later researchers.

3. A **methods** section should be the next part of the report. In this section the strategy used to carry out the study should be explained, including an explanation of how the subjects of the study were selected, what sort of research design was used, how the relevant data were collected, how the data were processed, and how they were analyzed. In addition, this section should include a discussion of any problems that arose in the process of carrying out the study and an account of how those problems were resolved.

4. The **findings** of the study should be reported next. First, the subjects of the study should be described in order to put the findings in context. It should be made clear whether the findings apply only to those from whom the data were acquired or whether the results may be legitimately generalized to a population the subjects represent. Next, the results of the data analysis should be reported in an objective manner, often including key tables and graphs that organize the findings. The bearing of those results on the hypotheses of the study should be made clear; that is, it should be reported whether the results lend support to the hypotheses of the study.

5. A **discussion** of the results should follow, including an evaluation of the theoretical and practical implications of the findings and a critique of how the study turned out. Although the section on the findings of the study should be limited to an objective report of the results, the discussion section provides an opportunity for the researchers to give their interpretations of what the findings mean. Suggestions may also be included about what should be done next to validate or to extend the findings of the study.

6. A list of **references** should follow the body of the report. Complete references to any sources used in connection with the study should be included.

7. **Appendices** should follow, containing any technical information not appropriate for inclusion in the body of the report. These appendices might include tables and graphs that either supplement the materials in the text or are considered too technical for inclusion there. In addition, any data collection instruments used should be included. If appropriate, other technical information relating to sample design, data processing, or data analysis may be included.

The research report should be complete enough that other scientists reading it can evaluate the study in terms of its adequacy and replicate it if desired. Of course, an article is necessarily shorter than a monograph. It seldom allows for the detailed reporting that is possible in a monograph. Nevertheless, a research article should include enough detailed information to allow others to judge the soundness with which the study was conducted and reported.

Writing Style

A formal **writing style** is usually recommended for a research report; however, that does not mean that the style should be ponderous. The more the writing style can be lightened up without compromising its message, the easier it will be for the reader to understand. For example, instead of being referred to as "the reader," the audience may be addressed as "you."

Technical writing often makes use of the **passive voice** rather than the **active voice.**[1] For example, a statement such as the following may be made:

> Funding agencies may insist on knowing how the findings of the proposed project will be circulated.

The expression "findings . . . will be circulated" is an example of use of the passive voice. The active voice is simpler and generally easier to understand. Translating the same passage into the active voice produces the following:

> Funding agencies may insist on knowing how the researchers will circulate the findings.

Of course, in technical writing the passive voice has a legitimate place. As Ivers says,

> Sometimes you may want to emphasize what has been done, using the passive voice—especially when you don't know or don't want to say who the doer was (for example, when the doer is unimportant or a vague "they"). . . . Avoiding [stultifying forms of the passive voice] will give you elbow room to use a few deliberate passive constructions for a desired effect without unduly weighing down your prose. (1991:121–22)

Another tendency in technical writing is to compose long sentences. Short sentences are easier to understand. Of course, the writer needs to exercise some judgment about breaking up long sentences into shorter ones. This can be overdone so that the result is a number of short, choppy sentences that do not convey the original meaning of the longer sentence. For example, on the first page of this chapter is the following sentence:

> There is an obligation to make results of research available to the scientific community so that other scientists can evaluate those results, incorporate them into their own work, or perhaps seek to validate them through further research.

According to the grammar checker software accompanying the word processing program used, this sentence is too long and should be broken up into

[1]The writing style of this chapter, for example, liberally illustrates the use of the passive voice.

shorter sentences. If this suggestion is taken too seriously, the result could be as follows:

> There is an obligation to make results of research available to the scientific community. Other scientists can then evaluate those results. They can incorporate them into their own work. They can also seek to validate them through further research.

Breaking up the original sentence into four separate sentences has changed the original meaning. In the original sentence the three possible actions of other scientists were presented as alternatives that might be pursued singly or in combination. The shorter sentences do not convey the same message. Rather, they imply that other scientists will take all three of the actions suggested.

Technical writing should be edited carefully to be as clear and simple as possible without sacrificing the message. It is often wise to use the services of a professional editor to accomplish this. Both the authors and the editor need to define clearly the audience being addressed by the report and need to write to that audience. This is a key point to keep in mind: Write to the audience who will be reading the report.

Vocabulary

Related to the subject of writing style is the question of the vocabulary used in the report. Scientists (particularly social scientists) are often criticized for writing in scientific **jargon.** Jargon may be divided into two categories: jargon that uses long, convoluted words and phrases designed primarily to give the text the appearance of scientific respectability rather than to communicate the message, and jargon that serves as a kind of shorthand to communicate the message to other scientists without wasting words. For example, in sociology the concept *social institution* has a technical meaning that sociologists understand. Consequently, writers can use the concept in a technical report without having to take the time and space necessary to define it and provide examples.

Each scientific discipline develops a specialized vocabulary that serves this shorthand function. If it is understood that a report is being written for members of the discipline, then the writer can use the specialized vocabulary to facilitate communication. On the other hand, if the report is being written for a wider audience, it may be necessary to translate ideas into commonly used words.

Unfortunately, many technical terms in sociology include words that are also used in common speech. For example, the term *group* is used in common, everyday language. It is also an important concept in sociology; however, in sociology it has a specific, technical meaning that sets it apart from its common usage. This is not a problem if the report is meant solely for sociologists. If the report is written for a wider audience, however, it should probably include definitions of the concepts mentioned.

Whenever the possibility exists that concepts used in a report may be misunderstood, either because they overlap commonly used words or because the audience is not clearly delineated, the safest course to take is to define specifically how the concepts are being used. If they are not defined specifically, then others who read the report cannot evaluate or replicate the research that was done.

Tables and Graphs

Tables and graphs are used two different ways in research. First, they are techniques for analyzing data. A table can be used to organize raw data and put them into a form that will assist the researchers in identifying patterns of relationships between relevant variables. A graph provides a visual representation of data that may be useful in evaluating their relevance for the study undertaken and for detecting aberrant features of their distributions. These types of tables and graphs are generally not for public consumption. Rather, they are analytical, working tools used by the researchers.

Second, tables and graphs are used as devices for presenting data in an organized and comprehensible manner. Technical reports, monographs, and articles in professional journals often include tables and graphs because they supplement the text materials and aid in understanding data analysis.

In using these forms of data presentation, report writers must exercise judgment about which tables and graphs to include. Overuse of these materials tends to obfuscate the narrative. Only tables and graphs that help to clarify the points being made or provide overall summaries of the data analyzed should be included in the text. More detailed or technical tables and graphs may be included in appendices for the sake of those who want to examine the data more completely.

When tables and graphs are included in the text of a report, the narrative should discuss them and tie them into the explanation of the results of the data analysis. If the writer decides that the results can be explained and discussed effectively without such materials, then they should be relegated to an appendix or omitted.

Documentation

Any sources used in the process of carrying out the research or in writing the report must be documented. Published materials that are used either in the form of a direct quotation or indirectly through paraphrasing should be properly referenced in the report. Unpublished materials such as working papers or personal communications from colleagues should also be referenced.[2]

Providing these references serves at least three important functions: It allows the reader to follow up on any interesting ideas that are presented in citations, it allows the reader to check the accuracy and the meanings of statements made in

[2]The proper format for referencing sources may be found in style manuals such as *The Chicago Manual of Style* (University of Chicago Press, 1993), Barzun (1985), Lee et al. (1990), and Shelton (1994), or in the frontmatter of journals such as *The American Sociological Review* or *The American Journal of Sociology*.

the report in connection with outside sources, and it protects the writers of the report from charges of **plagiarism.**

When there is any doubt about whether to cite a source, it should be cited. As the old saw goes, "It is better to be safe than be sorry."

OTHER ISSUES RELATED TO REPORTING

In this book we have repeatedly stressed the fact that research is a social phenomenon. It is no less true that the report-writing phase of the research process is social. Researchers interact with each other in the process of writing the report, they interact with those in a position to publish the report, and they interact with their audiences in the process of writing the report. This social nature of the reporting process brings up a number of issues that are considered here.

Writing as a Team Activity

Whenever research is carried out by a team, the writing phase of a project is necessarily a team endeavor. Although one researcher may be designated as the one to put the report together as an integrated whole, sections of the report probably will be written by different individuals or subgroups from the research team.

Because individual researchers have their own points of emphasis and their own styles of writing, integration of their contributions in **team writing** can be a major undertaking. For example, they may not agree on what should be included in the report or on the writing style and conventions to be used in the writing. Consequently, it is often necessary to reach compromises on these issues.

If the **conceptualization** phase of the research process is given sufficient time and attention in the initial stage of the project, then disputes over what should be included in the final report or what form the report should take may be avoided. Still, individuals have their pet interests and have a stake in putting some of themselves into the final product.

Resolution of disagreements about the report may be reached by designating some person on the research team as the one with the final word about what will constitute the finished product. If the research team is organized hierarchically, the person at the top of the hierarchy may assume this position. If the team is not organized hierarchically, the solution may be to designate one member of the team as the editor of the report. In either case it is important to give the designated person final say so that members of the writing team will take his or her decision as the final word.

Another possible resolution to problems of team research writing is to produce a series of reports, each dealing with a logical part of the final research product. Subteams of writers can then be assigned these separate writing assignments. It may be possible to put these subteams together in such a way that they will be able to work together in harmony. It is generally easier to assemble a harmonious writing team of a small number of people than it is when more people are involved. In the end, however, it may still be necessary to designate someone to review all of the individual reports to ensure that they represent the project as a whole.

A related issue is that of determining who will be included in the list of authors. It is conceivable that a member of the research team who was deeply involved in the work of the project may not contribute directly to the report writing. This is sometimes the case with graduate student assistants, and it may also be true of professional team members. The question, then, is whether they should be designated as coauthors.

It may be that a decision will be made to designate only those who participate in the writing as coauthors and recognize the contributions of others involved through footnotes, acknowledgments, or similar devices. If this is the case, it should be explicitly communicated to research team members at the time they are recruited for the project and should be made a condition for their employment on the project. If such an agreement is not reached ahead of time, it is best to include everyone's name on the final report.

Because of the likelihood that several reports or publications will come out of a research project, there is often sufficient opportunity for everyone on a project to share in the credit.

Some principal investigators on research projects have taken the position that because they pay graduate assistants to work on their projects, it is not necessary to list such employees among the authors of final reports or publications despite the amount of time and effort they have contributed. In a legal sense these principal investigators may be justified in this decision. From an ethical standpoint, however, everyone should be suitably recognized for their contributions. Furthermore, additional names in the list of coauthors do not necessarily diminish the recognition that will be received by any one of the authors.

Timing of Reporting

Another issue that arises out of team research is the timing of reporting study results. A member of the research team may become excited by potentially important or serendipitous preliminary results. Accordingly, he or she may be unable to resist the temptation to communicate these preliminary results to outsiders, including media representatives.

Such premature reporting may be counterproductive. It may have serious consequences for unfinished phases of a project, making them difficult or impossible to complete. It may turn out that additional data analysis proves the preliminary results to be in error. Premature reporting may even discredit the whole project.

Although it may not be possible to guard completely against premature reporting, steps may be taken to minimize risk. First of all, careful recruiting of research team members may minimize the risk. Recruiting experienced personnel whose employment history is free of unfortunate incidents of premature reporting will help to minimize risk. Second, researchers may be informed that, as a condition of employment, they must agree that they are not at liberty to release any information about the project without written permission of the principal investigator. Third, if researchers are involved in a project from its inception and if they are involved in its development, they may become committed enough that they have a stake in seeing it through to completion without divulging any preliminary results. Furthermore, if they are involved enough to have a grasp of the project as a whole, they are more likely to recognize that partial results are preliminary and that divulging those results would be premature. Researchers who are committed to the project as a whole can generally be trusted to protect the interests of the research team and the project.

Issues Related to Publishing

Because of the obligation to make research results available to others, it is desirable to publish in media that are widely circulated. At the same time, the publicatio should provide enough detail about the research so that colleagues will be able to evaluate it objectively. This presents a dilemma because the media with the widest circulation (i.e., newspapers and news magazines) are not the most desirable for publication because of their tendency to popularize the subject matter and limit the space devoted to reporting it.

As mentioned earlier, research monographs are desirable media for publication because they offer the most opportunity to report research thoroughly. Finding publishers to publish monographs is becoming more difficult, however, because of the increasing emphasis being put on making a profit from a book. Some of the publishing houses that carried limited-circulation, special-interest monographs in the past are now emphasizing the publication of textbooks because of their greater market potential. Other specialized publishing houses have gone out of existence.

University presses continue to be important sources for publication of research monographs because they are willing to take on specialized books with limited market potential. Although they are prepared to do short press runs, because of limited resources they must be selective in what they publish and are forced to put high price tags on their publications.

The other desirable medium for publishing research results is the professional journal. Professional journals publish technical articles reporting research in enough detail to satisfy the needs of professionals. Unfortunately, journals with wide circulation regularly receive many more manuscripts than they are able to publish. The turndown rates among leading journals such as the *American Sociological Review* and *The American Journal of Sociology* are as high as 95%. Even the lesser-known journals usually turn down more manuscripts than they accept.

Because of the competition to get published, authors of research manuscripts are often at the mercy of journal editors and editorial consultants. Many manuscripts are rejected because of matters of quality, either in the research or in the writing, but others are rejected simply because the subject of the research does not interest the editors. This is unfortunate because it has the effect of censoring some research findings that should be made available to colleagues in the field.

As a matter of fact, adequate circulation of research reports is a sociological problem that plagues the field of sociology as well as a number of other disciplines. When knowledge of what research has been done and what the results of that research were is not widely available, progress in a discipline is hampered.

There are a number of possible ways to ameliorate this problem. First, it would help if research grants provided enough funds to cover publication of the report of the project. Unfortunately, limited resources may lead researchers to assign publication costs a low priority in a research budget.

Second, the professional association of a discipline or some other body with financial resources may make a concerted effort to ensure that an exhaustive list of research will be reported in a medium devoted to research notes. Such notes will probably be rather sketchy because of space limitations, but information about how to contact the authors could be included with each note so that colleagues who are interested may pursue the subject further.

Third, the Internet and on-line publishing can make information about research widely available. At present, there are not enough professionals with access to the Internet to get the word out adequately. However, with sufficient effort it should be possible to make this type of communication widespread enough to meet the needs of the discipline.

SUMMARY

The final phase of the research process is reporting the results. Both research grants and research contracts usually include some provision for circulating the results of research. This is important because science is a public activity and there is an obligation to make research findings available to those who have a need to know.

Grants usually encourage wider circulation of results than do contracts. In fact, some contracts limit reporting to in-house research reports. When researchers are free to report research findings, a number of media are available. These include research reports, monographs, oral paper presentations, articles, edited collections, dissertations and theses, textbooks, popular periodicals, trade books, mass media outlets, audiovisual media, and the Internet. Several of these may be used to report on a single project.

Ideally, a research manuscript will provide sufficient detail to allow colleagues in the field to judge the quality of the research and replicate the study if so desired. The report should include an introduction to the research problem addressed, including the conceptual scheme used; a review of related literature; a description of the research methods used; a report of the findings of the research; and a discussion of the findings that ties them into the research question initially posed. In addition, supporting materials such as references and instruments used to collect data should be noted.

In writing a research report it is important to adapt the writing style and the vocabulary to the audience for which the report is intended. Comprehensible communication is a must! In order to make the manuscript as comprehensible as possible, tables and graphs are often included. It is also important to document any sources that were used in the research or the manuscript so that readers may follow up on points of interest to them.

Because most research is conducted in teams, report writing is usually a social activity. This fact leads to issues related to coordination of team writing, the timing of the circulation of research results, and publication problems.

TERMS TO KNOW

Active voice
Appendices
Audiovisual media
Conceptualization
Discussion
Doctoral dissertation
Edited collection
Findings
Internet
Introduction
Jargon
Literature review
Master's thesis
Media
Methods
Monograph
Oral presentation
Passive voice
Periodical
Plagiarism
Publication
References (documentation)
Research article
Research report
Team writing
Technical report
Textbook
Trade books
Writing style

ISSUES AND COMPARISONS

Ethical concerns in reporting results
How to construct good tables and graphs

EXERCISES

1. Select an article from one of the professional journals in sociology and read it thoroughly. Using the points made in this chapter, evaluate the article in terms of how adequately it covers the details of the research.

2. Pick a sociological topic that you are interested in researching. Go to the library and do a literature search on the topic. Make use of computerized search tools. Prepare a bibliography of sources you consider most relevant to the topic you searched.

REFERENCES

Barzun, Jacques, *Simple and Direct: A Rhetoric for Writers,* revised ed., University of Chicago Press, Chicago, 1985.

Chicago Manual of Style, 14th ed., University of Chicago Press, Chicago, 1993.

Ivers, Mitchell, *The Random House Guide to Good Writing,* Random House, New York, 1991.

Lee, Mary, Gloria Stephenson, Max Anderson, and Lynn Allan Lee, *The Handbook of Technical Writing: Form and Style,* Harcourt Brace Jovanovich, San Diego, 1990.

Roth, Julius A., *Timetables: Structuring the Passage of Time in Hospital Treatment and Other Careers,* Bobbs Merrill, New York, 1963.

Shelton, James H., *Handbook for Technical Writing,* NTC Business Books, Lincolnwood, IL, 1994.

CHAPTER TWELVE

THE ORGANIZATION OF RESEARCH

There are two perspectives from which the organization of research can be viewed: the way the **research tasks** are organized and the way the **research staff** is recruited and organized. In this chapter we give attention to both of these perspectives because they are interrelated. Without having the right research staff it is not possible to complete the tasks and accomplish the objectives of the research project. At the same time, these interrelated tasks must be spelled out clearly so that the work of the research staff proceeds in an efficient manner. In a very real sense, researching is an organized social event that leads to and underlies our claims to knowledge.

THE RESEARCH TASKS

A research project consists of conceptualizing, developing measurements of the concepts, selecting subjects to be studied, developing a research design to collect the relevant data, collecting the data, analyzing the data, and reporting the results.[1]

Most of the chapters of this book focus on these tasks. Chapter 2 discusses conceptualization, Chapter 3 deals with measurement, Chapter 5 deals with the selection of the subjects, Chapters 4 and 6–9 deal with the selection of a research design, Chapter 10 considers ways of analyzing data, and Chapter 11 discusses the alternatives for reporting the results of the research.

These seven tasks suggest an orderly process, proceeding from one step to the next until the research is complete and the results are available for public use. In fact, the **research process** is much more complicated than that because the tasks involved are generally not distinct. They are interrelated and often overlapping. Although conceptualization ideally is the first task of a project, for example, it sometimes continues to evolve as the research progresses. Likewise, final measurement decisions may be made in conjunction with the construction of the data

[1]The research tasks enumerated here were covered briefly in Chapter 1. A review of that part of Chapter 1 will be helpful in understanding the seven research tasks enumerated here.

collection instrument. Because of the fluid nature of the research process, management of the research must be flexible and must provide for unforeseen circumstances that alter the timelines established for accomplishing the various tasks.

It is customary in planning a research project to set up **timelines** for the accomplishment of each research task. Without such timelines it is difficult to figure the costs involved in accomplishing tasks and the resources necessary for their completion. Seldom does the actual progress of the research match the projected timelines exactly, however. According to Murphy's law, if anything can go wrong, it will. For example, the time allotted to collect the data may turn out to be insufficient. Some years ago one of the authors did an interview study of retired men to determine their adjustment to retirement. The interview schedule was short and could easily be completed in 10 minutes. The timeline for collection of the data allowed half an hour for each interview and sufficient time for the interviewers to travel from one subject's home to another's. When the interviewers started collecting data, however, they found that many of the respondents were grateful to have someone to talk to and wanted them to stay longer. Accordingly, interviewers often spent much more time with each respondent than the timeline allowed for (Loether, 1964:517–25). The timelines for the study were disrupted, but the subjects found the interview experience more satisfying than they might have otherwise.

Because the tasks involved in research are not distinct, the plan of a project is necessarily tentative and subject to revision as the project proceeds. No matter how familiar researchers are with the topic being researched and with the population being studied, their knowledge is still imperfect, and things will occur in the course of the research that call for some reevaluation of the research plan. In *Sociologists at Work: Essays on the Craft of Social Research* (Hammond, 1964), 11 sociologists wrote chronicles of their experiences in carrying out research projects. This book is particularly instructive because the authors reported how their research actually was done rather than how textbooks say it should be done.[2] What their accounts reveal is that research consists of a series of **decision points** that unfold as the project progresses. Peter Blau's account of his studies of bureaucracies describes one of these decision points,

> I did not anticipate the investigation of statistical records of performance. This was not merely an oversight. I wrote in a memo in the spring of 1948 that production records, which were a basic source of data in the famous study of work groups reported in *Management and the Worker* by F. J. Roethlisberger and W. J. Dickson [1939], would not be available for white-collar workers in public or private bureaucracies. . . .
>
> In my first week of orientation, I learned about the detailed and varied quantitative records kept in the federal agency on operations and on the performance of every agent. My interest was immediately aroused, and I started scrutinizing these records and abstracting information from them. (Blau, 1964:39)

[2]Most articles that appear in the sociology journals are cleaned-up accounts of how the research being reported was done. This cleaning process is not a deliberate attempt to mislead the reader. Rather, it usually results from pressures on the author to keep the text concise.

As a result of his discovery of fruitful data, Blau decided to incorporate them into his analysis, thus altering his original research plan. Such alterations in the research process are not at all unusual, as witnessed in the other accounts recapped in Hammond's book.

The lesson to be learned here is that the researcher should develop a careful research plan, anticipating as many potential problems and opportunities as possible, but realizing that contingencies will arise that must be dealt with in order to carry out the research.

INDIVIDUAL VERSUS TEAM RESEARCH

When a research project is being conducted by an individual, the **division of labor** is not problematic. Whatever work is done has to be done by the lone researcher. The tasks to be completed must still be scheduled and allotted sufficient time for completion, as is the case with any project, but the researcher normally does not have anyone else to turn to for assistance. An exception to this rule is the academic researcher who is able to enlist the aid of students to assist with some of the more mundane tasks (such as coding questionnaires). This work might be carried out as part of the requirements of a course, on a voluntary basis by students who want some research experience, or as work paid for by the researcher or from modest research funds available.

This was the most common model in earlier days. As William H. Sewell describes research in the 1930s,

> A lone scholar, with the assistance of a student or two, would undertake a research project with very limited funding, obtain information on a small non-probability sample, employ simple counting or cross-tabular procedures in the analysis of the data, write up the results, and hope to get an article or monograph published in one of the then limited outlets for sociological research studies. (Riley, 1988b:35)

This sort of **individual research** still exists but is less common than it was earlier. Academics are able to engage in such research with minimal funds because they may take advantage of university resources. Graduate students working on master's theses or doctoral dissertations usually do individual research, partly because of limited resources, but also because they are required to produce a product that demonstrates their ability to carry out a research project from inception to completion.

The computer has proved to be a boon to the individual researcher because it greatly reduces the labor involved in data analysis and report writing. However, the other research tasks are still formidable. As a result, research projects carried out by individuals tend to be limited to modest objectives such as cross-sectional studies of fairly specific research questions or field observations of individual sites. Furthermore, researchers who must collect their own data may have to be content with small samples or nonrandom samples and a conceptual scheme that includes fewer variables than would otherwise be the case.

Sometimes research projects are undertaken by what amounts to **research partnerships.** Two or three researchers may develop an interest in a research question and agree to pursue its answer together. This arrangement provides a larger labor pool than is the case with individual research, but it shares many of the same limiting characteristics. Limited funds and other resources may compel projects that are more modest in scale than is ideal. Thomas and Znaniecki's Polish peasant study (1918–1920), described in Chapter 9, is an early example of a research partnership between two scholars.

Increasingly, social science research is being carried out by research organizations. Some of these organizations are permanent, and others are specifically organized for and limited to the length of a particular project. Some are located in university settings, others are located in government agencies, and still others are set up as nonprofit or for-profit companies.

Team research is not a new phenomenon. During World War II the Research Branch of the U.S. Army conducted a series of studies that culminated in the four-volume series *Studies in Social Psychology in World War II* (Stouffer et al., 1949–1950). Several young scholars in sociology and other social and behavioral sciences who later became prominent in their fields got their early research experience with the Research Branch, either as civilians or as members of the Armed Forces. Another team research center that came into its own after the war was the Bureau of Applied Social Research at Columbia University, with which Paul Lazarsfeld was affiliated between 1950 and 1959.

In the private sector, public opinion polling organizations such as the Gallup Poll and the Roper Poll became prominent. However, their research is limited largely to survey or questionnaire research, whereas the research of the Research Branch of the Army and of the Bureau of Applied Social Research was more varied in approach.

Other private-sector research organizations focused on **applied research.** Rossi and Wright (1991) remark on the increasing emphasis that was put on evaluation research as a result of the Great Society programs of the mid-1960s and explain that whereas university-based researchers were slow to take advantage of opportunities in applied research,

> Private entrepreneurs . . . were quicker to notice and exploit the new emphasis on evaluation. Some existing firms that had not been particularly interested in the social sciences opened subsidiaries that could compete for social research contracts (e.g., Westinghouse). Others greatly expanded their social science research sections (e.g., the Rand Corporation). In addition, literally hundreds of new firms appeared on the scene, a handful of which became spectacular successes during the "golden years" (e.g., Abt Associates).
>
> By the middle of the 1970s, some 500–600 private firms existed primarily to bid on contracts for applied social research. As in other areas of corporate activity, a few firms garnered the majority of available funds. For example, in the period 1975–1980, 6 large research firms received over 60% of the evaluation funds expended by the Department of Education. (1991:88)

Rossi and Wright point out that Abt Associates at one time employed more PhDs in the social sciences than any one of the universities in the Boston area (1991:95).

In the Reagan years of the 1980s, there was a cutback in funding for the social sciences. Accordingly, many of the organizations doing social science research were downsized (Abt Associates cut its number of PhDs in half) or went out of existence. Nevertheless, the tendency to do research through organizations in universities, government agencies, and the private sector remains. This probably reflects the institutionalization of applied research and the greater sophistication in social science research, both in terms of testing more-elaborate theoretical models and in terms of technological advances that have made such tests feasible. In particular, the rapid progress of computer technology has facilitated sample selection, data collection, data analysis, and reporting of results.[3] Although this technology has also facilitated individual research, that level of research is still limited largely to small-scale projects.

Research organizations have the capacity to undertake the more ambitious projects with elaborate research designs and larger databases. Because these are the sorts of projects that are generally encouraged by the major funding agencies, young scholars who are just entering the field of sociology are likely to find opportunities for involvement in such team research efforts.

RESEARCH AS A SOCIAL ACTIVITY

Scientific research is itself a social activity. The lone researcher must still interact with others in the process of conducting a project. Social interaction takes place in making arrangements for a study, collecting the data, analyzing the data, and reporting the results.[4] Even the survey researcher who relies on mailed questionnaires as a source of data interacts indirectly with respondents through cover letters, follow-up letters, and the questionnaires themselves.

Solitary researchers whose data come from secondary sources and who spend many hours alone compiling those data also must be involved in social interaction. They interact with others in making arrangements to access the data. They may also interact with others in arranging for the analysis of the data once they have been collected. Furthermore, it is necessary to interact with others in preparing the results for publication or presentation and communicating those results. Many social processes and social structures are part of the context that makes research possible.

Team research, whether at the level of a partnership or at the level of a research organization, is even more social because of the interaction among the

[3]See Chapters 5–11 for examples of this computer technology.

[4]Chapter 1 discussed some of the social factors involved in research. Reviewing that discussion will reinforce what is being said here about the social nature of research.

researchers themselves. Researcher and staff member roles are defined, specifying the duties and obligations of each and indicating how each of those roles is related to the others. The more people there are involved in the organization, the more complicated the role network is and the greater the probability that the interactions that take place will be both direct (person-to-person) and indirect (through intermediaries).

Research generally involves a number of **stakeholders,** such as the funding organization, the researcher's host organization, the **principal investigator** and research staff, respondents involved in the research, and, perhaps, the interested public and professional audiences of research results. Felt obligations, competition, and friendships between these stakeholders can affect the outcome of research. For example, funders may expect the outcome to be favorable to their views or to have immediate and major implications, which may raise ethical issues for researchers (see Riley, 1988a, for further discussion of life as a researcher).

Norms and values about how best to conduct research have an impact on the outcome of research. Sometimes these norms have to do with quality standards, the **risks** of making mistakes, how open staff feel they can be about reporting discovered problems, or how **conflict** is resolved. It is helpful to have a research context in which individuals feel that their efforts are appreciated and count, in which they are challenged to high work standards and feel little personal risk in sharing potentially important insights and information about the research, feel a sense of trust and sharing an important venture, feel justly treated, and are motivated to contribute to the overall task of learning something new. Research organizations can have competitive norms in which staff who discover important problems with the research procedures or who have useful insights or skills feel that they cannot share this knowledge because of the consequences for themselves or others. In such cases, the quality of the research may suffer.

All scientific research, no matter what the discipline, has its social aspects; social scientists tend to be more involved in social interaction than scientists in some of the other disciplines, however, because the subjects of social science research are human beings or organizations of human beings.

Because social factors are involved in any research, they must be taken into consideration, and their impact on the project must be weighed in evaluating the outcomes. The researchers must ask themselves whether the social aspects of the research process had any deleterious or beneficial effects on the investigation of the research question. Any such effects must be factored into the researchers' conclusions.

FACTORS FAVORING TEAM RESEARCH

In an important sense, all research is team research. The investigator is involved with and depends on many others to accomplish even single-investigator research. Joseph Eaton recognized the trend in science toward planned team research as opposed to what he called "rugged individualism in research" (Eaton, 1951:708). Furthermore, he contended that there were several good reasons for this trend.

> First, the complexity of subject matter makes it increasingly difficult to approach any significant subject, particularly in the social sciences, with the skills and experience likely to be found in any one individual.
>
> A second factor in favor of teamwork is the enhancement of **intellectual stimulation** possible when different individuals focus on a single problem. Each person develops some stereotyped approaches and professional blind spots which tend to limit their capacity to observe. There is also the opportunity to clarify ideas when one must explain them to another who is sufficiently interested and informed to appreciate them. They are subject to criticism that tends to be constructive since it is motivated by a common goal rather than by competing incentives.
>
> Thirdly, team research facilitates the integration of theoretical assumptions of different scientific disciplines. Particularly in the social sciences, there are many contradictions and gaps in the theoretical framework which guides research.
>
> Finally, there is an opportunity for division of labor where one lone observer would be seriously handicapped. Psychological evidence summarized by Murphy, Murphy and Newcomb [1937] strongly suggests the theory that, all other factors being equal, group effort has a greater potentiality for accuracy than individual effort. (1951:708)

Eaton's third point speaks particularly to the situation in which the team carrying out the research is interdisciplinary; however, within the field of sociology itself several different theoretical and methodological approaches may well be represented among the members of the research team, depending on their academic backgrounds. Such variety in perspectives can give a project qualities that may add to the creativeness and fruitfulness of the research.

Eaton contends that an individual researcher is more prone to error than a research team. This may be the case if team members monitor the quality of each other's work. However, on some occasions lack of effective coordination of the efforts of team members may contribute to the commission of errors.

A fifth factor that might be added to Eaton's list is that research grants and contracts (with some exceptions) tend to be slanted in favor of research organizations rather than individual researchers. Consequently, individual researchers may be unable to compete successfully for much of the research money available.

PROBLEMS OF TEAM RESEARCH

A number of potential problems stem largely from the fact that team research is a social activity. In the first place, although the team members are assembled because of their professional skills, they are human beings subject to the same frailties as any other humans. Relationships that start out on a professional level tend to become personal as well. Consequently, team members react to each other in terms of their personalities as well as their professional capabilities. If the personalities of all of the team members are compatible, then things may go along smoothly. Often, however, team members encounter rough spots in relating to each other. In such cases disputes that start as professional disagreements (e.g., over technical aspects of the research process) may move to a personal level and disrupt the project. Often this affects how important information and insights are shared, and it can even become violent, as in a large study in which key staff members actually got into a fistfight over the interpretation of statistical findings. These sorts of eventualities must be anticipated and attempts to resolve or head them off must be taken at the recruitment level, as research roles are defined for the participants, or in the way the organization's climate of norms and values is established.

Another possible problem for team research is that team members usually differ in **professional status.** Some team members may be widely known for their past scholarship and others may be unknown. Some are more senior in experience than others. Some may be familiar with the subject matter being studied and others may be newcomers. Some may have PhDs whereas others do not. In the case of university-based research teams, in particular, it is usually the case that some members of the team are students and others are professionals. These differences in **status** must be dealt with in such a way that they do not interfere with the progress of the research. As Eaton says,

> A mutual adjustment to each other's status becomes essential. Status affects such things as the influence of their opinion in team consultations, the attention paid by outside observers to each member, the remuneration offered, and the credit given for their respective contributions. The difficulties of integrating different levels of prestige has [sic] been a primary stumbling block of many team research efforts. (1951:710)

Again, a clear-cut definition of the roles of researchers and staff members and communication of those definitions to all the members of the team can be very helpful in avoiding stumbling blocks to which Eaton alludes. Often those less familiar with the study area can make a special contribution by raising questions about underlying assumptions that might otherwise be skipped over and not examined.

Organizational size is another possible source of problems for team research. The more people involved in the organization, the more complicated the role network is and the more coordination of activities is needed. Organizations reach the point at which they become so large that it is not possible for all team members to have frequent direct contact with each other. At that point coordination of activities may become crucial to the success of the organization. The greater labor base available makes it possible for the organization to accomplish more, but, at the same time, more time must be devoted to managing it. As a result, there is no one-to-one relationship between the number of members added to the organization and the increment added to the labor base available to accomplish the work.[5] This princi-

[5]Of course, this principle is not limited to the operation of research organizations. It applies to organizations in general.

ple might be characterized as the rule of diminishing returns of organizational size. This can have important implications for planning a research organization because, using the principle as a basis for a cost–benefit analysis, it might be possible to determine the optimal size for the organization's staff. Optimal size in this context means that there are enough people to do the work but not so many that substantial human resources must be diverted to management functions. When research organizations become unwieldy because of simultaneous work on a number of projects, the problem is sometimes handled by breaking the overall organization into several semiautonomous research teams, each assigned to a separate project. Sometimes organizations use a functional organization (e.g., instrument design, sampling, data collection, analysis) in which one unit handles a certain aspect of all projects. This structure raises other issues about how knowledge is shared and activity is coordinated for any given research project.

Another important consideration in anticipating problems in team research is whether the team is organized as a **hierarchy.** A professional values autonomy and usually seeks to identify his or her position in a research team as that of one among equals. If a research organization is set up hierarchically and the principal investigator or **research director** sees his or her position as one of authority over other members of the team, there is likely to be friction. In discussing the role of the research director, Miller says,

> The research director takes his place in the center of all of the forces that have been described. His role is to direct group processes, ascertain group sentiment, and make decisions so that the research can be designed and executed with harmony and efficiency. He must see that role definitions for each member are clearly outlined. He must interpret the external demands on the project and relate them to his research personnel so that appropriate action is taken. He must come to recognize that he will get little opportunity to do field research himself. And he must accept the fact that some interpersonal friction will accompany his most valiant efforts to make group research palatable, especially during the early period when a number of individual researchers are learning to live together as group researchers. He will come to understand that each member of the group is concerned with his reputation as the result of his membership. He wants to have his say as to what others do when he feels his own standards are being violated. This is at once a source of group power and of group conflict. The director will often be challenged as to how these group motivations can be channeled. (1991:75)

The research director may avoid conflict by setting a collegial context for the researchers. Even though the research director is the principal investigator, with ultimate responsibility for a project, he or she can define that position as a buffer between the funding agency and his or her professional colleagues, protecting their status as researchers from outside influences.

However, if a research director conceives of his or her role as being in authority over the others in the system, that can lead to problems. The professionals on the team may resist attempts to control their activities and thereby impede the progress of the project. As a case in point, in one project in which the research director insisted that the researchers keep regular 9-to-5 hours, rebellion almost ensued.

The professionals on the team came and went as they wished, insisting that they worked long hours on the research whether or not they happened to be physically present. One made the point that his most creative ideas might occur to him at 3 A.M. and that he could not turn his brain on and off by the clock. The rebellion was avoided by a compromise that recognized both the autonomy of the professionals and the responsibility of the principal investigator for the progress of the project.

Miller mentions **job security** concerns of researchers as another source of potential problems in team research. When the research organization is not a permanent entity, the researchers are working with **soft money.** That is, their tenure on the project depends on the continuation of funding. Some projects are funded for definite periods of time and it is understood that at the end of the funding period the research staff will be terminated. Other projects have prospects of extending the period of employment by submitting proposals for project extensions or proposals for new projects. Miller says,

> As individual contracts begin to approach termination, personal insecurities mount and are intensified by group interaction. The feelings of insecurity are expressed in many different ways, which may include demands for more say in both policy and administrative decisions, safeguards for individual publication rights, and almost single-minded preoccupation with the acquisition of the next research contract. (1991:75)

Because these feelings of insecurity become more pronounced in the latter stages of a project, they can present particular problems because the preoccupation of the researchers is likely to disrupt progress at that crucial phase when data are being analyzed and final reports are being written. This tends to be a hectic period in any project, even when staff insecurity is not an issue. Often delays earlier in a project cut the time available for analysis in order to meet final deadlines.

A final potential problem area for team research relates to the **commitment** of the members of the research team. Researchers who are personally committed to a project tend to be more reliable and trustworthy in carrying out their duties than do hired hands. A common problem with survey research is that interviewers who are hired strictly as interviewers and are paid by the interview or by the hour are not as likely to give the work their best effort as are researchers who have been intimately involved with a project from its inception and who are on salary. These hired hands require attention, sometimes with close supervision and spot checking of their work to maintain quality.

Committed researchers, on the other hand, can generally be trusted to do the job with the intent to maintain quality because they have a personal stake in the outcome. It is in establishing this commitment that the potential for problems arises. If the members of the research team feel that they have had an important role in the development of the project from its inception, then they are likely to be committed. This requires that they be a part of the decision-making process as the project moves through the research tasks discussed earlier in the chapter. Because staff are often not hired until a project's initial proposal has been accepted and funded, involving staff from the beginning may be a problem. Involving everyone in the decision making sometimes complicates the whole process because it requires that compromises be reached to avoid alienating individual team members. In questionnaire construction, for example, items are sometimes included more because they are important to individual team members than because they are germane to the data collection process. Consequently, questionnaires designed by teams are neither the most efficient nor the most effective instruments for getting the job done. Furthermore, such questionnaires often take much more time to develop than they would if they were created by an individual researcher.

The task of accomplishing research objectives while keeping individual team members committed is often a delicate one. But it is important if the project is to be successful. Here is where expertise with interpersonal relations and an understanding of human nature are invaluable tools.

Eaton suggests what he calls **democratic teamwork** as a possible solution to this problem. He says,

> Occasionally scientific team research is conducted by a number of collaborators without any defined structure of authority and responsibility. Major decisions are made jointly. Different team members assume primary responsibility in those areas where the group considers them most competent. This method is in accord with professional traditions of scholarly autonomy and is most commonly found in university settings. . . . Some degree of inhibition of individual initiative is always implied when a team research effort is being considered. Under a democratic arrangement, however, the limits, their extent and substance, are not imposed by an outside authority. They are the product of the team whose members agree to them to accomplish their joint purpose. (1951:712)

In this sort of democratic teamwork arrangement, the person who takes on the role of principal investigator is, in effect, doing so to satisfy the requirements of a funding agency without actually assuming a position of authority within the research organization. Although this arrangement contributes to the maintenance of member commitment, it can also complicate the whole process of accomplishing the research tasks. The wheels of democracy sometimes move very slowly.

Although commitment by the research staff is crucial, it is also important to attempt to develop similar feelings among staff members (e.g., the clerical staff). Although their work roles may not be directly tied into the accomplishment of the research tasks, their behavior on the job can either enhance or hinder the progress of a project. In this regard, an orientation program for staff members can be important. If professionals take the time and effort to explain the nature of the project and point out how staff members' efforts fit in, those staff members may feel that they are more than just hired hands. One of the authors had the privilege of working with a professional who was particularly adept at involving the clerical staff in the activities of the research team. Staff members were included in discussions of strategies for carrying out research tasks and were asked their opinions about how the research team should proceed. As a result, those staff members began to identify themselves with the research and made special efforts to see that the work was accomplished accurately and promptly.

TASK–TEAM INTERDEPENDENCE

The point was made early in the chapter that there is interdependence between the research tasks to be accomplished and the research team assembled to accomplish them. From the start of a research project, the tasks and the team interact. How the tasks to be completed are defined and scheduled on the timeline is affected by the makeup of the research team. In turn, the composition of the research team depends on the specific research tasks. For example, if the research question under investigation calls for a field observation design, then the researchers recruited are likely to be different than they would be if the design called for was a survey. In other words, an explicit attempt is made to match the skills of the researchers recruited with the demands of the study to be undertaken.

This interaction between the demands of the study and the composition of the research team continues throughout a project. At times the demands of the study alter the behavior of the researchers (or may even alter the composition of the research team), and at other times the research team revises the tasks to be accomplished. Thus, there is an intimate relationship between the two that makes each research project unique. All of the factors discussed in this chapter are at play at the same time, each affecting each other and resulting in a research product that is not quite the same as it would have been if the specific tasks undertaken and the particular players in the process were different. To reiterate, scientific research is itself a social phenomenon subject to the same influences as any other social phenomenon, plus a few influences that are unique because of the kinds of activities engaged in by scientists. It is a social encounter that creates and underlies the quality of resulting scientific knowledge.

THE EDUCATION FACTOR

When research is carried on by a research team based in an educational setting, an additional dimension is added to this whole picture: the **education factor.** Although university research is devoted primarily to the advancement of scientific knowledge, it also serves the function of training students to carry on the work of the discipline or disciplines involved. Thus, in addition to the professional researchers, the research team usually includes student researchers (typically graduate students). These student researchers help accomplish the work of the project but, at the same time, they are supposed to be learning how to do research. As a consequence, how the research tasks are carried out and how the research team is organized is influenced by the need to make the experience an educational one for the students. In this regard Miller says,

> A professional researcher . . . wants to choose his problem, be given the proprietary right of publication for his work, and have control over his working conditions. The university is concerned that graduate students receive broad research training and not be employed at mere clerical tasks. The research design must be constructed in recognition of these concerns and the staff organized in optimum-sized working groups so that the best combination of professional staff and graduate students may be obtained. (1991:75)

What this implies is that these additional demands on the project will further affect the interactions between the research tasks and the research team and these, in turn, will further affect the final product of the research. A typical effect of having students as members of a research team is to slow the pace of the project. The professional researchers often must proceed at a more leisurely pace than they would normally do in order to provide the students with the opportunity to learn. Furthermore, students may be allowed to make mistakes that would not otherwise occur because one way to learn is to benefit from one's mistakes. Each of these circumstances has the effect of altering the course of the project and adding to the uniqueness of the whole process.

The degree to which the presence of students influences the research project depends on the relative weights given to the goals of advancing scientific knowledge and training students. Projects differ considerably in terms of how these two demands are balanced (or left unbalanced). Projects that are heavily weighted toward the demands of scientific knowledge are likely to tolerate less disruption of normal project activities by students than projects whose primary purpose is to provide an educational experience. Thus, the impact of the presence of students on a project is not a constant by any means. Nevertheless, their very presence on a research team is bound to have some effect even when an attempt is made to minimize their influence on project outcomes.

SUMMARY

This chapter dealt with the organization of social research. The term *organization* was used in two senses: the organization of the research tasks of a project and the organization of the research staff. It was pointed out that these two perspectives on organization are intimately interrelated and must be considered in relation to each other.

The research tasks were identified generally as conceptualization, measurement, subject selection, research design, data collection, data analysis, and result reporting. These are not seven distinct steps, but are interrelated and overlapping. Although timelines are set up for the accomplishment of these tasks, in reality they are seldom accomplished exactly as planned. The wise researcher anticipates opportunities and problems in carrying out a project and tries to make allowances for them so that the goals of the project will be accomplished.

Although individual research still exists, it is becoming less and less common, and team research is becoming more common. Factors favoring team research were reviewed. Even so-called individual research is often a team effort when one looks at the broader set of interactions and support of the investigator.

Problems of team research were considered. These include the consequences of the human factor, particularly in terms of personality differences and organization norms, even among skilled professionals; the problem of differences in professional status; the problem of organizational size; the problem of hierarchical organization; problems of security; and the problem of commitment.

The interdependence of research tasks and the research team was discussed. How each affects the other was considered and the consequences of such interdependence were pointed out. The additional factor of an educational mission in the case of university-based research was considered. The effects of attempts to balance the goal of advancing knowledge with the goal of training graduate students were pointed out.

All research (particularly social science research, in which humans are not only the researchers but often the focus of a study) is a social activity subject to all of the advantages and complications of any activity that involves the interaction of human beings. In Chapter 13 the additional factor of research resources is considered in terms of how such resources affect the progress and outcome of a research project.

TERMS TO KNOW

Applied research
Commitment
Conflict
Decision points
Democratic teamwork
Division of labor
Education factor
Hierarchy
Individual research
Intellectual stimulation
Job security
Norms
Organizational size
Principal investigator
Professional status
Research director
Research partnerships
Research process
Research staff (team)
Research tasks
Risk
Soft money
Stakeholders
Status
Team research
Timelines

ISSUES AND COMPARISONS

Social aspects of research
Impact of computer technology on research
Ethical concerns in team research
University-based research versus research in private research organizations
Task–team interdependence

EXERCISES

1. Arrange to interview a faculty member about the organization of one of his or her recent research projects. How does he or she describe the organization of the research in terms of the tasks to be done and the social organization? Ask about instances in which the organization of the research effort was especially beneficial to the knowledge the project developed and instances in which the organization posed problems. Write an organized statement summarizing the points made in the interview and your own reflections on ways to build strengths and avoid problems in organizing research.

2. List the ethical issues that might arise because of the social organization of research. How might these issues be handled?

3. Find an example of a report of results from team research. List ways in which the social organization of the research might influence its findings. What steps would you suggest to handle any problems you see?

REFERENCES

Blau, Peter M., "The Research Process in the Study of the Dynamics of Bureaucracy," in Philip E. Hammond, ed., *Sociologists at Work,* Basic Books, New York, 1964.

Eaton, Joseph W., "Social Processes of Professional Teamwork," *American Sociological Review* October 1951;16(5):707–13.

Hammond, Phillip E., ed., *Sociologists at Work: Essays on the Craft of Social Research,* Basic Books, New York, 1964.

Loether, Herman J., "The Meaning of Work and Adjustment to Retirement," in Arthur B. Shostak and William Gomberg, eds., *Blue Collar World,* Prentice Hall, New York, 1964, pp. 517–25.

Miller, Delbert C., *Handbook of Research Design and Social Measurement,* 5th ed., Sage, Newbury Park, CA, 1991.

Murphy, Gardner, Lois Murphy, and Theodore M. Newcomb, *Experimental Social Psychology,* Harper, New York, 1937, pp. 715–38.

Riley, Matilda White, ed., *Sociological Lives,* Sage, Newbury Park, CA, 1988a.

Riley, Matilda White, "Notes on the Influence of Sociological Lives," in Matilda White Riley, ed., *Sociological Lives,* Sage, Newbury Park, CA, 1988b.

Roethlisberger, F. J., and W. J. Dickson, *Management and the Worker,* Cambridge, MA, 1939.

Rossi, Peter H., and James D. Wright, "Evaluation Research: An Assessment," in Delbert C. Miller, *Handbook of Research Design and Social Measurement,* 5th ed., Sage, Newbury Park, CA, 1991, pp. 87–97. Originally published in Ralph H. Turner and James F. Short, Jr., *Annual Review of Sociology,* Vol. 10, Annual Reviews, Palo Alto, CA, 1984, pp. 332–52.

Stouffer, S. A., L. Guttman, E. A. Suchman, P. F. Lazarsfeld, S. A. Star, and J. A. Clausen, *Measurement and Prediction,* Vol. 4, Princeton University Press, Princeton, NJ, 1950.

Stouffer, S. A., A. A. Lumsdaine, H. Lumsdaine, R. M. Williams, Jr., M. B. Smith, I. L. Janis, S. A. Star, and L. S. Cottrell, Jr., *The American Soldier: Combat and Its Aftermath,* Vol. 2, Princeton University Press, Princeton, NJ, 1949.

Stouffer, S. A., E. A. Suchman, L. C. De Vinney, S. A. Star, and R. M. Williams, Jr., *The American Soldier: Adjustment During Army Life,* Vol. 1, Princeton University Press, Princeton, NJ, 1949.

Thomas, William I., and Florian Znaniecki, *The Polish Peasant in Europe and America,* Gorham Press, Boston, 1918–1920.

CHAPTER THIRTEEN

RESOURCE CONSIDERATIONS

No matter how carefully a research project is planned, if the resources necessary to do the work are not available the project will not come to fruition. Any project, regardless of how creative or important it is, must have adequate resources to accomplish the research tasks. When we use the word ***resources*** here we mean such things as labor, equipment, supplies, time, and space. First, there must be an appropriately skilled research staff to accomplish the work. Second, the proper equipment must be available to do the job. Third, the staff must have the supplies needed. Fourth, enough time must be allotted to each of the research tasks involved in the project. Finally, there must be adequate and appropriate space available within which to carry out the activities of the project. Of course, the basic resource necessary to obtain all of these is money.

A crucial question anyone wanting to do research must answer is "How will we (I) find the necessary financial support?" In an ideal situation, all of the necessary resources or the money needed to get them would be available. In the real world it does not work this way. Accordingly, researchers often must be salespeople as well as scientists in order to do the research they think is necessary or desirable. If they cannot sell their research ideas to someone or some organization willing and able to supply the money to accomplish it, then the project may never get beyond the planning stage. A key step in initiating research, then, is to identify potential sources of funding such as government agencies or foundations that are interested in the research topic and are in a position to offer the necessary financial support.

PROJECTING COSTS

Before approaching potential funding agencies for money, it is necessary to estimate how much a research project will cost. This step will immediately eliminate some agencies because projected costs exceed their grant limits.

The conceptualization phase of research is generally a prerequisite for costing out a research project. If the researchers have done a careful job of conceptualizing the potential project, then they will know what research tasks they need to carry out to answer the research question. Having identified those research tasks, they can use them as a basis for calculating project costs. For example, if they know how many hours of work will be involved in the project, they will have a basis for estimating labor costs.

In fact, estimation of labor costs is the key step in developing a research budget. Once the labor costs are estimated, they can be used as a basis for estimating other project costs. Estimates of labor costs must take into account the number of people with specific skills needed and the time required for them to complete the research tasks. It is also necessary to consider wage and salary rates and employee benefits (e.g., social security, workers' compensation, health plans).

The basic step in calculating overall labor costs is figuring the total number of hours of labor required for the project. In order to do this it is useful to break the project down into its constituent phases and estimate how much time will be required to complete each. Ackoff has suggested that a project might be broken down into the following phases to calculate a budget–time schedule: (1) planning, (2) conducting a pilot study and pretests, (3) drawing a sample, (4) preparing observational materials, (5) selecting and training personnel, (6) conducting a trial run, (7) revising plans, (8) collecting data, (9) processing data, and (10) preparing the final report (Ackoff, 1953:347).

Of course, the phases that enter into a specific research process may differ, depending on the nature of the particular study. Furthermore, although they are presented in numerical order here, the research process does not actually proceed neatly from one step to the next. Rather, the steps overlap and interrelate. Nevertheless, in estimating time needed to complete each of these steps it is usually possible to treat them as separate from each other.

It is helpful in projecting the resource needs of a project to have an even more detailed breakdown of the steps in the research process than Ackoff suggested. If the particular research design to be used (e.g., experiment, survey) is known, then it is possible to develop such a breakdown. Dillman (1982) studied the costs of conducting research through the use of mail questionnaires. In the process of analyzing his data, he broke the steps in a study into several specific tasks and figured the costs accordingly. Under the category of "General Costs," for example, he listed the following:

- Draw systematic sample from telephone directories or other sampling source
- Purchase mailout envelopes
- Purchase business reply envelopes
- Print questionnaires
- Graphics design of cover
- Telephone (toll charges)
- Supplies (miscellaneous)
- Type, proof, and store names in automatic typewriters (Miller, 1991:637)

Under "First Mailout" of the questionnaire he listed the following tasks:

- Print cover letter
- Address letters and envelopes

- Postage for mailout
- Prepare mailout packets
- Postage for returned questionnaires (business reply envelopes)
- Process and precode returns (Miller, 1991:637)

In addition to these two lists of tasks, Dillman provided detailed lists for each of the other phases of the study that he identified.

One of the most important costs is that of sufficient time for thinking! Often research projects are treated as if they were a mechanical process of data collecting and processing, but research is a thinking process. When data gathering is underfunded, it is tempting to squeeze time out of the analysis and reflection phases of a study. Often new things are learned as the research progresses or surprises happen, and that generally requires redoing some steps or figuring out some other way of approaching some aspect of the research. Funding estimates should respect the critical role of time to step back and think through the meaning of results and to plan further research steps if needed.

Because these lists are made up of specific activities, it is possible to anticipate the labor, equipment, supplies, time, and space needed at each step to carry out the work. Sladek and Stein (1981:60) call a budget based on such a detailed list of specific research tasks a functional budget. A **functional budget** is a tool used in the process of developing a final budget for a project. Consequently, it is not usually a part of the final **research proposal** submitted to a potential granting agency.

The first step in developing a functional budget is to figure labor costs. Once the labor costs have been estimated, it is possible to decide what equipment and supplies will be needed to support the labor detailed for each task. The equipment for a project usually may be divided into two types: permanent and temporary. The permanent equipment is purchased outright for the project and generally becomes the property of the grantee, whereas the temporary equipment is leased for the length of the project or the phase of the project for which it is needed. Supplies are consumables such as paper, printer ribbons, floppy disks, and pencils that must be replenished as the project goes on.

Time is naturally factored into the estimate of labor costs. It also must be considered in figuring costs for equipment and supplies because the timing for their use has bearing on the costs involved. For example, some equipment must be available for use during the length of the whole project, whereas other equipment may be needed for only one phase of a study (e.g., multiple telephones for several interviewers to use simultaneously in an interview study conducted by telephone).

Space is another important item in figuring the costs of research. The research staff must have space to carry out the work. This may include office space for clerical staff and researchers, laboratory space for computers and other equipment, and storage space for supplies. Space also enters the equation in another sense. If the research involves fieldwork such as observation or interviewing, then the researchers must be transported to the sites where those activities are to take place and their expenses paid while they are there. Consequently, travel costs including transportation, accommodations, meals, and incidental expenses must be calculated.

Once a tentative budget for a project has been developed, researchers can begin to explore sources of funding to determine whether there are agencies that would be interested in funding the particular project and whether those agencies are prepared to provide funds sufficient to carry out the research.

The budget developed for a project must be realistic. The amount requested should be sufficient to do the work, but it should not be padded. That is, it should not include expenses beyond what is actually needed. With regard to requesting sufficient funds, Sladek and Stein say,

> It is imperative, of course, to ask for enough money to conduct your project properly. Though this statement appears to be self-evident, many novices, inexperienced in budget preparation, short-change themselves by keeping their budgets unrealistically low in an effort to remain competitive. A "bare-bones" budget, or a budget that seriously underestimates costs, can lead to one of two undesirable situations.
>
> First, your proposal may be rejected. The reviewers, who will be knowledgeable about the costs of your proposed project, will recognize that you have not carefully considered all of the resources you will need. The reviewers will not know whether the underestimate was an oversight on your part or whether you really did not understand all of the ramifications of the work you were about to embark on. . . .
>
> Second, your proposal may be funded, but after the initial glow of excitement has passed, you may wish it hadn't been. Working on a project that is underfunded is extremely difficult, and when you are the one who is responsible . . . it can be downright unpleasant. In the cold light of day, when you realize that you don't have enough money for staff or travel or supplies, you may wish you had been more generous with yourself at the budget preparation stage. (1981:28–29)

With regard to the padded budget, they say,

> Just as it is a rule of thumb never to underestimate your project costs, it is equally important not to pad your budget with overestimates. According to Chuang-Tse, "to have more than enough is harmful. This is true of all things, but especially true of money." It is harmful to ask for more money than you need (to pad the budget) for two reasons.
>
> First, your proposal may be rejected. The reviewers will recognize any inappropriate costs in your budget, as well as those that are appropriate. They will have an excellent idea of what your project costs should be. Therefore, you should make every effort to estimate those costs reasonably. Failure to do so may negatively affect the reviewers' confidence in your ability to manage the funds once you receive them.
>
> Second, it is possible that your proposal will be funded at the padded level proposed. If this happens, you may not be able to spend all of the money even if you purchase luxury items and are not cost-conscious in your spending. If there are substantial funds left at the end of the project, it will appear to the grantors that you planned poorly. On a later occasion, when you really need all of the money you ask for, the grantors may not give it to you. (Sladek and Stein, 1981:30)

Estimating future costs for longitudinal research is especially risky because it often requires not only estimating changes in the cost of resources but also projecting how many people will still be alive and available for reinterview. A Canadian researcher found to her dismay that people lived considerably longer than had been projected by demographers.

Obviously, estimating the costs of a project is not a matter to be treated lightly. It is a long, tedious process, but the success or failure of efforts to obtain funding may depend on how carefully this process is carried out. As Krathwohl says,

> Developing the budget is an excellent test of how clearly and completely the project has been described. A clearly described project and precise work plan will be easily translated into budgetary terms. A vague one will be translated only with slow guesswork. (1988:88)

SOURCES OF FUNDING

The sources of funding for research fall into two broad categories: government sources and private sources. Government sources may be at the federal, state, or local levels. Private sources also may be found at each of these three levels. As a general rule for both government and private sources, the more local the agency, the more parochial its interests are likely to be and the more limited its funds. There are exceptions to this rule, however. For that reason alone it is important for researchers seeking funding to canvass the full range of potential sources. At times

"Major Funding. How much do you need?"

funding is available from agencies that, at first glance, may seem to be unlikely sources. For example, the American Philosophical Society has provided modest support for social science research projects on a variety of research topics.

Government Funding Sources

The federal government is a prime source of funding for social science research. Miller (1991) points specifically to the National Science Foundation, the U.S. Department of Justice, the National Institute on Aging, the National Institute of Mental Health, the U.S. Department of Education, the U.S. Department of Labor, the U.S. Department of Defense, and the National Endowment for the Humanities as major sources of funding for social science research projects. This list is by no means exhaustive, but it represents the sources that have funded social science research most often. Other agencies, such as the Social Security Administration and the National Institutes of Health, also encourage and fund social science research. (See Box 13.1.)

With the exception of the National Science Foundation, the government agencies listed generally limit their support to projects whose research questions relate directly to the areas of interest that are their major focus. The Department of Justice, for example, is a good source of potential funding for research questions dealing with crime, delinquency, the justice system, and correctional facilities. Similarly, the Department of Education is a potential funding agency for any research question relating to the subject of education.

The usual practice for most of the federal government agencies interested in sponsoring research is to publish **requests for proposals (RFPs)** specifying a list of research topics that they consider appropriate to fund. Researchers seeking funds for their projects must either find RFPs for which their research topic is appropriate or alter their topic to fit the guidelines of the RFPs.

The National Science Foundation is almost unique in its willingness to fund basic research on any topic that a social science researcher proposes, as long as it meets scientific standards. Unlike most other funding sources, the National Science Foundation does not require the grantee to demonstrate that the research will produce results that have practical applications. Schaffter remarks that this policy

BOX 13.1
WEB SITES

A number of sources of information about research funding can be found on the Internet. Searching by the name of an organization, "research funding," or specific topic area should be helpful. Many government agencies maintain such sites. For example, the National Science Foundation site is http://www.nsf.gov. Links to various funding agencies are maintained by some universities.

"permits to a maximum degree the freedom and independent action in the choice and conduct of research necessary for scientific progress" (1969:61).

Of course, the burden is on the potential grantee to convince a panel of proposal reviewers that the research will be of scientific value, is feasible, and is worth funding and that the researchers can accomplish their plans.

State and local government agencies seldom provide the same degree and kind of funding for basic research as the National Science Foundation. These agencies are more like the other agencies in the federal government, issuing RFPs for research on topics that interest them and promise to have practical applications. On the state level, such agencies are usually those dealing with the justice system, education, demography, health, or other social problems. On the local level, too, agencies focusing on these and related areas are those likely to issue RFPs. Often they require a geographic focus on their areas. It is not unusual at the state or local level for agencies to obtain money from the federal government for the implementation of applied programs (e.g., social service programs such as Head Start) that, as a condition of funding, require evaluation. Consequently, the grantee agency may issue an RFP seeking a researcher or researchers to evaluate the program. As was mentioned in Chapter 12, applied research of this type has become a significant part of all of the social science research taking place in the United States.

Private Funding Sources

The other major source of social science funding is the private sector. Several thousand private foundations in the United States provide funds for research. According to Miller (1991:593), five major funders of social science research are the Social Science Research Council, the Rockefeller Foundation, the Russell Sage Foundation, the Ford Foundation, and the Carnegie Corporation. In terms of staff size and assets, the big five are the following:

- Ford Foundation: staff members, 560; assets, $5.3 billion
- PEW Charitable Trusts: staff members, 50; assets, $2.3 billion
- Robert Wood Johnson Foundation: staff members, 103; assets, $1.9 billion
- Lilly Endowment: staff members, 21; assets, $1.7 billion
- Carnegie Corporation of New York: staff members, 53; assets, $637 million (Miller, 1991:594)

Private foundations generally fall into one of four types: independent foundations, company-sponsored foundations, operating foundations, and community foundations (Read, 1986:6).

The **independent foundation** is a "grant-making organization established to aid social, educational, religious, or other charitable activities" (Read, 1986:6). These foundations are endowed by individuals, families, or groups. Although they may have broad discretion in the kinds of projects funded, they usually have guidelines about the sorts of research they will fund and the specific scientific fields from which they will entertain proposals. It has been estimated that about

70% of these kinds of foundations limit their giving to local areas (Read, 1986:6). The Russell Sage Foundation is an example of such an independent foundation.

The **company-sponsored foundation** may legally be an independent organization, but it has close ties to a corporation that supplies the funds. The grants given tend to be related to the activities of the corporation and may be given primarily to organizations located in areas in which the corporation has facilities. The Dayton–Hudson corporation has such a foundation, which gives grants for a number of different sorts of activities, especially in areas where their stores are located. For some of these company-sponsored foundations, the bulk of the giving takes place just before tax time because the corporation may write off grants as a tax benefit.

An **operating foundation** is one that uses its resources to conduct in-house research or provide a direct service of some sort. This type of foundation makes few grants to outside organizations and, when it does, these grants are primarily to enhance the foundation's own research or other activities. Operating foundations are usually endowed by a single source but may accept donations from the public on a tax-deductible basis. Examples of operating foundations are university foundations that raise funds to support faculty research and other university activities.

Community foundations are publicly supported organizations that award grants for projects in their own communities. The grants given by these foundations are generally awarded to organizations based in the local community. In describing this type of foundation, Lauffer says,

> Cleveland established the first community foundation in the years immediately preceding World War II. There are now more than 300 others throughout the United States. Today they account for about 3% of all foundation assets and allocations in the United States. Initially established to ensure proper stewardship of trusts and bequests, community foundations now actively seek funds from individual and corporate donors. . . . Several report allocations from local government sources as well.
>
> Community foundations are concerned primarily with local needs. At one time they tended to sponsor only such cultural programs as the local philharmonic or a summer "concert in the park" series. Today they are increasingly involved in human service and community development activities. (1984:133–34)

Because of their local focus, the community foundations are potential sources of funding for a limited number of projects with a specific focus and applied orientation.

The first category of foundations, the independent foundation, includes most of the major ones for social science funding. The Ford, Rockefeller, and Carnegie foundations fall into this category, although the funds for their initial endowments came from corporations.

Applying for grants from foundations is generally less trying than applying for government grants. The foundations tend to be less demanding in their guidelines for preparation of proposals, and they are often more liberal in their budget requirements.

Identifying Potential Funding Sources

Universities and large research organizations are apt to have offices that specialize in locating sources of funding for potential projects. These may be called "the Office of Research and Funded Projects" or some similar title. If asked by a researcher, they will come up with a list of potential funding agencies, both government and private, and will obtain details about the proposal formats required. Such offices often assist in preparing the proposals in final form, working out budget details, and acquiring any signatures needed from university or organization officials. Some research offices also publish periodic lists of grants available, with subject matter covered, deadlines for proposal submissions, and so on. When such supporting services are available, researchers are left free to concentrate on the conceptual and substantive details of their potential projects.

If no supporting facility is available, then it is up to the researchers to identify the potential funding sources. The library is a key source of information about government and private funding sources. Miller (1991) lists four major sources of information about research grants that should be available in university libraries. The first of these is the *Guide to Federal Funding,* produced by the Consortium of Social Science Associations and edited by Susan D. Quarles (1986). The guide gives information about more than 300 federal programs that offer funding to social scientists.

A second source is the *Guide to Research Support,* published by the American Psychological Association (Dusek et al., 1987). It covers funding opportunities in the behavioral sciences by 180 federal programs and 55 private programs.

An annual publication that provides comprehensive information about funds available from government agencies, foundations, corporations, and other groups is the *Annual Register of Grant Support.* The twenty-ninth edition of this publication appeared in 1996.

Comprehensive information about private foundations with assets of $1 million or more is published annually in *The Foundation Directory* (Jacobs, 2000). This publication of the Foundation Center is kept current through semiannual supplements that also provide information about smaller foundations.

Most libraries also have books on research funding and grant acquisition (some of which have already been cited here). Some of these have chapters on how to research funding sources. Lefferts (1982) has a particularly comprehensive chapter, "Resources for Locating Funding Sources." Although it came out in 1982, it lists many sources that are still current.

An up-to-the-minute source of information for funding opportunities from federal government grants is the *Federal Register,* published by the government five days a week. Similarly, *The Commerce Business Daily* is a government publication that publishes RFPs from government agencies.

Obviously there is no dearth of information about funding sources. The problem is to sift through all of the information available to find a match between the research topic to be studied and the agencies that have related interests and adequate funding opportunities.

A Word about Matching Funds and Overhead

Whether funds are sought from a government or a private funding source, **matching funds** may be required. That is, the organization seeking funding must pledge to contribute a certain percentage of the project budget in the form of money or other resources. For example, a funding agency may require that the grantee cover 20% of the costs of a project. The grantee could do this by pledging to pay 20% of the costs across the board or could contribute resources such as office space, equipment, and supplies.

Other funding agencies require that budget items be divided into the categories of direct and indirect (**overhead**) costs. Grants may cover all of the **direct costs** and allow a certain percentage of the budget to pay for indirect costs. These **indirect costs** may include such items as accounting costs, rental of office space, and the costs of utilities to support that space. In the guidelines supplied by funding agencies, allowances for indirect costs are usually spelled out. In the case of universities and other research organizations that regularly do business with funding agencies, a percentage for indirect costs may be negotiated and may be used as a matter of course when any funding requests are submitted. These allowances are often generous (in some cases 50% of direct costs or more).

The implications of matching funds and overhead will be considered further later in this chapter.

GRANTS VERSUS CONTRACTS

Research funds are usually awarded in one of two forms: a research grant or a research contract. There are significant differences between these two types of awards. The **research grant** awards funds to researchers to carry out research on ideas that they have developed. A **research contract** generally provides the funds necessary to carry out research projects specified by the funding agency. In the case of funding agencies such as the National Science Foundation, researchers are allowed wide leeway in selecting the research questions to be studied. In other cases grant programs may be more restrictive in that they specify the general area of interest to which the research must be limited. For example, the Social Science Research Council (1996) announced a Sexuality Research Fellowship Program that began in 1997. The brochure announcing the program described the fellowships as follows:

> The Sexuality Research Fellowship Program seeks to cultivate new generations of scholars who address the complexity and contextual nature of human sexuality and explore links across disciplines, methods, and issues. The Sexuality Research Fellowships encourage researchers to formulate new research questions, generate new theories, and make contributions that link the study of human sexuality to the intellectual trajectory of their own disciplines.

This program still allows considerable leeway to researchers in formulating their research questions, but it limits those questions to the study of human sexuality.

Research contracts are likely to be more restrictive because they are usually limited to particular research questions of interest to the funding agency. For example, in 1996 the Federal Bureau of Justice Statistics was requesting funding to conduct a national study on campus sexual assault. Such a study would involve data collection from campus police agencies and college administrators, and from assault victims regarding their experiences with educational institutions and law enforcement agencies. Given the availability of the funds, the agency would then issue an RFP to potential researchers (American Statistical Association, 1996:9). Those competing for the funds would commit themselves to carrying out the specific research being solicited by the agency.

In the case of research contracts, although the research questions are specified by the agency, the particular approach used to answer those questions is usually decided by the potential researchers. That is, they take the research question specified by the RFP and, in written form, explain how they propose to go about answering the question. In this sense the contract may not differ from a grant. The big difference is in who formulates the research question to be answered (the researchers or the funding agency) rather than how the answer is pursued.

Another difference between grants and contracts is in the timing for submission of a research proposal. Grant funding agencies often have one or two deadlines each year for submission of proposals. Thus, researchers seeking funds have considerable time to prepare and submit their proposals. In the case of contracts, the period available for preparing a research proposal is usually short (seldom more than 90 days) because the timing of the research must be coordinated with the applied program to be evaluated. Potential researchers who do not get the RFP as soon as it is issued consequently have even less time to respond.

Another difference between grants and contracts is in the number of awards given. Grant-funding agencies often have a given number of dollars to award in any one year, and the number of projects granted depends on how expensive each is and how far the funds may be spread. In the case of the agency contracting for research, there is usually only one contract to be allotted for a project, and the amount of money allotted depends on the agency's resources. Competitors for the contract essentially bid against each other. The researchers who are deemed capable of carrying out the work and who submit the lowest bid usually are given the contract.

The final product of a research project also differs between grant research and contract research. In the case of grant research, the researchers usually have a variety of reporting forms from which to choose, in addition to a brief summary report to the funding agency. They may publish a monograph, publish articles, make presentations to professional organizations, or do some combination of these. In the case of the research contract, the usual reporting vehicle is a final report submitted to the funding agency for its use. Other forms of reporting may have to be specifically approved.

To summarize, the research grant allows greater latitude on the part of the researchers in deciding what is to be researched, allows more time for development of research strategies, provides funding opportunities for more than one project, and allows greater freedom in reporting the results of the research than does a research contract.

THE RESEARCH PROPOSAL

The most important ingredient in the quest for research funding is the research proposal. The proposal must convince those responsible for funding the project that it is worthwhile, of interest to the funding agency, and worth spending money on. In this regard Miller says,

> The purpose of a research proposal is to provide a statement establishing the objectives and scholarly significance of the proposed activity, the technical qualifications of the project director/principal investigator and his or her organization, and the level of funding required.
>
> The proposal should contain sufficient information to persuade both the professional staff of the agency and members of the scholarly community that the proposed activity is sound and worthy of support under the agency's criteria for the selection of projects or under specific criteria specified in the applicable proposal-generating mechanism. . . .
>
> Writing a proposal, like writing any other request, is a challenge in effective persuasion. Every agency has its own method for selecting proposals it wants to fund. Whatever the method used, individuals at the agency will be reading the proposal to determine how it fits into their funding pattern and how cogently the applicant has presented it. (1991:587)

Each funding agency has a set of guidelines for proposals it will consider. Some sets of guidelines are much more detailed than others. They list each item of information that must be included in the proposal and often tell you how much space should be allotted to each section.

In general, research proposals include the following information: a title page; an abstract that gives a succinct summary of the proposed project; an introduction that states the research question to be addressed, puts it into its scientific context, and explains its scientific and (if applicable) applied importance; a discussion of related research; a project narrative that describes how the research will be carried out; a discussion of the qualifications of the researchers to do the project, including resources they have to support the research; a timetable for accomplishing the work; and a budget detailing the financial support necessary to complete the project.

Whether the funding being sought is a grant or a contract, the proposal usually must provide the information listed here. Even though the funding agency is seeking researchers to contract for the work involved in a project that the agency specifies, the researchers competing for the contract are usually expected to supply the eight kinds of information listed here. Although the original idea may not be theirs, they will be expected to demonstrate through their proposal their understanding of the subject to be researched and their technical competence to do the work required.

When writing a proposal, it is very important to be responsive to the guidelines provided by the potential funding agency. As Lauffer says,

> There is, of course, no perfect pattern to recommend for all grant applications. If I were to suggest any single hard-and-fast rule, it is this: Follow exactly whatever instructions are spelled out by the prospective funder. (1984:231)

In reviewing the proposal, the panel of experts (or whoever reviews proposals) looks to see whether the proposal has followed the recommended guidelines and whether the information sought by the agency is provided.

What makes the proposal so important is the fact that it must stand on its own in making your case for funds. Because those judging a proposal may never have an opportunity to speak directly to the potential grantee, the proposal itself must convince them that the project deserves to be funded.

The Prospectus

If a researcher initiates an inquiry with a funding agency, it may be improper and a waste of time to submit a research proposal at the outset. Rather than spend a lot of time preparing a complete proposal only to find that it is not appropriate for the agency to which it is submitted, it might be better to submit a **research prospectus** first. A prospectus is a short document (usually five pages or less) that briefly and generally describes the project you have in mind. From reading the prospectus a contact in the potential granting agency can usually give you positive or negative feedback. If the feedback is positive, then you can proceed to develop a full-blown research proposal, using the guidelines provided by the agency. If the feedback is negative, then you have saved the time you would have devoted to writing the proposal and the time you would ordinarily have to wait while the proposal goes through a formal review process. Even if the feedback is not entirely positive, the contact in the funding agency may be able to suggest ways to modify a proposal to make it eligible for funding.

The ultimate function of the research prospectus is to test a research idea in a preliminary way, essentially asking the funding agency whether your idea has merit from their standpoint and whether you should pursue it with them. As Holtz says,

> An unsolicited proposal coming "out of the blue" with no advance discussion is extremely unlikely to be successful. Successful unsolicited proposals are usually the result of a personal discussion of ideas with individuals in the agency and some advance expression of interest by the agency. (1979:49)

PROBLEMS OF CONSTRAINTS

The **constraints** put on research by the basic need for resources may be counterproductive in their effect on the progress of science. In an ideal situation, scientists would have unlimited resources to pursue the research interests of their choice.

The early model for this in the arts was the wealthy patron who provided the artist with the funds necessary to pursue whatever project suited his or her fancy. At one point in his life after he was dismissed from his position at the École Polytechnique in 1846, Auguste Comte (known as the father of sociology) was supported by his disciples and admirers so that he could continue his work on positivism (Barnes, 1948:83). After a while, however, they balked at his demands for more support, and he was reduced to lecturing to anyone willing to pay to hear him.

A more modern version of the patron model is think tanks such as the Center for Advanced Studies at Princeton or the Center for Advanced Studies in the Behavioral Sciences at Palo Alto, or grants such as MacArthur Fellowships. Think tanks select scholars to support in residence for a limited time period (such as a year) so that they may pursue scholarly projects of interest to them. Similarly, MacArthur Fellowships are awarded to a limited number of people from diverse fields, including the arts and the sciences, for a 1-year period so that they may pursue their scholarly or artistic interests. Opportunities for creative activities of the researcher's choice are very limited; consequently, they fall far short of meeting the resource needs of the scientific community in general.

Researchers usually must turn to government or private funding agencies for project support. To some extent, funds from these agencies come with strings attached. That is, constraints are put on the activities of the grantees in terms of what they study, who they study, and how they use resources in the process of doing their studies. Grants awarded for basic scientific research tend to have fewer constraints placed on them than do other types of financial support. However, only about a third of the funds provided for research are dedicated to basic research. Likewise, funds awarded in the form of grants tend to have fewer constraints placed on them than contract funds. But contract research opportunities are becoming more available to researchers than grant research.

Because researchers must go where the money is if they want to do research, to some extent the funding agencies determine the directions in which a scientific discipline will advance. Characteristically, in the social sciences more money is available for the study of deviant behavior than for the study of normal social behavior. George Lundberg claimed in his lectures that only about 5% of human behavior is deviant and difficult to predict. If he was correct in his estimate, then one might argue that only about 5% of sociological research should be devoted to the study of deviant behavior. However, public concern tends to focus on social problems. Hence, when government funds are allocated for social research, those problems tend to get the lion's share of the resources. Furthermore, many private foundations that support research tend to have similar emphases on perceived problem areas.

To the extent that social problems steer research away from basic research on sociological problems, they can prevent sociology from progressing as a scientific discipline. (See Box 13.2.)

Of course, this does not imply that sociologists should desist from researching deviant behavior. After all, it is universal to all human societies. However, research on deviant behavior should be sociological research rather than social-problem–oriented research. In other words, deviant behavior should be approached as a subject for basic research in preference to applied research if it is to contribute to our

BOX 13.2
SOCIAL PROBLEMS VERSUS SOCIOLOGICAL PROBLEMS

There is an important distinction between a social problem and a sociological problem. A **social problem** is social behavior that is defined as undesirable by the public or the mass media. For example, robbery is perceived of as a social problem—a type of behavior that should be eliminated—by the public. Concern over this problem is often expressed in the mass media, and pressure is put on government officials at all levels to do something about it. Any kind of behavior that is perceived as being undesirable may be defined as a social problem. Its undesirability is based on a value judgment, however, rather than on an objective evaluation of how much it affects society.

A **sociological problem** is one that deals with social behavior not in terms of values, but in terms of the need to understand how such behavior fits into the larger social context. Sociologists seek to understand social behavior, and in doing so they study society and attempt to fit particular instances of behavior into the social system. They want to know how a particular form of social behavior relates to the system as a whole, how it affects the system, and the consequences of its effects on the system.

Returning to the example of robbery, that phenomenon can be viewed from either a social problem perspective or a sociological problem perspective. When the public views robbery as an undesirable phenomenon that must be controlled or eliminated, then it is being treated as a social problem. A government agency may solicit funds for research to discover how to control or eliminate robbery.

Émile Durkheim (1938) considered deviant behavior to be functional to society. Such deviant behavior includes robbery. From his viewpoint, deviant behavior was necessary because those who engaged in it could be apprehended and punished for their deviant acts. Deviants were punished to set an example for the other members of a society. They could see that if they committed deviant acts, they would be subject to the same punishment. The effect of this lesson was to get other members of society to conform to societal expectations of acceptable behavior and avoid deviance.

Durkheim felt that if there were no examples of punishment for deviance it would be difficult, if not impossible, to get society members to conform.

From this perspective, robbery could be studied in a sociological context rather than a social problem context. The interest would be in how robbery and the punishment associated with it serve as agents of social control. In contrast to the social problems approach to deviant behavior, Durkheim's approach was a sociological approach. He was attempting to account for deviant behavior in terms of how it fit into the scheme of things, rather than focusing on whether it should be eliminated. As a matter of fact, from his perspective, elimination of deviant behavior would be dysfunctional to society and could possibly lead to more sociological problems because of the disruptive effects on the ongoing social process.

store of sociological knowledge. The problem is finding support for such basic research.

There are more-extreme examples of pressure on researchers from funding sources. Some funding organizations, particularly those with strong ideological positions or profit motives, make clear what kinds of results are desired or expected from the research. It may also be clear that results that are not favorable to the funding agency or its pursuits are to be downplayed in any report. Researchers must avoid or guard against these pressures, perhaps in an explicit agreement about how findings are to be treated. This is one reason why research reports must report the source of funding and explain research procedures taken to avoid biasing effects of sponsorship.

Another constraint imposed on researchers by funding agencies is on the human subjects who may be studied. Government funding agencies, in particular, generally require assurances that the privacy, safety, and dignity of human subjects be preserved in the research situation and that they will be handled in an ethical manner.[1] At times such assurances invalidate the data being collected or rule out data collection altogether. In 1996 Congress threatened to pass a Family Privacy Protection Act that would greatly restrict research involving minors. The bill, H.R. 1271, was described in *Footnotes,* a publication of the American Sociological Association, as follows:

> H.R. 1271 requires prior written consent from a parent or guardian for any minor to participate in federally funded survey research, if the survey contains questions in seven categories. These categories include sexual behavior or attitudes, illegal and antisocial behavior, religious affiliations or beliefs, and mental or psychological problems. Currently, Institutional Review Boards may waive written consent provided an appropriate mechanism for protecting the children is substituted and after carefully weighing the nature and purpose of the research and the risk and anticipated benefit to the research subject. (1996:3)

In November 1995, Felice J. Levine testified on behalf of the American Sociological Association and a coalition of 35 professional organizations against passage of the bill. She made the point that the bill removed flexibility from the human subject protection process that could be detrimental to both the subjects' interests and the quality of the research.

Weighing the effects of research on subjects is not a simple process. Nevertheless, competent and responsible researchers should be able to evaluate and handle the importance of the research being conducted and any potential inconvenience or potential for other inappropriate consequences for the subjects of the study. When a funding agency has a definitive policy on this matter, the decision is taken out of the hands of the researchers. This essentially determines which research will be undertaken and which will not.

A third type of constraint placed on research by funding agencies involves the uses to which funds may be applied. When a research grant or contract is awarded, it is based on a budget submitted by the researchers seeking funding. Funds are allotted to specific budget categories such as labor costs, equipment, supplies, and travel. In many cases funds may not be transferred from one expenditure category

[1]The ethics involved in research on human subjects are discussed in Chapter 1.

to another without the permission of the funding agency. This constraint sometimes presents problems to researchers. Because serendipitous occurrences may require changes in the original research plans, researchers may find that it is necessary to transfer funds. If they do not have the authority to do so and if it is difficult to arrange such transfers with the funding agency, the progress of a project may be halted or seriously hampered. Researchers may have to ignore important insights that would lead them in slightly different directions than the research plan originally specified and continue as initially agreed upon. The outcome might be a project whose findings have less merit than they would have had with more flexibility in decision making.

A fourth constraint on research stems from the need to provide matching funds or to negotiate overhead for a project. If matching funds are required, the potential grantee must be able to provide the necessary finances or resources. This has the effect of reducing funding possibilities for researchers who do not have an organizational base such as a university or a large research corporation. Consequently, grant or contract applicants do not start on a level playing field, and researchers who are particularly qualified to carry out certain kinds of research may be eliminated from consideration.

When overhead is negotiated as a separate budget category, researchers who are not affiliated with an established organization may again be at a disadvantage. They will probably not have the same leverage to negotiate the percentage allowed that a university or large research organization would. Accordingly, they may end up with a budget that is not really adequate to perform all of the work necessary for a successful research effort.

Even researchers who do have an adequate organizational affiliation to handle matching funds or overhead may be at a disadvantage. Because the organization with which they are affiliated must be involved in the funding process, researchers surrender some of their authority to make research decisions. They must deal not only with the funding agency but also with the staff of the larger organization of which they are a part.

Typically, grants allow more flexibility in the use of funds than do contracts. Also, grants tend to be more liberal about altering project objectives when new insights arise. Even within the grants category, some granting agencies are more permissive than others in shifting project goals and transferring funds.

Essentially, decision making authority shifts from the researchers who are presumably best qualified to make the decisions to less-qualified employees or consultants of funding agencies or the larger organizations with which they are affiliated. In an ideal situation, the researchers would have all of the professional qualifications necessary to make sound decisions and the authority necessary to make them. Actual situations usually fall short of this ideal.

OTHER ISSUES

In addition to the constraints on research discussed earlier, other issues have an important bearing on the progress of research in the social sciences.

In the case of social science research in particular, politics may be a factor. Because of the kinds of research topics in which social scientists are interested, there are often political implications that affect funding decisions. For example, in the late 1990s illegal and legal immigration was a politically explosive subject. There were strong feelings on both sides of the political spectrum. Many politicians were of the opinion that immigrants were a vulnerable population to attack and that attacking them would be advantageous in increasing their own popularity with voters. Those on one side of this controversy argued that immigrants, both illegal and legal, used up public funds that could have been better spent on needy native-born citizens. Those on the other side argued that immigrants contributed more to the economy than they claimed in public services, thus increasing the funds available to the needy. In such a politically explosive atmosphere, it would be difficult for researchers to obtain funding for a value-neutral research project to study the facts of the situation.

Another issue that determines what research is done is the limited amount of money available through the funding agencies and the resulting competition for it. In some cases it is not the merit of the project being proposed that is the deciding factor in funding, but the skill with which the proposal is written. A whole industry has developed around the skills necessary to write successful proposals. For some people proposal writing (for both grants and contracts) has become a full-time occupation.

The unfortunate outcome of this emphasis on "grantsmanship" is that some projects that merit funding are passed over in favor of less important projects because the proposal writers for the latter are more adept salespeople. Because projects dealing with social problems tend to have an advantage over basic research projects to begin with, such topics combined with the skills of the proposal writer tend to upset the balance in favor of applied, short-run, problem-solving projects.

A related issue has to do with the panel of people who review project proposals for funding agencies. These people are usually selected on the basis of their professional expertise in the subject matter for which funding is available. Nevertheless, they tend to have personal biases about which topics are important to research and who is qualified to do the research. If their personal biases favor research on deviant behavior, for example, they may fund projects dealing with that subject in preference to projects dealing with normal behavior, despite the fact that the latter may have more scientific merit. They may also tend to favor applicants primarily on the basis of their university affiliation rather than on the merits of their proposals.

The fundamental problem is that resources are limited and applicants must compete for those resources. Those who are most successful in the competition are sometimes not those who would be funded if scientific merit alone were the criterion. The grantsmanship industry, with its assorted strategies for writing successful proposals, would not be needed if adequate funding were available for every project with scientific merit.

A final issue that stems from the fact that social science research is generally underfunded has to do with the greater frequency of cross-sectional as opposed to longitudinal studies. A major point this book has sought to make is that social behavior is dynamic rather than static, so much more attention must be given to longitudinal research. Longitudinal research is generally more costly than isolated cross-sectional studies. Limited funding tends to bias research in favor of a static model; as a result, our understanding of social behavior accumulates more slowly than is desirable.

SUMMARY

Acquiring adequate resources to carry out social research is crucial to the progress of sociology. Necessary resources include labor, equipment, supplies, time, and space. The key to acquiring these resources is funding. Both government and private agencies provide funds for research. A research proposal, including a budget, is essential in seeking research funds. If the potential project is carefully conceptualized, it will be possible to project costs for carrying out the work. Protecting time for stepping back and thinking through consequences of one's methods and the meaning of findings is essential. Given an overall estimate of costs, it is possible to search various sources to identify agencies that might be interested in and capable of funding the project.

The two major types of funding are grants and contracts. Grants tend to be broader in their scope than contracts and are more likely than contracts to support basic research. Applied projects, specified by funding agencies, are usually supported through contracts. Requests for proposals are the most common means used to encourage researchers to compete for contracts.

Proposal writing has almost become an art form. Projects that are funded are sometimes less important scientifically than those that are left unfunded. Those that are funded may be successful either because of the skills of the proposal writer in selling an idea or because the topic to be researched has important political ramifications. As a consequence, there has been a distortion in the progress of sociology as a field of scientific knowledge.

The need for resources, both financial and material, has constrained progress in sociology by slanting research in certain popular, applied directions by limiting who may be studied and limiting the authority to make research–relevant decisions. Furthermore, the limited nature of social science research funding has had the effect of slanting research toward a static model of social behavior rather than a dynamic model.

TERMS TO KNOW

Community foundation
Company-sponsored foundation
Constraint problems
Direct costs
Functional budget
Independent foundation
Indirect costs
Matching funds

Operating foundation
Overhead
Requests for proposals (RFP)
Research contracts
Research grants
Research proposals
Research prospectus
Research resources
Social problem
Sociological problem

ISSUES AND COMPARISONS

Basic versus applied research
Pressures on the research process resulting from how it is funded
Ethical concerns arising from resource considerations

EXERCISES

1. Decide on a research topic or research question. Then look up potential funding sources. What possible funding sources are there? What limitations and expectations do they appear to impose? What are the criteria for selection of projects? What guidelines do they provide for submitting requests for funding?
2. Develop a research budget. Select a modest research project you would like to carry out (or find an interesting research project reported in a journal article). Develop an organized and realistic budget for the project. Ask faculty, proposal writers, or departmental staff for information you need about salary rates for various types of staff, fringe benefits, overhead, and so on. You will have to make some guesses as well. On a separate page (referring to budget line items), indicate how you calculated each cost item and explain and justify the need for key expense items.
3. If your instructor makes available a research proposal with a budget for your review, review its organization and comment on the budget. Is it adequate for the project that has been proposed? Is it padded?

REFERENCES

Ackoff, Russell K., *Design for Social Research,* University of Chicago Press, Chicago, 1953. Reproduced in Miller, Delbert C., *Handbook of Research Design and Social Measurement,* Sage, Newbury Park, CA, 1991.

American Sociological Association, *Footnotes* May/June 1996;25(5).

American Statistical Association, *GSS SSS Newsletter* Summer 1996.

Annual Register of Grant Support, 29th ed., National Register Publishing Company, Wilmette, IL, 1996.

Barnes, Harry Elmer, *An Introduction to the History of Sociology,* University of Chicago Press, Chicago, 1948.

Dillman, Don A., "Mail and Other Self-Administered Questionnaires," in Peter Rossi, James Wright, and Andy Anderson, eds., *Handbook of Survey Research,* Academic Press, New York, 1982.

Durkheim, Émile, *The Rules of Sociological Method,* edited by George E. G. Catlin, The Free Press of Glencoe, New York, 1938.
Dusek, E. Ralph, Virginia E. Holt, Marti E. Burke, and Alan G. Kraut, eds., *Guide to Research Support,* 3rd ed., The American Psychological Association, Hyattsville, MD, 1987.
Jacobs, David G., *The Foundation Directory,* 22nd ed., Columbia University Press, New York, 2000.
Holtz, Herman R., *Government Contracts: Proposalmanship and Winning Strategies,* Plenum, New York, 1979.
Krathwohl, David R., *How to Prepare a Research Proposal,* 3rd ed., Syracuse University Press, Syracuse, NY, 1988.
Lauffer, Armand, *Grantsmanship and Fund Raising,* Sage, Newbury Park, CA, 1984.
Lefferts, Robert, *Getting a Grant in the 1980s: How to Write Successful Grant Proposals,* 2nd ed., Prentice Hall, Englewood Cliffs, NJ, 1982.
Miller, Delbert C., *Handbook of Research Design and Social Measurement,* Sage, Newbury Park, CA, 1991.
Quarles, Susan, ed., *Guide to Federal Funding,* Russell Sage Foundation, New York, 1986.
Read, Patricia E., ed., *Foundation Fundamentals,* 3rd ed., The Foundation Center, New York, 1986.
Schaffter, Dorothy, *The National Science Foundation,* Praeger, New York, 1969.
Sladek, Frea E., and Eugene L. Stein, *Grant Budgeting and Finance: Getting the Most Out of Your Grant Dollar,* Plenum, New York, 1981.
Social Science Research Council, *Sexuality Research Fellowship Program* (a brochure announcing the program), 1996.

CHAPTER FOURTEEN

DEVELOPMENTS AND PROSPECTS

How can one gain reliable knowledge? This is the basic problem that methods of research are meant to solve. In the preceding chapters we discussed the process through which research is accomplished. Starting with how research questions are generated, we traced the progress of the work through its intermediate stages, which deal with seeking answers to the research questions posed. Finally we focused on the stage at which the results are reported. At each stage we addressed the principal kinds of problems and issues that arise in most research projects.

THEMES

Throughout these chapters the following important themes were developed:

- Research questions focus on variable characteristics of the **cases** being studied. Explanations are sought to account for the fact that different cases have different scores on the characteristics of interest (that is why a characteristic that can have a distribution of scores is called a variable). For example, when cases under study are people who are employed full time, it may be of interest to account for the variability in their annual incomes.

- In order to account for variability, it is necessary to make comparisons. Without comparisons of some kind it is not possible to explain why some cases have higher scores on a characteristic than others, so it is not possible to answer the original research question posed. In attempting to account for differences in annual income, for example, attention might be focused on differences in the cases studied by gender and level of education.

- Social science research, like most scientific research, is ultimately interested in generalizing findings beyond the cases studied to a broad **class of cases.** Sometimes this broader population is bounded by time and place, but most often researchers are interested in establishing theoretical principles that apply to unrestricted (in time and place) classes of cases of some defined type, hence the interest in inferential logic of statistical tests, which permits reasoned generalization from sample to population. Case study research is also generally concerned with identifying **concepts** and **principles** that may apply more broadly and can be used in research aimed at generalizing findings.

- The social world, which is the principal subject matter of the social sciences, is a dynamic one. Consequently, research strategies used to study that world must focus primarily on process rather than structure and, when structure is addressed, it must be studied dynamically. That is, attention must be given to structure as a developing and evolving phenomenon rather than as a static form. For example, if the subject of research is the labor force, then research questions should deal with the ways in which a labor force develops and evolves rather than with its structure at a specific point in time. Throughout the book the point was made that longitudinal research must be given increasing emphasis over cross-sectional research if the discipline is to continue to progress.

- Research is a social process, and it must be considered in that light. Regardless of the scientific discipline being considered, whether it be physics or sociology, social influences affect the research from its inception to its completion.

However, there are additional complications to social science research that are less likely to enter into research in other disciplines. First, social scientists are more likely to interact with their sources of data than are most other scientists, and that interaction is likely to be more intrusive than it is for other disciplines. This is because the sources of social science data are usually human, and the cooperation of those human subjects is generally required in the process of data collection. Biologists may also have humans as their subjects, but much of their research allows them to collect data from such subjects in less obtrusive ways than the data collection techniques of social scientists.

Another complication faced by social scientists is that both they and their subjects have a similar life span. This limits the time frames they can use in collecting data and greatly complicates their study of long-term social processes.

Because of their social components, each research project is the product of negotiations and compromises between the various parties to the study. Therefore, cookbook recipes for conducting research are oversimplifications.

USES OF RESEARCH

As pointed out earlier, the motivation to do research may be to develop scientific principles or it may be to seek solutions to immediate problems. Because of the social context within which modern research is negotiated and carried out, there has been increasing emphasis on applied research to solve immediate problems. A whole industry has developed around the need to solve social problems and to evaluate programs designed to treat such problems. Although much of this research is carried out by private research companies, university researchers and university research centers are also in the competition for applied research contracts and grants.

In general, the research process discussed in this book is the same whether the research is aimed at the development of scientific principles (pure research) or the solution of immediate problems (applied research). Ways in which the uses of the findings (pure or applied) affect how the research proceeds have been discussed throughout the book. One obvious effect of the planned use of research results is which research projects get funded. When there is concern over perceived social problems, research that focuses on those problems is more likely to be funded. Furthermore, the research projects receiving this funding are likely to be more narrowly focused and to provide more short-term results than research projects aimed at developing scientific principles.

In light of the emphasis on applied research, sociologists must weigh the long-term consequences for the advancement of **scientific knowledge** and the discipline itself. Although some researchers welcome the funding opportunities provided by applied research projects, others worry that emphasizing applied research at the expense of pure research will lead society to treat symptoms in the short run rather than arrive at scientific principles that may provide basic solutions to problems in the long run.

Of course, not all research projects are exclusively pure research or applied research. It is often possible to carry out applied research projects that also have pure research implications. As a classic case in point, the American Soldier Series of research projects carried out by the Research Branch of the U.S. Army during World War II and published in four volumes under the title *Studies in Social Psychology in World War II* (Stouffer et al., 1949) were aimed at collecting information that could be used by the U.S. Army. In the process of doing the applied projects, however, the researchers came up with findings whose impacts on the field of sociology were more general. Such concepts as *reference group theory* and *felt deprivation* had theoretical significance that led to studies that fell clearly in the realm of pure research.

THE POINT OF IT ALL

As we have seen, scientific inquiry is directed toward four goals:

- Description of the state of some phenomenon. Often this involves description of the **relationship** between variable characteristics of a class of cases.

- Explanation of some phenomenon of interest. This often involves explanation of the relationship between characteristics.

- Prediction of future states of cases, such as the future age distribution of a population.

- Control of some situation. For example, research on the causes of delinquency may be done for the purpose of introducing changes that reduce delinquency.

Description is involved in achieving each of the other goals. Research methods often focus on how to make systematic, unbiased, accurate, and reproducible descriptions. But explanation is the primary pursuit of most scientific inquiry. There is an attempt to develop general principles that would enable one to answer "why" questions (e.g., "Why do some become criminals?" "Why are income and education related?"). Developing and testing potential explanations depends on good description of some aspect of the empirical world. The other goals of inquiry, prediction and control, are often emphasized in applied research, and they also depend centrally on description and on general principles developed to answer "why" questions.

Research is intimately tied to social contexts in which other goals are pursued as well. Increasingly research is conducted in organizations in which there is a strong stakeholder interest in gaining notoriety, being first with spectacular findings, publishing in certain journals, building a career, winning increased research funding, making a profit, reducing costs, achieving rapid turnaround, finding quick and simple answers, avoiding controversy, supporting past conclusions or current positions, maintaining "proper" organizational roles and standard operating procedures, or appealing to political interests. Scientists may also have multiple, perhaps conflicting roles in organizations. The social context of scientific work has an effect on knowing and inquiry.

Methods of scientific research are also changing. In the social sciences there are new study paradigms and new options for handling different aspects of research. Thus, methodological development is critical for the social sciences. In the following section we briefly introduce some developing aspects of research methods in the hope of challenging the reader to develop new ideas and explore further course work and experiences about new methods of inquiry.

THE PROCESS OF KNOWING

Scientific research as an inquiry process is characterized by four features. It is a knowledge-building process, attempting to add to what is already known. It is characterized by an openness and commitment to demonstrating how one knows what one claims to know. Research questions that are addressed have more than one potential answer; any hypothesized answer to a research question must be potentially falsifiable on the basis of research findings. Finally, researchers have an interest in generalizing findings to potential cases beyond the specific cases studied. This distinguishes scientific research as a human pursuit from other kinds of pursuit, such as finding only supportive evidence to build a case; stating as "findings" personal beliefs, opinions, and preferences that are not falsifiable or not supported by research findings; or using biased or inaccurate data or secret research processes that are not open to checking and **replication.** Even with training, the hopes and goals of rigorous scientific knowledge building are difficult to maintain.

Main building blocks of research and the main themes of inquiry discussed in earlier chapters are reviewed here. Just as the unfolding of superior inquiry is a social process, so is the flow of problematic research. We point to a few **families of flaws** that seem to unfold all too often in social science research. Following that, we will reflect on ways in which the options available to inquiry are or might be strengthened.

Concepts (or property concepts) point to phenomena of interest, such as gender, social class, organizational centralization, self-concept, and family, that are defined and labeled so they can be clearly communicated. Concepts bracket pieces of the real world that are thought to be related in some useful way, things a researcher notices as interesting and important. If these concepts point to something of durable interest in a field and if they prove to be useful in thinking about some phenomenon, then they tend to be more widely used to capture what is of scientific interest. Much work in the social sciences involves the identification and articulation of concepts or properties of some kind of case. A concept may be a property that a case either has or doesn't have. It may be a property such as age, in which cases may differ from each other over a whole range of potential values.

Cases are the entities to which concepts apply. For example, gender is a property of individual humans and centrality is a property of organizations. Scientific work involves identification of the class of cases to which concepts refer. Generally a class of cases is unbounded in time and place, an unrestricted class of cases. For example, researchers may be interested in generalizations about concepts such as functional ability among older people whenever or wherever they may be found, not only the few older people included in a particular study.

Relationships between concepts for a class of cases is the focus of most research. For example, how are age and income related for a class of cases such as Hispanic women? Inquiry typically examines cases to see whether certain property concepts are related to each other, or to see whether expected relationships are evident among a certain class of cases. When possible, general principles about relationships between concepts are developed and tested. These principles about relationships between concepts are the building blocks of explanations called **theory.**

Conditional relationships are principles about relationships that apply only under certain conditions. For example, threats to the existence of a group are related to a movement of the group's moral boundaries (what it considers proper or deviant), but this is true only under the condition that the group is a cohesive, interrelating group. The conditions are important to know. Many research contributions are devoted to identifying conditions under which certain principles operate differently for different kinds of cases. Because statuses such as social class, ethnic group, gender, and age often identify cases to which principles apply differently, these background characteristics are often routinely included in most social science research.

SCIENTIFIC CONTRIBUTIONS

Social science inquiry deals with concepts, cases, and the relationship between concepts for classes of cases. Scientific contributions come from discovering and refining concepts and the way they can be measured validly and reliably in different situations. Contributions are made in identifying and refining types of cases or interesting groups of cases that may show different results, such as studies of rural versus urban communities, older versus younger people, or larger versus smaller firms. Finally, contributions are made to information we have about the relationship of properties (concepts) for a given class of cases.

Why focus on concepts, cases, and relationships? An important reason is to be able to develop systematic knowledge about how the world works. This systematic knowledge is captured in generalizations or principles (however tentative) that can be used to predict what one will find for new, unstudied cases.

Theories are logically related sets of empirically based principles (and definitional axioms, qualifications, or conditions, as well as assumptions that may be made). The principles may be expressed in a casual way or they may be expressed quite rigorously (graphically as models or arrow diagrams, or mathematically or symbolically as an equation or set of equations). Principles in theories are generally logically related. Logical deduction is then possible. For example, a principle may state "If A then B," and another may state "If B then C." A further, implied principle could be deduced: "If A then C." The logical relationship between the various theoretical statements permits deduction of further implications. These can be tested in research and, if not refuted or modified by evidence, their support lends further credence to the whole set of theoretical statements from which they were deduced.

Most of the principles stated in science are probabilistic. That is, they state the likelihood (usually not a certainty) that a relationship of some type exists between concepts for a certain class of cases. A classic test of a theory involves logically deducing some kind of further statement (a hypothesis) and then conducting empirical research to see whether the data refute the deduction. Scientific inquiry is often focused on developing, refining, and testing theories. Theory development may take many forms. Grounded theory attempts to develop theory in the process of making field observations, starting with few, if any, preconceived ideas. Another approach to building theory is to start with a proposed theory, deduce implications, and test them. Both the inductive (research then theory) and the deductive (theory then research) approaches contribute to our storehouse of useful scientific theory and thus knowledge of some phenomenon.

It should be evident that a good theory has both practical and basic research value. It helps identify what to describe, and it helps explain relationships between concepts and the conditions under which they hold. This can lead to better predictions and possibilities for taking action to control undesired outcomes. Good principles that have a track record of being true in various relevant situations can help immensely in applied pursuits aimed at controlling or changing some situation.

Scientific explanation involves answers to "why" questions. For example, why do some people have higher incomes than others? One principle is that education and income are related: The higher the educational level, the more likely the person is to have a high income. Pursuing this further, why are income and education positively related in this way? The answer to that question leads to more detailed theory, perhaps a theory about the organization of labor markets in an increasingly technologically sophisticated era. The answer to the next "why" calls for research that would involve further principles and further linkages of them in theories of greater complexity. The **scope of a theory** is the breadth of the conditions under which principles in the theory apply.

Researchers contribute to explanations in all the ways noted above. The task of inquiry is a large one, and rarely can a single researcher make contributions in all areas. Thus, it is important to build on the results of past inquiry (often calling for a search of relevant literature) and promote teamwork among researchers who are contributing to certain aspects of an overall program of research.

The body of knowledge claimed by a scientific field consists of a range of things. It includes work on the various parts needed to address "why" questions: concepts, cases, relationships, tentative principles and conditions under which they hold, and statements of theories. The more-accepted part of scientific knowledge involves principles and theories checked out by empirical research. These are found in the written record of a field: its journals, research monographs, and grant reports. Thus, there is considerable emphasis on the publication of research results.

Findings and principles are most firmly accepted when they use acknowledged methods of study that meet accepted standards of quality, when results are made widely available so scholars can check and use the findings, and when findings have been replicated and checked by empirical research to see whether they hold up (or to identify the conditions under which they apply). Determining whether proposed findings derive from an inquiry process that meets these standards implies that there are interested, relevant, and able colleagues in a field who carefully review and react to proposed findings. These reviews can be found in peer judgments about proposed research projects (i.e., those proposed for funding), in journal and book publications subject to **peer review,** and in critical review articles about knowledge in some area. Scientists spend considerable amounts of time reviewing one another's work and publishing the methods and findings of their own research efforts. Although this process helps ensure the solid basis of knowledge-generating research, it also tends to perpetuate accepted perspectives.

DEVELOPING THE PROCESSES OF INQUIRY

Riley's (1963) research design decisions provide one way of organizing where it is that new methods are being developed. Figure 14.1 reproduces Riley's list, originally discussed in Chapter 4.

Nature of the Research Case

The social sciences have been adept at detailing different types of research cases in their inquiries, including studies with multiple levels of cases (e.g., individuals within families within neighborhoods within societies). For studies focusing on smaller components, broader units are coded as their context. For broader units,

FIGURE 14.1 Main Research Design Decisions (From Matilda Riley, 1963)

- **Nature of the Research Case**
  Alternatives include: an individual in a role in some collectivity, a dyad or pair of interrelated group members, subgroup, group, society, or combinations of these.
- **Number of Cases**
  Alternatives include a single case, a few selected cases, or many selected cases.
- **Sociotemporal Context**
  Alternatives include cases from a single society at a single period or cases from many societies or many periods.
- **Primary Basis for Selecting Cases (sampling)**
  Alternatives include cases selected to represent some population, cases selected for some analytical purpose, or both.
- **Time Factor**
  Static studies (covering a single point in time) or dynamic studies (covering a process or change over time).
- **Extent of Researcher's Control over the System under Study**
  Alternatives include no control, unsystematic control, or systematic control.
- **Basic Sources of Data**
  Alternatives include new data collected by the researcher to answer the research question or available data that are relevant to the research question.
- **Method of Gathering Data**
  Alternatives include observation, questioning, or combinations of these.
- **Number of Properties Used in Research**
  Alternatives include one, a few, or many properties.
- **Method of Handling Single Properties**
  Alternatives include unsystematic description or measurement of variables.
- **Method of Handling Relationships among Properties**
  Alternatives include unsystematic description or systematic analysis.
- **Treatment of System Properties**
  Alternatives include unitary (properties such as "type of government," which cannot be broken down into some sum of individual properties) or collective (properties such as "crime rates," which are aggregated from properties of individuals within the system).

individual characteristics may be averaged or aggregated as analytic characteristics of these broader units. More recently, techniques for simultaneously handling multilevel units have been developed. These techniques depend on computer approaches.

Number of Cases

With widespread use of computers it is easier to use very large data sets or to link several large data sets for analysis. For example, large national surveys in important policy areas use very substantial samples (20,000 and larger). In some cases, such as the General Social Survey, regularly repeated sampling can permit combining annual data sets into larger samples that cover a span of years, and the total number of cases is very large. A larger sample facilitates use of more-sophisticated statistical modeling techniques. At the other extreme, there is more interest in case studies of larger units such as societies at some historic point or whole social movements. Which research strategy yields more knowledge in the long run is a matter of debate, but each furthers sociological knowledge, raises new questions to pursue, and challenges existing theory.

Sociotemporal Context

Most research is located in the time and place of the researcher. Studies using settings that cut across time and place are needed. New options available to the researcher include multinational studies, in which similar surveys are conducted in a number of different societies. Systematic cross-national comparisons can then be used for cross-societal analysis. The existence of historic archives of easily used data (e.g., on-line historic documents and library references, accumulations of archived survey data, and newspaper files) has meant that a range of temporal settings can be examined systematically. We anticipate that this trend will continue.

It is unclear whether contemporary research methods courses are preparing students for the issues specific to broader sociotemporal contexts. Many archives are bounded by the sociopolitical units that fund them or traditional survey convenience (e.g., eliminating nonadults, institutionalized groups, and those without phones or homes). Thus, studies that are specifically designed to gather comparable data that bridge place and time are still rare. More attention must be devoted to the organizational and persistence skills and funding needs involved in such research.

Sampling

General household samples often use telephone lists or random-digit dialing techniques. These often depend on computer archiving and screening of phone numbers. There are increasing problems of potential bias caused by unlisted phones, people with multiple phones (e.g., cellular phones, home business phones, pagers), call forwarding, answering machines, and call screening. There is increasing use of probability sampling, although samples often use standard exclusions such as eliminating people in institutions or the various hard-to-sample populations.

The Time Factor

With computer archives and repeated large-scale surveys, it is possible to have at least aggregate data available over a modest time span. Data that follow individuals over time are harder to come by. Societal emphasis on quick findings may work against developing extensive through-time data sets.

Researcher Control over the System under Study

Laboratory research is becoming less common. Instead, there is more emphasis on studying systems in which an investigator has little or no control over critical features such as the allocation of the independent variable treatment to cases. In the United States there appears to be increasing reluctance on the part of potential respondents to trust the data-gathering process or the possibilities of confidentiality and to require some clear benefit for participation.

Basic Sources of Data

There has been a rapid growth of standardized data sets that are archived and available in computer-usable form. Increasingly, new data from large samples of standard or general populations are being archived and made available for other researchers to use. Data from the U.S. Census are increasingly available in various computer-usable forms. Most new data in the social sciences appear to be from surveys or case studies.

Method of Gathering Data

Although observation and questioning are still the basic ways in which data from humans are obtained, the way these are implemented in research is changing. Video recording is becoming more widespread. Telephone interviews often use computer-assisted interviewing (CAI), which simplifies branching, random ordering of questions, tailoring of questions for types of respondents, and data input. Textual data can be entered into a computer file for analysis by optical character reader (OCR) scanners. Many text files are already available in computer form. Telephone interviews can be directly recorded on tape for clearer sound and easier transcription. Multiple speakers can be recorded using electronic technology that keeps different speakers separated. Portable computers may aid in-person interviewing and field note-taking. Computers also may improve the speed and accuracy with which various databases can be linked for special research purposes.

Number of Properties Used in Research

Although it is increasingly possible to link data sets, so that the number of variables available for use in analysis can be quite large, the question often is whether the available variables contain measures demanded by a project. Another problem is the ratio of the number of variables to the sample size. It is generally a good strategy to have many times more cases than variables for a stable analysis. Availability of large data sets permits using more variables simultaneously in the analysis. Although ethical and privacy issues are involved, linking data sets that exist in computer file form creates the possibility of combining many variables in an analysis.

Method of Handling Single Properties

In an era of many surveys it is easy to assume that most properties to be measured can be adequately measured by established, structured questions that can be handled in a quantitative or statistical way. From our point of view, much more attention must be devoted to developing valid and reliable measurements for the range of important social science concepts. It would be helpful if rewards for scholarly work more fully recognized creating and checking measurement procedures, including scales, as a valid scientific pursuit in a research career. Clearer conceptual definitions would be helpful in this process.

With computer resources, textual data will increasingly become used, and the problem of developing valid and reliable indicators of concepts from these data must be addressed. A variety of qualitative and quantitative approaches to text analysis are becoming available. Some analysis techniques (e.g., Lisrel) are combining the analysis of measurements with modeling linkages between concepts. There is a need to tailor measurements better to relevant populations. New measurement models are being developed (item response theory in psychology, for example), and these appear to be promising for sociological research.

Method of Handling Relationships between Properties

There has been a rapid growth in quantitative techniques for handling the relationship between variables. This includes the further development of techniques to handle nominal and ordinal variables with two or more response categories. Again, the growth in computer power has made possible the rapid growth in statistical techniques for modeling various patterns of relationship between properties. Somewhat less well developed are procedures for more systematically handling the relationship between variables in qualitative research.

Treatment of System Properties

Properties of social systems are treated as unitary (global) when the overall system is classified directly. System properties are also treated as collective (analytic) when subunits are measured and these measures are combined to represent the system as a whole. Classifying a society by its form of government would be a unitary treatment, and averaging individual ages to represent a society's age would be a collective treatment of a variable. But many other features of systems beg for systematic measurement. Computer-based network analysis is one example of possibilities for measuring more-complex aspects of social interaction. More work is needed in this area.

SOCIAL PROCESS OF INQUIRY

In this book we have tried to highlight some of the features of research as a social pursuit. Inherently, research is a team pursuit. Collaboration as co–principal investigators or collaborating specialists is common. Also common is collaboration with students and other research team members, with specialists who assist for only a time, with colleagues who provide feedback on study ideas, and, often, with someone in a field setting who provides access and insight for a study. Even when an investigator appears to be the sole investigator on a project, relationships with others make that possible. At minimum, there are the audiences toward which the findings are being directed and those in the setting who help minimize disruptions for the researcher. This may seem obvious, but it has many important implications for research. The social organization of research influences how research is designed and conducted and the conclusions that are drawn. Thus, social factors underlie research claims in the same way that planned design features do. After all, the *achieved* design features underlie knowledge claims in any study. In this book we have attempted to point to things that influence how and whether planned research is achieved.

Families of Flaws

Just as the process of developing sound research is a social process, some inquiry processes lead to what we call families of flaws. One problematic decision or a certain type of interest leads to a series of related flaws. Some examples follow.

- **Aimlessness.** Some research projects start without a clear question in mind about what is being sought. Often this happens when a group decides that "research" is a good thing to do next or when the investigator is inexperienced or forced to do a class project. The lack of a question may stem from a group's inability to agree on a question, or it may simply be overlooked in the rush to gather data. Often it happens when an interesting data set is available and the researcher decides ahead of time that it will be used. Without a question, data gathering becomes an opportunistic or voyeuristic collection of interesting topics. The case and the population of cases to be used are ad hoc, accepted without question, or undefined. The data that may be gathered are generally treated simplistically; single-item responses are described or lists of individual responses are quoted. The process ends in a jumbled way with no answers because there was no question to be answered.

- **No variation.** Sometimes research is developed rather well but decisions are made that result in no variation in key variables. In other words, sampling decisions may be made that result in no variation in the dependent variable. For example, studies of why some students perform well often result in decisions to study students who have top grades "to see what they did to perform so well." The result is a sample with no relevant variation in student performance—everyone selected has top grades. Thus, no statement can be made about why these students do well (because what they did might have been done by everyone anyway). It is a fatal flaw. The lack of variation often is not noticed explicitly, and the analysis ends up describing responses of those who were sampled, which may be interesting but don't answer the initial research question.

■ **Missed contributions.** Another flaw family that may not be fatal is one in which a research team and research context are set up with people who have special expertise and knowledge that aren't used. This may happen when a rigid organizational structure makes it inappropriate to seek out expertise that may be at hand. It sometimes happens when a principal investigator feels he or she is expected to know it all and is reluctant to ask someone else for an opinion. This flaw family is common when the opinions of people at lower levels in an organization are considered less valuable or worthwhile and thus are discounted or ignored. As most researchers know, the diligent secretary often knows a lot about what is actually happening in research, but such people are rarely asked and their knowledge is rarely used. It also happens when there is strong competition between parts of a research team that are not encouraged to communicate openly. Sometimes research organizations are so risky for individuals that there is great reluctance to express ideas or provide unpopular information. And there are research organizations that hustle research through with an eye to the bottom line, where the party line is so strong that contrary ideas are discouraged. These missed opportunities diminish the quality of inquiry and increase the chance that errors will go undetected or unreported.

■ **Have method, will research.** The logic of research generally flows from the research question and what is required to answer it. Sometimes a researcher, because of narrow methodological training or a value commitment to a particular research method, decides to use it regardless of the demands of the research question. Narrow experts are often narrowly used, assumptions are largely ignored, and the result is more an illustration of the method than a pursuit of an answer to a research question. Often the connection between a stated research question and the rest of the research becomes strained and illogical. Sometimes significant findings are missed or ignored as the research focuses on proper use of the method.

■ **Biased research.** Bias is always a potential in inquiry, and careful researchers openly consider the possibilities and try to avoid or analyze them. But some settings heighten the likelihood of systematic bias in a certain direction and decrease the likelihood that the biases will be noticed or analyzed. Sometimes this happens when the stakes are high: Funders are expecting supportive findings, ideological positions of the researcher or his or her organization dictate a certain view of the subject matter, certain methods or skills are left unquestioned, or certain outcomes are seen as "good" or "politically correct." The chance of biased inquiry contexts is one reason that research reports and ethics statements often demand a knowledge of the type of research organization, the sources of funding, and conflicting organizational affiliations of researchers.

As we have seen, the research setting often has important consequences for the research itself and its findings. Usually, highly competitive, strongly hierarchical settings or those that have other primary goals than knowledge building (particularly those that emphasize short-term or spectacular results) are problematic for careful, systematic inquiry. What features of a research setting support and contribute to good scientific inquiry? Often they appear to be settings that value individual contributions, promote communication, are neutral about the outcome, and permit sufficient time to think things out, plan, develop and check procedures, and reflect on the analysis and findings. Where are these found? Better research settings are often found in universities and nonprofit organizations and some enlightened government and commercial firms. A person who wants to become a skilled researcher should consider the consequences of different kinds of organizational settings on their quality of work and check settings against these criteria.

IN CLOSING

Increasing access to more powerful and portable computers will continue to have a very important impact on social science research. (See Box 14.1.) The strength is in the limitless possibilities for quickly conducting all aspects of research. The

BOX 14.1
USEFUL INTERNET ADDRESSES FOR RESEARCH

American Sociological Association: http://www.asanet.org
Content analysis:
  MCCA, a computer content analysis program: http://www.clres.com/
  Resources: http://www.gsu.edu/~wwwcom/content.html
  VBPro, a content analysis procedure: http://excellent.com.utk.edu/~mmmiller/

Database search of the Internet: http://odwin.ucsd.edu/data

General Social Survey (GSS) data (data from national surveys from 1972): http://www.icpsr.umich.edu/gss/ or http://www.soc.qc.edu

Idea Works, a company that provides various expert systems that aid in sample selection and research design: http://www.ideaworks.com/

Interuniversity Consortium for Political and Social Research: http://www.icpsr.umich.edu

Methods resource links: http://www.siu.edu/~hawkes/methods.html#data

National Institutes of Health (funding source): http://www.nih.gov

National Science Foundation (funding source): http://www.nsf.gov

Sampling lists: Example of a commercial survey research company that provides sampling lists: http://www.worldopinion.com

Social Science Research Council, research and funding source: http://www.ssrc.org

Sociology links: http://www.princeton.edu/~sociolog/links.html
U.S. Census information: http://www.census.gov

potential weakness stems from the hidden nature of computer software routines. Perhaps future research will include steps to check the quality and accuracy of computer programs used in research. We would expect an increasing accumulation of knowledge in the form of computer programs called expert systems that permit access, linking, and use of theoretical principles and empirical findings that are entered into the system. There is a serious need for replication of prior findings. What a human researcher needs to engage successfully in serious, superior scientific inquiry must be understood better and this knowledge used to develop better research settings. As the theme of this book suggests, greater attention must be directed to the consequences of research contexts and the kinds of contexts that maximize research quality.

TERMS TO KNOW

Cases
Class of cases
Concepts
Conditional relationships
Families of flaws
Peer review
Principles
Relationships
Replication
Scientific explanation
Scientific knowledge
Scope of a theory
Theory

ISSUES AND COMPARISONS

The role of ethics in research
Characteristics of research (falsifiable, generalizable, knowledge-building, demonstrated knowledge)
Research goals (description, explanation, prediction, control)
Theory then research (deductive) versus research then theory (inductive)
Research (inquiry) as a social process
Supportive inquiry contexts

EXERCISES

1. Explore the Internet to identify and examine different sources of information on a research method and data that might be used.
2. Think about situations you have experienced in which you do your best inquiry. List the key characteristics of the inquiry contexts that make the most difference for you. Then identify available research settings in which you can find the strengths that you would need. If you were to be hired to do first-rate research, what conditions would you demand to maximize your potential for making solid research contributions?

REFERENCES

Riley, Matilda White, *Sociological Research: A Case Approach,* Harcourt Brace, New York, 1963.

Stouffer, Samuel A., et al., *Studies in Social Psychology in World War II,* 4 vols., Princeton University Press, Princeton, NJ, 1949.

APPENDIX

HOW TO CREATE RANDOM NUMBERS FOR RESEARCH

Random numbers are one of the most useful items in research. They are used to select a sample randomly that is intended to be representative of a defined population. They are also used to assign cases randomly to experimental and control groups. In fact, at many points in research using random numbers is either necessary or very helpful. For example, question order might be randomized for each respondent to offset question order effects (and permit a study of question order as well), interviewers might be randomly assigned to cases to be interviewed to offset interviewer effects (and, again, permit the study of these effects), and interviews or documents to be analyzed might be randomly ordered to reduce the effects of skill and fatigue on data collecting or coding. In fact, random ordering of interviewing helps prevent problems when unexpected events intervene during the data collection phase of research (a random sample will have occurred before and after the unexpected event, permitting analysis of the effect of the event and separate analysis of the pre- and postevent data. Random subsamples of interviews might be recontacted to check on interviewing procedures, and observations in the field might occur on random days and times to ensure that all potential times are covered.

The key feature of randomness is that each possible outcome has a known (generally equal, depending on how it is done) chance of being selected. That means that the selection is protected against systematic biasing factors such as the researcher's subtle preferences or other inadvertent biases. Examples of potential biases include the following situations:

- Certain kinds of subjects are assigned to be interviewed first when interviewers are learning their jobs.
- In using alphabetical lists, the Andersons are interviewed first and the Zeldichs last.
- Interesting documents are coded first and the boring ones given less-focused attention later.
- Questionnaires are mailed to central city zip codes first, before the study is widely known, and those to suburban zip codes are mailed later, leaving the possibility that a relevant news report could intervene.

Here we will illustrate the use of random digits for the purpose of selecting a sample from a sampling frame or finite list of cases in a population. Similar procedures can be used for other randomization situations. To start with, one needs to know the following:

- The number of cases in the sampling frame (number of cases to choose from). These must be numbered sequentially and uniquely.
- The number to be selected (desired sample size).

There are several ways to get random digits for research purposes.

USING PRINTED LISTS OF RANDOM DIGITS

Tables of random digits are often provided as an appendix in statistics books. Two tables of random digits are provided at the end of this appendix. You can create your own table of random digits by following instructions for using a spreadsheet program (given in this appendix) or by using this feature of some standard statistical packages.

To use a table of random digits:

1. First, sequentially number cases in the sampling frame or population so they can be identified by number.

2. Then identify how many digits make up the largest number you want (e.g., the total number of cases to choose from in a population or sampling frame). For example, if there are 284 students in the freshman class that you want to sample, then three-digit random numbers are needed (from 001 to 284).

3. Decide how you will go through the table of random digits and where you will start. Decide where the x-digit field (e.g., three-digit field to sample from the 284 students in the freshman class) is going to be in the table (usually x contiguous numbers). Decide how you will proceed through the table (e.g., going down the columns in the table or starting at the top of the page with the next set of x contiguous digits). Choose a starting point haphazardly (or perhaps randomly). For example, drop a pencil point on a page (without looking) and take the nearest x-digit number as a starting point.

4. Write down random digits. Move through the table from the starting point you chose. Write down each random x-field number. Skip over numbers in the table that are outside the range of case ID numbers (e.g., in the student example, random numbers in the table that were 285 and larger would be skipped because the population includes only 284 potential cases). If you are sampling without replacement, omit duplicate numbers as well. If you are sampling with replacement, data from the multiply-selected cases would be duplicated (the number of times that that case number came up in the random digits) and used in the analysis.

USING SPREADSHEET PROGRAMS

A large number of random digits can be created using a spreadsheet program such as Excel, which has a random number generating function. The calculation equation can be created for one cell, and the equation can be copied to any number of cells in the spreadsheet to create as many random digits as needed for some research purpose such as drawing a sample, randomly assigning cases to experimental and control groups, or deciding in what order to interview. The procedure given here is for Excel, but similar procedures can be used in other spreadsheet programs.

Creating a Page of Random Digits

1. Establish a new spreadsheet and highlight the first cell in column A (A-1). Type in the following formula: = 100000 * RAND()
2. Enter the formula. You will see a random number with up to five digits before the decimal (the number of zeros in the above equation). To test this out, touch function key F9, and the formula will recalculate and show a different random number.
3. Format the number to show only the integer part of the number (for viewing convenience) by clicking on "Format," then "Cells," then "Custom," and scroll to "0," which is the symbol for whole numbers.
4. Now, using the Copy function, copy the formula from cell A-1 to a sufficient area of the spreadsheet (e.g., to column I and down to row 50, depending on the size of page you ultimately want to print).
5. Print the page of random digits. If you want another page of random digits, touch F9 and print the new page.
6. Use the random digits as indicated earlier. Note that the spreadsheet program omits leading zeros. You will have to treat missing leading zeros as zero.

Creating a Tailored List of Random Digits for Sampling

1. Number the cases in the population or sampling frame. Identify how many potential cases there are.

2. Establish a new spreadsheet and highlight the first cell in column A (A-1).

3. Enter the following formula, substituting the appropriate number for *LOW* and *HIGH:* = LOW + ((HIGH – LOW) * RAND())

LOW is the lowest random digit you want (usually 1); *HIGH* is the highest random digit you want (usually the total population size). Enter the formula. You will see a random digit with a decimal.

4. Format the number in this cell to drop decimal values. Click on "Format," then "Cells," then "Custom," and scroll to choose "0," the symbol for integer values. To test this, touch function key F9, and the formula will recalculate. If you see values you did not intend, check the equation.

5. Now, using the Copy function, copy the formula from cell A-1, down column A to the number of random digits you need for the study. Usually this is the intended sample size (plus some—perhaps doubled—to take account of missing data, nonresponses, or sampling without replacement). Once the formula is entered, you will have a list of random digits for use in sampling.

6. Print the list of random digits. If you want another set of random digits, touch F9 and print the new list.

7. Select cases from the population or sampling frame with the ID number that matches the random number. Use the random digits in the order listed. If sampling without replacement, skip previously used ID numbers. If sampling with replacement, duplicate the data ultimately derived from a case the number of times it is chosen in the process of selecting a sample.

RANDOM DIGIT PROGRAMS

There are several special-purpose random digit programs that automatically format (e.g., sort, omit duplicate numbers for sampling without replacement) random digit lists, but they are generally privately written and not widely available. You could write your own program in a language such as C, Fortran, Pascal, or Basic.

Some statistical packages such as ProStat (Poly Software, International, P.O. Box 526368, Salt Lake City, UT 84152) include a math command that defines the number of rows and columns and fills it with random digits between specified low and high values.

Tables of Random Digits

	COLUMN 1	COLUMN 2	COLUMN 3	COLUMN 4	COLUMN 5	COLUMN 6	COLUMN 7	COLUMN 8
Row 1	38010	70809	28963	32279	3942	55115	92642	47681
Row 2	88039	24424	88841	53148	88518	96097	36246	66034
Row 3	21988	06333	64055	78062	20248	69412	57311	65567
Row 4	50519	41801	58520	08007	69798	55773	90453	13305
Row 5	65644	12804	38325	76817	79855	72544	20258	39619
Row 6	88078	20860	47093	18321	46034	59844	27771	33928
Row 7	57898	91176	65540	11755	63445	46140	91317	54594
Row 8	36079	29652	57459	65537	57514	52249	03995	75449
Row 9	80252	44085	03312	94775	13815	75857	20838	99939
Row 10	88136	71883	68807	63613	89751	87819	95140	67496
Row 11	75099	19667	80990	83348	75518	49970	93120	51275
Row 12	30509	92201	89336	83328	12317	96150	07135	26096
Row 13	62326	07101	30729	73588	88367	74745	96340	03256
Row 14	45767	31842	23593	01528	20984	13705	02626	35555
Row 15	50210	90116	16808	54536	40804	04248	01536	57375
Row 16	51913	89169	83013	92899	02604	24436	07739	02717
Row 17	10099	24039	79727	36917	37452	80340	56253	23484
Row 18	33856	28451	11568	10650	88951	01259	70408	01390
Row 19	24995	31932	67173	89171	46275	96072	97167	78605
Row 20	05901	76681	60101	59438	27618	29264	97323	54412
Row 21	67919	42282	12109	03777	16758	13919	54922	65221
Row 22	64835	78662	69184	73185	99629	57568	08170	13287
Row 23	72670	30450	60534	11815	14234	33173	30640	48591
Row 24	93079	68025	58736	36487	36922	40792	01743	61031
Row 25	26743	63406	20410	34538	89819	21481	92659	04803
Row 26	54311	10980	71478	74692	27813	16516	18623	67895
Row 27	56211	03211	80805	95801	16951	36075	74678	66608
Row 28	51283	60720	34644	31291	70411	91208	71996	37333
Row 29	84372	33343	71124	27864	85878	22744	59139	85789
Row 30	16868	88443	06554	07992	70338	99638	97666	60562
Row 31	87785	68370	13883	44251	66696	70222	53105	23300
Row 32	94186	78217	15737	62203	96298	59564	16072	19407
Row 33	94644	58006	90188	10831	45361	68590	48432	38828
Row 34	02110	42733	37463	16059	48172	62542	52463	12354
Row 35	06994	77598	81107	75844	08487	64463	67065	38921
Row 36	37442	24724	80919	36723	49477	45192	28350	71439
Row 37	01583	18570	57000	61718	25775	62632	07977	63037
Row 38	48075	39907	23411	26912	59658	44623	30865	30792
Row 39	10326	38844	61818	26895	84544	42456	28523	67804
Row 40	78551	47394	10439	71967	11124	33631	41993	53082
Row 41	18250	32074	79351	88205	35869	53947	85942	64511

	COLUMN 1	COLUMN 2	COLUMN 3	COLUMN 4	COLUMN 5	COLUMN 6	COLUMN 7	COLUMN 8
Row 1	98540	22429	73944	97490	76680	38179	87121	56427
Row 2	29624	87080	87340	567	28671	59323	38707	68019
Row 3	17895	94847	22246	31545	27819	05917	47315	50721
Row 4	50436	25662	88780	67200	47658	60078	69345	78846
Row 5	75884	81637	06808	31625	57806	78316	54776	29003
Row 6	61329	31793	39081	56045	44877	27708	45139	37056
Row 7	06946	48100	79007	87767	88857	28171	91173	08835
Row 8	85346	32661	68813	29859	20243	33062	63956	10614
Row 9	85540	16929	45423	41027	52929	81227	71934	19453
Row 10	65227	14535	82272	30899	07475	18775	93157	70122
Row 11	79651	19464	88372	68177	66444	95494	25249	50739
Row 12	19706	9154	94052	99132	16737	39792	63570	52901
Row 13	95431	65215	15359	20832	62326	00238	56652	32251
Row 14	38307	67571	00789	22837	81489	31225	53346	00543
Row 15	19976	75277	02612	37703	37880	40334	25875	94624
Row 16	35075	16985	92241	95374	06209	20943	12555	81824
Row 17	55235	96572	13927	88789	52201	37728	61594	10899
Row 18	71448	94558	40136	74139	10310	29273	54303	68449
Row 19	22294	86763	05352	59117	97041	93939	52069	11071
Row 20	57519	98283	98409	12868	37877	96163	69746	13832
Row 21	90947	29821	95317	27775	69260	29920	02893	00273
Row 22	51989	86216	58880	58379	17497	37440	31210	21923
Row 23	31402	62907	62493	74803	29218	51014	64966	96044
Row 24	36450	73039	64887	09881	15608	64148	91288	32784
Row 25	38796	95186	39393	97110	49096	50120	96704	67781
Row 26	19514	71510	72880	15808	55696	11896	86385	14211
Row 27	55055	57869	03792	34262	15315	59617	56689	76075
Row 28	19688	16353	83423	54095	23575	54353	92988	18040
Row 29	55829	09005	61388	20022	14642	63791	15166	63679
Row 30	60660	83702	84091	88002	22235	05977	31696	35374
Row 31	83445	29688	42593	18666	14733	06506	14865	86650
Row 32	06574	37785	72051	97694	18855	97861	41409	80839
Row 33	34758	86734	44870	90981	96250	06372	4051	14915
Row 34	81824	35980	41851	22831	43214	79994	19902	03584
Row 35	97106	48272	33105	46392	27973	97190	78503	57373
Row 36	07488	21300	17982	75674	44003	34042	96010	40614
Row 37	87519	04192	35819	74811	58920	59356	15430	40046
Row 38	11233	56989	35071	84820	84387	12378	83392	42578
Row 39	63957	78204	18456	33367	09338	34741	66654	85963
Row 40	33048	28786	05214	56316	77195	75141	95179	70438
Row 41	27069	88994	50552	83304	47211	91215	94936	34322
Row 42	12576	19457	85633	40787	45069	95532	51112	59060

GLOSSARY

access (Ch. 8) In research, the process of contacting and obtaining the responses of subjects. Often the process of gaining access is complicated by gatekeepers who control access to dependent subjects (e.g., parents giving permission to interview their children).

accretion measures (Ch. 9) Measures of things that are built up as byproducts of social action (e.g., measuring the height of fingerprints on glass display cases in a museum to determine the likely age of those who viewed the display).

achieved design (Chs. 1, 14) The actual procedures a researcher is able to implement that underlie the researcher's findings. Often research procedures are not achieved in exactly the planned way, and this may make a substantial difference in the way findings are supported.

aesthetic statements (Ch. 1) Statements about what a person appreciates or likes.

anonymity (Ch. 7) Condition in which an investigator does not know the identity of a person or case and thus cannot associate a response with a particular person. It is contrasted with **confidentiality.**

applied research (Chs. 1, 12, 13) Research with the ultimate aim of solving a problem or providing guidance in making a policy or reaching a decision about how to proceed.

archival data (Chs. 1, 7, 9) Data (text or numeric) that have been gathered previously and are stored for future use, often by others.

arrow diagram (Ch. 2) A graphic that uses arrows to show the relationships among independent, dependent, and control variables in a theoretical model. It is useful in showing the theoretical relationships a researcher is considering.

association (Ch. 10) Statistically, the relationship between variables. Various coefficients can be used to summarize the strength and direction of such a relationship.

basic research (Chs. 1, 13) Research that focuses primarily on developing new knowledge, often expressed as a new theory or the testing of hypotheses derived from a theory. This contrasts with research that focuses on some practical problem or description of a specific group. Most research is a blend of basic and applied components, emphasizing one or the other.

bias (Chs. 3, 9, 10) Systematic error that is involved in measurement due to some known or unknown factor. For example, people may systematically understate their ages or overstate their family incomes.

bivariate analysis (Ch. 10) Analysis of pairs of variables to see how they are related or associated. The relationship of social class and age is an example of a bivariate relationship. Often one of the two variables is an independent variable and the other is a dependent variable.

case, unit of analysis (Chs. 2, 3, 14) The defined entity that is sampled and scored or measured on variables of interest in a research project. A case is defined in terms of its substantive characteristics and their location in time and place. In sociology a case often is a human individual, a group, an organization, or a society. It can also be social entities such as "the father–child role relationship" or "a dyad." In research, a group or population of these cases is targeted for examination.

case study (Chs. 4, 8) A study of a single (or, in practice, a very few individual) cases. Generally this permits a more detailed or involved examination of the selected cases.

cause (Ch. 10) A theoretical idea about the relationships between concepts such that some have exclusive influence on others. To demonstrate that data from a study support hypotheses about a causal relationship (e.g., that *X* causes *Y*), investigators must demonstrate that there is an association between the two variables, that the time order of impact of the two variables is such that the cause precedes the effect, and that the relationship is not spurious (i.e., no unaccounted for variable explains away the *X–Y* relationship).

central tendency (Ch. 10) The tendency for scores in a distribution to cluster around some central value that may be designated as a representative value for that distribution. The average age of people in a population is an example of such a representative value.

chance differences (Ch. 6) Differences between groups that stem from random processes such as sampling, in which the chance of inclusion of somewhat different types of cases in the groups accounts for some or all of the difference between the groups. For example, the mean age may differ between two groups sampled from the same population simply because of the chance that one group included somewhat older people than the other group. These differences can be assessed with inferential statistical tests. Chance differences may also play a role in measurements from unreliable measurement processes.

cluster sample, random (Ch. 5) A sample in which the population of cases is divided into clusters or groups (e.g., homes grouped by census areas or individuals grouped by counties) and clusters are randomly selected. All cases in the selected clusters are used unless the sampling plan calls for a second stage of random sampling within the selected clusters.

concept (Chs. 1, 14) A property or characteristic of some case or unit of analysis in which one might be interested.

conceptual definition (Ch. 3) A definition of a concept that serves as the basis for theoretical discussions about the concept and its relationships to other concepts (e.g., a verbal definition of concepts such as age, social class, or anomie). A conceptual definition is the basis for developing a measurement procedure that is used in gathering data in a research project. A conceptual definition is the standard by which the validity of the measurement procedure is judged. Conceptual definitions, like other definitions, often tell how the concept of interest is like similar concepts and how it differs from them.

conceptualization (Ch. 11) The process of identifying and defining some phenomenon of interest and connecting these ideas to past theory that may be relevant. Conceptualizing the phenomenon now called social class is the subject of many important books. Conceptualizing important concepts is a key step in research.

confidentiality (Ch. 7) Situation in which the researcher knows the identity of the respondent but promises not to reveal it to anyone or write up the findings so that the identity of a case can be discovered. See **anonymity** for a contrasting concept.

construct validity (Ch. 3) A way to demonstrate empirically that an operational definition of a concept matches its conceptual definition. Construct validity involves showing that measurements are correlated in ways that are expected, given the conceptual definition. Demonstration in data that expected correlations with other variables exists.

content analysis (Ch. 9) The analysis of text treated as research data. This is done by human coders who are trained to read and categorize text, or by a computer program that either aids in hand coding or includes the rules for examining text automatically.

context of research (Ch. 1) The social, political, economic, organizational, and physical setting of research.

continuous variable (Ch. 3) A variable whose scores merge into one another without gaps. Precision of measurement of the scores is limited only by the measurement instrument. For example, age is a continuous variable that could be measured in terms of years, months, days, hours, minutes, seconds, or fractions of seconds depending on the availability of a precise measurement instrument.

contracts, research (Ch. 13) Research funding for a specific, planned project often designed by the funder. Contrast with research **grants.**

control and experimental groups (Chs. 4, 6) Critical contrasting groups found in many types of research but most often discussed in experimental research. The experimental group is exposed to the stimulus or independent variable. The control group generally is not exposed to the stimulus but may receive a placebo, which is exposure to a "treatment" like that received in the experimental group but without the critical independent variable. Experiments often contrast more than one experimental group with one or more control groups.

control variable (Chs. 3, 10) A variable used to determine whether other factors may influence the relationship between the independent and dependent variables.

convenience sample (Ch. 5) A sample selected because it is convenient for the researcher. For example, a university researcher may study social groups in a nearby town.

correlation (Ch. 10) The relationship between variables. Often this refers to specific kinds of statistical measures of the relationship between variables.

covert research (Ch. 8) Research conducted so that subjects are unaware they are being studied. The research operation is kept secret without disclosure to the subjects and without their informed consent (e.g., observing public behavior in a park).

cross-sectional study (Ch. 4) Research that is done at one point in time. Surveys often are done at one point in time. This contrasts with trend studies or panel studies that gather data and make comparisons over time.

data (Ch. 1) Data are (a plural noun) the recorded measures that come from research (e.g., number codes for answers in a questionnaire, observational records, or textual information). Analysis of data leads to relevant research findings.

data archives (Ch. 9) See **archival data.**

data point (Ch. 4) An item of data; the response of a case to a variable. These are usually represented by a single number code in a data set.

demonstrated knowledge (Ch. 1) A principle of scientific research that claims of knowledge must be based on research whose procedures are explained and can be replicated by others. A demand that one be able to show how one knows what one claims to know.

dependent variable (Chs. 2, 10) A variable that is treated in a research project as an outcome or to be dependent on other prior variables in an arrow diagram that shows how variables are related to each other. Sometimes *dependent variable* is used for variables that are the focus of analysis or explanation.

design options (Ch. 4) If research design is seen as a set of decisions about features of a study (e.g., the case, sample type and size, when and where cases are found, as in Riley's paradigm), then the set of things one can choose from constitutes the design options available to the researcher. The task is to pick a compatible set of options that will lead to sound research data to answer the research question at hand.

discrete variable (Ch. 3) A variable defined to have categories that are not continuous. Family size and most count variables are discrete, as are marital status, occupation, and whether one owns or rents one's home. There are no potential responses in between the specified categories.

disproportionate stratified random sample (Ch. 5) Stratified sampling in which the probability of selection is different for different strata (e.g., rare strata may be oversampled to have enough cases for a study). See **stratified random sample.**

distorter variable (Chs. 3, 10) A variable that changes the direction of a relationship between an independent and a dependent variable when it is not taken into consideration. For example, a positive relationship may appear to be negative, or vice versa.

double-blind experiment (Ch. 6) An experiment in which neither the researcher nor the subject knows whether the subject will receive the experimental treatment (i.e., whether the subject is in an experimental or control group).

dynamic models (Ch. 4) Conceptual models of phenomena in which change through time is a central feature (as opposed to **static** models).

error, sampling (Ch. 5) See **sampling error.**

errors, data preparation (Ch. 9) Errors that result from the process of coding data into a form for analysis. Good research involves careful checking for these kinds of error.

evaluative statements (Ch. 1) Statements about how something compares to a standard that the person may want to use.

existential statements (Ch. 1) Statements made by researchers about what they find to exist (relationships between variables, general principles, descriptive findings, etc.).

experiment (Ch. 4) A type of study in which groups of cases are compared and the experimenter controls which case gets the treatment (or independent variable) and other aspects of the research setting. Usually cases are randomly assigned to experimental and control groups.

experimental and control groups (Chs. 4, 6) See **control and experimental groups.**

experimenter bias (Ch. 6) Systematic error in data caused by the presence or activities of an experimenter. For example, an experimenter may more closely examine cases in an experimental group than cases in a control group.

exploratory research (Ch. 2) Research intended to search for something such as a good hypothesis to answer a research question or to enrich the researcher's understanding of some phenomenon. Often exploratory research leads to future research that tests new formulations and ideas on broader populations.

external validity (Ch. 6) The extent to which the results of an experiment can be generalized beyond the cases actually included in the experiment.

face validity (Ch. 3) Judgment that an operational definition should logically measure the concept it is designed to measure (e.g., the judgment that asking respondents their birthdates will result in data necessary to determine their ages). Face validity is also called logical validity.

facts (Ch. 2) The basis of research, specific instances of some empirically verifiable outcome that is found in some specific time and place.

falsifiability (Ch. 1) The ability of a hypothesized answer to a research question to be shown to be false as well as not false.

field (Ch. 4) The place where subjects are located and where research data are gathered.

finite population (Ch. 5) A defined universe of cases to which a theory or a research question is assumed to apply that is limited in size, time, and location. In contrast, see **infinite population.**

generalizability (Ch. 1) The ability of research findings to be applied not only to the specific cases included in a study but also to a broader class or population of cases.

grants, research (Ch. 13) Funding for research in which a granting agency generally requests proposals for research and accepts proposals but lets the researcher guide the study. The granting agency may or may not specify research topics eligible for funding.

Guttman scale (Ch. 3) A procedure to check a series of items thought to measure different strengths of a concept validly and to arrange themselves in a cumulative order.

Hawthorne effect (Ch. 6) An effect (noticed in an early time-motion study in a plant in that town) in which some aspect of the context (such as an experimental group "feeling special") leads to outcomes that may enhance, reduce, or otherwise affect the measured outcome variables.

hierarchical organization (Ch. 12) An organization with positions arranged so that some positions report to and are controlled by other positions above them, such as workers, supervisors, division managers, vice presidents, and company president.

hierarchy, status (Ch. 12) A hierarchy of positions in society or an organization in which power, prestige, and financial rewards are greater for higher positions than for lower ones.

hunches, authority, and experience (Ch. 1) In contrast to scientific research, hunches about what is true, referring to some authority's statement about what is true, or general observation and personal experience often become used as ways people may come to know something. The key to scientific research is in being able to show how one knows what one claims to know so that others can follow the same procedures to check out the truth of the knowledge claims.

hypothesis (Ch. 2) A proposed answer to a research question. Hypotheses are generally statements about how variables are related to each other (causally or otherwise) and conditions under which these relationships are expected. Research may explore in search of good hypotheses or test existing hypotheses. Better hypotheses in research are those that are obviously connected to theory.

hypothesis-testing research (Ch. 2) Research designed to see whether a given hypothesis is supported.

independent variable (Chs. 2, 6, 10) A variable that is thought to influence another dependent variable (a cause factor). Research often is designed to test the hypothesis that independent variables actually have the influence they are hypothesized to have on other (dependent) variables.

indirect cost (overhead) (Ch. 13) Grant or contract funding for research often includes general maintenance expenses that are not specific project costs (e.g., regular office space, available telephone line, heat and electricity, standard office computer connection, existing labs). Universities often have a prenegotiated rate for research, such as 40% of the research project's direct costs. This is added to the project's direct costs in establishing the total grant amount.

inference (Ch. 5) The logical process of reasoning from general principles to their logical implications. In statistics, inferences are made from empirical knowledge gained from a carefully drawn probability sample to the larger population from which the sample was drawn. For example, generalizations about opinions of U.S. adults can be inferred statistically, within limits of sampling error, from a random sample survey.

infinite population (Ch. 5) A theoretical notion about a class of cases that is not bounded by time or place. All mothers, wherever they exist or whenever they may exist in the past, present, or future, would be an infinite population. Often scientific theories are about infinite classes of cases, but information about such a broad class of cases can be gained only by dealing with available, finite populations, developing sound theoretical principles, and continually challenging and testing these principles on different finite samples.

informants (Ch. 8) Subjects in a study who are chosen and interviewed because they have knowledge about some situation or event. Sometimes subjects are also asked to be respondents when a researcher is interested in their opinions or characteristics. The subjects who are interviewed in a study may be asked to be informants or respondents or, sometimes, both. Generally the criteria for choosing informants are different than those for choosing respondents.

internal validity (Ch. 6) Concern that the proposed cause is actually what produced the effect of interest in an experiment. An experiment is internally valid if it is designed and conducted in such a way that all alternative explanations of the observed outcome can be ruled out.

interval measurement (Ch. 3) A variable conceptually and operationally defined so that categories of the variable are mutually exclusive and exhaustive, the categories have a defined order from high to low, and a unit of the variable is defined so that the difference between categories is known (e.g., degrees Fahrenheit).

intervening variable (Ch. 10) In a conceptual model developed for some research purpose, some variables may be "between" an independent and dependent variable. A process may have an outcome because an independent variable influences an intervening variable, which in turn produces an outcome for a dependent variable. Intervening variables play a double role in research; they are dependent with respect to the preceding independent variable as well as independent with respect to the following dependent variable.

item analysis (Ch. 3) A procedure used to check the relationship between proposed summated scale items and the overall scale.

key informant (Ch. 8) Another word for informant in a study, in this case, one of the main selected informants.

knowledge-building pursuit (Ch. 1) One of the key features defining scientific research. The researcher has the intent of building knowledge.

kurtosis (Ch. 10) A characteristic of a distribution of scores: the extent to which the distribution is peaked around a narrow range of scores. *Leptokurtosis* means more peaked than normal, *mesokurtosis* means normally peaked (in a statistical sense), and a *platykurtic* distribution is flatter, with scores less concentrated than normal. In statistics, quantitative measures can be computed to measure this feature of a distribution of scores.

laboratory research (Ch. 4) Research conducted in settings where the researcher has considerable control over who receives an experimental treatment, for example, and control over other conditions of the research. This is often a specially equipped room or laboratory where extraneous factors are eliminated.

levels of measurement (Ch. 3) A scale representing different degrees of refinement in measurement instruments. The four levels usually identified are **nominal, ordinal, interval,** and **ratio.** Refer to the definitions of these terms.

longitudinal study (Ch. 4) Research conducted over time in which time is a variable.

macro-level theory (Ch. 2) Theory at the level of larger-scale units in which cases are societies or organizations. See **theory.**

matching (Ch. 6) A way of assigning subjects to experimental and control groups in which the groups are made equivalent.

matching by overall group distributions (Ch. 6) An attempt to match control and experimental groups on the overall distribution of one or more variables rather than having identical cases. For example, the average age or percentage female would be made identical across experimental and control groups.

matching case by case (Ch. 6) An attempt is made to have identical, matched subjects, one subject assigned to the experimental group and one to the control group.

matching funds (Ch. 13) Some funding agencies require that the researcher or the researcher's organization provide part of the funding for a proposed research project. Often the fund match takes the form of use of facilities or donated time, but it may also be actual funds.

measurement error (Ch. 3) Unsystematic, random error involved in the process of making measurements. These errors average out to zero (some are overestimates and some are underestimates). Systematic error is called **bias.**

micro-level theory (Ch. 2) Theory at the level of small-scale units in which cases may be a given type of role, an individual social actor, or small groups such as families. See **theory.**

monograph (Ch. 11) A book that describes how research was carried out and reports a single or set of related research results.

multistage sampling (Ch. 5) Sampling in which more than one sampling process (identifying a population of cases and selecting a sample of those cases) is used. For example, a multistage cluster sample may randomly select clusters and then, at a second stage, randomly select cases from the selected clusters. Two or more stages may be used.

multivariate analysis (Ch. 10) Analysis that involves the simultaneous examination of the relationship between three or more variables. Multivariate statistical techniques such as multiple regression build on bivariate analysis that involves relationships between pairs of variables.

nominal level measurement (Ch. 3) A variable conceptually and operationally defined so the relationship between categories of the variable is one of simple difference (e.g., state of residence).

nonrandom sample (Ch. 5) Any sampling procedure that does not use strictly random sampling procedures or one in which the probability of selection is not known (e.g., convenience samples).

observer (Ch. 1) The researcher or person who conducts observations of some subject, event, or situation. The person doing the observing must be as free from bias as possible.

operational definition (Ch. 3) An indicator that can be used in research to classify cases into categories of a concept. Usually there can be many operational definitions of a given concept, some more useful, precise, valid, or reliable than others.

optimum allocation stratified random sample (Ch. 5) Stratified sampling in which both the size of the strata and the variability of cases within the strata are used to determine the number of cases to be sampled from each stratum. See **stratified random sample.**

ordinal level of measurement (Ch. 3) A variable conceptually and operationally defined so categories of the variable are mutually exclusive and exhaustive and the categories have a defined order from high to low on the concept but the difference between categories is not defined or known (e.g., favorable to unfavorable attitudes toward something).

panel study (Chs. 4, 7) Longitudinal research in which the same subjects are reinterviewed one or more times over time.

paradigm (Ch. 2) An approach or perspective (with assumptions) about some phenomenon that guides the identification of key variables and how they may produce the effects of interest. Sometimes aspects of the paradigm are implicit, but better research is developed from explicitly identified paradigms. See also **scientific paradigm.**

parameter (Ch. 5) A characterization of some aspect of a population, such as the average age or standard deviation of household income. Sample statistics (results of data drawn in a sample) are used to estimate population parameters. How a sample is drawn (e.g., a probability sample) aids in making supportable generalization of sample statistics to population parameters.

participant observation (Ch. 8) A study in which the researcher participates in the event while he or she is making observations for research purposes. This is contrasted with nonparticipant observation, in which the researcher does not participate but takes the role (usually) of researcher or writer. Researchers may take aspects of each observer role during the course of the research.

physical units (Ch. 9) Units defined according to some physical boundaries such as a city block, a census tract, or a book (in content analysis). These are often used in sampling areas to study or textual units to code.

placebo (Ch. 6) A treatment of a control group that includes most features of the real treatment except its critical aspect. For example, in a drug study the control group gets a sugar pill of the same size and look as the real drug that is given to the experimental group. This helps rule out noncritical aspects of the treatment that may become alternative explanations of findings.

population (Ch. 5) In sampling, population is the universe from which the sample is drawn. A population of cases to which research findings are to be generalized must be identified. Some populations of interest to researchers are finite and others are infinite. See **finite population** and **infinite population.**

population elements (Ch. 5) These are the cases or units of interest in a research project that make up the population to be sampled and, later, inferentially described.

precision (Ch. 3) The number of categories distinguished in the measurement. A variable that uses only low, medium, and high would be less precise than one that used 10 categories. Usually, greater precision is sought.

predictive validity (Ch. 3) Validity of a measurement (operational definition) that is established by seeing whether the measurement can predict known classifications of cases.

principal investigator (Ch. 12) Usually the person (or persons) who proposes the research, is granted funding, and is responsible for overseeing the conduct of the research. This is often a legally specified position and often limited by funder rules to a single person.

probability sample (Ch. 5) A sample in which cases are drawn from a population with a known probability of being drawn. That probability, although known, may be equal or unequal across cases.

property space (Ch. 3) The logical combinations of categories of variables that define all the potential types of cases one might describe. For example, the property space of gender and home ownership would produce combinations of man/owner, woman/ owner, man/renter, and woman/renter. Examining the possible combinations may lead to expanding or combining categories or be used in measurement of more-complex concepts.

proportionate stratified random sample (Ch. 5) Sampling in which strata are identified and cases are selected from different strata at the same rate. For example, if a 10% sample is taken of one stratum, then a 10% sample is taken of all other strata. This contrasts with disproportionate stratified sampling, in which the rate of sampling varies between different strata (rare strata may be oversampled). See **stratified random sample** and **disproportionate stratified random sample.**

proposal, research (Ch. 13) A written document (usually) that describes the ideas behind a proposed research project as well as how it is to be conducted, with a budget describing needed resources. The proposal is often submitted to funding agencies for resources to conduct the research. Graduate students may be asked to prepare a research proposal on their dissertation research, which their dissertation committee will examine, revise, and approve as part of the education process.

prospectus, research (Ch. 13) A short document that describes the general idea and procedures of a research project before preparation of a full proposal. Some funding agencies ask for the shorter version and select researchers, who will then be asked to prepare a full proposal.

qualitative analysis (Ch. 8) Analysis in which the investigator uses qualitative data (e.g., text, pictures, observational records) to reach conclusions. Generally this involves in-depth examination of all available data and careful scholarship and checking on the part of the investigator, but without the systematic assistance of statistical analysis of quantitative data.

qualitative secondary data (Ch. 9) Nonquantitative data such as videotapes, pictures, and textual data that are archived and available for future research use.

quantitative secondary data (Ch. 9) Data expressed in coded, usually numeric form that are archived and available for future research use.

quota sample (Ch. 5) A nonprobability sampling procedure in which quotas are established for data-gathering staff so that the sample, overall, will reflect known aspects of the population on variables of interest. For example, an interviewer may have a quota of 50% men and 50% women to be found and interviewed.

random assignment (Ch. 6) Assigning cases to groups (e.g., treatment or control in the case of an experiment) in a manner that is random so the probability of being in a given group is the same for all cases.

random cluster sample (Ch. 5) See **cluster sample, random.**

random measurement error (Ch. 3) See **measurement error.**

random numbers (Ch. 5) Digits that appear with equal (or known) probability. A table of random numbers is one that has an equal likelihood of any given digit appearing at any place in the table. In the whole table, there are essentially equal numbers of each digit. Random numbers can be found in a published table or generated by a computer program, and they are used in randomly selecting cases into a sample and in randomly assigning cases to groups.

random sample (Ch. 5) A sample in which the elements (cases) in a defined population have a given chance of being drawn into the sample. Usually this probability of being drawn is equal from case to case.

random selection (Ch. 5) Selecting cases randomly, as in random sampling.

ratio level of measurement (Ch. 3) A variable conceptually and operationally defined so that categories of the variable are mutually exclusive and exhaustive, the categories have a defined order from high to low, and a unit of the variable is defined so that the difference between categories is known. In addition, the scale of the variable has a meaningful zero point representing absence of the characteristic (e.g., family size, amount of family income).

reactivity (Ch. 9) The possibility that a measurement process is influenced by factors deemed to be outside the research. Reactive measurement processes are those in which the research and researchers are likely to influence the outcome of the measurement. Nonreactive measures are those in which there is little or no chance that research activity can influence the measurement.

recording units (Ch. 9) In content analysis, defined cases about which data are recorded. In textual research a paragraph in a report may be the unit that is coded on relevant variables. These scored recording units may be aggregated in research to arrive at an overall measure of a whole article, which may be the unit used in the analysis of the data. See **content analysis.**

referential units (Ch. 9) In content analysis, referential units refer to objects or events that appear in the medium being analyzed. These objects or events might be particular people, ideas, or countries, for instance. In analyzing fiction books, the characters included in the book are an example of defined referential units.

reliability (Chs. 3, 8) The extent to which random errors are involved in the measurement process. Random errors average out to the true value, but more unreliable measures have the potential for greater error in one direction or another. Reliability is distinguished from bias, which is systematic error that tends to be in one direction (too low or too high, for example) and is a validity problem. Data to evaluate reliability of a measure are often test–retest or split-half. See **split-half reliability** and **test–retest reliability.**

replication (Chs. 4, 6, 14) The repeating of a research project using the same (or similar) design to see whether the same or similar results occur. This is critical to generating knowledge. Sometimes replications are carried out on somewhat different populations or with somewhat better techniques that are thought to be of the same type as the original research.

representative sample (Ch. 5) A sample designed to represent some specific population on characteristics of interest to the study. Random sampling is more likely to result in a representative sample than is nonrandom sampling.

request for proposals (RFP) (Ch. 13) Funding organizations or those who would like research to be done on some topic generally describe their interest and ask for appropriate researchers to submit proposals on how the study could be carried out. When the funder specifies the research design and is looking for someone to carry it out, the request is usually called an RFC (request for contract) rather than a request for proposals.

research designs (Ch. 4) There are many standard, general approaches to research in the social sciences. These have names such as *field observation, case studies, experiments, surveys, longitudinal studies, laboratory research,* and *research using secondary data.* Each label suggests characteristic choices among alternative sets of research methods.

research methods (Ch. 1) How a study is conducted, including all aspects such as conceptualization, measurement, data gathering, and analysis.

research question (Ch. 1) Critical to all research, a research question states what a researcher wants to know about some topic. It ends in a question mark! Good research questions (see Ch. 2) guide all aspects of research.

research topic (Ch. 1) A research topic points to some general phenomenon about which the researcher wants to know something. Topics might include crime, social class, people in nursing homes, student performance, etc. A research question specifies what one wants to know about a research topic (see research question).

Riley's 12 key research decisions (Ch. 4) A list of 12 key research decisions that an investigator makes, knowingly or not, in carrying out a piece of research. These represent a pattern of choices that determine how the research is carried out and how the findings are supported.

sample (Ch. 5) A subset of a defined population of cases used in most instances to estimate population values (parameters). How the sample is drawn determines how well one can demonstrate that the sample is representative of the population from which it is drawn.

sample size (Ch. 5) The number of cases included in a sample. This is traditionally symbolized as N (i.e., $N = 100$).

sampling error (Ch. 5) The error that would be expected by chance in random sampling. By chance the result of a sample may be higher or lower than the true value that would be obtained if the whole population were accurately enumerated. Thus, one could think about a whole distribution of sample outcomes based on repeatedly sampling the same unchanged population. A standard deviation of that theoretical distribution (called a standard error) is used as a measure of sampling error. Larger probability samples have less sampling error, in general.

sampling frame (Chs. 5–7) The finite list of population elements that is actually available for sampling. An important concern is that a sampling frame be as close to the defined population as possible. The phone book, for example, may be a sampling frame of households in a community but it is likely to miss families who move and those who cannot afford phones or who do not list their numbers.

sampling units (Ch. 9) Defined cases that are drawn into a sample. These may be census tracts, blocks, individuals, or organizations, for example.

sampling with replacement (Ch. 5) A sampling strategy in which a case, once drawn into a sample, is returned to the population so it has a chance of being drawn again as sampling proceeds. This strategy focuses on kinds of cases rather than unique cases, and replacement keeps the population composition unchanged for subsequent draws. If a case is drawn more than once, multiple measurements are recorded.

sampling without replacement (Ch. 5) Once a case is drawn, it is set aside so that no case can be drawn into the sample twice. In small samples this alters the composition of the population and limits the range of possible samples that may be drawn.

scale (Ch. 3) A set of items (statements or questions) designed to measure a respondent's position with respect to a theoretical concept such as an attitude, interest, or property. A scale may be designed to measure a respondent's attitude toward marriage, for example.

scientific laws (Ch. 2) Statements of the relationship of variables that have been sufficiently tested to be taken as true for some class of cases.

scientific paradigm (Ch. 2) An approach or perspective (with assumptions) about some phenomenon that guides the identification of key variables and how they may produce the effects of interest. Scientific paradigms are widely held and guide how research can best be done. Innovation may lead to a scientific revolution in which a new paradigm may challenge and ultimately replace currently used paradigms.

scope of theory (Ch. 2) Scope is the breadth of the class of cases to which a theory applies, as well as the range of phenomena it includes (e.g., carpenters in Wisconsin in 1998 or all carpenters wherever and whenever they exist).

secondary data (Ch. 9) Data that have been previously gathered and archived in some form so they are available for future research.

secondary data research (Ch. 4) Research involving archival data, whether qualitative or quantitative.

simple random sample (SRS) (Ch. 5) A simple random sample is one in which each case in the population has an equal chance of being drawn into the sample and each possible sample has the same chance of being drawn as any other sample. This is in many ways the standard against which other sampling plans are compared. In a simple random sample, sampling is done with replacement. See **sampling with replacement.**

skewness (Ch. 10) The tendency of scores in a distribution to vary more in one direction from the central value of the distribution than in the other direction. The result of skewness is an asymmetric distribution. If the scores vary more below the central value than above, the distribution is said to be negatively skewed. If they vary more above than below, the distribution is said to be positively skewed.

snowball sample (Ch. 5) A type of nonprobability sample in which new cases to be included in a study are identified by cases that are included in a sample. Respondents refer the investigator to other cases of the desired type (e.g., a person with a rare disease may know others with the same disease, and the person may refer the researcher to them for inclusion in the study).

social context of research (Ch. 1) The social context of research includes norms and expectations, social networks and teams, organizational arrangements, and social action involved in research. Research is a social process as well as a logical and empirical process.

soft money (Ch. 12) Temporary research funds (e.g., grant or project funds) as opposed to regularly recurring funds, such as university funds a state may budget for salaries or other regular operations.

split-half reliability (Ch. 3) Reliability of a scale that is determined by correlating summed responses to one half of the scale items to the other half of the scale items.

spurious (Ch. 10) A spurious relationship is a relationship between variables that can be shown to disappear when other antecedent variables are controlled. Thus, other factors appear to cause the outcome rather than the ones expected.

stakeholders (Ch. 12) Those who are interested and concerned about a research project. Stakeholders often express their opinions or attempt to influence what happens in research according to their beliefs.

static models (Ch. 4) Research models that focus on the current state of a system or relationship between variables rather than focusing on processes of change and how certain states of a system affect later stages.

statistic (Ch. 5) A value of some variable based on sample data. The corresponding value of that variable for the population from which the sample is drawn is called a parameter or population parameter. The mean of a sample is called a statistic, and the mean of the population is called a parameter. Inferential statistics help justify the inferential leap from statistics to parameters.

statistical controls as pseudo-matching (Chs. 3, 6, 10) When matching of cases is not possible, two groups can be statistically adjusted on control variables so that a fair comparison of groups can be made. For example, if two cities with different average ages were to be compared and one had a special program for the elderly and the other did not, the comparison could be improved by statistically controlling for the age differences. This approach to making groups comparable is usually problematic because of all the potential variables that must be controlled. See discussions of experimental versus survey research advantages and disadvantages.

stimulus (treatment) (Ch. 6) The treatment or independent variable applied to selected cases in a study.

stratified random sample (Ch. 5) A defined population is divided into a mutually exclusive and exhaustive set of strata (subpopulations), and cases are randomly selected from each of the strata. Strata are usually defined in terms of known characteristics of the population (e.g., gender or region of residence).

stratified sample (Ch. 7) A sample in which the population is stratified in terms of prior information about some variable. A sample is taken from each stratum.

summated scale (Ch. 3) A scale in which responses to items are summed. Item analysis techniques are designed to see whether scale items validly reflect the same variable.

suppressor variable (Ch. 3, 10) Suppressor variables are those that have the effect of decreasing the strength of relationship between an independent and dependent variable when the suppressor variable is not taken into account.

surveys (Chs. 4, 7) A pattern of research design decisions that emphasizes large representative samples of available populations and cross-sectional data gathering. See the chapters and Riley's decision paradigm for details.

syntactical units (Ch. 9) In content analysis, sentences or grammatical units of text that can be identified and scored on relevant variables.

systematic sample (Ch. 5) A sample in which listed cases are selected using some fixed interval (e.g., every *k*th case). This is not a probability sample.

systematic sample with random start (Ch. 5) A random process is used to determine which case is the starting case in systematic sampling (e.g., a random start at some case numbered 1 through the interval size used in sampling). Then systematic sampling at a given interval is used. This makes the sampling plan a probability sample because the chance of a case being drawn can be computed, although it puts constraints on which cases are drawn once the random start is established.

tautology (Ch. 2) A statement that is true by definition.

test–retest reliability (Ch. 3) A way to test reliability of some measurement instrument by using it on the same cases at two points in time. If the two measures are highly correlated (assuming no instrument effect or change in the phenomenon being measured), the measurement process is seen as reliable.

thematic units (Ch. 9) In content analysis, this refers to coding textual data in which themes are identified and classified.

theoretical perspective (Ch. 2) A proposed theory that helps guide research to test it or provides guidance in identifying relevant variables and relationships to use in a research project.

theory (Chs. 2, 14) A logically interrelated set of proposed or accepted scientific laws about some phenomenon. Theory acts as the answer to "why" questions ("Why do three-person groups sometimes end up as a pair and an isolate?") Theory provides a possible answer that could be the subject of research to test the application of the theory.

Thurstone method of equal-appearing intervals (Ch. 3) A scale-checking procedure in which responses of judges are used to identify items that behave as if they are measuring a given concept. See **scale.**

trade publications (Ch. 11) Publications written for public consumption and sold in general-purpose bookstores.

treatment (Ch. 6) See **stimulus (treatment).**

trend study (Ch. 7) Longitudinal research in which a group (but not necessarily the same individuals) is reinterviewed. For example, annual surveys of a sample of U.S. residents may be used to trace trends over time in rates of divorce or crime.

unit of analysis (Ch. 2) See **case.**

unit of measurement (Ch. 3) The concept or construct of that which is to be subjected individually to the measurement process, such as a year or month in measuring age, or $1,000 in measuring income.

univariate analysis (Ch. 10) Analysis of data that focuses on the distribution of single variables. By contrast, bivariate analysis focuses on the relationship of pairs of variables, and multivariate analysis focuses on the simultaneous relationship of three or more variables.

unobtrusive measures (Ch. 3) Measurement processes that are not noticed by subjects. Observation in public spaces is often unnoticed by subjects and thus unlikely to affect their behavior. Studies of historic documents would probably be unobtrusive for those who created the documents.

validity of experiments (designs) (Chs. 6, 8) The extent to which the results of an experiment support the position that the proposed cause is actually what produced the effect of interest (see **internal validity**) and whether the results of the experiment may be generalized (see **external validity**).

validity of operational definitions (Ch. 3) The extent to which the formal and operational definitions of a concept correspond to each other. (In other words, are you measuring what you intended to measure?)

variability (Ch. 10) The necessary ingredient in research: differences between cases on some variable. Scientific research is directed toward explaining this variability.

variable (Ch. 3) A property or characteristic of some class of cases that researchers identify and define conceptually. Variables are defined to have categories in terms of which a class of cases may vary.

weighting (Ch. 5) Weights are used in analyzing samples in which cases are drawn with differing probabilities (e.g., in disproportionate stratified random sampling). Oversampled cases are down-weighted and undersampled cases are up-weighted to reflect accurately the population from which they came.

BIBLIOGRAPHY

Ackoff, Russell K. (1953). Design for social research, Chicago: University of Chicago Press.

Allison, Paul D. (1984). Event history analysis: Regression for longitudinal event data, Newbury Park, CA: Sage.

Annual Register of Grant Support, 29th ed. (1996). Wilmette, IL: National Register.

Bailey, Carol A. (1996). A guide to field research, Thousand Oaks, CA: Pine Forge Press.

Barton, Allen H. (1964). The concept of property space in social research, in Paul F. Lazarsfeld and Morris Rosenberg, eds., The language of social research, Glencoe, IL: Free Press of Glencoe, pp. 40–53.

Barzun, Jacques. (1985). Simple and direct: A rhetoric for writers, rev. ed., Chicago: University of Chicago Press.

Becker, Howard S. (1984). Problems of inference and proof in participant observation, in George J. McCall and J. L. Simmons, Issues in participant observation, Reading, MA: Addison-Wesley.

Berelson, Bernard. (1952). Content analysis in communications research, New York: The Free Press.

Bonjean, Charles M., Hill, Richard J., and McLemore, S. Dale. (1967). Sociological measurement: An inventory of scales and indices, San Francisco: Chandler.

Brent, Edward E., Jr., Scott, James K., and Spencer, John C. (1988). EX-SAMPLE: An expert system to assist in designing sampling plans, Columbia, MO: Idea Works, Inc.

Campbell, Donald T., and Stanley, Julian C. (1963). Experimental and quasi-experimental designs for research, Chicago: Rand McNally.

Coffey, Amanda, and Atkinson, Paul. (1996). Making sense of qualitative data, Newbury Park, CA: Sage.

Converse, Jean M., and Presser, Stanley (1986). Survey questions: Handcrafting the standardized questionnaire, Newbury Park, CA: Sage.

Couch, Carl J. (1987). Researching social processes in the laboratory, Greenwich, CT: JAI Press.

Cresswell, John W. (1994). Research design: Qualitative and quantitative approaches, Newbury Park, CA: Sage.

Davis, James A. (1985). The logic of causal order, Sage University Paper 55, Newbury Park, CA: Sage.

Denzin, Norman K., ed. (1994). Handbook of qualitative research, Newbury Park, CA: Sage.

Dillman, Don A. (1978). Mail and telephone surveys: The total design method, New York: Wiley.

Dillman, Don A. (1982). Mail and other self-administered questionnaires, in Peter Rossi, James Wright, and Andy Anderson, eds., Handbook of survey research, New York: Academic Press.

Dusek, E. Ralph, Holt, Virginia E., Burke, Marti E., and Kraut, Alan G., eds. (1987). Guide to research support, 3rd ed., Hyattsville, MD: American Psychological Association.

Edwards, Allen L. (1957). Techniques of attitude scale construction, New York: Appleton-Century-Crofts.

Emerson, Robert M. (1983). Contemporary field research: A collection of readings, Boston: Little, Brown.

Foundation Center. (1996). The foundation directory, 18th ed., New York: Columbia University Press.

Fowler, Floyd J., Jr. (1995). Improving survey questions: Design and evaluation, Newbury Park, CA: Sage.

Glaser, B., and Strauss, A. L. (1967). The discovery of grounded theory: Strategies for qualitative research, Chicago: Aldine.

Habenstein, Robert W., ed. (1970). Pathways to data: Field methods for studying ongoing social organizations, Chicago: Aldine.

Hammond, Phillip E., ed. (1964). Sociologists at work: Essays on the craft of social research, New York: Basic Books.

Holtz, Herman R. (1979). Government contracts: Proposalmanship and winning strategies, New York: Plenum.

Ivers, Mitchell. (1991). The Random House guide to good writing, New York: Random House.

Johnson, Allan G. (1995). The Blackwell dictionary of sociology: A user's guide to sociological language, Oxford: Blackwell Publishers.

Kish, Leslie. (1965). Survey sampling, New York: Wiley.

Krathwohl, David R. (1988). How to prepare a sociological proposal, 3rd ed. Syracuse, NY: Syracuse University Press.

Krippendorff, Klaus. (1980). Content analysis: An introduction to its methodology, Newbury Park, CA: Sage.

Kuhn, Thomas. (1970), The structure of scientific revolutions, 2nd ed., Chicago: University of Chicago Press.

Labaw, Patricia. (1980). Advanced questionnaire design, Cambridge, MA: Abt Books.

Lauffer, Armand. (1984). Grantsmanship and fund raising, Newbury Park, CA: Sage.

Lee, Mary, Stephenson, Gloria, Anderson, Max, and Lee, Lynn Allan. (1990). The handbook of technical writing: Form and style, San Diego: Harcourt Brace Jovanovich.

Lefferts, Robert. (1982). Getting a grant in the 1980s: How to write successful grant proposals, 2nd ed., Englewood Cliffs, NJ: Prentice Hall.

Levine, Joel H. (1993). Exceptions are the rule, Boulder, CO: Westview.

Liebow, Elliot. (1970). A field experience in retrospect, in Glenn Jacobs, ed., The participant observer: Encounters with social reality, New York: Georg Braziller.

Loether, Herman J., and McTavish, Donald G. (1993). Descriptive and inferential statistics: An introduction, 4th ed., Boston: Allyn & Bacon.

Lofland, John, and Lofland, Lyn H. (1984). Analyzing social settings, 2nd ed., Belmont, CA: Wadsworth.

Madge, John. (1962). The origins of scientific sociology, Glencoe, IL: The Free Press.

Madge, John. (1965). The tools of social science: An analytical description of social science techniques, Garden City, NY: Doubleday.

Marsh, Robert M. (1967). Comparative sociology: A codification of cross-societal analysis, New York: Harcourt Brace.

Miller, Delbert C. (1991). Handbook of research design and social measurement, 5th ed., Newbury Park, CA: Sage.

National Opinion Research Center. (1991). General Social Surveys, 1972–1991: Cumulative codebook, Chicago: University of Chicago.

Osgood, Charles E., Suci, George J., and Tannenbaum, Percy H. (1957). The measurement of meaning, Urbana: University of Illinois Press.

Parton, Mildred. (1950). Surveys, polls, and samples: Practical procedures, New York: Harper and Brothers.

Payne, Stanley L. (1951). The art of asking questions, Princeton, NJ: Princeton University Press.

Quarles, Susan, ed. (1986). Guide to federal funding, New York: Russell Sage Foundation.

Read, Patricia E., ed. (1986). Foundation fundamentals, 3rd ed., New York: The Foundation Center.

Reynolds, Paul D. (1982). Ethics and social science research, Englewood Cliffs, NJ: Prentice Hall.

Riley, Matilda White. (1963). Sociological research: A case approach, New York: Harcourt Brace.

Riley, Matilda White, ed. (1988). Sociological lives, Newbury Park, CA: Sage.

Schaffter, Dorothy. (1969). The National Science Foundation, New York: Praeger.

Schuman, Howard, and Presser, Stanley. (1996). Questions and answers in attitude surveys: Experiments on question form, wording and context, Newbury Park, CA: Sage.

Sechrest, ed. (1979). Unobtrusive measurement today, San Francisco: Jossey-Bass.

Shelton, James H. (1994). Handbook for technical writing, Lincolnwood, IL: NTC Business Books.

Sladek, Frea E., and Stein, Eugene L. (1981). Grant budgeting and finance: Getting the most out of your grant dollar, New York: Plenum.

Strauss, Anselem, and Corbin, Juliet. (1997). Grounded theory in practice, Newbury Park, CA: Sage.

Sykes, J. B., ed. (1982). Concise Oxford dictionary of current English, Oxford: Clarendon Press.

Sykes, Richard E. (1978). Toward a theory of observer effects in systematic field research, *Human Organization*, 37:2 (summer) 148–56.

Tuma, Nancy B., and Hannan, Michael T. (1984). Social dynamics: Models and methods, Orlando, FL: Academic Press.

Webb, Eugene T., Campbell, Donald T., Schwartz, Richard D., Sechrest, Lee, and Grove, Janet Belew. (1981). Nonreactive measures in the social sciences, 2nd ed., Boston: Houghton Mifflin.

Weitzman, Eben A., and Miles, Matthew B. (1995). Computer programs for qualitative data analysis: A software sourcebook, Newbury Park, CA: Sage.

Yamaguchi, Kazuo. (1991). Event history analysis, Newbury Park, CA: Sage.

Yin, Robert K. (1994). Case study research: Design and methods, 2nd ed., Applied Social Research Methods Series #5, Newbury Park, CA: Sage.

Zeller, Richard A., and Carmines, Edward G. (1980). Measurement in the social sciences: The link between theory and data, Cambridge, UK: Cambridge University Press.

INDEX